ICCA
CONGRESS SERIES NO. 3

VIIITH INTERNATIONAL ARBITRATION CONGRESS
NEW YORK, 6–9 MAY 1986

KLUWER LAW AND TAXATION PUBLISHERS
DEVENTER · ANTWERP
LONDON · FRANKFURT · BOSTON · NEW YORK

INTERNATIONAL COUNCIL FOR COMMERCIAL ARBITRATION

COMPARATIVE ARBITRATION PRACTICE AND PUBLIC POLICY IN ARBITRATION

GENERAL EDITOR PIETER SANDERS
with the cooperation of the
T.M.C. Asser Institute for International Law, The Hague

Distribution in the USA and Canada
Kluwer Law and Taxation Publishers
101 Philip Drive
Norwell, MA 02961
USA

Library of Congress Cataloging-in-Publication Data
International Arbitration Congress (8th : 1986
New York, N.Y.)
Comparative arbitration practice and public policy in arbitration.

(ICCA congress series; no. 3)
At head of title: International Council for Commercial Arbitration.
"VIIIth International Arbitration Congress, New York, 6–9 May 1986"—Series t.p.
1. Arbitration and award—Congresses. 2. Public policy (Law)—Congresses. I. Sanders, Pieter. II. T.M.C. Asser Instituut. III. International Council for Commercial Arbitration. IV. Title. V. Series.
K2400.A55 1986 347'.09 87–2689
ISBN 9–06544–296–0 342.79

D/1987/2664/40

ISBN 90 6544 2960

Table of Contents

Preface

This Volume is the third in ICCA's Congress Series. Previous Volumes contained the proceedings of the Hamburg Congress 1982 on *New Trends in the Development of International Commercial Arbitration and the Role of Arbitral and Other Institutions* and the proceedings of the Lausanne interim meeting of 1984 on *UNCITRAL's Project for a Model Law on International Commercial Arbitration.* The present Volume covers ICCA's VIIIth Congress, held in New York, May 1986.

The Congress dealt with two subjects, each in a separate Working Group. The topics of discussion were "Comparative Arbitration Practice" and "Arbitration and Public Policy". This Volume presents the excellent papers written by the Rapporteurs and Commentators on their subjects. For their names, reference may be made to the Table of Contents of this Volume. In order to facilitate discussion during the Congress, the reports were sent in advance to all participants who registered in time.

The discussion in *Working Group I* on "Comparative Arbitration Practice" focused on a Hypothetical Case prepared by Judge Howard M. Holtzmann and Professor Giorgio Bernini. The papers prepared by the Rapporteurs and Commentators addressed the specific questions of the Hypothetical Case.

At the Congress, Working Group I followed a unique procedure. Each Rapporteur and Commentator did not present his or her entire paper at one time in the traditional way, but instead the various questions of the Hypothetical Case were taken up one after another, and the Rapporteurs, Commentators, and participants discussed the questions one at a time. Following that same structure, in this Volume each question of the Hypothetical Case is presented individually. Immediately after each question we reproduce the portions of the papers of the Rapporteurs and Commentators that respond to that particular question. The full text of each paper is this included, but the material is arranged by question. Special thanks go to Judge Holtzmann who undertook the painstaking work of organizing the material in this way in order to facilitate a comparative study. Those who wish, in addition, to have the text of any of the Reports or Comments in its original form may order copies at cost price from the T.M.C. Asser Institute.*

Working Group II on "Arbitration and Public Policy" was conducted along more traditional lines. Four Rapporteurs presented papers on separate aspects of the topic, and views were presented by six Commentators. In this Volume, the full texts of the Reports are reproduced in the same order in which they were presented at the Congress, followed by texts of the Comments. This Working Group was chaired by Dr. Ottoarndt Glossner, Prof. Dr. Rafaël Eyzaguirre Echeverria, Prof. Ivan Szász and Mr. Tang Houzhi.

In addition to the Reports and Comments, several interesting written *Communications* were received and valuable and interesting oral *Interventions* were made in both Working Groups. Due to limitation of space it has not been possible to reproduce these Communications and Interventions in this Volume. Lists of the Communications and Interventions are to be found on pages 172–173 and 363–366. Those who are interested may obtain copies at cost price from the T.M.C. Asser Institute.*

Thanks are due to the American Arbitration Association which was the able host of the New York Congress. Thanks are also due to the Department of International Commercial Arbitration of the T.M.C. Asser Institute and in particular to Mrs. Judy Freedberg, Department Head, for invaluable assistance in the editing of this Volume.

We hope this Volume will be a useful source of information for all those interested in arbitral proceedings as conducted in different parts of the world and in the world-wide role public policy plays in arbitration.

Schiedam, November 1986

Pieter Sanders
General Editor

* Orders for copies should be addressed to:

Department of International Commercial Arbitration
T.M.C. Asser Institute
Alexanderstraat 20–22
2415 JM THE HAGUE
The Netherlands

THE WHITE HOUSE

WASHINGTON

April 15, 1986

I am pleased to send warm greetings to all those gathered for the VIIIth International Arbitration Congress of the International Council for Commercial Arbitration.

Arbitrators render valuable assistance to the business community in resolving disputes. For over six decades, the people of this nation have benefitted from the services of the American Arbitration Association, your host organization. Its impartial experts, working in the private sector, have resolved thousands of disputes.

Today, world trade has increased to a level requiring a more expansive and effective system for dispute resolution. In promoting and developing such a system, international arbitrators can help to lessen conflict, promote harmony, and bring world peace closer to fulfillment.

New York will soon be the site of ceremonies celebrating the 100th birthday of the Statue of Liberty, our symbol of freedom and hope. May this be an inspiration to you in your endeavors for peaceful settlement of disputes through arbitration.

On behalf of all Americans, I wish you a most productive and enjoyable meeting. God bless you.

Ronald Reagan

STATE OF NEW YORK
EXECUTIVE CHAMBER
ALBANY 12224

MARIO M. CUOMO
GOVERNOR

It gives me great pleasure to extend greetings to all in attendance at the VIIIth International Arbitration Congress of the International Council for Commercial Arbitration.

Since 1926, when the State of New York enacted a modern arbitration statute, arbitration has been a vital mechanism for the settlement of disputes in this State.

That same year, the American Arbitration Association was founded. It is especially fitting that on its 60th anniversary, the American Arbitration Association is hosting the first International Arbitration Congress to be held in America.

The members of the International Council for Commercial Arbitration and the participants of its VIIIth Congress represent many geographical areas and economic systems. Your efforts to develop and expand the use of international commercial arbitration are of the utmost importance in achieving and maintaining harmony in international trade relations. Honored by your presence, we welcome you to our State; and we extend our best wishes to you for a most worthwhile Congress.

Welcome to New York State, and best wishes for a successful and enjoyable Congress.

Mario M. Cuomo

March 17, 1986

THE CITY OF NEW YORK
OFFICE OF THE MAYOR
NEW YORK, N.Y. 10007

May 6, 1986

To All In Attendance
Eighth Annual International Arbitration Congress
International Council for Commercial Arbitration
The Waldorf-Astoria
New York, New York

Greetings:

On behalf of the City of New York, I welcome the International Council for Commercial Arbitration and its Eighth International Arbitration Congress.

Your host organization, the American Arbitration Association, was founded in our City sixty years ago.

Robert Coulson and his able associates have combined their talents to make this the most productive Congress to date.

To those who have come to this gathering from nations throughout the world, I extend special greetings in the confident hope that you'll return home with a sense of great accomplishment and with pleasant memories of New York...which I modestly claim to be the greatest City in the history of the world.

With all good wishes to Professor Pieter Sanders and his distinguished colleagues.

Sincerely,

Edward I. Koch
Mayor

Opening Address of Robert B. von Mehren

Chief Judge Sol Wachtler, outgoing ICCA President, Pieter Sanders, incoming ICCA President Giorgio Bernini, President Robert Coulson, Ladies and Gentlemen.

Welcome to New York City: Welcome to the VIIIth International Arbitration Congress of the International Council for Commercial Arbitration.

I pondered how I should greet this Congress – a Congress whose basic working themes are "Comparative Arbitration Practice" and "Public Policy in Arbitration" at its opening. I thought that my greeting would be insufficient without certain elements: It should relate, at least metaphorically, to New York City, it should concern arbitration, and it should have some relevance to our working themes.

I have chosen, therefore, to welcome you to this Congress within the framework of a famous unusual arbitration. The arbitration that I have in mind was brought before a single arbitrator; there were three claimants; the sole arbitrator consulted independently with each claimant; the award was "motivated" but not "reasoned"; and the consequences of the award led to a legend and to some of the most wonderful poetry and painting of the western world.

This arbitration was not conducted under the aegis of any arbitral body as such and the award was not filed in any dossier. Enforcement was not sought from any international or state judicial body. Instead, the award drew divine attention, led to tragedy and was challenged on the plains of Mars.

Since the award was not formally recorded, I cannot quote it directly. I can, however, draw upon a number of ancient and contemporary sources to present the facts, the award and its consequences. I have chosen to base my summary largely upon a modern account by the author, poet and classicist, Robert Graves.

Perhaps it is both relevant and interesting to present a summary of this case as it might be organized in a modern American law school classroom.

SUMMARY OF THE ARBITRATION

The Appointing Authority: He was almighty and consequently found it unnecessary to consult with any court of arbitration or to present "lists" to the parties. Neither ICC or AAA procedure here. Instead, he acted on the basis of divine authority and divine pique.

The Sole Arbitrator: A herdsman of royal blood, chosen by the divine appointing authority because he was "as handsome as . . . [he was] wise in the affairs of the heart" (Robert Graves, *The Greek Myths* (Penguin Books) p. 270)).

The Claimants: Three women of divine quality intensely jealous of each other.

The Terms of Reference: As the Wicked Queen put it in Snow White: "Mirror, Mirror on the wall, who is the fairest of them all."

The Procedure Adopted: The sole arbitrator adopted the civil law approach of direct involvement by the tribunal in the fact-finding process. No American procedure here – no interrogatories, no demands for documentary production and no pre-hearing depositions.

As Robert Graves describes the proceedings, the appointing authority advised the sole arbitrator that it was for the sole arbitrator to determine the procedural rules. Graves writes:

> " 'Will it be enough to judge them as they are?' Paris asked Hermes (the representative of Zeus), 'or should they be naked?'
> 'The rules of the contest are for you to decide,' Hermes answered with a discreet smile.
> 'In that case, will they kindly disrobe?' Hermes told the goddesses to do so, and politely turned his back." (*Id.* at 271.)

The Claimants: Aphrodite, Athena and Hera complied with the procedural direction of the tribunal and the arbitration continued with examination by the sole arbitrator of each claimant individually and privately.

The disadvantage of direct contact between the tribunal and the claimants without the presence of counsel is vividly demonstrated by this case. Again, I quote Robert Graves:

> "Aphrodite sidled up to him, and Paris blushed because she came so close that they were almost touching.
> 'Look carefully, please, pass nothing over. . . . By the way, as soon as I saw you, I said to myself: "Upon my word, there goes the handsomest young man in Phrygia! Why does he waste himself here in the wilderness herding stupid cattle?" Well, why do you, Paris? Why not move into a city and lead a civilized life? What have you to lose by marrying some one like Helen of Sparta . . .?' " (*Ibid.*)

The Award: Aphrodite solemnly swore to Paris that Helen would fall head over heels in love with him and "Paris, without a second thought, awarded her the golden apple." (*Id.* at 272).

The Arbitrator's Fee: Helen of Sparta, described by Aphrodite to be "as beautiful as I am, and not less passionate."

The Reception of the Award: By his judgment, Paris incurred the hatred of both Hera and Athena; they plotted the destruction of Troy; the Trojan War followed and led to the fall of that city and to the death of the arbitrator.

★ ★ ★

My arbitration – the judgment of Paris – raises procedural and public policy issues which I am sure all of us will be able to address with more authority after the Congress.

So without more ado, I say that it is my pleasure to welcome you not to Paris but to New York and to award to all of you not a golden apple but "The Big Apple". It is our pride and pleasure to have you here.

Welcoming Address of Professor Pieter Sanders

As Chairman of ICCA, I would like first of all to express how pleased we were to receive the invitation of the AAA to hold our VIIIth Congress in New York. After Paris, Rotterdam, Venice, Moscow, New Delhi, Mexico City and Hamburg, we now for the first time have a Congress in the United States.

ICCA's activities are, in broad outline, twofold. First of all, ICCA, along with the host organization, participates in the organization of international arbitration conferences where topics of great interest for the development of international commercial arbitration are dealt with on the basis of reports written by experts on the subjects of the conference. These reports are distributed well in advance of each meeting to those who register in time. Participants may then come to the conference well prepared for the discussion.

Secondly, ICCA has an extensive publication program: its *Yearbooks* are well known. *Yearbook* XI (1986) just came from the press and is available here, as are all ICCA publications. This eleventh Volume again provides in its 700 pages a wealth of information on international commercial arbitration. It also contains, for the first time, an *Index* of all arbitral awards published in the *Yearbooks*. This 45-page Index of the subjects dealt with in the arbitral awards will be of great assistance to lawyers and arbitrators when they want to know how international arbitrators have decided previously in similar cases. With the Hamburg Congress, ICCA started the publication of its *Congress Series*. The New York Congress Book will be no. 3 in this series. Participants will receive it before the end of this year.

Relatively new is ICCA's third publication: the *International Handbook on Commercial Arbitration*. This is a loose-leaf edition. Here you find national reports on practically all countries where international commercial arbitration currently takes place. These reports are regularly updated in the loose-leaf. Annexed to each national report are all relevant legal texts. This, of course, includes the Arbitration Act or the relevant part of the Code of Civil Procedure of the country concerned.

Both activities of ICCA – its congresses and interim meetings on the one hand, its publications on the other – have a common denominator: the promotion of commercial arbitration as a means of solving disputes arising out of international trade. Both activities are aimed at improving the quality of the arbitral process and, where possible, to better conditions under which this private settlement of disputes takes place.

ICCA is a non-profit organization. Its Council Members devote their time and energy to the goals of ICCA without any remuneration. The same applies to those who function as general editors for ICCA's publications. The ICCA Council, as such, is quite an idealistic group. It is presently composed of 32 members, all experts in arbitration. They come from 17 countries, representing all the different systems of arbitration in the world. ICCA has been recognized by the United Nations and is a so-called non-governmental organization, an NGO. As such, we advise and assist the UN and, particularly, the UNCITRAL in its arbitration work. This was already the case with the UNCITRAL Arbitration Rules (1976), followed by the UNCITRAL Conciliation Rules (1980) and more recently in the preparation of the UNCITRAL's Model Law on International Commercial Arbitration (1985) on which project ICCA held a meeting in Lausanne in 1983, attended by more than 500 participants. In fact this was a massive hearing on the Model Law project.

We are often approached with the question "How can I become a member of ICCA?" The answer is, I am sorry to say, simply: "You can't." We enlarged the maximum number of members recently to 36 but the few seats which we still have available will be occupied by representatives of countries or regions we deem still not sufficiently represented. Their choice is made, with great care, by ICCA's Council in the old-fashioned way of cooptation.

From the time of the first Congress in Paris (1961), ICCA was privileged to have Jean Robert as Chairman until I took over in Mexico. With great respect we all remember the period during which he guided ICCA and we are happy to welcome him here today as Honorary Chairman of ICCA. After this Congress I will be succeeded as Chairman of ICCA by Professor Giorgio Bernini. We are all convinced that in the years to come ICCA will be efficiently and eloquently chaired by him.

In two years time, we will hold our next interim meeting in Tokyo, Japan on 31 May–3 June in 1988. This meeting will be hosted by the Japan Arbitration Association and the Japan Shipping Exchange, Inc. The subject of this meeting will be Arbitration and Conciliation in that region. I am also happy to announce that we received an invitation from the Stockholm Chamber of Commerce to hold our IXth Congress in Stockholm in 1990. Tokyo and Stockholm will be the places of our next meetings.

The use of international arbitration is steadily increasing. In response to this increased use of arbitration as a means of settling disputes many national legislators have during the last decennia improved the conditions under which arbitration takes place. These modern arbitration laws are favourable to arbitration in that they seek to allow the parties the greatest possible autonomy while protecting the interests of the parties by providing mechanisms for assisting the arbitration process in going forward and assuring the parties a fair hearing. In general, enforcement of awards has been facilitated by reducing the formal requirements and limiting the grounds for refusal. Conversely, the grounds for setting aside of awards have been more strictly defined as well.

Similarly, many arbitral institutions have modernized their procedures by adapting their rules or adopting new types of procedures: conciliation, mini-trials and various forms of alternative dispute resolution. There has been a proliferation of international arbitration centres, creating a stimulating competition to provide the best possible services under the most favourable legal and – I may add – meteorological climate.

Unification and harmonization of arbitration practice have been promoted by the wide and increasing adherence to international arbitration treaties. Today 69 States have adhered to the New York Convention. Similarly, the Washington Convention has now been adhered to by 92 States.

The subjects of this Congress are good examples of ICCA's efforts to assist in the development of international commercial arbitration. *Arbitral practice* in various legal systems will be compared and examined. Participants will return home to their own legal systems with an increased understanding of other systems. *Public policy* will also be examined. In the past a broad application of public policy has sometimes hindered the course of international commercial arbitration. In the coming days, different visions of public policy will be discussed and the ideas expressed at this Congress may later find their expression in new definitions of "international" public policy.

In this way, ICCA seeks to illuminate new ideas, providing a forum where all points of view may be heard.

Let me terminate this address by now expressing our sincere thanks to the AAA and the Congress Coordinator Mrs. Rosabel Everard Goodman and her staff for the excellent organization of this meeting and by wishing all of you interesting and happy days in the fascinating scenery of New York.

Guest Address of the Honorable Sol Wachtler

I am privileged to welcome the Eighth International Arbitration Congress to New York State and to New York City. I am privileged to be with you.

As I am privileged to be a Judge, particularly during these times when our court and the court system in this State are being tested as never before. Last year the courts of this State resolved 2½ million cases. That's ten times more than all the cases resolved in the entire federal court system in the same year. And the kinds of cases we have! In New York State, of course, we probably have the most imaginative lawyers in the world. Certainly the most imaginative criminals.

In the last few years we had to decide if fish had the right to breathe in the Hudson River. We had to decide that the Grand Central Terminal should stand, and that the blue laws should fall.

We had to tell a parent of an infirm young child that that child had a right to live. And we told a terminally ill elderly patient that he had a right to die. We said that a man could be found guilty of raping his wife, that an obese woman could not be fired simply because she was obese if she could do the work assigned to her.

Matters which weren't dreamed of a decade ago are now coming into our state courts.

On the civil side, we are seeing consumer protection being fostered by class actions. Environmentalists have made the courtroom their battleground. We see affirmative action suits to eliminate discrimination and student unrest moving from behind the barricade and into the courtroom. We are witnessing the enormous increase in the use of our courts which is the mark of our litigious and free society.

The people who seek access to our courts are entitled, in our democratic society, to have the courts redress the wrongs done them. Historically, the role of law and the courts has been a creative force in regulating social, economic and political affairs of our republic.

But having said that we recognize the fact that with this influx of litigation, the courts are literally drowning, and mind you, I have spoken only of the civil side.

On the criminal side, where people look to the criminal courts for salvation – people who live behind triple-locked doors because of their fear of crime, a caricature of a society which prides itself on civil liberties, the courts are practically helpless in dealing with the volume.

This morning New York City had 26,000 cases in the Criminal Court and only 60 Judges available to try them.

But coming back to the civil courts and commercial litigation, the congestion in the courts is only one by-product of our litigious society. The other, of course, has been manifest in the escalating costs of doing business. The costs of not only maintaining the courts but of insuring against the astronomical boxcar verdicts of juries.

So we look for alternatives.

Agreements to submit disputes to arbitration were once viewed adversely as an improper attempt to preclude judicial review. The Appellate Courts in this State and nation have completely altered that view.

Arbitration is now well recognized as an effective and expeditious means of resolving disputes between willing parties desirous of avoiding the expense and delay frequently attendant to the judicial process. Not only do we support and urge the process but, I can assure you, and those who have participated in the process in the State can attest to the fact, that there has been an even-handedness as confirmation of awards relates to parties – domestic or foreign.

As further evidence of our positive reception to the arbitration process, I would just like to note, by way of boasting, that New York State was the first in this country to fund community dispute resolution centers within our court system.

Last year, 77,000 contract disputes were referred to these centers, which exist in 52 of our counties and are available to 97% of our State's population.

And if there is any doubt with respect to the efficiency of that system, as compared with the regrettable court delays, I tell you that the time from referral to one of our resolution centers to the time of final disposition averages 15 days.

Once again, I welcome all of you to this Congress. I tell you, without hesitancy and without meaning to over dramatize, that we look to the arbitration and the alternative dispute resolution process as one of the ways in which we can keep our court system alive.

And make no mistake about it, the maintaining of our court system is one of the most important aspects of maintaining our civilization because, as those students of history will tell you, the decline of every great civilization has been preceded by a failure in that civilization of the justice system.

Working Group I
Comparative Arbitration Practice

Chairmen: Judge Howard M. Holtzmann
Professor Giorgio Bernini

Hypothetical Case for Use in a Comparative Study of Arbitration Practice in Various Legal Systems

*by Judge Howard M. Holtzmann**
*and Professor Giorgio Bernini***

I. INTRODUCTORY NOTE

The purpose of this hypothetical case is to provide a framework for a systematic comparative examination of typical *practices* followed in various parts of the world in conducting an international commercial arbitration. In using the word "practices" we mean the elements of arbitral procedure that arbitrators have discretion to determine because they are not specified in the national law governing the arbitration or in the arbitration rules agreed to by the parties.

Parties from different countries who engage in international transactions often agree that any disputes arising from their contracts will be resolved by arbitration in a third country under rules that provide that the sole arbitrator – or the chairman of the arbitral tribunal – will usually be of a nationality other than the nationalities of the parties. In such cases, businessmen and their lawyers may be uncertain concerning the practices that are likely to be followed by arbitrators who may come from a different legal system.

Wise arbitrators and understanding lawyers can find ways flexibly to accommodate arbitration practices of different legal systems. An international arbitration will, however, go forward more efficiently – with fewer surprises and less cost – if the parties and the arbitrators know *in advance* what practices are likely to be followed in conducting the proceeding.

The lawyers of the parties will, of course, familiarize themselves with the legislation of the place of arbitration that may govern their arbitral proceedings. Likewise, they will study whichever arbitration rules may have been chosen by the parties. National legislation and arbitration rules, however, do not answer all of the questions; they usually leave broad areas to be determined by agreement of the parties or, where there is no such agreement, to be decided by the arbitral tribunal. This hypothetical case is designed to explore how arbitrators from different legal systems typically approach procedural questions on points as to which they have broad discretion under the applicable law and governing arbitration rules. For it is these matters of *practice* that may be unknown to parties

* Chairman, International Arbitration Committee and Past Chairman of the Board, American Arbitration Association; Member, Iran-US Claims Tribunal; Vice President of ICCA.
** Professor of Commercial Law, Bologna University; Member of the Executive Committee of the Associazione Italiana per l'Arbitrato; Lawyer; President of ICCA.

who come from different legal systems and who have different professional training and backgrounds.

Advance knowledge of such practices is important for the parties because it will help them to prepare their cases more effectively and to present them in a manner that is more likely to persuade the arbitral tribunal. It is valuable for sole arbitrators, and tribunal chairmen, because it will help them to understand – and not be shocked by – actions of a party that are different from the ones to which they are accustomed under their own law and in the light of their own legal and cultural backgrounds. It will also be useful for party-appointed arbitrators in assisting them to understand their colleagues and thus in promoting collegiality within the arbitral tribunal.

It must be understood that even within any one legal system there is no single arbitration practice that is equally applicable in all cases. Practices vary in different trades, in different transactions and to meet differing needs. We can, at best, hope to illuminate through this hypothetical case certain tendencies that are likely to occur in arbitrating a dispute arising out of a complex international commercial transaction of the type that frequently arises in world trade.

It must also be recognized that some of the arbitration rules used in international transactions provide answers to many questions of procedure – indeed, that is one of the great values of utilizing such rules. Arbitration rules do not, however, provide all the answers, because most, quite wisely, leave broad areas of discretion to the arbitral tribunal to adopt detailed procedures designed to meet the needs of particular cases. For this hypothetical case, we have assumed that the parties have agreed upon the UNCITRAL Arbitration Rules (hereinafter called "the Rules"). We have done so because they are among the rules that leave wide areas of procedure for determination by the arbitrators. They provide, that

> "[s]ubject to these Rules, *the arbitral tribunal may conduct the arbitration in such manner as it considers appropriate*, provided that the parties are treated with equality and that at any stage of the proceedings each party is given a full opportunity of presenting his case." (Art. 15, para. 1; emphasis added.)

By examining an arbitration case conducted under these Rules it is therefore possible to observe how arbitrators from different legal systems are likely to deal with a number of vital questions of practice. We emphasize that in addition to the UNCITRAL Arbitration Rules there are other rules sponsored by various arbitral institutions that can be effectively used in international cases. Many, if not all, of the same questions of arbitral practice arise under those other rules.

We describe below a typical dispute in international trade. We then present various specific questions of practice that are likely to arise at each stage of arbitrating the dispute. Each Rapporteur was asked to respond to each of those questions from the standpoint of how an arbitrator from his legal system is likely to view the questions. The Commentators were invited to give further insights based on practice in their countries and regions. Active participation by members of the audience who attended the Working Group was encouraged.

The Rapporteurs and Commentators were chosen for their wide diversity of legal backgrounds, including common law, civil law and socialist law. Developed and developing countries were represented, as were various economic systems. The Rapporteurs and Commentators came from East and West Europe, North and Latin America, the Middle East, the Far East and Africa. Thus their responses reflect a broad spectrum of experience.

The Rapporteurs were (listed alphabetically):

Michael F. Hoellering – General Counsel, American Arbitration Association, New York, USA

J. Martin H. Hunter – Solicitor, London, England

Sigvard Jarvin – General Counsel, ICC Court of Arbitration, Paris, France

Sergei N. Lebedev – Head of the Chair of Private International and Civil Law, Moscow Institute of International Relations; President, Maritime Arbitration Commission at the USSR Chamber of Commerce and Industry, Moscow, USSR; Vice President of ICCA

Each Rapporteur presented written answers to all of the questions of the hypothetical case. Those answers appear below immediately following each question. (The answers are presented in the alphabetical order of the Rapporteurs' names.)

The Commentators were (listed alphabetically):

Jacques El-Hakim – Professor at the University of Damascus; Attorney, Damascus, Syria

Shinishiro Michida – Dean and Professor at the Faculty of Law, University of Kyoto, Japan; Member of ICCA

Tinuade Oyekunle – Barrister and Solicitor of the Supreme Court of Nigeria; Financial Secretary of the Nigerian Arbitration Association, Lagos, Nigeria; Vice President of ICCA

José Luis Siqueiros – President of the Interamerican Bar Association; Past President of the Mexican Academy of International Commercial Arbitration; Member of ICCA

Tadeusz Szurski – President of the Court of Arbitration at the Polish Chamber of Foreign Trade, Warsaw, Poland; Member of ICCA

The Commentators each presented written answers to some – but not all – of the questions of the hypothetical case*. Due to limitation of time, they were requested to respond only to those questions as to which practice in their region is different from that described by the Rapporteurs, or as to which particular information or

* *See also*, Communication to the Working Group "Answers to Questions of the Hypothetical Case from the Point of View of an Arbitrator in Italy", G. Mirabelli, Past Chief Justice of the Italian Supreme Court (copy available from the Department of International Commercial Arbitration, T.M.C. Asser Institute, The Hague, The Netherlands).

emphasis would be helpful to outsiders who appear before arbitrators from the region. Where a Commentator prepared a written answer to a question, that answer is printed below following the answers of the Rapporteurs. (These answers also appear in the alphabetical order of the authors' names.)

In addition to answering the specific questions of the hypothetical case, the Rapporteurs and Commentators were invited to write briefly concerning general aspects of arbitration in their areas. These appear below under the heading "General Comments" and are printed following the answers to the hypothetical case. These General Comments are important for a full understanding of each author's answers to the questions of the hypothetical case because they often explain various broad concepts that influenced those answers. Also, several of the General Comments express important qualification and reservations. Thus, Professor Lebedev expressed a view also shared by other authors:

> "A reservation seems appropriate to be made that the answers presented in this Report reflect the purely personal opinion of the author: it is quite probable that many respective questions in specific arbitration, depending on the circumstances of a case and the individual arbitrators involved, might well be resolved in a different manner."

Approximately 30% of the time of the Working Group was devoted to interventions from members of the audience. There were a total of 75 interventions. Each intervenor was invited to present a brief summary of his views. A number of the intervenors also submitted written communications. Space will not permit reprinting in this volume of these summaries of interventions and communications. They are, however, available from the Department of International Commercial Arbitration of the T.M.C. Asser Institute in The Hague, The Netherlands, from whom copies can be obtained.

II. DESCRIPTION OF THE HYPOTHETICAL CASE

Hightech Corporation ("Hightech") is organized under the laws of the nation of Machinia. It has offices and a factory in Machinia. It designs, manufactures and installs complex computer systems that can be used by mining companies for a variety of purposes, such as analyzing data to determine the most profitable places to mine, making maps and maintaining accounting records.

Steelco Corporation ("Steelco") is organized under the laws of the nation of Metalia. It has offices and several iron ore mines in Metalia. In order to operate most efficiently and profitably it needs to analyze a great deal of data concerning the content of various ore bodies in its mines, and concerning its operating costs, such as its expenses of transportation and energy. It desires also to improve its ability to make financial projections and to consolidate its accounting records.

In 1983, Steelco entered into a contract with Hightech under which Hightech was required to manufacture and install a large computer and peripheral equipment ("the System") to be specially designed to meet Steelco's business requirements. The contract provided that the System would include certain equipment that Hightech warranted was covered by a valid patent that it owned and that did not infringe patents of others. Hightech was also required to train twenty Steelco employees to operate the System.

The contract also provided that Steelco, at its own expense, was to construct a building near its offices in Metalia in which the System was to be installed. Under the contract, Steelco was responsible for installing air-conditioning equipment in the new building in order to maintain the proper atmospheric conditions to keep sensitive parts of the System from burning out. Specifications for this air conditioning were provided by Hightech and were attached as an annex to the contract.

Both parties expected that the System would improve the efficiency of Steelco's operations and increase its profits.

The contract was signed on 1 March 1983. It required that the System be manufactured and installed within two years, that is by 28 February 1985. By that time the System had to be capable of passing a series of performance tests specified in the contract.

The contract price was 10 million Machinian dollars. The contract required payment of $1 million on the date it was signed. An additional $3 million was required to be paid when the main computer was delivered in Metalia. Steelco has made both of these payments, totalling $4 million.

Payment of the remaining $6 million was required by the contract within 30 days after the successful completion of the specified performance tests. There were no letters of credit.

By 28 February 1985, the System had been installed but had not yet successfully completed the performance tests. The System had broken down several times and failed to perform accurately. On 1 March 1985, Steelco gave written notice terminating the contract on the ground that Hightech had failed to fulfill its obligations. In the letter of termination, Steelco asked for the return of the money it had paid and for compensation for lost profits it would suffer due to late delivery of the System.

Steelco asserted that there were engineering reports in Hightech's files that showed that Hightech had known for a long time that the System had serious technical defects. Steelco also alleged that another reason why it terminated the contract was that it had received a letter from one of Hightech's competitors, Supertech, asserting that Hightech's patent was invalid and that the System infringed patents owned by Supertech. Supertech threatened that if Steelco used the System it would be liable to pay royalties to Supertech.

Hightech argued that the termination of the contract was improper. It contended that the only reason there was delay in completion of the performance tests was that Steelco had failed to install proper air-conditioning equipment as required by the contract, causing sensitive parts of the System to burn out. Moreover, Hightech asserted that the System had been damaged by Steelco's own employees when they attempted to operate it. Hightech said its patents were valid and did not infringe any Supertech patents.

To these contentions, Steelco responded that any fault in the air conditioning was due to incomplete specifications provided by Hightech, and that mistakes, if any, by Steelco employees were due to improper training by Hightech. Hightech replied that the air-conditioning specifications and the training it had provided were as complete as usual trade customs required.

Both parties agreed that if Steelco had to go to another supplier to purchase a substitute system it could not receive delivery for at least two more years.

The parties discussed the dispute, but were unable to resolve it. The contract contained the following arbitration clause:

> "Any dispute, controversy or claim arising out of or relating to this contract, or the breach, termination or invalidity thereof, shall be settled by arbitration in accordance with the UNCITRAL Arbitration Rules as in force on the date of this contract.
> (a) The appointing authority shall be the Neutralian Arbitration Association.
> (b) The number of arbitrators shall be three.
> (c) The place of arbitration shall be Neutraliaville, Neutralia.
> (d) The language to be used in the arbitral proceeding shall be English."

Steelco filed a Notice of Arbitration under the Rules (Art. 3). It alleged that Hightech had breached the contract by (i) failing to deliver on time a System that performed in accordance with the contract specifications, and (ii) furnishing a System that infringed Supertech's patent thereby exposing Steelco to liability for royalties to Supertech. Steelco demanded the return of the $4 million it had paid to Hightech, plus interest. Steelco also demanded at least $10 million damages for profits that it would lose because it would have to continue to use its existing obsolete methods for two years or more, while awaiting delivery of modern computers from some other supplier.

Hightech denied any breach of contract and counter-claimed for the remaining $6 million of the contract price, plus interest.

Each party asked to be awarded the costs of the arbitration, including its expenses for legal representation.

III. QUESTIONS AND ANSWERS REGARDING THE HYPOTHETICAL CASE

The questions set forth below would all arise in the arbitration between Hightech and Steelco. Under the Rules and the law of Neutralia, the arbitrators have power to answer these questions in whatever way they consider appropriate. Each Rapporteur was asked to imagine that arbitration in Neutralia is the same as in his own legal system and to answer each question on the basis of customary practice in his system. Where more than one answer is appropriate, the Rapporteurs were invited to state their preference, or what they believe would be the preference of most other arbitrators who share their legal background. Where there is no customary practice, the Rapporteurs were asked to indicate the answer that a Neutralian arbitrator would most likely give.*

* Lawyers, arbitrators, witnesses and others involved in an arbitration are not, of course, invariably male. While recognizing and welcoming that, we have nevertheless avoided the use of "his or her," or similar cumbersome devices. Rather, for purposes of simplicity in writing, we have adopted the convention that the masculine pronoun refers as well to females.

A. Composition and Staff of the Arbitral Tribunal

HYPOTHETICAL CASE

The Rules provide that each party shall appoint one arbitrator. (Art. 7(1)) The lawyer for Hightech sat in his office thinking about who might be the arbitrators in the case. He wondered whether to recommend to his client that it designate an arbitrator from Machinia in order to ensure that the arbitral tribunal included a person familiar with Machinian business customs and culture, or whether an arbitrator from another country might be better able to persuade a third-country chairman. Also, he was not sure how best to advise his client concerning the most desirable professional qualifications for the arbitrator it would appoint. He knew that in some parts of the world lawyers are usually chosen as arbitrators, whereas elsewhere technical people expert in the factual subject matter of the dispute are preferred. Should he advise his client to appoint a lawyer experienced in commercial and international law, or would it be preferable in this case to appoint an engineer who could better understand the technical aspects of the System and the air conditioning? He guessed that the Chairman of the arbitral tribunal would probably be Neutralian, and felt that the case would proceed more smoothly if Hightech appointed an arbitrator who had the professional qualifications that were consistent with Neutralian practice. But he knew nothing about Neutralian practice.

In Metalia, Steelco's lawyer was worrying about the same thing. Should he advise his client to designate a Metalian arbitrator? Should his client appoint a lawyer or an engineer? Because the largest part of Steelco's claim was for lost profits, its lawyer also considered whether it might be best to appoint a financial specialist who was familiar with the methods for projecting lost profits in future years.

Thus the first questions of practice faced by the two lawyers were:

QUESTION 1

Should a party choose a party-appointed arbitrator from his own country?

ANSWERS TO QUESTION 1

MR. HOELLERING

More often than not a party appoints as arbitrator an individual from his own country – one who is familiar with the business customs and culture of that country.[1] There are other considerations, however, which may influence a party to appoint a person of a different nationality from his own. The anticipated background and orientation of the presiding arbitrator, the place of arbitration, the language of the proceedings, the applicable substantive law, the reputation of a particular nominee, a connection with another venue which may prove

1. *See* Stein and Wotman, *International Commercial Arbitration in the 1980's*, note 5 on page 154, *infra*, at 1701.

significant – any of these factors may influence a party's decision to appoint an arbitrator who is not a national of his own country.

MR. HUNTER

There is no rule imposed by English law. Neither is there any general practice. It would be natural, and perfectly proper, for each party to want to appoint a person who is "pre-disposed", in a general sense, towards its own political, business and cultural attitudes. To appoint someone of his own nationality, however, may create an impression of collusion or bias. It may be better to appoint someone from another country for reasons of "tribunal psychology". Many awards are achieved by the formation of a majority between the presiding arbitrator and one of the party-nominated arbitrators; and a presiding arbitrator may well be more inclined, in general terms, to join with a party-nominated arbitrator in agreeing upon a majority award if, in addition to actual independence, he has a greater *appearance* of independence. An arbitrator of different nationality from the party who appointed him may be preferable in this context.

MR. JARVIN

In the majority of ICC cases the party-appointed co-arbitrator will have the same nationality as the party who nominates him. We believe that parties prefer to have their own nationals as co-arbitrators, since they are thereby guaranteed that at least one person on the arbitration panel will understand the cultural, legal and economic environment of the party. It would be too strong a word to speak about a tendency, but in recent times it has been noticeable that parties appoint as co-arbitrator a person who is well known as an international arbitrator or as an international specialist in a particular field irrespective of whether that person has the same nationality as the party. The authority of a well-known person on the panel will, in the party's mind, presumably, have a greater influence on the outcome of the case than the nationality of the arbitrator.

Well-informed parties to an ICC arbitration will know that the Court, when appointing a chairman – who should come from a third country – will avoid having two arbitrators of the same nationality on the panel in order not to establish a majority in terms of nationality. If Hightech's lawyer supposes that Steelco intends to appoint a Metalian arbitrator and the ICC a Neutralian chairman, and if Hightech's lawyer would like to avoid having a Neutralian chairman, he might consider nominating a Neutralian co-arbitrator. That way, the ICC would look elsewhere for a chairman, e.g., in a third country, such as Undeterminia, and the panel would not be dominated by two Neutralian arbitrators.

If Hightech's lawyer supposes that Steelco will appoint a Metalian co-arbitrator and is happy with a Neutralian chairman, he might think it wise to appoint a Metalian co-arbitrator himself in the hope that the chairman would be more inclined to listen to his co-arbitrator than to the co-arbitrator appointed by Steelco.

If Hightech's lawyer anticipates that Steelco will default and not propose an arbitrator, he will consider Article 2.6, second paragraph of the Rules of the ICC which provides that the Court of Arbitration of the ICC will request a proposal from the National Committee of the ICC in Metalia. Therefore, Hightech's lawyer will know that there will most probably be a Metalian co-arbitrator, and Hightech's lawyer can make his nomination accordingly.

PROF. LEBEDEV
Choice of an arbitrator, especially in *ad hoc* arbitration, has a distinctively individual character, and depends mainly on the personal preferences of those who have to make the choice and on their factual knowledge of potential candidates able and willing to undertake the mission of an arbitrator.

In any case, it should not be assumed that Hightech will necessarily prefer to choose a citizen of Machina as an arbitrator, and Steelco a citizen of Metalia. It cannot be excluded that Hightech, as well as Steelco, might prefer to appoint a citizen of Neutralia as an arbitrator.

PROF. EL-HAKIM
An arbitrator well-acquainted with the law applicable to the case or to the arbitral procedure or having the same nationality or legal background of the arbitrator(s) or of the President of the arbitral tribunal will certainly be more suitable. Nevertheless, most parties will select an arbitrator of their own nationality, because:

a. They are more acquainted with him.
b. He would be more available and is more aware of their problems and needs.
c. They think he might be more devoted to their interests.

MRS. OYEKUNLE
No customary practice has emerged on this point. Careful consideration will, firstly, be given to the particular facts of the case. For example, if the complex computer systems are to be installed in a very remote part of Africa where there is minimal rural electrification and the atmospheric temperature is very hot and humid, the pollution created by dust, gasfumes and waste is very high and there is no pipe-borne water. The water in use in the mines is piped one thousand miles from the nearest river and it is only in use at high tide seasons; the water supply is supplemented by boreholes. It may require the appointment of a party-appointed arbitrator who is from Africa and who understands the local conditions in the area. Such an arbitrator will appreciate that the specifications for air conditioning suitable for maintaining the proper atmospheric conditions in the place where the computer systems are to be located were not adequate and thereby attributed to the failure of the system to perform accurately.

Another advantage of appointing an arbitrator who understands the geography of the location is his additional knowledge of the political, business and cultural attitudes of the country as indicated in the Report of Mr. Hunter.

Any decision reached on this point also depends on who is likely to be appointed as the Chairman of the arbitral tribunal and also as the co-arbitrator. For instance, if the Respondent in this case (Hightech) is likely to appoint an arbitrator who is familiar with the peculiarities mentioned above and the Chairman who will be appointed by the appointing authority is also to possess knowledge of such peculiarities (having regard to his previous experience in similar matters), the Claimant may decide to appoint an arbitrator from another country.

It will definitely not be in the interest of the Claimant to have the three arbitrators on the arbitral tribunal come from highly sophisticated societies that lack knowledge of conditions in remote areas with no pipe-borne water and minimal rural electrification. For example, in such a case, any air-conditioning specifications must have added to them specifications for powerful generators to sustain consistent power for the air-conditioning systems.

Depending on these peculiar factors, a Claimant may prefer a party-appointed arbitrator from his own country.

On the other hand, if the Claimant felt that, in spite of all the existing peculiarities, an expert who is likely to be appointed by the arbitral tribunal or called by him, the other party or both parties will adduce such evidence as to clarify the peculiar situation, amongst other things, he may decide to nominate an arbitrator of a different nationality from his own.

QUESTION 2

What professional qualifications would be customary for the party-appointed arbitrators in a case of this type (i.e., lawyer, engineer or financial specialist)?

ANSWERS TO QUESTION 2

MR. HOELLERING

The professional qualifications of party-appointed arbitrators in international arbitration proceedings will depend on each party's evaluation of the various issues to be decided by the arbitral tribunal. In the United States, experience suggests that when the issues are primarily legal, the party-appointed arbitrators will be lawyers experienced in commercial and international law. When the issues are technical, the party-appointees will be chosen for their technical expertise in the subject matter of the dispute. Where both significant legal and technical issues combine in a single case, the parties will generally try to find arbitrators with qualifications in both areas.

The factual background of the case indicates that both legal and technical issues are involved. In reaching an award, the arbitral tribunal will need to consider not only questions of contract interpretation and patent law, but also a range of technical issues relating to the computer system, the performance of the air conditioning, the adequacy of the specifications for the air-conditioning system, and the significance of engineering reports relating to system performance and patent validity.

Given the range of these issues, it is likely that counsel for both parties will recommend designation of an arbitrator with solid technical and legal qualifications, such as an attorney with extensive experience in the computer field, patent law and international trade. However, the preference of parties with regard to the qualifications of party-appointed arbitrators will vary, and there is no predominant pattern – some will prefer a lawyer/arbitrator, others, in view of the technical aspects of the case, an engineer as the party-appointed arbitrator.

Were this case one in which all three arbitrators were to be selected under the rules of the American Arbitration Association, consultations between the parties and the Association might well result in the designation of a panel consisting of a lawyer, an engineer and a financial specialist. The joint selection of the entire panel by both parties, with AAA assistance, will facilitate the inclusion on the panel of the broadest range of expertise. The AAA has a roster, searchable by computer, of over 3,000 qualified arbitrators to serve on international cases. These arbitrators provide the Association with extensive data regarding their education and professional background, expertise and range of experience. It is highly likely that an appropriate panel could be drawn from this large database to resolve the Steelco-Hightech dispute.

To ensure that its factual contentions and legal arguments can be communicated effectively and appreciated by the arbitral tribunal, each party will want to appoint an arbitrator with both legal and technical qualifications. The choice of a financial specialist is not likely, since consideration of Steelco's claim for lost profits is contractual in nature, and information on this aspect of the case may be provided by expert testimony.

One author has noted that it is important to consider both the law of the arbitral forum and that of the country where enforcement will be sought when choosing a party-appointee. "The issue is essentially one of striking a balance between the requirement that the tribunal be impartial and recognition of the right of the parties to select persons in whom they have confidence. These objectives are not, of course, necessarily inconsistent and various ways of organizing an arbitral tribunal reflects differing approaches."[2]

In response to a survey conducted by the American Arbitration Association,[3] 59 American attorneys, law firms and corporations indicated the factors most important to them in their choice of an arbitrator. The breakdown of those responses was as follows:

Importance:	*Very*	*Somewhat*	*Not*
Knowledge of applicable law	37	20	1
Knowledge of particular industry	31	26	1
Recognized international arbitrator	11	24	22
Language ability	41	9	8
Membership in arbitration societies	5	14	38
Nationality	11	32	14

MR. HUNTER

There are no specific requirements, but it is usual for parties to nominate persons who are familiar with arbitration law, and arbitral practices and procedures. Other than in certain special types of arbitration (mainly outside the commercial

2. De Vries, *Practical Aspects of International Litigation–Arbitration*, Proceedings of the American Society of International Law 64 *Am.J.Int'l L.* No. 4, p. 251 (1970).

3. *See* Coulson, *Survey of International Arbitration Procedures*, in American Arbitration Association, *Arbitration & the Law, 1981*, p. 228; *see also* Coulson, *A New Look at International Commercial Arbitration*, 14 *Case W.Res.J.Int'l L.* 359 (1982). *See also* answer to Question 14, *infra*.

field, such as rent review arbitrations under leases) it would be rare for a party to nominate an arbitrator who has no knowledge of arbitration law and practice.

In England, many lawyers, engineers, surveyors, accountants, shipbrokers and commodity traders and other persons with professional qualifications have received specific training in arbitration law and practice; for example, by attending seminars and conferences, or by taking the relevant examinations to attain Fellowship of the Chartered Institute of Arbitrators, a body which runs a number of training programmes and a pupillage scheme.

In this particular case, if the present Rapporteur was Steelco's lawyer, he would advise his client to nominate a lawyer as arbitrator. The primary issues are of a legal nature (interpretation of the contract specification; the patent issues). Secondary issues, such as performance of the computer system, quantification, etc., are usually readily understood by lawyers having an appropriate background. We are not told the substantive law applicable to the issues, but probably a lawyer, very possibly not from Metalia (see the answer to Question 1), but familiar with the legal system and generally "predisposed" to Metalian political and cultural attitudes, would be suitable.

If the present Rapporteur was Hightech's lawyer, he might have the advantage of knowing who Steelco had nominated. Similar considerations would apply, but since Hightech's case depends so strongly on showing that the equipment supplied was in accordance with the specification, there would be a temptation to nominate an expert in the computer field, even assuming that Steelco had nominated a lawyer.

Whether representing Steelco or Hightech, the present Rapporteur would place no great significance on nominating someone familiar with Neutralian (English) procedural law. He would assume that the presiding arbitrator would be suitably qualified for this purpose.

MR. JARVIN

He would most certainly be a lawyer, experienced in the kind of questions that will arise in this case. Where a lawyer needs technical advice he normally appoints an expert who can enlighten the tribunal. The opposite, i.e., a tribunal composed of technicians who take legal expertise, is not seen in practice.

The overwhelming majority of arbitrators in ICC cases are lawyers. In a sample study, made in 1983, of arbitrators (co-arbitrators as well as chairmen) in 100 cases and including cases processed under different legal systems – i.e., not only civil law which is my task when answering this questionnaire – the percentage of lawyers and non-lawyers was the following:

94 lawyers, out of which 52 law practitioners
20 in-house lawyers
13 law professors
9 judges

6 non-lawyers, out of which 2 chief accountants
2 chief engineers
2 consultants

100

PROF. LEBEDEV

It is practically excluded that a financial specialist will be chosen as an arbitrator by Steelco, unless Steelco is 100% sure that the outcome will be successful and, hence, that the only problem in the arbitration will be the problem of calculation of damages (lost profits). In a serious international arbitration case, like this one, such belief is unjustifiably and excessively optimistic.

There are certainly no grounds for doubting the great importance of the technical issues arising in this case, for Hightech as well as for Steelco (were there inherent defects in the System, was it possible and when to have the system functioning, what was the state of air-conditioning equipment, were the third-party patents infringed, etc.), and these considerations may be a good incentive for choosing a highly qualified engineer as an arbitrator. It is unlikely, however, that he will be equally competent in all of the above-indicated technical questions. Besides, it is not the expertise and even not the finding of the "technical truth" in the course of arbitration that is meant here. It will be necessary, in any case, to evaluate from the legal standpoint the facts of a technical nature which may be considered by the arbitrators as proved. It is submitted that even for Hightech – although proving the perfection of the System might seem to guarantee success in the arbitration – it would be questionable not to pay attention to the legal aspects of the case by appointing an engineer, unless he is a specialist in the area of the principal technical issues in dispute and has at the same time practical experience of participation in arbitrations, at least in so-called "technical arbitration".

No doubt, a candidate for arbitrator having both technical and legal knowledge, although not of the same depth, would attract the attention of any party. Touching upon, for example, the area of merchant shipping, it might be noted that in various cases – from shipping to collisions – persons who have diplomas as captains and as lawyers are often appointed as arbitrators. Experts in patent law specializing in certain technical areas may serve as another example.

However, in the absence of such candidates for this case, it is most likely that Hightech, and even more so Steelco, will prefer to choose an arbitrator from among lawyers who may be scholars or practitioners specializing in legal problems of international trade, transfer of technology, etc., having experience in international arbitrations and, consequently, are familiar with the legislation and practice of several foreign countries. Being inclined to this solution, we are also taking into consideration traditional attitudes to commercial arbitration itself which, with all its peculiarities, is conceived as an alternative to court proceedings and under any circumstances as a legal institution.

MRS. OYEKUNLE

On the facts of the case, a lawyer experienced in international arbitration law and commerce would be preferred.

HYPOTHETICAL CASE A. cont.

The Rules contemplate that the two party-appointed arbitrators will agree on a third arbitrator, who will be the chairman. (Art. 7(1).) The lawyers for Steelco and Hightech were not sure whether it would be permissible to communicate *ex parte* with the party-appointed arbitrators designated by their clients to discuss ideas concerning the desired qualifications of a person who would be chairman, or the names of individuals who would, or would not, be desirable. Both lawyers knew that under the Rules all arbitrators are expected to be impartial and independent, and that the party-appointed arbitrators are held to the same standard as the chairman. (Arts. 9 and 10.) Both lawyers knew that it would not be permissible to have *ex parte* communications with any arbitrator after the arbitral tribunal had been formed. Each wondered, however, whether it would be acceptable under Neutralian practice to discuss with the arbitrator appointed by his side matters relating to the selection of the third arbitrator (but not the merits of the dispute).

QUESTION 3

Is it permissible for a party to discuss *ex parte* with the arbitrator it appointed matters relating to the selection of the third arbitrator?

ANSWERS TO QUESTION 3

MR. HOELLERING

Assuming that Neutralian arbitration practice is similar to that in the United States, it is permissible for a party or its counsel to discuss with its arbitrator-appointee matters relating to the choice of the third arbitrator. Commonly discussed would be ideas concerning the desired qualifications of a chairman, or the names of individuals who would or would not be desirable. However, since the UNCITRAL Rules, which govern our hypothetical case, as well as the AAA's Supplementary Procedures for International Arbitration, contemplate that all arbitrators, including those appointed by a party, shall be neutral, it would not be appropriate for a party or its counsel to discuss with its arbitrator-appointee other aspects of the case.[4]

MR. HUNTER

In England there is no specific rule or ethical guideline. It is a somewhat personal matter for individual arbitrators. The present Rapporteur, as a party-nominated arbitrator, finds it acceptable – and indeed positively helpful – to discuss with the party appointing him the *general* qualities required in the third arbitrator for a

4. In certain domestic arbitration arrangements, such as in labor-management and certain commercial arbitrations, the parties sometimes provide for the use of non-neutral party-appointed arbitrators. Ordinarily, under US law, such arbitrators can be sympathetic to the position of the party who appointed them, but *ex parte* communication on, and prejudgment of, the merits of the case are not permissible. Even party-appointees are expected to serve and decide the case on a neutral basis.

particular case, e.g., professional qualifications, nationality, competence in languages and so forth.

The present Rapporteur prefers such discussions to be with the nominating party's lawyers, rather than with the party or its executives directly (because lawyers will find it easier to understand where the dividing line lies beyond which the conversations may become unacceptable by compromising the independence and impartiality of the arbitrator); and he prefers not to discuss specific names although, exceptionally, a list of "possibles" by way of example may be helpful. The final choice must always be with the arbitrator, if that is what the arbitration clause specifies.

MR. JARVIN

There are no specific rules or guidelines for *parties*, and the question that might arise would rather be whether it is permissible for the *co-arbitrator* to discuss matters relating to the selection of the chairperson without endangering his impartiality. The answer is that it is permissible for the arbitrator to discuss with the party appointing him the general qualities of the chairperson (training, experience, language, etc.) without going into a discussion on the merits of the case.

PROF. LEBEDEV

At first sight, such discussions might have some positive value, in particular, to prevent the parties from being dissatisfied and from making objections and challenges in regard to the third arbitrator, who was approved by the parties before his appointment. However, a proposal as to the prospective third arbitrator made by an arbitrator after approval of the party that appointed the latter may well cause doubts and suspicions, whether justified or not, on the part of the other party-appointed arbitrator and, what is more important, of the other party, making it more difficult, rather than easier, to arrive on an agreement on the candidate. Although the law does not directly deal with this question, it is believed that the general rule regarding impartiality and independence of arbitrators (Arts. 9, 10 of the UNCITRAL Rules) should be considered as valid not from the time when the arbitral tribunal is formed, but as of the time when an arbitrator is appointed; therefore, *ex parte* consultations between the arbitrator and the party who appointed him regarding the choice of the third arbitrator will not be encouraged. It is a quite different situation and not only acceptable, but even desirable, when the two arbitrators together, after they have agreed upon the prospective third arbitrator, but before his official appointment, discuss the candidate with the parties.

PROF. EL-HAKIM

Although the discussion between the party and the arbitrator will not be officially recorded, it will, nevertheless, take place in almost all cases. Under local laws, such a discussion does not violate any explicit rule, although it does not comply with strict ethics, except if the discussion is restricted to the general requirements that are supposed to be suitable to the President. Practically, contacts between one party and the arbitrator it has appointed go much beyond those limits, although they are difficult to prove and even if they are proven, they will not necessary lead to the annulment of the procedure.

MRS. OYEKUNLE

There is no legal or customary rule against this practice. It is, therefore, permissible. In fact, it is very useful to advise the party, although not by emphasising the appointment of a particular person as Chairman but, by indicating list of possibles. In fact, this consultation is necessary in assisting the party, having regard to the intricacies of issues which are likely to come up during the arbitration. Such a complex matter requires the appointment of a capable Chairman who will direct the proceedings in an independent and impartial manner. The Chairman appointed should also be capable of giving the parties equal treatment and a full opportunity of presenting their case.

DR. SZURSKI

Although the general rule as to impartiality and independence of arbitrators will always be considered by a Polish arbitrator as being valid as of the time he was appointed, in principle, most arbitrators will treat the consultation with the parties, and particularly with the parties' lawyers, on matters concerning the selection of a third arbitrator as being practically justified and as not violating that general rule. Such an approach, however, can be expected only as regards *ad hoc* arbitrations in more complicated cases as, e.g., that between Steelco and Hightech. It must, however, be underlined that the practice of consultations between arbitrators and the parties or their lawyers as regards the choice of the presiding arbitrator happens rather rarely within the framework of the Court of Arbitration at the Polish Chamber of Foreign Trade, where most of the arbitrators inscribed on the list know each other and having received (according to the Rules) the statements of claim and of defense before the choice of third arbitrator, easily reach mutual consent as to the most suitable person to be the chairman of the tribunal in a given case.

Among the reasons which may justify the practice in question of consultations, mention may be made of the following:

- such consultation can help to avoid choosing as the third arbitrator a person with regard to whom a party may have reservations or even bad experience from its own past practice, which fact otherwise might not have been known by the arbitrator.

- since the choice of a third arbitrator needs the agreement of the other arbitrator, in practice, consultations with the party or the party's lawyer as to the third arbitrator may result only in the elimination of a person who is not acceptable to a party; in no way will it put the other party in an unequal position.

HYPOTHETICAL CASE A, cont.

Under the Rules, if the two party-appointed arbitrators fail to agree on the third arbitrator, the appointment will be made by the appointing authority, which in this case is the Neutralian Arbitration Association. (Art. 7(3).) The Steelco and Hightech lawyers each tried to guess what type of person the Neutralian Arbitration Association would appoint as chairman, if it were called upon to act in this case.

QUESTION 4

What professional qualifications would be customary for the chairman in a case of this type (i.e., lawyer, engineer or financial specialist)?

ANSWERS TO QUESTION 4

MR. HOELLERING

The hypothetical case provides that the arbitration will be conducted under the UNCITRAL Rules, administered by the Neutralian Arbitration Association. In the United States, the leading arbitral institution which serves as appointing authority and provides administrative services under the UNCITRAL Rules is the American Arbitration Association. The AAA, when appointing a presiding arbitrator, would follow the list procedure set forth in Article 6(3) of the UNCITRAL Rules.[5] An advantage of this approach is that the parties are provided with greater opportunity to select a third arbitrator who is mutually acceptable and possesses the level of expertise considered appropriate.

In view of the claims between Steelco and Hightech, such a list would consist of eight to twelve individuals, including attorneys, engineers, computer experts, financial specialists and any other persons whose professional and business experience are relevant to the issues in dispute. The background of the third arbitrator would thus depend entirely on the mutual preference of the parties with regard to the names on the list provided by the administering agency.

In the event that a third arbitrator could not be appointed from the lists submitted, the Association would most probably appoint an attorney with technical qualifications in the computer field and expertise in international trade. Well-qualified attorneys, particularly with prior arbitration experience, are often appointed as presiding arbitrators in international cases, to deal with the legal complexities and facilitate the procedural aspects of such cases.[6] Most likely, to ensure his independence and impartiality, he should be of a nationality other

5. Art. 6(3) provides that the appointing authority will transmit to each party identical lists of at least three names from which the parties may delete the names of candidates to which they object, and number the remaining names in the order of preference. The list is then returned to the appointing authority within fifteen days.

6. *See* AAA Commercial Arbitration Rules sects. 13 and 15. The results of a survey of American practitioners indicate that parties generally prefer to select arbitrators from a list, rather than have the arbitral agency make a selection on its own initiative. *See* Coulson, *Survey*, note 3 *supra*.

than that of either party. The appointment of a Neutralian lawyer would not only satisfy this requirement, but also ensure the designation of a chairman familiar with the procedural law of the place of arbitration.

MR. HUNTER

A lawyer with specific experience of the Neutralian (English) law and practice of arbitration. This would almost certainly be the case where the appointment of the third arbitrator was made by agreement between the arbitrators appointed by Steelco and Hightech respectively (UNCITRAL Rules, Art. 7(1)).

If the appointment is made by the London Court of International Arbitration, called upon to act as appointing authority under Article 7(3) of the UNCITRAL Rules, it is almost certain that an experienced Neutralian (English) lawyer–arbitrator would be appointed from its panels of arbitrators. The appointing authority would, however, first use the "list system" specified in Article 6(3) of the UNCITRAL Rules, and would propose a number of potential presiding arbitrators from its panels to give the parties an opportunity to make a joint choice from the list. The appointing authority would also comply with any wishes expressed jointly by the parties, and would give consideration to any views expressed unilaterally by one party; but the chairman of the tribunal in a case of this kind would almost invariably be a lawyer unless the parties agreed otherwise.

MR. JARVIN

Reference may be made to the sample study of 100 arbitrators described in the answer to Question 2.

Whenever the Court invites a National Committee to propose a chairperson, it submits a description of the case for the Committee's guidance. Each committee is free to propose one or several arbitrators. The majority of committees submits one name only for approval by the ICC Court. On the National Committee level, various methods are used to find the most appropriate chairperson. In some countries special sub-committees who deal only with the proposals of arbitrators to the Court have been set up. The local sub-committee consists of lawyers and businessmen familiar with the legal community in their country and able to contact prospective arbitrators quickly to find out if they are willing and able to take on a case.

PROF. LEBEDEV

Due to the considerations stated in connection with Question 2, and especially in the light of the general concept of arbitration, the Neutralian Arbitration Association is most likely to include on the list of prospective third arbitrators to be proposed to the parties (Art. 7(3), Art. 6(3) and (4) of the UNCITRAL Rules) mainly lawyers having the qualifications which were discussed in regard of a lawyer appointed as an arbitrator by the party. This, of course, does not exclude the possibility of including on the list appropriate engineers or financial specialists alongside the lawyers. In general, however, the appointment of a lawyer, on the one hand, and the above qualification requirements, including a comparative law perception, on the other hand, for the third arbitrator, as contrasted with the party-appointed arbitrator, are pre-determined additionally by the functions of the third arbitrator related to the organization of the arbitration proceedings (see, for example, Art. 31(2) of the UNCITRAL Rules). The Arbitration Association would even more willingly accept this approach in case the list-procedure was deemed inappropriate. On the other hand, if the list-procedure was used and both parties preferred to appoint not a lawyer, but an engineer or financial specialist named in the list of the Arbitration Association, such preference would be considered binding for the Association.

MRS. OYEKUNLE
It would be customary to appoint a lawyer as chairman in a case of this type.

HYPOTHETICAL CASE A. cont.

The Steelco and Hightech lawyers knew that in some legal systems it is the practice for the arbitral tribunal to appoint a secretary (sometimes called a "registrar") to assist it in conducting a complex case, even when the case is administered by an arbitral institution. The two lawyers imagined that it was likely that the chairman would be guided by Neutralian practice on a matter such as this, on which the Rules contained no specific provisions.

QUESTION 5

Is it customary for the arbitral tribunal to appoint a secretary? If so, what is his function?

ANSWERS TO QUESTION 5

MR. HOELLERING
The extent of secretarial or administrative assistance available to the arbitral tribunal usually depends on whether the parties have provided for an institution to administer the arbitration. Where an administering authority has been named, a range of such services will be provided by the arbitral institution; where no institution is involved, however, it is not customary for the arbitral tribunal to appoint a secretary. Rather, these functions are performed by the arbitral tribunal itself, most often by the presiding arbitrator.[7]

In this case, the parties have named the Neutralian Arbitration Association as appointing authority under the UNCITRAL Rules. American Arbitration Association procedures applicable to those rules specifically provide for rendition of administrative services when mutually requested by the parties or by the arbitral tribunal. The additional functions the AAA would perform include transmittal of oral and written communications among the parties and the arbitral tribunal other than at hearings; working with the arbitrators to establish

7. In those cases where the tribunal chairman is a partner in a law firm or a retired judge, a junior lawyer employed by the firm or a paralegal may be assigned the function of secretary.

the date, time and place of hearings and giving advance notice thereof to the parties; arranging for hearing rooms, stenographic transcripts and interpreters, where necessary; and making arrangements for arbitrator fees and advance deposits of such fees on account, in consultation with the parties and the arbitral tribunal.[8]

It is also customary for the AAA to assign a tribunal administrator to each case administered under its auspices. The administrator is charged with handling, from start to finish, the administrative aspects of the case, and providing administrative assistance to the tribunal throughout the arbitral proceeding.[9]

MR. HUNTER

It depends on the type and size of case, and whether the chairman of the tribunal has the inclination and facilities to undertake the administrative tasks.

Although Article 38(c) of the UNCITRAL Rules implies that the tribunal may incur expenses in respect of "assistance", it could be imprudent for the tribunal to incur the cost of a secretary (sometimes called a registrar) without the agreement of the parties. However, a case of this size would clearly justify the appointment of a secretary.

His functions would vary, depending on the inclinations of the chairman of the tribunal and the lawyers for the parties. They would, however, be purely administrative. He might organize the hearing room, engage stenographers, rent photocopy machines, check transcripts, arrange for the typing and copying of the award, arrange the finances and the correspondence between the tribunal and the parties. Unlike the situation prevailing in some continental types of arbitration, particularly of the public international law type, he would not carry out research into legal issues for the tribunal, and (although he might be present and keep minutes) he would not participate in the private deliberations of the tribunal. It is a fundamental principle of English arbitration law that the tribunal may not delegate the function of determining the issues.

MR. JARVIN

It has not been customary, except for Swiss arbitral tribunals. However, there is a tendency towards appointing a secretary also with other tribunals, particularly Scandinavian[10] and French.

The Secretary usually assumes the functions of a clerk:[11] he arranges meetings, books hotels and makes reservations for hearing-rooms and travel; files, keeps and retrieves documents; keeps the record at hearings; undertakes legal research upon the arbitrator's instructions.

---

8. *See generally* American Arbitration Association Procedures for Cases Under the UNCITRAL Arbitration Rules (available from the AAA).

9. AAA Commercial Arbitration Rules sect. 4.

10. *Arbitration in Sweden* (1984), page 80: "The appointment of and the fees to be paid to an attorney to serve in the capacity of secretary for the proceedings require the prior approval of the parties. *It is the normal practice to make such an appointment in large or complex cases*".

11. Pierre Jolidon, *Commentaire du Concordat Suisse sur l'Arbitrage*, Berne (1984), pages 242, 243: "In the framework of the ICC Court of Arbitration, neither the parties nor the tribunal can validly charge the secretary with the administration of evidence. As a rule, one may compare the tasks of a secretary with those of a registrar of a state court although they are not identical." (Original in French)

It is questionable whether the secretary should assist at deliberations among the arbitrators and whether he should draft the award. In ICC practice this is not encouraged since it risks giving to the secretary an influence and role that comes too close to that of an arbitrator. The secretary must not sign the award.

The ICC is presently preparing a memorandum for arbitrators defining the powers and limits of the secretary.

PROF. LEBEDEV

Bearing in mind that under the arbitration clause in the contract the Arbitration Association is only to act as "the appointing authority", the arbitral tribunal in a matter of such complexity is most likely to desire a secretary having legal background. His functions may include making various arrangements and the handling of technical matters as instructed by the arbitral tribunal or the third arbitrator: correspondence with the parties; mailing documents; providing premises for the conduct of the hearings; hiring of stenographers and, if necessary, interpreters; preparing minutes of the sessions (see Question 57), etc.

PROF. EL-HAKIM

Arbitrators very seldom appoint a secretary. However, when a Chamber of Commerce appoints as arbitrator a businessman with no legal background, he often appoints as "secretary" a lawyer who practically manages the arbitration, gives his legal opinion to the arbitrator and drafts the award. When the latter is challenged before the courts examining the claim for leave of enforcement (exequatur), such violations do not lead to the annulment of the award, as it should under the laws in force. For instance, the Court of Appeal of Damascus decided (judgment no. 808 on 22 September 1982) that the legal counsel appointed by the arbitrator to assist him in the way described above is a "legal expert" who does not differ from any technical expert and his advice to the arbitrator does not affect the award, especially when the arbitrator has the power of *amiable compositeur*. Such a judgment obviously violates the basic principles of law, since expertise is only authorized in technical matters not in legal ones, otherwise, the expert would usurp the powers of a judge or an arbitrator. It shows, however, how obvious legal rules can be ignored in case law.

When a secretary is appointed, it is, however, excluded that he be present in the deliberations without affecting their secrecy.

MRS. OYEKUNLE

It is not customary for the tribunal to appoint a secretary but in such a complex case as this, such appointment may be important. The secretary's role will be mainly administrative.

DR. SZURSKI

The view expressed by the Rapporteurs that in such a complex case as that between Steelco and Hightech, the arbitral tribunal will most probably appoint a

secretary should be shared. However to answer Question 5 in a direct way the following should be said: It is not an established custom to appoint secretaries in *ad hoc* arbitrations in Poland. It depends on the complexity of the case and on the practical possibilities of the chairman of the arbitral tribunal.

Chairmen of arbitral tribunals, who are of Polish nationality, usually try to avoid the additional expenses entailed in appointing a secretary of the tribunal and use their own secretarial facilities. However, for the purpose of keeping records at the hearings, a secretary is usually appointed. A different rule prevails in the Court of Arbitration at the Polish Chamber of Foreign Trade where all administrative services are carried out by the Secretariat of the Court and where each arbitral tribunal is provided a recording secretary who is directly responsible for the file and for administration of the case.

It seems worthwhile to add that, at present, arbitral tribunals having their seat in Poland will also most probably use the secretarial and administrative services of the Court of Arbitration at the Polish Chamber of Foreign Trade, availing themselves of the possibilities provided for in the newly issued "Rules of Arbitrations *Ad Hoc* Administered by the Court of Arbitration at the Polish Chamber of Foreign Trade."

B. Legal Representation

HYPOTHETICAL CASE

The Rules provide that parties may be represented by the lawyer of their choice (Art. 4), but are silent as to whether lawyers must submit powers of attorney. Hightech's lawyer came from a legal system in which lawyers for parties in arbitration were not expected to submit to the tribunal a power of attorney evidencing their authority to act in the case. Steelco's Metalian lawyer was accustomed to a requirement that each lawyer submit a power of attorney. Neither knew the practice in Neutralia.

QUESTION 6

Should the lawyers for the parties submit powers of attorney to the arbitral tribunal? If so, what, if any, formalities should be observed with respect to the document?

ANSWERS TO QUESTION 6

MR. HOELLERING

It is not customary in the United States for lawyers to submit formal powers of attorney to the arbitral tribunal. Either a letter of appearance from the attorney to the other party and the administering authority, a telephone call or correspondence from the attorney, or the physical appearance of the attorney at the arbitration hearing, is sufficient.[12]

MR. HUNTER

No, this is not normally necessary. It is customary, both for the tribunal and for the other party, to accept the accreditation of a party's lawyer without formality. A letter on the headed notepaper of a firm of solicitors stating:

> "we represent Steelco, the claimants in the above arbitration"

would normally be accepted without question. It would be serious professional misconduct for a lawyer to claim that he has authority to represent a party if this is not true.

If a party, or the tribunal, were (exceptionally) to demand that a lawyer prove formally his credentials to represent his client, then a letter of authorization from that client, duly executed in accordance with its articles of association (constitution), would suffice. A power of attorney would never be required.

MR. JARVIN

There does not seem to be a firm practice. Arbitrators from civil law systems treat the problem differently, and they demand the production of powers of attorney in less than half of the cases. Lawyers are well advised to be prepared to produce one on an arbitrator's request, established according to the criteria governing where the power of attorney was made.

PROF. LEBEDEV

In the absence of direct instructions in the arbitration law or in the arbitration rules applicable to this arbitration, the solution of the question concerning representation and power of attorney depends to a certain extent on the characterization of arbitration adopted in the given country, i.e., whether it is considered to be of a procedural, substantive (contractual) or *sui generis* nature. It is submitted, nevertheless, that from any point of view it will be necessary at least to present some kind of power of attorney entrusting a particular person with representation of the party in arbitration (in relation to the other party, as well as to the arbitrators). However, when proceeding from a strictly procedural characterization, apparently it should be admitted that the form of the power of attorney, as well as the scope of the representative's powers, are determined under the rules of the country of arbitration, dealing with representation in court. Speaking of Soviet law, it might, in particular, mean that authority of the representative to withdraw a claim, in full or partially, to admit a claim or to agree to an amicable settlement should be expressly stated in the power of attorney (see, for example, Art. 46 of the Code of Civil Procedure of the Russian Soviet Federative Socialist Republic (RSFSR)).

On the contrary, if arbitration is considered as contractual, the form as well as the period of validity of the power of attorney should be determined under the law

12. *See, for example,* AAA Commercial Arbitration Rules sect. 22.

of the place where the power of attorney was issued; it is sufficient, however, to satisfy the requirements of the Soviet law as to the form of the power of attorney (see, for example, Art. 5661 of the Civil Code of the RSFSR). On the other hand, under the contractual characterization, the power of attorney of general tenor for the conduct of the arbitration case might be considered as authorizing the representative to perform any acts in the arbitration, except for those specifically excluded by the power of attorney.

Taking into account available practice, we believe that it would be correct to use, in essence, the second approach, although not because of the contractual qualification of arbitration, but rather by way of analogy with the law, while considering arbitration as a *sui generis* institution.

It should be taken into account, however, that under Article 4 of the UNCITRAL Rules, a party, wishing to be represented by certain persons, must communicate in writing "the names and addresses of such persons" to the other party. Being sent also to the arbitral tribunal, such written communication from authorized executives of Steelco and Hightech is most likely to be treated as a proper power of attorney unless any further formalities are mandatorily imposed by the laws of their respective countries.[13]

PROF. EL-HAKIM

A power of attorney is required by the laws of most Arab countries. In a court procedure, that power must be authenticated (Art. 105 of the Syrian Procedure Code).

PROF. MICHIDA

It is reported that in Great Britain and the United States, the parties' attorneys need not ordinarily submit powers of attorney to the arbitral tribunal, and that in Civil Law countries, arbitrators demand production of powers of attorney in less than half the cases.

In Japan, lawyers who represent parties customarily submit powers of attorney. The Rules of the Japan Commercial Arbitration Association and the Rules of Maritime Arbitration of The Japan Shipping Exchange, Inc. provide for powers of attorney (Rule 7(4); Sect. 5, Sub-Sect. 5).

MRS. OYEKUNLE

No. It is not necessary to submit powers of attorney to the arbitral tribunal. Communication by letter, telex, cable, telephone, etc. may be sufficient.

DR. SZURSKI

Unlike in England, USA and some European countries, in Poland, the power of attorney will be requested from any representative of a party, lawyers included. On the other hand, no formalistic approach as to its form should be expected. The power of attorney need not be in a separate document. It will be sufficient to grant

13. Under the Maritime Arbitration Commission (MAC) Rules of Procedure (para. 4(2)): ". . . Attached to the Statement of claim filed by a Representative shall be a power of attorney or another document evidencing the powers of the Representative."

it in writing to the arbitral tribunal; of importance is only the scope of the authorization.

Unless the power of attorney provides for any restrictions as regards its scope, it will be treated *ex lege* as authorizing the legal representative to perform any act in arbitration proceedings and as comprising the right to withdraw or to admit a claim as well as to settle the dispute amicably.

In case of any restriction in the power of attorney as to the authority of the legal representative, the arbitral tribunal may be inclined to admit the statements of the legal representative exceeding the scope of the power of attorney only on the condition of their later formal confirmation by the party concerned.

It should be added that in practice the arbitral tribunal will admit any statement in the proceedings signed by a lawyer without attachment of the power of attorney but it will demand presentation of the power of attorney at the hearing.

HYPOTHETICAL CASE B. cont.

The lawyers for Steelco and Hightech each wondered whether it was advisable to employ Neutralian lawyers to work with them.

QUESTION 7

It is customary for foreign parties in a case like this to have a local lawyer as one of the members of its legal team?

ANSWERS TO QUESTION 7

MR. HOELLERING

It is customary, but not required, for foreign parties to have a local lawyer as a member of their legal team. There are several reasons why counsel for both Steelco and Hightech would want to employ local counsel. Primarily, an experienced arbitration practitioner can guide the parties with regard to the applicable local procedural law, thus ensuring compliance where necessary to guarantee the enforcement of the resulting award. Secondly, since it is likely that one or more members of the arbitral tribunal will be Neutralian attorneys, the participation of local counsel will facilitate the presentation of the foreign party's case in a manner consistent with the professional experience of these members of the tribunal. Finally, if it becomes necessary for a party to participate in legal proceedings relating to the arbitration, qualified local counsel, required by the courts, will already be familiar with the case and will be available without delay to represent the party's interest.[14]

14. For example, motions to compel arbitration, motions to confirm the resulting award, and motions seeking any relief in aid of arbitration will require local counsel admitted to practice in the courts of the jurisdiction where relief is sought.

MR. HUNTER

It is always prudent for a party to take advice from a local lawyer at the place of arbitration at the outset of the arbitral proceedings. The question of whether or not a local lawyer should be engaged as a permanent member of the legal team for the conduct of the arbitral proceedings probably depends not so much on the *place* of arbitration, but more on the people involved.

Thus, if the chairman of the tribunal is a retired Neutralian (English) judge or a senior lawyer whose practising experience is mainly in the domestic courts, then it would be sensible for a party to include an English practitioner in the legal team, because the chairman's approach to procedural issues is likely to have a bias towards traditional English court procedures.

Conversely, if the presiding arbitrator is a "civil" lawyer (or, say, an English internationally orientated lawyer with a known predisposition towards non-adversarial practices) it might be imprudent for a party's presentation at the oral hearing to be dictated by an English lawyer with a primarily domestic practice, whose ideas of procedure may be dominated by rules of evidence which are only appropriate for adversarial proceedings.

English lawyers would be required in the event that any application to the courts became necessary either during or after the arbitral proceedings.

MR. JARVIN

There is no definite answer. It depends on several circumstances, *inter alia*, the amount in dispute, the place of arbitration and the law applicable to the arbitration (procedural rules and rules on the merits).

Where the place of arbitration is thought to require special knowledge of local procedure (such as Switzerland with its Concordat) or where the custom is that a local lawyer must be involved (e.g., UK with its split bar system), it is customary to have a local lawyer, irrespective of the amount in dispute.

In large ICC matters, there is a clear tendency for parties to be represented by lawyers from their own country as well as a local lawyer at the place of arbitration.

PROF. LEBEDEV

Participation of local lawyers in arbitration is not at any rate imperative. Whether to hire them or not depends fully on the discretion of each party. Considering, however, that arbitration proceedings, at least in part not covered by the UNCITRAL Rules, are subject to the law of the country of arbitration, assistance of the lawyers of that country in a difficult case like this may be very useful for the parties. Such a conclusion may be even more compelling if also the substantive law of that country turned out to be applied (for example, due to agreement reached by the parties in the course of arbitration proceedings).

MRS. OYEKUNLE

Such appointment is not imperative but useful. The practice is growing particularly for foreign lawyers to have a local lawyer as one of the members of their legal team. This is particularly important having regard to the case-stated procedure under the Arbitration Act of the Law of the Federation of Nigeria and the power of the Court to remit matters referred or any of them for the reconsideration of the arbitrators or umpire.[15] A local lawyer may also be of immense assistance in advising on the peculiar political, social, economic and customary practice of the place of arbitration in addition to rendering advice on the procedural and/or substantive law of the forum where that law is applicable.

Where there is a reference to the local court as required by the Arbitration Act, the qualified local legal practitioner[16] who has audience in the local court will be able to represent the interest of the party whose legal team of lawyers he has joined. Only citizens of Nigeria are entitled to have their names enrolled as Legal Practitioners of the Supreme Court of Nigeria *except* where reciprocal treatment has been granted by the Attorney General by regulations after consultation with the Bar Council.[17] Such reciprocal treatment will however be withdrawn where it has ceased for both parties.

C. Contents of the Statements of Claim and Defense

HYPOTHETICAL CASE

The lawyer for Steelco was faced with the need to make decisions concerning the contents of the Statement of Claim. He wanted his Statement of Claim to satisfy the Neutralian chairman, but he did not know what a Neutralian chairman would wish in a case such as this. The Rules require that the Statement of Claim include a statement of the "facts supporting the claim," the "points at issue," and the "relief or remedy sought." (Art. 18(2)) The Rules, however, gave Steelco's lawyer no guidance as to how much detail should be included. Similarly, the lawyer for Hightech wondered how much detail to provide in his Statement of Defense and in the counterclaim that would be included therein. He, too, wanted to satisfy the Neutralian chairman. (Art. 19(2)–(4))

QUESTION 8

How much factual detail should be included in the Statements of Claim and Defense?

ANSWERS TO QUESTION 8

MR. HOELLERING

In large international cases, whether conducted under UNCITRAL Rules or other arbitration rules, it is customary for the parties to file a more detailed Statement of Claim and Defense than in domestic cases. The chairman is likely to expect

15. Arbitration Law (Cap 10) Laws of Lagos State of Nigeria Sect. 11(1), Sect. 15.
16. Legal Practitioners Act 1962, Sect. 3.
17. Arbitration Act (Cap 13) Laws of the Federation of Nigeria and Lagos 1958 Sect. 9, Arbitration Law (Cap 10) Laws of Lagos State of Nigeria 1973 Sect. 9. See also note 16.

sufficient detail in such statements which will provide at least as much information as is contained in the factual statement of the hypothetical case. This is consistent with the intent of Articles 18 and 19 of the UNCITRAL Rules, which provide that the arbitral tribunal is to receive information regarding the nature of the dispute and the remedy sought by each party, in advance of the proceedings and in greater detail than was provided in the initial notice of arbitration.

MR. HUNTER

In general, Statements of Claim and Defense in English arbitration proceedings contain sufficient factual detail (a) to define the issues (because it is not necessary under the UNCITRAL Rules, or usual under English arbitration procedures, for "terms of reference" to be drawn up) and (b) for the other party to know with adequate particularity both the underlying facts and the legal basis for the claims.

The respondent is entitled to know in advance what he has to answer (otherwise it may be said that he has not had a full opportunity to present his case – see UNCITRAL Rules, Art. 15).

"Trial by ambush" is discouraged in English arbitration, and if new contentions are put forward at a late stage this will often lead to adjournments and delay. However, it is not generally necessary for the parties at this stage to set out the *evidence* on which they rely. A party who, without a reasonable excuse, introduces new facts at a stage which necessarily leads to an adjournment of the hearing will normally be penalized by an appropriate order in relation to the additional costs caused by the adjournment.

The position under the UNCITRAL Rules may be slightly different from the general practice in non-administered arbitration in England, because Article 22 of the UNCITRAL Rules envisages the possibility of further written statements in which, presumably, the parties may amplify the initial Statements of Claim and Defense provided by each party. However, the present Rapporteur considers that a wise claimant will present the relevant facts as comprehensively as possible at the first stage, because failure to do so will inevitably lead to opportunities for the respondent to create delays.

MR. JARVIN

Statements of Claim and Defense are as a rule fairly detailed. They contain statements of the case, of the relief sought, and legal arguments and references to case law, and sometimes, reference to witnesses to be heard. Written evidence is generally included. A copy of the arbitration clause or agreement must be submitted,[18] otherwise the claimant runs the risk that the request be rejected in the absence of a *prima facie* arbitration agreement.

In appreciating that it is dangerous to generalize, it can be said that it is a practice with UK and US lawyers to be detailed. Parties from developing countries do not often have legal representation and their presentation is then very sparse. Eastern Socialist countries usually submit more of a skeleton picture of the dispute in the request for arbitration. Civil Law parties and their lawyers

18. Art. 3(2) of the ICC Rules.

move in the direction of US and UK practice and present much detailed information with the request for arbitration, enclosing voluminous documents.

PROF. LEBEDEV

In the absence of any tactical considerations in favour of another solution, the claimant wishing "to satisfy the Neutralian chairman" should include in the Statement of Claim in detailed manner all facts having relevance from the claimant's standpoint. In such a situation it would be most appropriate for the defendant to act similarly, especially in regard to the additional facts and those facts which in his opinion were not stated by the claimant correctly or in full.

PROF. MICHIDA

On this Question, the Questionnaire prepared by the Chairman rephrases the Question, adding the word "complete" as follows:

> "A complete statement of facts should be included in the Statement of Claim and Defense."

It is reported that in Great Britain a wise claimant will present the relevant facts as *comprehensively* as possible at the first stage, and in the United States the parties customarily file a more *detailed* Statement of Claim and Defense than in domestic cases. (Emphasis supplied.)

The Civil Law report states that Statements of Claim and Defense are as a rule *fairly detailed* and, aware of the custom of UK and US lawyers to be detailed, Civil Law parties and their lawyers are moving in the direction of US and UK practice and present *very detailed* information with the request for arbitration, enclosing *voluminous* documentation. (Emphasis supplied.) My impression is that the British and United States practices reflect the influence of traditional court litigation, and that the Civil Law movement is emulating Anglo-American practices.

The response of the Japan Commercial Arbitration Association and the Japan Shipping Exchange, Inc. to this question is that a statement of fact that supports the claim or defense, or that makes the issues clear, is sufficient in arbitration, because the details of the case are to be presented in the hearing.

As to the documents to be filed with an application for arbitration, the Rules of Maritime Arbitration of The Japan Shipping Exchange, Inc. provide for "[d]ocuments in support of his claim, if any" (Sect. 5). As to a supplementary filing, those rules state:

> "2. Where the Supplementary Statement and documentary evidence (if any) have been filed, the Office shall forward the duplicate of the Supplementary Statements and respective copies of the further documentary evidence (if any) to the Respondent, and instruct him that, if he has any objection thereto, he shall file his Supplementary Statement within fourteen (14) days after despatch thereof.
>
> "3. In the event of any further Supplementary Statement and documentary evidence being filed, the procedures provided in the preceding Sub-Section shall be repeated." (Sect. 9)

The Rule of the Japan Commercial Arbitration Association provides:

> "Rule 7: A person requesting arbitration ... shall submit the following documents . . .
>
> "(1) A written request for arbitration;
>
> . . .
>
> "(3) The original or a copy of any documentary evidence supporting the claim in the request for arbitration;
>
> . . .
>
> "Rule 12: A party which has requested arbitration or has made a counterclaim may make a change of request or counterclaim (hereinafter called 'change'). Provided that, after the Tribunal has been established such change shall be made only with the approval of the Tribunal."

These rules make it possible for a party in dispute to apply for arbitration quickly without extensive legal documentation, and also to avoid having the application incite a tense confrontation between the parties. They are in keeping with what I have described as the amicable texture of Japanese arbitration proceedings. Because, as a method of dispute resolution, arbitration differs fundamentally from court adjudication, it is fitting that, even at its earliest stage when the application for arbitration is filed, its amicable atmosphere be safeguarded.

MRS. OYEKUNLE

The Statements of Claim and Defense should be as detailed as possible in order to lay out the picture of the whole case to the arbitral tribunal and to avoid unnecessary waste of time in bringing out new issues at a later stage and permitting delay which prolongs the arbitration and increases cost. It is particularly important where the arbitration law of Nigeria applies; any delay by the claimant in specifying his case may make him vulnerable to a recalcitrant respondent who will use any excuse to delay the case or ask for a reference to court to pronounce on certain procedural or substantive issues.

HYPOTHETICAL CASE C. cont.

Both lawyers wondered how much legal argument to include when describing the "points at issue." Should each, for example, state his position on what law governs the substance of the dispute and include specific references to that law?

QUESTION 9

How much legal argument should be included in the Statements of Claim and Defense?

ANSWERS TO QUESTION 9

MR. HOELLERING

It is customary for detailed legal arguments to be reserved for the hearing, or for closing arguments, post-hearing briefs and memoranda of law. It is the custom and practice in international arbitration, however, for each party to outline the legal theory of its claim, defense or counterclaim, and to state its view as to the applicable governing law, in addition to the facts, in the Statements of Claim and Defense.

MR. HUNTER

It is interesting that Articles 18(2) and 19(2) of the UNCITRAL Rules appear to require statements of the *facts* relied upon, but not a statement of legal principles.

Is it assumed that the tribunal will make its own enquiries into the relevant law? Or, alternatively, obtain the legal arguments in a further written statement provided under Article 22, or at the hearing?

In an English court case the written pleadings simply state the propositions of law relied upon by the parties, without citing authorities or providing detailed arguments to relate the relevant legal principles to the facts of the case. Legal argument is reserved for the oral hearing.

There is no rule, or general customary practice, in English arbitration. If the lawyers representing the parties are primarily experienced in domestic court work, they may follow the rules applicable to written pleadings in court when preparing a statement of claim in an arbitration. Those more experienced in the field of arbitration, particularly international arbitration, would normally ensure that the legal arguments are set out quite fully in the Statement of Claim submitted under Article 18(2) of the UNCITRAL Arbitration Rules, and would refer to the legislative texts and other authorities relied on. Where the Statement of Claim has in fact set out detailed argument, the Respondent would no doubt feel compelled to do the same by way of reply in his Statement of Defense.

MR. JARVIN

Legal argument should be fairly detailed in the Statements of Claim and Defense. A statement of what law applies is of the greatest importance to assist the Court to choose the national committee that will be invited to propose an arbitrator where the parties have not agreed on the choice. Legal arguments are welcome to help the Court assess the complexity of the matter, which influences the choice of arbitrator, and the likely time that the arbitrator will spend on the case; this in turn influences the amount of fees that will be payable to him, for which the parties will be asked to pay an advance.

Detailed legal argument at the early stage of the arbitration will enable the arbitrator to draw up more accurate terms of reference. Early settlement negotiations are facilitated if both sides know the strength of the arguments of the other side.

PROF. LEBEDEV

Although the UNCITRAL Rules, in contrast with many other arbitration rules, do not require the inclusion of legal arguments in the Statement of Claim (Art. 18(2)), there are no obstacles to do this if the party so wishes.

Apparently, it can hardly be expected that the dispute between the parties may be decided exclusively on the basis of contract provisions, i.e., without using rules of law applicable to the contract. If there are no doubts as to the applicable law (for example, it is clear that the arbitral tribunal, guided by the conflict of law rules of the country of arbitration, will hold the law of Metalia applicable as the law of the place (?) where the contract was concluded), it seems quite logical, at least from the standpoint of usual practice for the presiding arbitrator, to expect from Steelco detailed legal substantiation of its claims including references to the respective rules of Metalia law, especially those justifying termination of the contract. Accordingly, a similar approach on the part of the defendant would seem appropriate in regard of his objections to the Claim and of the Counterclaim.

If the question of applicable law gives rise to doubts, it may hardly be rational for the parties at this stage, i.e., before this question is decided, to give detailed legal arguments – for example, by the claimant on the basis of Metalian law and by the defendant on the basis of Machinian law. It is submitted that in a situation like this, the arbitral tribunal, including the presiding arbitrator, would consider with full understanding, brief and general legal argument of the parties in the Statements of Claim and Defense with concentration on the explanation of their positions regarding the applicable law in order for this issue to be solved (as a preliminary one) by the arbitrators, or by agreement of the parties themselves (including, for example, an accord in favor of the law of the country of arbitration).

MRS. OYEKUNLE

There are no specific rules as to how this should be done. The Statements of Claim and Defense can be as detailed as possible including statements of facts and law, but usually legal arguments of principles of law and cases applicable are reserved for oral arguments which are generally summarized at the close of the hearing when the lawyers on either side make their submissions. The advantage of having a detailed Statement of Claim is the urge it gives to the respondent to reply in detail to all the issues raised in the Statement of Claim so that the element of surprise, for either side, is reduced if not completely eliminated.

HYPOTHETICAL CASE C. cont.

The two lawyers also observed that the Rules required them to state the "relief or remedy sought." Steelco's lawyer was particularly worried about how to state the demand for lost profits because, although his client had made various calculations, he knew from experience that further analysis made in the course of preparing the case for trial might result in somewhat different amounts. Also, it was not yet certain how long it would take Steelco to find another supplier and how long it would take that supplier to deliver computers. In view of the circumstances, should he simply state, "Claimant demands compensation for the damages it has suffered," without indicating a specific amount? Or should he write, "Claimant demands $14 million, plus interest, and reserves the right to prove any further damages at a later stage of the arbitration proceedings"? He wondered how a Neutralian arbitrator would react to these or other possible alternatives.

QUESTION 10

How specific should the demand for relief be?

ANSWERS TO QUESTION 10

MR. HOELLERING

Each party's demand for relief should be as specific as possible. It is best to specify at the outset the amount of claims that are ascertainable, and to indicate those in which an amount cannot yet be specified. And if relief other than monetary damages is sought, such as rescission or other equitable relief, this, too, should be included in a party's demand for relief.

Frequently, claims, counterclaims and set-offs are stated as indeterminate amounts in international arbitration proceedings. Occasionally, with some claims determined and others not, a minimal figure will be set to indicate the size and nature of claims. Either way, a party reserves the right to prove its full damages when all the facts are known, and will not be precluded from seeking amounts higher than the original base claim figure, provided the basis of the claims remains the same.

The demands for relief filed by the parties, in the instant case, were sufficiently specific. Steelco demanded return of the $4 million partial payment with interest, and an additional $10 million in damages for lost profits. Hightech counterclaimed for the remaining $6 million of the contract price, with interest. Amounts in excess due either party would still be determined over the course of the arbitral proceedings.

Since the UNCITRAL Rules expressly provide for recovery of attorneys fees and costs,[19] the parties properly sought reimbursement of its arbitration costs and legal fees, as well.[20]

MR. HUNTER

Very specific. It should include, for instance, any claims in respect of interest and costs in addition to all other substantive reliefs claimed. The reason for this is that, because there will not normally be a separate "terms of reference" signed by the parties and the arbitrators, it will be the Statements of Claim and Defense submitted under Articles 18 and 19 which establish the mandate, or mission, of

19. *See* Art. 38.

20. Although arbitration costs are awarded by the arbitrators under US law, attorney's fees are not deemed awardable absent an express agreement by the parties to that effect. Agreements to arbitrate under the UNCITRAL Rules would constitute such an agreement. *See, for example,* NY Civ. Prac. Law 7513; Uniform Arbitration Act sect. 10; *Matter of Central School District No. 1 (Double M. Construction Corp.)*, 46 A.D.2d 800, 361 N.Y.S.2d 47 (2d Dept. 1974). *But see J. R. Snyder Co., Inc.* v. *Soble*, 226 N.W.2d 276 (Mich. App. 1975) (failure timely to object to award of counsel fees resulted in waiver).

the tribunal. Parties should therefore be meticulous in specifying their claims and counterclaims.

It is not essential to supply detailed calculations or evidence as to quantification of claims for damages at this stage of the arbitral proceedings.

MR. JARVIN

The second alternative is preferable, for reasons set out in the answer to Question 9 and for the following reasons.

In ICC practice, the relief sought is usually set out in the request for arbitration, where it can be determined.

To know the amount in dispute *is important for the Court* since it will influence the decision as to the number of arbitrators if the number has not been agreed between the parties. As a rule of thumb, the Court will appoint a sole arbitrator where the amount in dispute is less than one million dollars and three where more. (This does not apply to cases where an Eastern Socialist country is party; in those cases there are almost without exception three arbitrators).

The amount in dispute will also determine the advance on costs that the parties will be asked to pay to the ICC. The advance is calculated according to a schedule set out in Appendix III to the Court's Rules.[21] Where no amount in dispute has been specified, the Court will fix an advance according to its discretion.

The amount is *important for the arbitrators* to know, since their probable fees will be based to a great extent on that amount. The Schedule III to the Court's Rules gives a minimum and a maximum amount within which range the Court will fix their final fees.

The relief if not specified in the Request for arbitration, may be determined later, up till the time for the drawing up of the Terms of Reference. Thereafter, no new claims may be made (see Art. 16 of the Court's Rules, which sets out the conditions under which new claims may be made after the Terms of Reference are established).

PROF. LEBEDEV

Since the claimant demands recovery of damages, the arbitral tribunal is most likely to expect that Steelco at least indicate the approximate amount and method of calculation of that part of the damages which represents lost profits. Such indication, on the one hand, permits the arbitrators to have a clearer picture of the case on the whole and, on the other hand, does not prevent the claimant from later changing or increasing the amount of damages sought, because such increase, in our opinion, cannot be considered as "amendment of the claim" that under Article 20 of the UNCITRAL Rules may or may not be allowed by the arbitral tribunal.

MRS. OYEKUNLE

The demand for relief should be as specific as possible because anything not specifically claimed may not be granted. The grant of any relief not specifically

21. For a quick reference to the calculation of the arbitrator's fees and the Court's administrative expenses, refer to Guide to Arbitration, ICC Publication No. 382, Paris 1983, pages 45–46.

claimed or proved may lead to the award being set aside or remitted to the arbitral tribunal. Such a course of action will have the effect of prolonging the matter and increasing the cost which will completely defeat the essence of arbitration.

HYPOTHETICAL CASE C. cont.

The Rules state that each party "may" annex to its Statement of Claim or Defense "all documents he deems relevant or may add a reference to the documents or other evidence he will submit." (Art. 18(2); *see also* Art. 19(2)) Both lawyers observed that the use in the Rules of the word "may," instead of "shall," permitted them wide flexibility. Each wondered what to do. Would it be better, for example, to annex the full text of (i) the contract, (ii) the specifications, (iii) correspondence relating to the formation of the contract, (iv) correspondence or other documents relating to the alleged performance or non-performance of the contract, such as shipping documents, inspectors' reports, correspondence with Supertech concerning the patent issue, etc., and (v) documentary evidence of customary trade practice? Or would it be better at this stage of the case to include only a reference to those documents?

QUESTION 11

Should supporting documents be annexed to the Statements of Claim and Defense? If so, what documents? Or should there only be a reference to documents that will be submitted at a later stage of the proceeding? Or should there be neither attached documents nor references thereto?

ANSWERS TO QUESTION 11

MR. HOELLERING

It is customary for the parties to annex basic documents to the Statements of Claim and Defense. There is considerable variety, however, as to which material may be included. In the Steelco-Hightech dispute, the documents appended might include the contract, the disputed system specifications and selected items of correspondence on key aspects of the dispute supporting the filing party's position. Taken together, the Statements of each party, with annexed supporting documents, would provide the arbitral tribunal with a good overview of the general facts and legal theories on which the parties' claims are based.

MR. HUNTER

In an English arbitration which is not governed by a set of arbitration rules, it would not be normal to provide copies of supporting documents, or even a list, at the statements of claim and defense stage. However, some crucial documents might be referred to, or quoted, in the text.

In institutional arbitrations in England, the relevant rule would be followed.

For example, the ICC Rules (Art. 3(2)) require the claimant to include in his "Request for Arbitration":

> "such documentation . . . as will serve clearly to establish the circumstances of the case".

The LCIA Rules have no such requirement as regards the initial stages of the arbitration.

In the present Hypothetical Case, in which the UNCITRAL Rules apply, it is optional under Article 19 for the parties either to annex documents, or to give references to them, or to do neither. The present Rapporteur considers that a prudent claimant will annex the documents *on which he relies* at the statement of claim stage, in order to minimize subsequent delays.

MR. JARVIN

Supporting documents are generally annexed. The contract, the specifications and the correspondence relating to the alleged performance of the contract would probably have been submitted by civil law trained lawyers in a case like this. Correspondence relating to the formation of the contract and documentary evidence of customary trade practices, on the other hand, would only be submitted if they were likely to be at issue in the case, e.g., if the defendant could be supposed to contest the validity of the contract.

As a general rule, civil law trained arbitrators expect to receive sufficient documentation to get an overview of the case (facts and law), *but nothing more.*

The practice of particularly common law trained counsel to submit every possible piece of paper is met with little understanding on the part of civil law counsel and arbitrators. A party who is under an obligation to submit every possible document (which seems to be the case in the US where the lawyer might otherwise risk a negligence suit) should do so only if he gives clear guidance to the arbitrator on which documents he will rely, setting out their importance for the case. No arbitrator will read heaps of documents without knowing if they are important to the case or not and the practice of flooding the Court's secretariat and the arbitrators with hundreds of kilos of paper rarely pleases anyone, apart from the international courier companies.

PROF. LEBEDEV

On the basis of customary practice in the country of arbitration, the arbitral tribunal is most likely to expect that at least principal documents supporting the claimant's and defendant's positions will be annexed to the Statements of Claim and Defense, including the contract, specifications, documents concerning tests of the computer and air-conditioning equipment, correspondence with Supertech about patents, etc. On the other hand, it is hardly possible for the arbitral tribunal to have objections if the claimant and / or the defendant would prefer at this stage only to make references to respective documents, since such a course is expressly provided for in Article 18 of the UNCITRAL Rules. If, however, no documents were annexed to the claim and no references to documents were made by the claimant, the arbitral tribunal is most likely at its own initiative or upon request of the defendant to require the claimant (or, in another situation, the defendant) to present within a certain period of time "a summary of the documents and other evidence, which that party intends to present in support of the facts in issue set out in his statement of claim or statement of defense" (Art. 24(2) of the UNCITRAL Rules).

MRS. OYEKUNLE

Yes. Supporting documents are generally annexed to the Statements of Claim and Defense. Where documents are not annexed to the Statements of Claim and Defense, they are generally submitted during oral arguments and admitted as exhibits. The practice of annexing relevant documents in order to concretize and give a full picture of the case of either side as well as save time, is gradually evolving. It is, however, provided under the provisions of the arbitration law applicable in the place of arbitration (Nigeria) that "any party to a *submission* may sue out a writ of subpoena ad testificadum or a writ of subpoena duces tecum, but *no person shall be compelled under any such writ to produce any document which he could not be compelled to produce on the trial of an action.*[22]

A *submission* in this case is defined as "a written agreement to submit present or future differences to arbitration, whether an arbitrator is named therein or not.[23]

In spite of the above legal provision, the parties in the case under consideration would still be free to attach the following relevant documents, in order to fully prove their case: the contract signed on 1 March 1983 for the manufacture and installation of the computer system, the specifications for the air conditioning, correspondence with Supertech about the patents, documents concerning the tests of the computer and air-conditioning equipment, documentary evidence of the payment of the $4 million and the letter of acknowledgement (if any), correspondence with Hightech on the faulty performance of the system and its not meeting the performance tests, finally, the letter from Steelco giving notice of termination of the contract to Hightech on the ground of failure to fulfil its obligations.

HYPOTHETICAL CASE C. cont.

Both lawyers wondered what the arbitral tribunal would do if it found the Statements of Claim or Defense, or both, to be insufficiently detailed, or that key documents were not annexed.

This question raises the interesting philosophical problem of the extent to which arbitrators should take the initiative to shape the proceeding, or whether, instead, they should leave such matters in the hands of parties. It is an issue that will arise again in connection with Questions 17–19.

---

22. *See* note 17.
23. Arbitration Act (Cap 13) Law of the Federation of Nigeria and Lagos 1958, Sect. 2.

QUESTION 12

If a party were to submit a Statement of Claim or Defense that the arbitral tribunal considered insufficiently detailed, would the arbitrators, without any request from the other party, order a more detailed submission?

ANSWERS TO QUESTION 12

MR. HOELLERING

Although arbitrators do have the power to request amplified Statements from any party, it is not customary for them to do so, absent a request from the other party. Given the increased emphasis placed on the case management function of the arbitral tribunal, however, it is likely that, particularly in international cases a greater number of requests for more detailed Statements will be issued in the future.

MR. HUNTER

Yes. The present Rapporteur understands that this is one of the purposes of Article 22 of the UNCITRAL Rules.

In English non-administered arbitration, the tribunal would probably leave it to the parties to ask for orders directing more particularized written submissions; although an experienced chairman, or sole arbitrator, might well write to the parties prior to the hearing to suggest that the parties should amplify the written material submitted, so as to avoid the hearing being unproductive.

MR. JARVIN

Probably yes. Under the Rules of the ICC, the arbitrator has a duty to "establish the facts of the case by all appropriate means".[24] Arbitrators having a civil law tradition would not find it difficult to apply this duty by ordering further particulars from a party whose statements seem incomplete. In Swedish arbitration law, the arbitrators may take steps to call for evidence.[25] In French international arbitration, likewise.[26] Under the Swiss Concordat, the parties are free to agree on the procedure to be followed. Such agreement may include a provision that the arbitrator should have no power to intervene *ex officio* with regard to evidence, which seems to indicate that arbitrators in the absence of such

---

24. Art. 14(1) of the ICC Rules.
25. *Arbitration in Sweden* (1984), page 117, which goes on to state that this ability may be useful in cases where parties are not represented by Counsel. However in normal cases the aribitrator will act only in a ministerial capacity and summon witnesses etc. at the request of the parties.
26. Patrice Level in *Droit et pratique de l'arbitrage international en France*, FEDUCI, 1984, page 64: "If one sees the ICC Rules as the expression of a certain wisdom, one should admit that it is within scope of the arbitrator's function and power to order all appropriate measures such as expertise, appearance of the parties and testimony, even if neither party has so requested . . . It is nevertheless essential that the arbitrators not take such measures without notifying the parties and inviting their comments on the measure ordered and the results." (Original in French)

exclusion are free to apply all means they find appropriate.[27] To order a more detailed submission would be accepted practice in ICC arbitration as long as the arbitrator respects the duty to communicate everything to the other party (*le principe de contradictoire*).

PROF. LEBEDEV

Proceeding from the fact that the degree of thoroughness in stating the positions of the parties depends in general upon their own discretion, the arbitral tribunal is unlikely to order at its own initiative a "detailization" by the party of his Statement of Claim or Defense, that in fact meets the requirements of Article 18(2) and Article 19(2) of the UNCITRAL Rules.

PROF. MICHIDA

It is reported that in the United States, arbitrators do not customarily order a more detailed submission of a Claim or Defense, if the opposing party did not request such an order.

The Rules of The Japan Commercial Arbitration Association provide in relevant part as follows:

> "2. The Tribunal may, when it deems necessary, request the submission of evidence or the voluntary appearance of a witness or an expert witness." (Rule 26)

MRS. OYEKUNLE

Parties are required to prove their case. The Arbitral Tribunal would rarely order a more detailed submission without a request from the other party except to clarify issues that require elucidating, particularly in a complex case such as the one under consideration. Both parties must, however, be informed. Moreover, since the arbitration clause in the contract provides that UNCITRAL Arbitration Rules shall apply, applying that rule will be recognized and the tribunal shall be able to decide on what further written statements shall be required from the parties in addition to the Statement of Claim and the Statement of Defense.[28]

DR. SZURSKI

In its desire to make the proceedings efficient and at the same time to clarify, as much as possible, all legal and factual aspects of the case already before the hearing, the Polish arbitrator – as a rule – will not be inclined to fix the date of hearing until he has received the most important information and data about the case. A rule which is followed in practice is to limit the hearing mainly to clarification of doubts arising out of documents and to give the parties the possibility to support their positions by evidence which could not have been presented by way of correspondence (like hearing witnesses and experts) as well as to hear oral pleadings. It can be expected that to reach this effect, the Polish arbitrator may request certain "detailization" of the Statement of Claim or

27. Jolidon, *op. cit.* pages 340 and 342, 2nd para.
28. Art. 22 UNCITRAL Rules.

Defense on his own initiative (contrary to the US arbitrator as referred to by Mr. Hoellering).

D. Terms of Reference

HYPOTHETICAL CASE

The Rules contain no provision either requiring or excluding preparation of "terms of reference," such as under the ICC Rules. The arbitral tribunal, exercising its power to "conduct the arbitration in such manner as it considers appropriate" (Art. 15(1)), is thus free either to require terms of reference or not. The lawyers of Steelco and Hightech do not know whether a Neutralian chairman would be accustomed to having terms of reference and therefore might wish them.

QUESTION 13

Should terms of reference be prepared? If so, what should be included? What would be the role of the arbitrators in preparing them? Would all three arbitrators be involved, or only the Chairman? Who should sign the terms of reference?

ANSWERS TO QUESTION 13

MR. HOELLERING

Unless arbitration is conducted under ICC Rules, it is not customary for terms of reference to be prepared. A further "submission" agreement, executed by the parties at the time of arbitration, is unnecessary since "future disputes" clauses are considered valid, irrevocable and enforceable under the United States Arbitration Act.[29] In our hypothetical case, the UNCITRAL Rules, together with the Statements of Claim and Defense, will serve to clarify the power and authority of the arbitral tribunal with respect to the dispute.[30]

Although formal terms of reference are not required or customary, practitioners have indicated a preference for a statement of issues, together with relevant documents, which the arbitrators would receive and have an opportunity to review prior to the commencement of hearings.[31] Rather than define the scope of the proceedings and arbitral authority, however, as do terms of reference, the purpose of such a statement would be to capsulize the factual and

29. 9 U.S.C. sect. 1. Chap. 2 of the US Arbitration Act implements the UN Convention in the United States.

30. *See* UNCITRAL Rules Arts. 15–29; 32(1). *See also* Rhodes and Sloan, *The Pitfalls of International Commercial Arbitration*, 17 *Vanderbilt J. Int'l L.* 19, 38 (Winter 1984).

31. Coulson, *Survey*, note 3 *supra*. Suggested topics for inclusion in such terms of reference may be found in McClelland, *International Arbitration: A Practical Guide for the Effective Use of the System for Litigation of Transnational Commercial Disputes*, 12 *Int'l Lawyer* 83 (Winter 1978).

legal issues of the controversy and serve as an informational springboard to the tribunal.[32] To the extent that sufficient information is not contained in the statements of claim and defense, it may be provided during or following the pre-hearing conference.

When terms of reference are required, as they are by the ICC Rules,[33] they are drawn up by the arbitral tribunal in consultation with the parties, and each arbitrator participates in their preparation. When agreement has been reached, the terms of reference are signed by both the parties and the arbitrators.

MR. HUNTER

"Terms of Reference" are virtually unknown in England, except in ICC arbitrations in which they are mandatory under Article 13 of the ICC Rules. There is no requirement for terms of reference in London Court of International Arbitration (LCIA), and the present Rapporteur cannot imagine any circumstances in which the tribunal or the parties would suggest executing formal terms of reference in an LCIA arbitration.

Exceptionally, in non-administered arbitration, the tribunal might ask the parties to sign terms of reference if, for example, it wanted the parties to agree on a specific basis for the fees of the arbitrators, or some unusual procedural directions.

Another reason might be where it is envisaged that enforcement proceedings may be necessary in a jurisdiction where there must be a submission agreement, or compromise, *after* the dispute has arisen.

MR. JARVIN

In arbitrations taking place according to the Rules of the ICC Court of Arbitration, the arbitrator's mission is defined in a document called "Terms of Reference". This document shall include, amongst others, particulars of the applicable procedural rules.[34] Parties who have not agreed in their contract on what procedure to adopt – and parties very rarely do agree – still have a chance to agree by the time they come together with the arbitrator and the other party for the drafting of the terms of reference. According to Article 11 of the ICC Rules, the parties, and failing them, the arbitrator may agree on a procedure by reference to a municipal procedural law or to any other procedure acceptable to the parties or the arbitrator. The freedom of choice is complete, and there are examples of different procedural laws being combined to be used for different aspects of the procedure.

A survey made at the Court's Secretariat in 1985[35] showed that out of a total of 151 terms of reference signed by the parties and the arbitrator, express reference was made to a municipal procedural law in 27% of the cases. In 11% of the cases,

---

32. One author has noted that terms of reference, or some other statement on issues and procedure, is a desirable first step in the conduct of international arbitration. *See* Goekjian, *The Conduct of International Arbitration*, 11 *Law of the Americas* 409, 419 (Fall 1979).

33. Art. 13 of the ICC Rules specifies the particulars of such terms of reference.

34. ICC Arbitration Rules, Article 13 (1)(g).

35. Andreas Reiner: "Die Wahl des anwendbaren Verfahrensrechts in Rahmen der ICC – Schiedsgerichtsbarkeit", paper presented at an arbitration day arranged in Vienna on 30 May 1985, page 11.

there was a reference to municipal law, albeit in a weaker language, and in 6% of the cases, the terms of reference mentioned equity and fairness as the principles governing the procedure. In the majority of the terms of reference, 56%, there is merely a reference to Article 11 of the ICC Rules, which sends the ball back to the arbitrator, since he has to settle the procedure where the parties cannot agree.

One often finds, in addition to a simple reference to Article 11 of the ICC Rules, that one or more aspects relating to evidence is expressly treated in the terms of reference. What is allowed as evidence, when and how it should be presented, whether cross-examination should be permitted, etc. is of particular concern to arbitrators where they themselves come from different legal systems or where a non-civil law system is represented among parties' counsel. The following extract from a recent case illustrates how an arbitral tribunal resolves that procedural problem:

> "The hearings were conducted in the English language, a language with which all three members of the Tribunal are conversant. Because the parties had not settled the procedure to be followed, it was settled by the Tribunal under Article 11 of the Rules of the ICC Court of Arbitration to follow a modified version of the Anglo-American mode of procedure, since two of the Arbitrators and the English counsel representing the parties were familiar with that mode. Some of the witnesses were examined and cross-examined by Dutch lawyers, and a few were examined and cross-examined by a lawyer from the United States of America, but the vast majority of the witnesses were examined and cross-examined by English barristers. The changes in the normal Anglo-American mode of procedure were at least 3 in number: (1) The witnesses were unsworn, (2) the cross-examination was to be "brief", and (3) most importantly, instead of all the claimant's witnesses being examined and cross-examined on the claimant's whole case, and the respondent's witnesses likewise, the issues were divided into several topics, and the claimant's and respondent's witnesses were examined and cross-examined on each topic. On each topic the witnesses were examined by the counsel for the party who called them, cross-examined by counsel for the other party, re-examined if counsel thought it advisable, and recross-examined if counsel thought it advisable." (3840/RP 22.5.85)

The terms of reference should be signed by the arbitrators and the parties. In ICC practice, it sometimes happens that a party refuses to sign the terms of reference. The Court then approves them if it is satisfied that there exists a prima facie agreement to arbitrate under the Rules.

One of the advantages of drawing up terms of reference and having them signed by the parties is that such a document may cure possible insufficiences relating to the arbitration agreement. In some legal systems, it is, for instance, questionable whether parties can submit to arbitration disputes which do not yet exist, by means of an arbitration clause inserted into a contract.[36] By the signing of terms of reference for an existing dispute, the parties refer to arbitration that particular dispute, and dispel possible doubts as to their consent to submit to arbitration. The terms of reference then serve as useful written evidence of the source of the arbitrator's powers.

In ICC practice, the role of the arbitrator in the preparation of the terms of reference varies widely. In some cases the Chairman of the tribunal asks the

36. *See* Samir Saleh: *Commercial Arbitration in the Arab Middle East*, London, 1984, pages 48–50.

parties to submit draft terms of reference. In other cases the parties prepare lists of issues to be included, but leave the drafting of the terms of reference to the arbitrator. In yet other instances, the arbitrator prepares a draft terms of reference based on the Request and the Response and circulates it among the co-arbitrators and the parties for comments. A fourth approach is to draw up and sign terms of reference at a meeting of all persons concerned after a secretary has typed the terms of reference under the arbitrator's instructions and/or dictation in the presence of the co-arbitrators and the parties.

Other advantages of preparing terms of reference are that it offers the parties and the arbitrators an opportunity to fix procedural rules for the arbitration, to define clearly the scope of the dispute, to fix a schedule for hearings, presentation of evidence, etc. Last, but not least, the discussions that take place when preparing terms of reference sometimes lead to a settlement of the dispute.

The arbitrator must avoid indicating at the stage of preparing the terms of reference what solution he intends to give to the dispute. The terms of reference contain a true statement of the parties' respective claims, but not an analysis by the arbitrator of how he intends to resolve the dispute. If the parties get the feeling that they are forced into a situation where they are asked to compromise or subscribe to solutions on the merits, the exercise of drawing up terms of reference may become a lengthy and difficult one.

PROF. LEBEDEV

The existence of the arbitration clause is considered in the country of arbitration as eliminating the necessity of drawing up any additional documents (terms of reference, submission or *compromis*) when a dispute has arisen and is referred to arbitration. Hence, the powers of the arbitrators generally cover all the issues in dispute which may be raised by the parties in the Statements of Claim and Defense or in the course of the proceedings, unless these issues go beyond the arbitration clause.

Such approach, of course, does not prevent the parties from agreeing, for example, by writing terms of reference, to restrict the powers of the arbitrators to specific issues, to set a time limit for making the award, etc. Should such a document be drawn up, it is not necessary that it be signed by the arbitrators.

PROF. EL-HAKIM

1. Terms of reference are often useful to summarize the case and its basic issues or fill a gap in the claim or the arbitration agreement. But they pre-suppose the common agreement and cooperation of both parties, the lack of which may cause lengthy discussions that delay the procedure (sometimes for several months). This may be used by a reluctant respondent or his lawyer to obstruct the normal course of the procedure. Although some arbitration rules (e.g., Art. 13(3) ICC Rules) authorize the institution supervising the arbitration to adopt the terms established by the arbitrator(s) despite the objections raised by one party, such terms cannot then add anything substantial to the content of the arbitration agreement and will, therefore, be useless.

2. Although the role of the Chairman in establishing those terms should be predominant, it all depends on the initiative and capacity of all the arbitrators. As

in drafting the award, it is up to any one of the arbitrators or even to the parties' lawyers to establish draft terms of reference, which are then submitted to the other arbitrators or parties' lawyers for discussion and approval.

PROF. MICHIDA

It is reported that under the Rules of the ICC, terms of reference must always be prepared and in Great Britain, the Soviet Union and the United States, they are not required.

In Japan, unless arbitration is conducted under the ICC Rules, terms of reference are not prepared. The preparation of terms of reference is regarded as too time consuming. It can impede the prompt commencement of the arbitral process and could adversely affect the possibility of an amicable settlement of the dispute. See, Comment on *Question 62, The Role of Arbitrators in Settlement.*

MRS. OYEKUNLE

There are no specific provisions for the preparation of terms of reference under the laws of the place of arbitration (Nigeria) but there is nothing preventing the arbitral tribunal and the parties from having one prepared to identify issues for arbitration. The arbitral tribunal is likely not to proceed with such preparation where both parties object.

DR. SZURSKI

The preparation of terms of reference in the meaning of the ICC Rules is not practised in arbitrations in Poland and other countries of the East-European region, the arbitration clause being considered as a sufficient basis for the conduct of arbitral proceedings within the scope of claims, defense and counterclaims. It does not signify that the arbitral tribunal itself or together with the parties cannot define certain issues to be followed.

Terms of reference as provided for by the ICC Rules of Arbitration, besides some undoubted advantages as pointed out in the Report of Mr. Jarvin, have also one great disadvantage: the need for the participation of the parties in their preparation may, in practice, prolong the arbitral proceeding (and it often does) even for considerable lengths of time, particularly, when one party is interested in such prolongation.

E. Pre-Hearing Conference

HYPOTHETICAL CASE

The Rules contain no provision either requiring or excluding a pre-hearing conference between the arbitral tribunal and the parties. The Hightech lawyer had been counsel in a case before the Iran–United States Claims Tribunal, and he knew that tribunal had developed a practice of holding pre-hearing conferences and had established a "Guideline" that described various topics for discussion at such a conference. (*See* 1 Iran–US C.T.R. 98 (1983).) In addition, he knew that some arbitral institutions also encouraged pre-hearing conferences as a way to clarify the issues and expedite the proceedings.

Based on his experience, the Hightech lawyer thought that the topics it would be helpful to discuss at a pre-hearing conference in this case could include (i) clarifying the issues, (ii) identifying any issues to be considered as preliminary questions, (iii) determining what further written statements should be presented, (iv) arranging exchanges of documentary evidence, (v) considering whether experts will be needed, (vi) determining various procedures to be followed, and (vii) establishing a schedule for future proceedings. He wondered whether a Neutralian chairman was likely to call a pre-hearing conference, or would be favorable to a suggestion to hold one.

QUESTION 14

Is it customary to hold a pre-hearing conference in this kind of case? If so, what topics would be discussed?

ANSWERS TO QUESTION 14

MR. HOELLERING

It is customary to hold pre-hearing conferences, especially in large, complex cases. Such conferences may be conducted by the administering authority;[37] however, both when an institution is or is not involved, such conferences frequently are conducted also by the arbitral tribunal.[38] Experience indicates that pre-hearing conferences can be of great value in expediting otherwise involved and protracted arbitration proceedings.[39]

Topics customarily discussed at pre-hearing conferences include: (1) clarification of claims and counterclaims; (2) stipulation of uncontested facts; (3) exchanges of lists of witnesses, including expert witnesses, with outlines of their testimony; (4) advance filing of documents, exhibits and briefs; (5) requests by either party for the other to submit documents; (6) identification of possible issues for preliminary decisions by the arbitral tribunal; (7) preparation of a glossary of terms and names for the benefit of the panel and stenographic

---

37. Rule 10 of the AAA's Commercial Arbitration Rules, under which many international arbitrations in the United States are conducted, specifically provides that "[a]t the request of the parties or at the discretion of the AAA a pre-hearing conference with the administrator and the parties or their counsel will be scheduled in appropriate cases to arrange for an exchange of information and the stipulation of uncontested facts so as to expedite the arbitration proceedings."

38. Rule 29 of the AAA's Patent Arbitration Rules provides that "[u]nless the parties agree otherwise, a preliminary hearing with the parties will be scheduled by the arbitrator to specify the issues to be resolved and to stipulate uncontested facts. Consistent with the expedited nature of arbitration, the arbitrator shall, at the preliminary hearing, establish (i) the extent of and a schedule for the production of relevant documents and other information, the identification of any witnesses to be called and a schedule for any hearings to elicit facts solely within the knowledge of one party and (ii) a schedule for further hearings to resolve the dispute."

39. In fact, such pre-hearing conferences may be preferred by parties. *See* Coulson, *Survey*, note 3 *supra*.

reporters; (8) scheduling of hearings; (9) ground rules for the hearings; (10) consideration of whether pre-hearing or post-hearing briefs will be submitted; (11) language of the proceedings; (12) provision of hearing rooms; and (13) provision for stenographic record and interpreters where necessary.[40]

MR. HUNTER

Yes. In England it would be called a "preliminary hearing" or "preliminary meeting". (The present Rapporteur prefers the latter, so that "hearing" may be reserved for sessions at which the tribunal receives oral argument or evidence on issues to be determined.)

The purpose of a preliminary meeting is to establish the procedural framework for the arbitration, and to determine how each issue may be dealt with in an orderly manner, e.g., the exchange of written submissions, how the evidence is to be presented, how experts (if any) will be used and so forth. The tribunal will invariably try to lead the parties into agreement on procedural matters. However, if the parties cannot agree, the tribunal will issue "directions", as soon as practicable after the preliminary meeting, after hearing each party's point of view.

In small cases the tribunal may often try to deal with these matters in correspondence in order to avoid the expense of convening a preliminary meeting. The present Hypothetical Case would clearly justify a preliminary meeting.

MR. JARVIN

Yes. In ICC arbitration a meeting for the preparation of terms of reference often serves as a pre-hearing conference. Since the issues are identified in the terms of reference, it is customary to deal with procedural points – such as exchange of documents, establishing a schedule for future proceedings – in a separate order, issued simultaneously with the terms of reference and signed by the arbitrators only. However, the procedural issues and the schedule are often included in the terms of reference document itself.

PROF. LEBEDEV

Although a "pre-hearing conference" with the participation of the arbitrators and of the parties is not customary, there are no formal obstacles to hold one. It seems that, upon request of one of the parties and more so of both parties in a case like this, the arbitral tribunal would hold such conference, but after the presentation of the Statement of the Claim and Statement of the Defense. Apart from discussing such matters as a schedule for future proceedings, clarification of points in dispute, presentation of additional explanations and evidence, appointment of experts, if any, etc., this conference may also be used, if the parties so agree, for settling preliminary issues which may have come out of the Statements of Claim and Defense, namely, issues regarding applicable law and

40. *See, for example*, Poppleton, *The Arbitrator's Role in Expediting the Large and Complex Commercial Case*, 36 *Arb.J.* 6 (Dec. 1981); Hoellering, *Pre-Arbitration Conference: Can the Big Cases Be Expedited?*, *N.Y.L.J.*, June 12, 1972, p. 1, col. 3.

the tribunal's jurisdiction over certain aspects of the case. The arbitrators will, undoubtably, notify the parties of their intention to consider such preliminary issues.

PROF. EL-HAKIM
Pre-hearing conferences are unusual in Arab countries. The arbitrator(s) or the president of the arbitral tribunal usually sets a schedule for the hearings and the exchange of documents and pleas, sometimes after considering the parties' requests in that respect.

PROF. MICHIDA
It is reported that pre-hearing conferences are usually held in Great Britain, civil law countries and the United States, but that they are not customary in the Soviet Union.

In Japan, pre-hearing conferences are not customary. My impression is that the prevalence of pre-hearing conferences in Great Britain, civil law countries and the United States once again reflects habits acquired in court adjudication. In judicial proceedings, however, pre-trial conferences are not necessarily simple matters. See, e.g., Rule 16 of the Federal Rules of Civil Procedure of the United States.

In the Hypothetical Case, Hightech and Steelco agreed to settle the dispute in accordance with the UNCITRAL Arbitration Rules. However, the UNCITRAL Arbitration Rules, unlike the Federal Rules of Civil Procedure, do not expressly provide for a pre-trial conference. Still, the arbitral tribunal could conduct a pre-hearing conference, since Article 15(1) provides that the tribunal may conduct the arbitration in such manner as it considers appropriate. Among the factors I believe it should consider in deciding whether to do so are: (1) How much time will it consume? (2) Are such conferences customary in Steelco's country, Metalia; Hightech's country, Machinia; or in Neutralia? (3) Do the practices in both parties' countries differ?

Japanese practice generally prefers the early commencement of hearings, with less formal and less complicated rules, in keeping with what I have denominated the amicable texture of Japanese arbitration. Occasionally, however, in response to the parties' convenience in international cases, some pre-hearing conferences have been held.

MRS. OYEKUNLE
Yes. It is customary to hold a pre-hearing conference in this kind of case. Topics that would be discussed include amongst other things, the following:

a. Time of delivery Statements of Claim and Defense
b. Discovery and inspection of documents
c. Arrangement of any matters which will shorten or facilitate the hearing
d. Fixing time, dates and place for hearing
e. Procedure that will be adopted at the hearing
f. In such complex matter, the need for secretarial service, etc.

DR. SZURSKI

Unlike in England or the US, pre-hearing conferences are not customary in arbitrations in Poland. It is, however, not excluded that in a complicated case like Steelco-Hightech, the arbitral tribunal might convoke such a conference to clarify certain points arising from the Statements of Claim and Defense and to schedule the future proceedings. Of course when convoking such a pre-hearing conference the arbitral tribunal will inform the parties of the topics foreseen for discussion.

QUESTION 15

Even if a pre-hearing conference is not customary, would a suggestion to hold one be received favorably?

ANSWERS TO QUESTION 15

MR. HOELLERING

The parties and the arbitral tribunal would most likely be receptive to the idea of a pre-hearing conference, even if such a conference were not customary. Arbitrators generally strive to accommodate the reasonable requests of the parties, particularly when such requests are likely to facilitate orderly and expeditious arbitral proceedings. In light of the "universal preference . . . for a prehearing conference, arranged by the agency,"[41] the suggestion to hold such a conference would most probably be well received by the parties and the arbitrators alike.

MR. HUNTER

If the parties agree that a preliminary meeting should be held, then the tribunal *must* convene one. Conversely, if they agree that there should *not* be such a meeting, the tribunal is similarly bound. These are merely examples of the principle of party autonomy.

If one party requests a preliminary meeting, but the other objects, the tribunal would usually lean in favour of granting the request (on the basis that if any party wishes to be heard on any issue, even a procedural one, then that wish should be granted).

If the tribunal itself makes the suggestion to the parties that the arbitrators would value a preliminary meeting, it would be rare for the parties not to comply with the suggestion.

MR. JARVIN

It depends on the costs involved. In a case involving complex procedural points there may be more reasons for convening the parties even if they live far apart, than in a case presenting few problems on procedure.

The arbitrator would be receptive to a request for holding a pre-hearing

41. Coulson, *Survey*, note 3 *supra* at 240.

conference if he has reason to believe that a settlement could be the result, particularly if the terms of reference were prepared without a meeting with the parties.

PROF. EL-HAKIM
Probably not.

MRS. OYEKUNLE
Yes, if it is agreed to by both parties.

QUESTION 16

If a pre-hearing conference is held, would the arbitrators, when giving notice to the parties, also inform them of the topics to be discussed?

ANSWERS TO QUESTION 16

MR. HOELLERING
When arrangements for such conferences are being made, it is customary to inform the parties of the proposed topics for discussion. Although notification to the parties of the proposed conference agenda is discretionary with the arbitral tribunal, experience has shown such meetings to be more effective when everyone knows in advance what is to be discussed. Such notice will facilitate discussions and help ensure that all parties are prepared to address those topics.

Where the pre-hearing conference is conducted by the administrative staff of the AAA, rather than by the arbitrators, it is customary to advise the parties of the topics for discussion.[42]

MR. HUNTER
Yes. The tribunal would normally send a provisional agenda to the parties – and would invite them to add any other matters they wish to discuss.

MR. JARVIN
Yes. The meeting will be more effective when everybody knows in advance which topics will be discussed and decided.

MRS. OYEKUNLE
Yes. Previous information on the topics to be discussed will facilitate the deliberation at the pre-hearing conference.

42. *See* AAA Commercial Rules sect. 10. A checklist of discussion topics, including all of the items specified in answer to Question 14, is utilized by AAA staff in conducting the conference.

F. The Extent to Which the Arbitral Tribunal Will Initiate and Establish Procedures not Expressly Provided in the Rules

HYPOTHETICAL CASE

When Hightech's lawyer was considering whether the arbitral tribunal would require preparation of terms of reference or would call a pre-hearing conference, the question arose in his mind whether a Neutralian arbitrator would take the initiative to establish procedures that are permitted but not expressly provided for in the Rules, or whether he would do so only if first requested by at least one of the parties. He also wondered whether the arbitral tribunal would first ask the parties for their views before establishing such a procedure. And he was uncertain whether the arbitral tribunal would establish such a procedure if *one* of the parties objected, or over the objection of *both* parties. These questions raise the issue of the respective roles of the parties and the arbitrators in shaping the proceedings.

QUESTION 17

Would the arbitral tribunal take the initiative to establish procedures that are permitted but not expressly provided for in the Rules?

ANSWERS TO QUESTION 17

MR. HOELLERING

Although the matter is within the tribunal's discretion, there are good reasons why the arbitrators are likely to establish such procedures. It has come to be recognized, especially in large and complex cases, that arbitrators should actively seek to manage the proceedings, so as to achieve expeditious, economical and just dispute resolution.[43] The broad discretion granted to the arbitral tribunal by the UNCITRAL Rules and arbitrator training programs generally conducted by the AAA serve to encourage such an approach.[44]

MR. HUNTER

Yes. If they think that such procedures are desirable for the efficient conduct of the proceedings, they would normally take this initiative by making a proposal to the parties. If the parties agree to the proposal, there is no problem. If the parties agree not to adopt the proposal, the tribunal is bound by that agreement.

If one party accepts, but the other party does not, then the tribunal would

43. *See* Poppleton, *The Arbitrator's Role*, note 40 *supra*; Holtzmann, "What an Arbitrator Can Do to Overcome Delays in International Arbitration," in *Justice For A Generation*, a collection of papers presented at the Annual Meeting of the American Bar Association, London, July, 1985, p. 335.

44. *See generally* Hoellering, "The Training and Development of Commercial Arbitrators," in International Council for Commercial Arbitration, *Yearbook Commercial Arbitration*, Vol. X, p. 551 (1985).

decide (using its powers under Article 15(1) of the UNCITRAL Rules) after giving consideration to the opposing views of the parties.

MR. JARVIN

In terms of reference there is invariably some mention of procedure. Generally, it is very limited and gives few details, merely referring to the Rules of the ICC, and, when these are silent, to rules which the arbitrators may decide. For arbitrators from civil law countries, to establish a detailed procedure is an exception rather than the rule. More often, they reserve the right to fix procedural rules as they go along and limit "procedure" to establishing a schedule for exchange of documents and pleadings and for hearings.

Here are a few typical examples from ICC practice:

(1) Arbitrators: *Tunisian*, *French*, *Libyan*, sitting in *Paris*.
Parties: *Swiss* claimant, *Libyan* defendant.
"*Le droit applicable à la procédure est celui prévu par le Règlement de la Cour d'Arbitrage de la CCI. Le tribunal ordonnera toutes mésures d'instruction qu'il jugera opportunes.*"

(2) Arbitrator: *Danish*, sitting in *Copenhagen*.
Parties: *Swedish* claimant, *German* defendant.
"Claimant and defendant have exchanged briefs. Oral hearings will be held in Copenhagen. A delay will be fixed for submission of any further documents and of a list of witnesses to be heard at the hearing."

(3) Arbitrator: *Swiss*, sitting in *Paris*.
Parties: *Italian* claimant, *Japanese* defendant.
"The place of arbitration is Paris. However, the arbitrator may hold hearings and summon the parties, representatives, experts and witnesses to appear at any place which he will determine after consultation with the parties to be appropriate for the accomplishment of his task.
The arbitral procedure is that prescribed by the ICC Rules, edition 1975, and in situations where these Rules are silent, by the *Code de Procédure Civile du Canton de Vaud*.
The arbitrator shall preliminarily decide in an interlocutory decision the issue of the language of arbitration."

(4) Arbitrator: *Lebanese*, sitting in *Paris*.
Parties: *German* claimant, *Yemen* defendant.
"Applicable law:
The rules of conciliation and arbitration of the ICC, and, failing that, those determined by the arbitrator."

(5) Arbitrators: *Jordanian*, *Egyptian* and *Lebanese*, sitting in *Athens*.
Parties: *Egyptian* claimant, *French* defendant.
"Applicable Procedural Rules.
Rules of the ICC Court of Arbitration. The tribunal shall determine the procedures to be adopted and it will not be bound by the Law of Civil Procedure and the Law of evidence of any Municipal Law."

PROF. LEBEDEV

It seems unlikely that the arbitrators at their own initiative would order a procedure which is not provided for in the UNCITRAL Rules, for example, a conciliation procedure. It is submitted that even within the arbitration proceedings proper when the arbitrators consider it desirable to carry out some procedural acts, which are not expressly provided for in the UNCITRAL Rules, but practised in the country of arbitration (for example, to order the parties to jointly compare and check their calculations), the arbitrators are most likely to find out the attitude of the parties beforehand and would not make an order if both parties object. On the other hand, depending, of course, on the nature of the procedure proposed by the arbitrators, the objections of only one of the parties may be rejected by the arbitrators pursuant to Article 15(1) of the UNCITRAL Rules, under which the arbitral tribunal ". . . may conduct the arbitration in such a manner as it considers appropriate . . .".

PROF. EL-HAKIM

Yes, if they are customary in the country of the arbitrators or the president and do not violate a mandatory provision in the law governing procedure.

MRS. OYEKUNLE

Yes, provided both parties agree to adopt such procedures.

QUESTION 18

Would the arbitral tribunal seek the comments of the parties before ordering a procedure that is not expressly set forth in the Rules?

ANSWERS TO QUESTION 18

MR. HOELLERING

Experience indicates that where arbitrators have directed procedures not expressly set forth in the Rules, almost invariably they have solicited the comments of the parties before ordering such procedures. At times, arbitrators will suggest supplementary procedures in draft form, and invite the comments of the parties before procedures are finally adopted.

Because arbitration is essentially a consensual process, arbitrators generally seek the participation and voluntary cooperation of the parties.[45] The arbitral tribunal will want to consider in advance the objections of any party to the proposed procedure, to assure that the parties are treated with equality, and that

45. "The consensual and voluntary characteristic of the arbitration process is a source of gratification to arbitrators. Arbitrators are not thrust upon the parties; they are *selected* by them. . . . Arbitrators, on the whole, will try to accommodate themselves to the procedural expectations and the well-established and accepted usages of the parties – but only to the extent that those procedures are helpful to them in their understanding of the case and to the fulfillment of their mission and functional responsibility." Seitz, *The Arbitrator's Lot*, 38 *Arb.J.* 51 (Mar. 1983).

the proceeding is conducted with due regard to the right of each party to present its case.

MR. HUNTER

Yes, see the answer to Question 17 above.

MR. JARVIN

Yes. If arbitrators call a meeting for the drafting of terms of reference, which is usually the case, procedural questions will be discussed and parties have an opportunity to comment on the arbitrator's proposed order.

If the terms of reference are established after an exchange in writing, also procedural issues may be discussed in writing. In all circumstances the arbitrators are likely to seek the parties' comments.

MRS. OYEKUNLE

Yes, the arbitral tribunal will normally seek the comments of the parties before ordering a procedure that is not expressly set forth in the Rules.

QUESTION 19

Would the arbitral tribunal order a procedure that is not expressly set forth in the Rules if *one* party objects? If *both* parties object?

ANSWERS TO QUESTION 19

MR. HOELLERING

Under appropriate circumstances, it is possible that the arbitral tribunal may order a procedure not expressly set forth in the Rules, over the objection of a party. It is less likely that the tribunal will order such a procedure over the objections of both parties, unless convinced that the procedure will serve the ends of fair and efficient arbitration, and comport with legal standards by which the conduct of arbitrators is measured. As stated above, however, because parties are free to mutually agree on the rules governing the proceedings,[46] arbitrators are not likely to initiate procedures to which all parties mutually object. Where the initiative for such procedures comes from the AAA, such procedures are not implemented if both parties object.

MR. HUNTER

Possibly, if one party objects (using its discretion under Art. 15(1) of the Rules). Not if *both* parties object (this would offend against the principle of party autonomy). See the answer to Question 17 above.

46. "Arbitration is essentially a creature of contract, a contract in which the parties themselves charter a private tribunal for the resolution of their disputes." *Astoria Medical Group* v. *Health Insurance Plan*, 11 N.Y.2d 128, 227 N.Y.S.2e 401, 403.

MR. JARVIN

There are few examples hereof in ICC practice, but the situation might well arise where the arbitrators would feel more comfortable to have a set of procedural rules fixed. The arbitrator has a duty to arrive at an award which is enforceable at law. If the parties cannot agree on a procedure, the arbitrator must take care that the procedure applied by him is in conformity with the law of the country where the arbitration takes place; otherwise he risks that recognition and enforcement may be refused under the New York Convention, Article V(1)(d). To order a procedure complying with the local requirements might then be a practical solution.

MRS. OYEKUNLE

The arbitral tribunal will not order a procedure objected to by both parties and will also hesitate to do so even where one party objects. Under the law of the place of arbitration, the objecting party may delay proceeding by making a reference to the court to state a case on the issue. Although under Article 15(1) of the UNCITRAL Rules, the arbitral tribunal may conduct the arbitration in such manner as it considers appropriate, there is a *proviso* that the parties be treated with equality and that at any stage of the proceedings each party be given a full opportunity of presenting his case. Unilateral enforcement of a procedure not acceptable to the parties may also affect enforcement of the award.

G. Pre-Hearing Procedures Concerning Documents and Discovery

HYPOTHETICAL CASE

The lawyers for Steelco and Hightech did not know what procedures concerning documents the arbitral tribunal might order in advance of the hearing. A number of questions arose in their minds and they were uncertain how a Neutralian arbitrator might wish to proceed. These questions raise aspects of the issue of "discovery" in arbitration, a matter on which there has been a great deal of misunderstanding.

Article 24 of the UNCITRAL Arbitration Rules permits the arbitral tribunal to order parties to submit summaries of documents and exchange documents, but does not require the arbitrators to do so. The inquiry raised by Question 20 is whether arbitrators are likely to exercise this power, or whether they will leave the initiative largely in the hands of the parties.

QUESTION 20

Would the arbitral tribunal order submission of summaries of documents and other evidence before the hearing as permitted, but not required, in Article 24(2) of the Rules?

ANSWERS TO QUESTION 20

MR. HOELLERING

It is customary for the arbitral tribunal to order submission of summaries of documents and other evidence before the hearing.[47] One of the primary objectives of the pre-hearing conference or preliminary hearing, as discussed in Questions 14–16, *supra*, is to arrange for the exchange of necessary information among the parties and the tribunal, so as to shorten and expedite the entire arbitration process. Although former practice, patterned after US domestic arbitration, did not favor the advance exchange of information, international arbitration has evolved to permit and even encourage this procedure.[48]

An overwhelming majority of American practitioners polled indicated that arbitrators should receive briefs and relevant documents in advance of the hearings. Most felt that the administering agency should have the authority to require pre-hearing submission of documents and briefs.[49]

MR. HUNTER

It would be unusual for a tribunal to request the parties to submit summaries of contemporary documents.

It would be more common for the tribunal to request the parties to submit:

a. confirmation that the parties do not propose to submit any further documents (or, alternatively, if so, then to request that they should be submitted well in advance of the hearing);
b. where a massive volume of documents has already been submitted, a list identifying specifically the most important documents on which special emphasis is to be given at the hearing;
c. written statements, or summaries, of the oral evidence to be presented at the hearing.

MR. JARVIN

Probably not. Civil law trained arbitrators would require an exchange of documents, possibly a statement in advance of witness statements.

---

47. *See* Salter, *International Commercial Arbitration: The Why, How and Where*, 88 *Comm'l L.J.* 381 (Aug.–Sept. 1983).

48. For an illustration of the conduct of international arbitration in the United States prior to this evolutionary stage, *see generally* Holtzmann, *The Basic Principles of Presenting Evidence in an American Commercial Arbitration*, 9 *ICA Arb.Q.* 3 (Apr.–June 1974); Coulson & Holtzmann, *Presenting Evidence in American Commercial Arbitrations*, paper presented to the Symposium on Analysis of Differences in the Ways of Presenting Evidence in Arbitrations Held Under the Civil and Common Law Systems, Interim Meeting, International Organizing Committee, International Council on Commercial Arbitration, London, 1974; Sandifer, *Evidence Before International Tribunals*, 1975, Univ. Press of Virginia, Charlottesville. For a discussion of the more modern practice, *see* Holtzmann, "What an Arbitrator Can Do . . .," note 43 *supra*; Stein, *Pre-Hearing Discovery in International Arbitration in the US*, *Forum New York*, Vol. 2, No. 1 (1985, World Arbitration Institute) (available from the AAA).

49. *See* responses to Questions 20 and 14, respectively, in Coulson, *Survey*, note 3 *supra*. Of 59 respondents, 50 indicated that arbitrators should receive documents in advance, and 49 thought that the agency should have the authority to require such submissions.

The civil law arbitrator would normally read the documents presented in the case before the hearing, he has no obligation to come to the hearings with an *esprit vierge*. If after having studied the request and defense, and after having established the terms of reference the arbitrator finds that a summary would be necessary or facilitate his understanding of the issues, he might order a submission of summaries, but not otherwise.

The following extract of terms of reference might be illustrative. The case is between a US and a UK party, the place of arbitration is Brussels, the arbitrators are Belgian, French and British, and the parties are represented by French and British counsel.

Procedural Rules

1. There will be two hearings; the first devoted to the hearing of witnesses and experts and the second devoted to the oral argument.

The first hearing will take place in Brussels or Paris from the 1st to the 4th of July.

The second hearing will take place in Geneva on the 24th to the 26th July.

The matter of damages will, if necessary, be the subject of a third hearing.

2. Reasoned requests for the submission of documents in the possession of the other party can be presented to the arbitrators (with copy to the other party) up to three months before the beginning of the first hearing.

The arbitrators will have discretion to order or to refuse the submission.

3. Expert opinion can be presented to the arbitrators (with copy to the other party) up to six weeks before the beginning of the first hearing and comments thereon can be presented up to three weeks before such beginning.

4. The list of witnesses to be called will be presented to the arbitrators (with copy to the other party) up to three weeks before the beginning of the second hearing.

A short memorandum, indicating the facts and points of law to be discussed at the hearing, can be presented to the arbitrators (with copy to the other party) up to three weeks before the beginning of the second hearing.

PROF. LEBEDEV

Most likely, the presiding arbitrator would wish to use the right granted by Article 24(2) of the UNCITRAL Rules in order that the other party and the arbitral tribunal can have at least a summary of documents and other evidence supporting the position of each party, before the hearing.

MRS. OYEKUNLE

It is not customary for the arbitral tribunal to order the submission of summaries of documents and other evidence before the hearing as permitted in Article 24(2) of the UNCITRAL Rules. However, if it was agreed by the parties at the pre-hearing conference to submit summaries of documents and other evidence before the hearing, the arbitral tribunal would respect their desire to do so.

DR. SZURSKI

It is not customary for a Polish arbitrator to order the submission of summaries of documents and other evidence before the hearing.

The approach of a Polish arbitrator in more complex cases will be most probably similar to that presented in the Report of Mr. Hunter, particularly as regards requesting the parties to submit documents further to those submitted with the Statements of Claim and Defense as well as regards requesting the attachment of a list of most important documents for the hearing.

QUESTION 21

Would the arbitral tribunal arrange for the parties to exchange before the hearing any documentary evidence in addition to that submitted with their Statements of Claim and Defense? If so, would the arbitral tribunal refuse to accept at the hearing any documentary evidence not previously submitted to the other party, unless satisfied that there was a good reason for the failure to do so?

ANSWERS TO QUESTION 21

MR. HOELLERING

The answer to the first question depends on the extent to which documentary evidence or reference thereto was annexed to the Statements of Claim and Defense. If the parties had not already done so, it is likely that the arbitral tribunal, wherever possible, would require the parties to provide each other with copies of documents to be presented at the hearing. Usually, these would include the exchange or reference to such basic materials as the contract, engineering specifications, key reports and important pieces of correspondence.

It is unlikely that the arbitral tribunal would refuse to accept pertinent documentary evidence not previously submitted to the other party. Failure of the arbitrators to accept material and relevant evidence provides a statutory basis for the invalidation by the courts of the arbitration award,[50] although the courts are not eager to second-guess the arbitrator in matters of evidence. Admission of such documents at a later stage of the proceedings, however, is with the understanding that the other party must be given time to examine them and offer rebuttal testimony.

MR. HUNTER

i. Yes. The tribunal would certainly take steps (using its power under Article 24(2) of the UNCITRAL Rules if necessary) to ensure that the parties give to each other (and to the tribunal) any further documentary evidence on which they propose to rely at the hearing.

ii. If, notwithstanding the above, a party does produce new documents then the tribunal would exercise its discretion. Exceptionally the tribunal might simply refuse to admit such new documents; more commonly it would allow them to be admitted, and would grant the opposing party any reasonable opportunity it wishes to respond, making the appropriate directions as to any additional costs incurred by any necessary adjournment.

---

50. 9 U.S.C. sect. 10(c); Uniform Arbitration Act sect. 12(4). "Discovery, American Style," however, is generally unavailable in arbitration. *See* McClendon, *Alternative Methods* note 5 on page 154 *infra* at 985–6.

MR. JARVIN

The answer to the first question is yes.

The answer to the second depends on the attitude of the other party, it being remembered that the arbitrator has a duty to assure that both parties have an opportunity to present their case and defense. Any submissions that come as a surprise to another party endanger that principle.

But it may also depend on what the arbitrators have ordered the parties to do with respect to the presentation of documents. If a time limit has been set the arbitrator would not permit the presentation of further documentary evidence after the expiry of the time limit, at least normally and unless he thinks there was a good reason for the party's failure.

Below are two examples of terms of reference that may be illustrative. The first is extracted from an arbitration taking place in Paris, with three civil law arbitrators (Belgian–French–French) and one French and one US counsel.

"a. Within sixty (60) days after notification to the parties of the transmission of these Terms of Reference, duly signed, to the Court of Arbitration, the Claimant shall submit its Detailed Presentation with possible documentary evidence. Within sixty (60) days after its receipt thereof the Defendant shall submit its Detailed Presentation, with possible documentary evidence. Along with its Detailed Presentation each party may submit 'Witness Statements'.

b. After receipt of the Defendant's Detailed Presentation, the arbitrators shall decide the manner in which possible additional expert testimony and reports shall be submitted and considered. If the arbitrators decide to appoint one or more independent experts pursuant to art. 14.2 of the ICC Rules, the parties shall be notified of this decision and granted a period of at least fifteen (15) days within which they may submit comments as to the identity and proposed terms of reference of said expert(s). After the reports from said expert(s) have been received, each party may submit observations. Observations of the Claimant must be submitted within thirty (30) days of receipt of the report(s), and those of the Defendant must be submitted within thirty (30) days of receipt of the Claimant's observations or, if the Claimant does not submit any observations, within sixty (60) days of reception of the report(s).

c. The arbitrators shall, if necessary, request the parties to submit any document relating to the issues subject to litigation.

d. The arbitrators shall, if necessary, hear live testimony from persons they deem it necessary to hear. All testimony shall be given under oath. A record shall be made of the arbitration hearings.

e. Within ten (10) days after the closing of the final hearing, each party may, at its option, submit a Closing Brief but no additional documentary or other evidence."

The second example is from an arbitration in Basel, with three civil law arbitrators (Belgian–Belgian–Swiss) and two Belgian counsel.

"In its Statement of Defense, the Respondent must comment in detail on the Claimant's claims and contentions of fact, and should indicate the nature of evidence and the documents in its possession which shall also be produced.

If the Respondent's brief does not comply with the above, the Chairman of the Tribunal will set a deadline for the Respondent to remedy these shortcomings. If the Respondent fails to do so, it will be assumed that the Respondent acknowledges the factual contentions of the Claimant and waives its right to controvert them.

The Claimant's reply memorandum shall be submitted by March 15, 1982, and the Respondent's rejoinder memorandum shall be submitted by April 4, 1982. The failure to comply with these deadlines will be deemed a waiver of the right to submit such reply or rejoinder.

The submission of the rejoinder memorandum ends the exchange of briefs, unless the Chairman authorizes the filing of further briefs for special reasons."

PROF. LEBEDEV

Although it would not be typical, the arbitral tribunal of course may, especially at the suggestion of one of the parties, set a limited period of time for them to present any additional evidence, which they consider essential. However, even after doing so, the arbitral tribunal is unlikely to refuse any of such evidence not presented within the set period of time, but at a later time, before hearings are closed (see also Question 53).

PROF. MICHIDA

Since a method for distributing the other party's documentary evidence already exists in Japanese arbitrations, as explained in the comment on *Question 8 Contents of the Statements of Claims and Defense*, this question is not entirely relevant to Japanese practice. Institutional arbitration rules expressly set forth the number of documentary items to be filed.

MRS. OYEKUNLE

See comments on Question 14 *supra*.

The arbitral tribunal would arrange for the parties to exchange before the hearing any documentary evidence in addition to that submitted with their Statements of Claim and Defense, particularly where the parties had agreed at the pre-hearing conference to submit such documents. The arbitral tribunal would rarely refuse to accept at the hearing any documentary evidence not previously submitted to the other party, but the arbitral tribunal must ensure that the other party has the opportunity to examine the documents and reply to them.

DR. SZURSKI

The position of a Polish arbitrator will coincide with that presented in the Report of Professor Lebedev.

QUESTION 22

Should voluminous and complicated data be presented through summaries, tabulations, charts, graphs or extracts in order to save time and costs? If so, would the arbitrators arrange for the other party to have the opportunity to review the underlying data on which the summary, charts, etc., allegedly are based?

ANSWERS TO QUESTION 22

MR. HOELLERING

There is general agreement that parties should be encouraged to present data through written summaries, charts or drafts wherever possible, in order to save time and money. All of us have learned that "a picture is worth a thousand words;" extensive testimony and hearing time may be saved by presentation of complex material in a visual form. It is also customary for counsel, the arbitral institution or arbitrators to arrange for underlying materials to be furnished to the other party sufficiently in advance of the hearing in order to permit intelligent study of such documents.

MR. HUNTER

i. Tribunals often find visual aids helpful, and indeed any material in graphical or tabulated form, particularly in complex technical cases. If a party wishes to present material in this form it would be unusual, and possibly improper (because a party must be given a proper opportunity to present his case) for the tribunal to refuse to accept it.

ii. Plainly the evidentiary weight of any such material is virtually non-existent if the underlying data for such material is not made available both to the tribunal and to the other party. Any reasonable request by a party for such underlying data would undoubtedly be received sympathetically by the tribunal.

MR. JARVIN

Yes to both questions.

Any mode of presentation that makes it easier for the arbitrators to understand the parties' arguments should be welcomed, supposing always that the underlying data can be checked on a party's or arbitrator's demand.

PROF. LEBEDEV

Each party, apparently, is entitled, being liable to prove the facts relied on (Art. 24(1) of the UNCITRAL Rules) to use technically justified methods for the simplication of the presentation of voluminous data to the arbitral tribunal and the other party. It may be assumed with certainty, however, that the arbitral tribunal, at the request of the other party, as well as at its own initiative, would order the production of original data, if the "substitute" as presented gives rise to doubts (Art. 24(3) of the UNCITRAL Rules).

MRS. OYEKUNLE

Yes, such presentation would help to clarify issues in complicated cases such as this. Such a procedure will have the advantage of saving on the time and cost of the hearing.

Yes, the arbitrators would arrange for the other party to have the opportunity of reviewing the underlying data on which the summary, charts, etc. allegedly are based.

DR. SZURSKI
The arbitral tribunal will most probably welcome any presentation of a complex material in a simplified and visual form. However, in case of any doubt with respect to data so presented, the arbitral tribunal, on its own initiative, or on request of the opposite party, will order the presentation of original documents.

HYPOTHETICAL CASE G. cont.

The Steelco lawyer was aware that in some cases arbitral tribunals have told the parties that, unless a party makes timely objection before the hearing, documentary evidence (such as copies of letters, telexes, invoices, shipping documents, checks or other payment orders, etc.) will be accepted as being genuine and as having been received in the ordinary course of business. For example, a letter will, without further proof, be accepted by the arbitrators as having been written on the date on the copy submitted, as having been signed as shown, and as having been received by the addressee, unless challenged by the other party. Steelco's lawyer planned to present documentary evidence of this type and thought it would save time and cost if such a simplified procedure for proof were to be adopted by the arbitral tribunal. He did not know, however, whether the Neutralian chairman would initiate or approve of such a procedure.

QUESTION 23

Would the arbitral tribunal establish simplified procedures for proving the authenticity and delivery of ordinary business documents?

ANSWERS TO QUESTION 23

MR. HOELLERING
Absent challenge, the authenticity of documents and other physical evidence is assumed.[51] Because conformity with legal rules of evidence is not necessary in arbitration proceedings,[52] it is customary for documents to be self-identifying wherever possible. Thus, they will will be admitted into evidence without formal authentication, except where a party objects.[53] This practice will generally meet with the approval of the presiding arbitrator.

Questions about the authenticity of a document may be raised at the time it is

51. Goekjian, *The Conduct of International Arbitration*, note 32 *supra* at 420.
52. Arbitration, as an informal process, customarily does not require adherence to strict rules of evidence, absent an agreement to the contrary by the parties. *See, e.g., Bell Aerospace Co.* v. *UAW*, 500 F.2d 921 (2d Cir. 1974). Evidentiary rules, which are exclusionary in nature, evolved in the context of jury trials, to protect lay persons serving as jurors from hearing prejudicial testimony. Arbitrators, like judges, as experienced practitioners and experts in their field, need not be so protected.
53. *See* Brower, *International Commercial Arbitration: Its Increasing Role, Special Nature, and Utility as an Alternative Means of Dispute Resolution*, remarks prepared for delivery at a meeting of the Young Lawyers Division, American Bar Association, Atlanta, Ga., Jul. 30, 1983.

offered into evidence, and need not be raised in advance. Failure to object to evidence offered, however, may result in waiver.[54]

For example, Steelco may wish to introduce a report by an independent engineering firm relating to the insufficiency of the cooling system designed by Hightech. Hightech would probably not object to the document's authenticity, assuming the original document, or a photocopy, were offered into evidence.

MR. HUNTER

Not on its own initiative. An English presiding arbitrator would expect the parties to produce for the tribunal an "agreed bundle". "Agreed" in this context means that the authenticity of the documents in the bundle is not challenged, although of course their interpretation or evidentiary weight may be disputed. If the parties fail to produce an "agreed bundle", which quite often occurs where a party is represented by lawyers who are not English, then the arbitration simply proceeds on the basis of two separate sets of papers, in which many of the documents are duplicated.

Where the authenticity of documents is in issue they will normally be isolated into a separate "not agreed" bundle. The parties will then make their submissions in relation to these documents, and the tribunal may at that stage ask for such further evidence of authenticity, proof of delivery, etc., as it considers appropriate, before it determines the issue between the parties in relation to the documents.

MR. JARVIN

Generally not on the arbitrator's own initiative, but certainly on request.

PROF. LEBEDEV

If the authenticity and delivery or mailing of such documents as letters, telexes, bills, shipping documents, etc., copies of which are submitted by one of the parties, is not questioned by the other party, the arbitral tribunal accepts these copies as evidence. If there is a dispute, it would be for the party relying on a copy to establish its worth.

MRS. OYEKUNLE

The question here is what exactly is meant by the words "Simplified Procedures"? The interpretation of such words would have different meanings when applied to different cases and their facts. In a case such as the one under consideration, complex technical questions might arise and the arbitral tribunal has to be very conscious of the type of simplified procedures they would adopt. Although the arbitral tribunal has very wide discretion in dealing with the case, the parties must at any stage be given equal opportunity to prove their case. If the type of simplified procedures proposed would assist in clarifying issues at stake, they would be adopted subject to the approval of both parties. The arbitral

54. *See, for example,* AAA Commercial Arbitration Rules sect. 38; *Pierre* v. *General Accident Ins. Co.*, 111 Misc.2d 88, 457 N.Y.S.2d 376 (Saratoga Cty. 1982) (failure of claimant to object to continuation of proceedings after raising objection to unsworn testimony amounted to waiver).

tribunal must, however, ensure that the simplication would not vitiate the award, because enforceability of an award is of the utmost importance.

HYPOTHETICAL CASE G. cont.

Steelco's Statement of Claim asserted that it believed that there were engineering reports in the files of Hightech that indicated that Hightech had known for a long time that the System had serious technical defects, but Steelco said it did not have copies. Steelco's lawyer thought that those reports would help to prove Steelco's case. He noted that the Rules contain a provision that the arbitral tribunal "may require the parties to produce documents, exhibits or other evidence." (Art. 24(3)) He knew that practices relating to discovery in arbitration varied in different parts of the world. A number of questions arose in his mind.

QUESTION 24

Would the arbitral tribunal take the initiative to order a party to produce documents from its files? If not, should the other party make a formal request to the arbitrators to do so?

ANSWERS TO QUESTION 24

MR. HOELLERING

While arbitrators increasingly take an active role in the conduct of arbitral proceedings, they generally expect each party to present its case in the manner most advantageous to its position. Thus, it is unlikely that the arbitral tribunal would, at the outset, take the initiative to order production of documents from a party's file. Arbitrators are granted this power, however, both under the law and the UNCITRAL Rules.[55] American parties have indicated that they support the arbitrator's authority to order the production of necessary documents within the sole control of one party.[56]

In terms of the hypothetical case, file documents regarding system design or other disputed matters may be crucial to Steelco's case against Hightech. It would thus be the responsibility of Steelco's counsel to formally request from the arbitral tribunal an order directing production of the desired engineering reports in advance of the hearings.

55. *See* US Arbitration Act sect. 7; UNCITRAL Rules Art. 24(3). The AAA Commercial Arbitration Rules sect. 31 provide that "[t]he Arbitrator, when authorized by law to subpoena witnesses or documents may do so upon the Arbitrator's own initiative or upon the request of any party." This Rule reflects US arbitration practice generally. *See also* Stein and Wotman, *International Commercial Arbitration in the 1980's*, note 5 on page 154 *infra* at 1705.

56. *See* Coulson, *Survey*, note 3 *supra*.

MR. HUNTER

Yes. The tribunal may request a party to produce documents from its files if it considers that this would assist it in its task.

However, for practical reasons the tribunal will normally leave this until a relatively late stage – either shortly before the hearing, or even during the hearing itself, because the existence of particular documents or files sometimes only emerges during the course of the oral evidence being given by witnesses.

This means that the parties themselves (knowing what they are likely to have on each other's files) will usually be ahead of the tribunal in this respect, and will ask the tribunal for an order that the documents should be produced.

MR. JARVIN

First question: No. Second question: Yes.

The ICC Arbitration Rules (Art. 14) stipulate that the arbitration "shall proceed . . . to establish the facts of the case by all appropriate means". This would leave him room for asking a party to produce documents from his files. In practice the situation can be described as follows:

Should a party wish the other party to produce a certain document, he usually addresses that party directly or through the tribunal as intermediary, requiring production of that document. In case the other party does not oblige, the first party may apply to the arbitral tribunal requesting the tribunal to order the other party to produce the document. Should the tribunal be satisfied that the document requested may be assumed to have importance as evidence and also be relevant, the tribunal will request the other party to produce it.

PROF. LEBEDEV

The right of the arbitral tribunal to require a party "to produce documents, exhibits or other evidence" (Art. 24(3) of the UNCITRAL Rules) may be exercised by the tribunal at its own initiative as well as at the request of the other party.

It is submitted, however, that just an indication by Steelco in the Statement of Claim or otherwise that according to the information available to Steelco there are documents in the files of Hightech (engineering reports, reports of external consultants, etc.) confirming the presence of defects in the System, would hardly by itself impel the arbitral tribunal to exercise the above-mentioned right. More likely, an express request by Steelco would be needed.

It is also more likely that the arbitral tribunal would satisfy such a request in regard of a specifically identified document (by the date, at least approximate; name of the author; event, for example, test in connection with which the document was made, etc.).

PROF. EL-HAKIM

Under the Syrian Code of Procedure (Art. 524) all the arbitrators (or one of them upon delegation by the others for a specific formality) carry on the investigation of the case and sign the respective minutes. Such broad terms seem to give arbitrators the widest powers to establish the facts, produce documents and receive other evidence.

PROF. MICHIDA
To "order" a party to produce documents is regarded as somewhat incompatible with the arbitration process in Japan. Section 19 of the Rules of The Japan Shipping Exchange, Inc. provides:

> "The Board may, irrespective of there being any request by either party, *request*. . . from the parties presentation of further documents . . . in order to elucidate the points in dispute." (Emphasis supplied.)

The words "may request," once again, reflect the amicable texture of the Japanese arbitration process.

DR. SZURSKI
The answer is similar to that presented in the Report of Mr. Hunter.

In case the arbitral tribunal finds that in the files of one of the parties there is a document which is important to the objective resolution of the dispute, it will undoubtedly request such party to produce that document. The arbitral tribunal will request a party to produce any document also on motion of the other party if it should be satisfied that the requested document may be of importance as evidence.

HYPOTHETICAL CASE G. cont.

Steelco's lawyer could not identify the engineering reports precisely. He did not know how many existed, their dates or whether they were written by employees of Hightech or by one of its several outside scientific consultants.

QUESTION 25

Would the arbitral tribunal order production only of specifically described documents? Or would it be willing to require production of all documents of a generally defined type?

ANSWERS TO QUESTION 25

MR. HOELLERING
While it is always preferable for a party to request an order for the production of specific documents, this is frequently not possible, especially where the desired documents are within the exclusive control of the opposing party. In such a case, the arbitral tribunal will be responsive to a request for documents of a generally defined type, so long as the request is not unreasonable or overly burdensome for the other party.[57]

57. *See, for example,* AAA Patent Arbitration Rules sect. 31, which provides that "[t]he Arbitrator may subpoena witnesses by describing with reasonable particularity the matter on which testimony is required and directing the subpoena to an organization which will be responsible for designating an appropriate witness. . . ."

If Steelco were to demand production of all of Hightech's engineering files, for example, such a request most probably would be denied as unreasonable. A more specific request for engineering files directly relating to the design of Steelco's system, however, would be honored.

MR. HUNTER

The way in which a tribunal would exercise its power under Article 24(3) of the UNCITRAL Rules depends on the type of case, and on the reactions of individual arbitrators.

Most English arbitrators would try to strike a balance between an order so general as to be unduly burdensome (or which may be categorized as a "fishing expedition") and an order so limited as to permit the party against whom it is made the opportunity to "hold up its sleeve" documents which would genuinely assist the tribunal in determining the issues.

Thus, an order – whether made on the initiative of the tribunal or at the request of a party – will normally relate to classes of documents specified with reasonable particularity; for example, in the present Hypothetical Case:

> "Hightech's internal memoranda and technical reports (whether internal or made by external consultants) relating to performance tests carried out up to 28 February 1985".

MR. JARVIN

First question: Yes. Second question: No.

It is generally not sufficient simply to ask for production of unspecified documents which may be of importance for the case. Each and every document must be identified and specified. This is a difference in comparison with the Anglo-Saxon discovery of documents, which has no direct equivalent in civil law countries, which do not have a system by which the parties are required to have lists of the documents which are or have been in their possession, custody or power relative to any matter in question between them in the action supplemented by a right of a party to inspection of the documents of the other party.

PROF. EL-HAKIM

Under the Egyptian and Syrian laws on evidence (Art. 21), the party requesting that his opponent be ordered to produce a document must describe it, indicate its contents and its relation to the case with evidence that it is in his opponent's possession. Such precisions seem to exclude the possibility, for the arbitrators, to order the production of a generally defined type of documents. Examination and expertise on the parties' accounting books are, however, excepted.

MR. SIQUEIROS

Under Latin American laws, specifically under Mexican law, no official inquiry can be made, neither by a court nor by any other authority (arbitral tribunal), to ascertain if merchants do or do not keep regular accounting books. Likewise, no court may, at the request of any party, order delivery or make a general examination of the books, registries, accounts and documents of merchants, save only in cases of general administration, liquidation of the company, management for account of a third party, or in case of bankruptcy.

Except in the aforementioned cases, the presentation of the books and documents of merchants can only be ordered at the request of a party or *ex officio*, when the person to whom they belong has an interest or liability in a matter involving such production. The examination shall be made in the place where the books, registries or documents are habitually kept or in any other place which the parties designate by mutual agreement; such examination shall be made in the presence of the merchant or of the person appointed by him and shall be limited to those issues which have a direct relationship with the action brought on the case in question.

If the books are not in the place where the court (arbitral tribunal) which orders their examination sits, the examination shall be made where the books actually are without compelling their transference to the place where the lawsuit rests.

QUESTION 26

What can the arbitral tribunal do if a party fails to comply with an order to produce documents?

ANSWERS TO QUESTION 26

MR. HOELLERING

If a party fails to comply with a pre-hearing order to produce documents, further consideration of the matter may be taken up at the oral hearing. It is rare, however, for a party to disobey an order of the tribunal, in the absence of justifiable circumstances, such as unavailability of the requested evidence. Doing so may cause the arbitral tribunal to draw a negative inference from the failure to produce a requested document at the time of award.[58]

With regard to documents located in the United States, the United States Arbitration Act provides that the requesting party may also seek judicial enforcement of a subpoena issued by the arbitral tribunal. While this rarely occurs in practice, once the subpoena is reaffirmed by the courts, refusal to obey it will subject the offending party to the penalty of contempt of court.[59]

MR. HUNTER

The tribunal has two basic options. The first, and most usual, would be to "draw an adverse inference" (that is to say, if it was admitted that documents existed, but the party refused to produce them, it would assume that they contained material damaging to that party's case). The second would be to initiate an

58. *See generally* Stein and Wotman, *International Commercial Arbitration in the 1980's*, note 5 on page 154 *infra* at 1705.

59. 9 U.S.C. sect. 7. *See also* Wilner, ed., *Domke on Commercial Arbitration*, (rev. ed.) sect. 24.03 (1984) Callaghan & Co., Wilmette, Illinois).

application to the High Court under the Arbitration Act 1950, s.12(6)(b) which states:

> "The High Court shall have, for the purpose of and in relation to a reference, the same power of making orders in respect of:
>
> . . .
>
> (b) discovery of documents and interrogatories
>
> . . .
>
> as it has for the purpose of and in relation to an action or matter in the High Court."

Such an order may be of limited value in that neither Steelco nor Hightech is English, and may not have assets within the jurisdiction of the English Court. However, in an exceptional case, the tribunal might consider it appropriate to involve the supportive powers of the court in this way. Note also that (a) a party could make an application to the court under this section and (b) that such an application (either by the tribunal or by a party) would be possible under Article 27 of the UNCITRAL Model Law.

A more difficult situation arises not where a party refuses or fails to produce documents which clearly or admittedly exist, but where the party against whom the order is made says "no such documents exist". The tribunal then has to decide whether it believes this assertion. If the documents would be of substantial importance, the tribunal may wish to examine witnesses orally on oath.

MR. JARVIN

In *France* the arbitrator cannot do anything to force a party to comply with an order to produce documents. If a party refuses, the arbitrator will draw its consequences from such refusal.[60]

In *Italy* an arbitrator's procedural orders do not have imperative force and can never be executed coercively. Like the judge the arbitrator can draw conclusions from parties' behaviour.[61]

In *Switzerland* as well the arbitrator will draw his conclusions from the parties' behaviour.[62]

In *Sweden* the Arbitration Act confers upon the arbitrators a general power to call for the production of evidence and the arbitrators are entitled to assign evidentiary weight to the fact that evidence is not forthcoming. It should be observed that the arbitrators may not impose fines or use other means of constraint to compel attendance of a witness or the production of a document. And they cannot administer oaths (as regards witnesses) or truth affirmation (as regards parties), which means that the criminal sanctions for perjury are not applicable. But there is a procedure available to compel a witness to attend and give evidence on oath or oblige any person to produce a document. This is by means of the courts. A party who wishes evidence to be taken in this way must ask for the approval of the arbitrators, and if they consider the measure necessary, the

60. Reply by René Sanson to Questionnaire on Evidence in preparation for the IVth ICC Seminar on East–West Arbitration, hereinafter referred to as "Reply to Questionnaire".

61. Italian reply to Questionnaire, prepared by Professor Edoardo F. Ricci, Milan.

62. Swiss reply to Questionnaire, prepared by the Swiss Arbitration Association.

party can apply to the district court where the witness or the holder of the document happens to be heard, or the document produced, and has means of backing up its words by sanctions.[63]

In summary, the answer to Question 25 is that the arbitrator generally has no coercive powers, but must limit himself to taking a party's attitude into consideration.

PROF. LEBEDEV

If a party declares that the requested document does not exist at all and the arbitrators have no confidence in the opposite conclusion, they, evidently, have nothing to do but accept this as a fact.

If a party does not deny the existence of a document but refuses to produce it, the arbitral tribunal, although it is not empowered to take enforcement measures against a party, may, in making the award "on the evidence before it" (Art. 28(3) of the UNCITRAL Rules), take into account the fact of such refusal and come to certain negative conclusions, etc., when it ultimately evaluates the whole of the available evidence related to the respective issue in dispute.

Here we assume that the law of the country of arbitration does not give the above-mentioned powers to the arbitrators and at the same time does not provide for the possibility to request assistance from the courts of this country. It should not be excluded, however, that when the law of Machinia (like the current law and practice of several countries) provides for the courts' assistance (by letters-rogatory) to the arbitral tribunals, including those sitting abroad, the arbitrators might turn to the court of Machinia in order to get from Hightech some specific evidence, especially when it may be done under the law of Machinia only by the arbitrators and not by Steelco.

PROF. EL-HAKIM

Under some laws, e.g., Art. 24 of the Egyptian law on evidence and Art. 23 of the Syrian law on evidence) the other party may submit an unauthenticated copy of the document which his opponent has refused to produce and that copy may be regarded as a true copy of the original.

DR. SZURSKI

A Polish arbitrator will rather exceptionally "draw an adverse inference". If a party refuses to produce a document the existence of which it does not deny, a Polish arbitrator will treat such a refusal as a negative fact which at the time of the evaluation of all of the available evidence may influence his position in favour of the other party.

It is not excluded that in case such a document is of exceptional significance, the arbitral tribunal will endeavour to obtain the document by requesting the assistance of the courts.

63. Swedish reply to Questionnaire, prepared by the Swedish National Committee of the ICC.

HYPOTHETICAL CASE G. cont.

Steelco's lawyer considered two ways to discover in advance of the hearings exactly what engineering reports existed in Hightech's files. The first way was to question the President of Hightech in person and in the presence of his lawyer (i.e., "take his desposition") and the second was to put written questions to him to be answered in writing (i.e., "interrogatories"). He knew that in some legal systems such discovery procedures are typical in court cases and may, in certain circumstances, also be utilized in aid of arbitration, whereas in other systems such pre-hearing discovery by oral or written questions is unknown. He wondered what the attitude of a Neutralian arbitrator would be toward ordering such discovery.

QUESTION 27

Would the arbitral tribunal order a party to answer, in advance of the hearing, oral or written questions put to it by the other party? If so, what can the arbitral tribunal or a party do if the party that receives such an order refuses to comply with it?

ANSWERS TO QUESTION 27

MR. HOELLERING

Generally, United States arbitration law and practice do not favor the applicability to arbitration of pre-hearing discovery devices available in court actions. It is not unusual, however, particularly in large cases, for the parties to voluntarily agree, or for the arbitral tribunal to authorize a limited use of such oral or written questions, particularly in favor of a party who has the burden of proving a particular issue. An order by the arbitral tribunal for a party to respond to such questioning would only issue upon a showing of necessity or good cause. This is in keeping with the objective of speeding up the hearing.

As one author has noted, "[t]he concept of wholesale document discovery, endless interrogatories and multiple depositions of your adversary's employees [available in judicial proceedings] is completely alien to international commercial arbitration. This places a real premium on your investigating and preparing your own case, anticipating the other side's evidence as much as possible, and then applying in the hearings true 'on your feet' skills."[64]

In the hypothetical case, Steelco may wish to seek the use of oral or written questions in discovering essential facts from the designers of the air-conditioning system recommended by Hightech and the computer system manufactured by Hightech. Hightech, on the other hand, may wish to interview Steelco employees responsible for the air-conditioning and computer systems, or question the contractors responsible for installation of the air conditioning.

If a party to the arbitration were to refuse to comply with such an order, the

---

64. Brower, *International Commercial Arbitration*, note 53 *supra*.

tribunal, in its discretion, may preclude future testimony on the issue, or may draw a negative inference from the refusal to answer.[65] A party may also seek an order for discovery in aid of arbitration from the courts. Such orders are most rarely granted, however. Although the courts do have discretion to grant such relief in appropriate cases, they have done so only upon a showing of exceptional circumstances.[66] This practice furthers the American judicial policy of minimal interference with the arbitration process.[67]

MR. HUNTER

Pre-trial depositions of witnesses are virtually unknown in English court procedures. However, unless the parties agree otherwise, the tribunal may proceed as it wishes. Depositions or interrogatories would be ordered very rarely, but the tribunal might take this course if it felt – exceptionally – that it would result in a genuine saving of time at the hearing, and thus lead to an overall saving of costs (after taking into account the costs involved in the deposition process).

If a party refuses to comply with an order for depositions or interrogatories, either the tribunal or a party could apply to the court under the Arbitration Act 1950, s. 12(6)(b) (see the answer to Question 26) or sub-section (d) which provides that the court may order the:

> ". . . examination on oath of any witness before an officer of the High Court or any other persons, and the issue of a commission or request for the examination of a witness out of the jurisdiction."

The exercise of this power by the court is discretionary and it may be that the judge would be unwilling to make such an order at the pre-hearing stage of the arbitration.

MR. JARVIN

No. Depositions are not customary in continental European legal systems. If the parties agree, one may presume that the arbitrator would order a party to answer questions in advance, but it is not generally done and the arbitrator would lack means of enforcing such a decision.

The Rapporteur cannot remember having come across any case involving civil law arbitrators where the tribunal ordered depositions or interrogatories.

---

65. A refusal to comply by a nonparty witness, however, may fall outside the scope of authority of the arbitral tribunal.

66. *See* Page, *Pretrial Discovery and Arbitration, N.Y.L.J.*, 15 January 1975, p. 1, col. 1.

67. "The essence of arbitration is resolving disputes without the interference of the judicial process and its strictures. When international trade is involved, this essence is enhanced by the desire to avoid unfamiliar foreign law." *Cooper* v. *Ateliers de la Motobecane, S.A.*, 57 N.Y.2d 408, 442 N.E.2d 1239, 456 N.Y.S.2d 728, 732 (1982). *See also Moses H. Cone Mem. Hospital* v. *Mercury Construction Corp.* — U.S. —, 103 S.Ct. 927 (1983) (notes minimal judicial interference policy "in view of Congress's clear intent, in the [US] Arbitration Act, to move the parties to an arbitrable dispute out of court and into arbitration as quickly and easily as possible." 103 S.Ct. at 940.

PROF. LEBEDEV

Although it is not at all usual, there are hardly any formal obstacles for the arbitrators at the suggestion of the claimant to order the defendant to answer in writing before the hearings the concrete questions put forward in such an order, especially when they are connected with proving the presence or absence of evidence (see, for example, Art. 24(3) of the UNCITRAL Rules). The consequences of the defendant's non-compliance with such an order of the arbitrators are essentially the same as indicated in connection with Question 26.

PROF. EL-HAKIM

Under many Arab Codes of Procedure, the court may put questions to either party, either by itself or at the request of the opposing party. A refusal to answer those questions may be regarded by the court as an acknowledgement of the opposing party's claims. Such provisions may apply, by analogy, to arbitration.

PROF. MICHIDA

It is reported that in the Soviet Union, although it is not usual, there are hardly any formal obstacles to an arbitrator ordering a party to answer in writing in advance of the hearing.

In Japan, the arbitral tribunal would not issue such an "order" (see the comment on Question 24) nor even "request" an answer, in advance of the hearing. The reason? Were that done, it would adversely affect the possibility of a speedy compromise settlement of the dispute. This approach is another expression of the amicable texture of Japanese arbitration.

MRS. OYEKUNLE

No, the arbitral tribunal would not order a party to answer in advance of the hearing oral or written questions put to it by the other party. The arbitral tribunal has the option to put such questions directly to the party during the hearing in order to clarify points or adduce necessary evidence. Although the arbitral tribunal may seek the supportive powers of the court to make such an order, such a cause of action should be avoided because the process is very slow and may lead to unnecessary delay. A party to the proceedings may not exercise the same restraint, however, as the arbitral tribunal in referring to the court. A party who feels strongly about obtaining such answers to such written questions may take advantage of the powers of the court to issue such orders. In addition to the power of the court to issue the order under the municipal law, Article 27 of the UNCITRAL Model Law also avails the arbitral tribunal or a party with the approval of the arbitral tribunal the opportunity of requesting assistance in taking evidence from a competent court of the State. It is said that the court may execute the request within its competence and according to its rules on taking evidence.

The possibility of the court assisting in taking evidence is available but the congestion of the court in the African Region[68] will result in delay in the arbitral proceedings and increase cost.

H. Submission of Further Written Statements Before the Hearing

HYPOTHETICAL CASE

The Rules leave it to the discretion of the arbitral tribunal to decide whether submission of further written statements, in addition to the Statements of Claim and Defense, will be required, or permitted, before the hearing. (Art. 22.) The lawyers for Steelco and Hightech did not know what the arbitral tribunal was likely to do in this case.

QUESTION 28

Should pre-hearing briefs be submitted?

ANSWERS TO QUESTION 28

MR. HOELLERING

Although the Statements of Claim and Defense serve to indicate the nature of the controversy and relief sought, in general terms, pre-hearing briefs are almost always filed, as well, in substantial international arbitration cases. The pre-hearing brief provides each party with an opportunity to address the facts and legal arguments it plans to prove in the arbitral proceedings.

Well-prepared briefs are of great assistance to the arbitrators. Additionally, they contribute to the orderliness of the hearings and serve to expedite the proceedings. As one commentator noted, a number of American practitioners feel that "prehearing briefs . . . help to direct the arguments to the issues in a logical fashion. . . . If such briefs are not submitted in complex cases, the arbitrator may be required to waste time at the hearing helping the parties to organize their presentations. Briefs may contribute to a realistic presentation, forcing the parties to focus on the strengths and weaknesses of their case."[69]

MR. HUNTER

Such a procedure would not be familiar to an English arbitrator, at least in the American usage of the word "briefs" (which has a different meaning in England). The present Rapporteur does not understand exactly what the word "briefs" means in this context; or what they might be expected to contain. The UNCITRAL Rules give no guidance.

---

68. Courts are generally congested with cases in the African Region and matters in court are not speedily dealt with due to many reasons amongst which are shortage of courts, mode of taking evidence, shortage of judges, inadequacies in the court process, shortage of supportive staff and equipments, etc.

69. Coulson, *Survey*, note 3 *supra* at 242.

If an English arbitrator felt that the Statements of Claim and Defense, and any "further written statements" submitted under Article 22 of the UNCITRAL Rules were inadequate, he might suggest that still further material or argument in written form should be produced in order to shorten the hearing. Alternatively, if the existing written statements were very complex and voluminous he might ask each party to submit some form of summary. However, it is almost inconceivable that he would ask for anything in written form which merely repeated material that had already been submitted, or in some way was to be regarded as a substitute for the oral argument at the hearing.

The present Rapporteur certainly considers that each party should present its arguments of law and contentions of fact comprehensively in written form prior to the hearing. "Trial by ambush" is not appropriate in the context of international commercial arbitration. If the earlier written statements have not performed this function (because there have been no full "memorials") then the submission of additional pre-hearing written documents from the parties appears in general to be desirable.

MR. JARVIN

Yes, if a party so wishes. The arbitrators would normally invite the parties to exchange further pleadings before the main hearings. If the Request for Arbitration and the Defense are detailed and address factual and legal points in detail, a further exchange of "briefs" before the hearing might be superfluous.

PROF. LEBEDEV

Depending on the circumstances, the question of the necessity and procedure of submissions by the parties of additional written explanations in the case might be decided most rationally in the course of pre-hearing conference (Sect. E).

It is submitted, however, that if the parties have not set forth their legal arguments in the Statements of Claim and Defense (Question 9), the arbitral tribunal, according to Article 22 of the UNCITRAL Rules, will give them an opportunity to do so in the form of additional written statements, which, like the Statement of Claim and Statement of Defense, should be filed first by the claimant and then by the defendant. The same procedure is most likely to be determined for the submission of further statements ("repliques" – "dupliques"), since the last word should be granted to the defendant.

PROF. MICHIDA

It is reported that in the United States, pre-hearing briefs are almost always filed in substantial international arbitration cases, and that in the civil law this may be done if the party wishes. Here too, it seems to me that the practices in the United States and the civil law are influenced by the lawyers' practices in court litigation.

On the other hand, it is reported that in Great Britain such a procedure would be unfamiliar to an English arbitrator – and that it is almost inconceivable that he would ask for anything in written form which merely repeated material that had already been submitted, or in some way was to be regarded as a substitute for the oral argument at the hearing.

My comment on this question is the same as that of the Rapporteur on Great

Britain. Arbitration differs from court litigation as a dispute resolution method. There is no inherent necessity to adopt practices used in court proceedings. What is the best procedure in arbitration will depend upon the circumstances of each case and the existing practices in both parties' countries. The answer to this question requires that one of the major goals of arbitration be kept in mind, namely efficient dispute resolution. This, in turn, entails consideration of the costs of settlement, including attorneys' fees. In this area, too, the Japanese practice reflects the amicable texture of Japanese arbitration procedures.

DR. SZURSKI

The position of a Polish arbitrator may be supposed to be similar to that presented in the Report of Mr. Hunter.

QUESTION 29

If pre-hearing briefs are submitted, is it customary for both parties to file them on the same date? Or would the claimant file first?

ANSWERS TO QUESTION 29

MR. HOELLERING

It is customary for both parties to file pre-hearing briefs on the same date. The date would be set sufficiently in advance of the first hearing to permit the arbitral tribunal and the parties to review the briefs fully.

When arbitration is administered by the American Arbitration Association, whether under UNCITRAL Rules or under its own rules, distribution of the briefs to the tribunal and to all parties is handled by the Association. If both parties are to submit briefs on the same date, and only one does so, distribution will be held up until both briefs are received.

MR. HUNTER

Most experienced English practitioners, whether arbitrators or lawyers representing parties, would regard the simultaneous exchange of documents containing written *argument* (as opposed to the simultaneous exchange of lists, bundles of documents or experts' reports) as a sham exercise which leads, at best, to delay and general aggravation; at worst, to procedural unfairness. Accordingly, any such exchange would nearly always be sequential, not simultaneous, with the claimant submitting his brief first.

MR. JARVIN

Claimant would file first.

DR. SZURSKI

It is submitted that the arbitral tribunal will act in a way as presented by Professor Lebedev [in Question 28].

QUESTION 30

If pre-hearing briefs are submitted, would the claimant then be permitted to submit a pre-hearing reply brief ("replique") and the respondent be permitted to submit a pre-hearing rejoinder brief ("duplique")? Would the submissions of the reply and rejoinder be simultaneous?

ANSWERS TO QUESTION 30

MR. HOELLERING

It is not the practice for the parties to file supplemental rejoinder and reply briefs. Depending on the complexity of the case, and on the particular circumstances of the matter, however, the arbitral tribunal may permit or suggest such filings in order to clear up unresolved preliminary questions of fact and law, in the interest of expediting the arbitral proceedings. If submission of supplemental briefs of this nature were permitted, filing of the briefs normally would be simultaneous, unless reasons for a different order of filing existed.

MR. HUNTER

All this would be very unfamiliar territory to the chairman of the tribunal where Neutralia is England. No doubt he would accede to the wishes of the parties, or an agreed view amongst his colleagues, but (assuming that adequate written statements have been submitted under Articles 18, 19, 22 and 24 of the UNCITRAL Rules) he would regard the "briefs" as an expensive waste of time and effort, and not likely to be of assistance to the tribunal. He would rather get on with the hearing without delay. As to mechanics, the present Rapporteur assumes that if the original pre-hearing briefs had been submitted simultaneously, then so would any reply or rejoinder briefs. Otherwise, it would all be done sequentially.

MR. JARVIN

First question: Yes. Second question: No.

But it should be understood that the filing of pre-hearing "repliques" and "dupliques" shall not be thought to be a custom; it will depend on the case whether such briefs will be deemed desirable at all or whether they, on the contrary, could be seen as delaying the arbitration. Arbitrators will play an active role and order and/or admit filing on request according to circumstances.

I. Determination of Preliminary Issues

HYPOTHETICAL CASE

Under the Rules, a plea by a respondent that the arbitral tribunal lacks jurisdiction over any issue must be raised not later than in the Statement of Defense. (Art. 21(3)) Accordingly, Hightech in its Statement of Defense asserted that the arbitral tribunal does not have jurisdiction over the issues of whether Hightech had breached the contract because its patent on the System was allegedly invalid and allegedly infringed patents owned by Supertech. Hightech's position is that questions of patent validity and infringement are not capable of settlement by arbitration. Hightech did not challenge the jurisdiction of the arbitral tribunal to determine the other issues in the case.

The lawyer for Hightech wanted an answer to the jurisdiction question at an early stage in the proceeding, because the task of preparing the defense would be simplified if he did not have to enter into complex technical matters of patent validity and infringement. The rules permit the arbitral tribunal to decide on a plea relating to its jurisdiction as a preliminary matter, or to proceed with the arbitration and rule on the plea in the final award. (Art. 21(4))

QUESTION 31

Should the arbitrability of the issues of patent validity and patent infringement be decided as preliminary questions? If so, why? If not, why not?

ANSWERS TO QUESTION 31

MR. HOELLERING

The arbitrability of the patent validity and infringement questions in the hypothetical case should be decided as preliminary matters. Whether or not such complex, technical issues need be arbitrated will significantly affect the scope of arbitration, in terms of the evidence to be presented, the witnesses to be called, and the necessary level of discovery.

Although questions of patent validity, infringement and interference are now within the domain of arbitration due to recent amendments to the US patent laws,[70] Supertech, the challenger of Hightech's patent, is not a party to the arbitration. Therefore, any decision on the merits of patent validity and infringement issues, if considered by the arbitrators to be germane to the underlying dispute, can only bind Steelco and Hightech.[71]

If the arbitral tribunal decides that the patent issues, or some of them, are not arbitrable, an early decision to that effect will significantly reduce and expedite the arbitral proceedings. An early decision that they are arbitrable will likewise clarify the scope of the proceedings, for which the parties must prepare.

MR. HUNTER

Yes. Because, if they are not arbitrable under the relevant applicable law, it is better to know this fact as soon as possible. In England it would be possible for an interim award on a preliminary issue of this kind to be tested in court. (Because, if the tribunal decided that these issues were arbitrable, an application could be

70. 35 U.S.C. sect. 294 (1983); 35 U.S.C. sect. 135(d) (1984).
71. 35 U.S.C. sect. 294(c).

made to the court claiming that the tribunal was acting in excess of its authority.) Thus the matter could be finally resolved at an early stage of the proceedings, at least as far as their validity in the place of the arbitration is concerned.

It seems inappropriate for the parties to incur the expense and effort of arbitrating these issues, only to find – at the *end* of the arbitration – that the tribunal had acted in excess of its authority. (The policy of the UNCITRAL Model Law is similar; see Art. 16(3).)

MR. JARVIN

This is difficult to answer.

The patent infringement issue is one of the grounds relied upon by Steelco; the other being alleged late delivery. The arbitrators might prefer to deal with the late delivery issue rather than the patent issue in a partial award if they consider that the late delivery issue involves less extensive evidence than the patent issue. A partial award might induce the parties to settlement negotiations; if the arbitrators are able to arrive at a partial award on one issue faster than on the other, this might be a reason for them to decide that issue as a preliminary question.

PROF. LEBEDEV

If Hightech states that the dispute is not arbitrable in respect to the alleged breach by it of contract guarantees regarding patents, it is submitted that the arbitral tribunal is most likely to decide this issue as a preliminary one and not to postpone this decision till the final award is made. First, it follows from Article 21(4) of the UNCITRAL Rules that the arbitrators should act so "in general". Secondly, a plea formulated as mentioned above may well be solved by the arbitrators without – and hence before the hearings of the case on the merits – examination of all facts, etc. Finally, this approach itself, to be used "in general", i.e., whenever practicable, facilitates the conduct of the case in arbitration for the parties to the greatest extent by clarifying the framework of their possible claims and objections.

PROF. EL-HAKIM

There is no provision in Arab laws denying arbitrators jurisdication over patent issues. However, if the settlement of those issues involve a third party which is not a party to the arbitration agreement, such an issue will then be regarded as a preliminary question to be settled by the competent court.

PROF. MICHIDA

It is reported that in the United States, as a result of 1983 and 1984 amendments to the US patent laws, questions of patent validity and interference may now be arbitrated. However, many countries have different systems for determining patent validity, entrusting such matters to the Patent Office and the regular judicial system. Japan is one such country. Therefore, the question of the validity of Hightech's patent, whose challenge by Steelco is advanced as a reason for cancelling the contract, should be decided as a preliminary matter.

However, there is no single patent right that is valid throughout the world. The Paris Convention for the Protection of Industrial Property provides:

> "Patents applied for the various countries of the Union by nationals of countries of the Union shall be independent of patents obtained for the same invention in other countries, whether members of the Union or not." (Art. 4 bis)

Therefore, in the light of this *lex locus* rule of patent rights, it is desirable for further discussion to make clear in which country "a valid patent that [Hightech] owned" (Hypothetical Case, page 22) was obtained, and from which countries "patents owned by Supertech," Hightech's competitor (Hypothetical Case, page 23), were obtained.

MRS. OYEKUNLE
The arbitrability of the issues of patent validity and patent infringement will usually be decided as preliminary questions. On the facts of the case, Hightech warrantees on the manufactured computer and peripheral equipment were said to be covered by a valid patent that it owned, and Hightech's patent did not infringe the patents of others. Steelco in its Statement of Claims alleged amongst other things, that "Hightech furnished a system that infringed Supertech's patent and thereby exposed it to liability for royalties to Supertech". Thus if it is decided that the issues of patent infringement are arbitrable, a decision on that matter may have a significant effect on the arbitration proceedings. An early decision would definitely have the effect of clarifying the scope of the proceedings.

DR. SZURSKI
The commentator shares the opinion expressed in the Report of Professor Lebedev.

J. Testimony of Parties

HYPOTHETICAL CASE

The lawyers of Steelco and Hightech both were aware that under some legal systems a party cannot be a witness. (*See, e.g.*, Sandifer, *Evidence Before International Tribunals*, Revised Edition, 1975, pages 349–366.) They were uncertain as to Neutralian practice in this respect.

Both lawyers knew that a great deal of misunderstanding and confusion can arise in arbitrating an international case because of different approaches to the question of the admissibility of parties as witnesses. They were aware of an actual example from a recent case. The case involved a dispute over alleged breach of contract between an American party and a party having a civil law background. Article 25(2) of the UNCITRAL Rules states that "if witnesses are to be heard, 15 days before the hearing each party shall communicate to the arbitral tribunal and the other party the names of the witnesses he intends to present and the subject upon . . . which such witnesses will give testimony". The lawyer for the American party gave notice that he would call as witnesses two high executives of the claimant corporation. They were the only representatives of the claimant who had participated in the negotiation of the contract. The American lawyer considered their testimony vital to proving his case.

Upon receiving the notice of the claimant's two witnesses, the respondent wrote the following letter to the arbitrators:

> "Both Mr. Jones and Mr. Smith (we have changed the names to preserve confidentiality) introduced by the claimant as witnesses, hold managerial positions in the claimant corporation and are interested parties in the case. Mr. Jones has been the founder and sole owner of the company, and Mr. Smith admits that he was the principal person who negotiated and signed the contract. Therefore, both are the ultimate and principal beneficiaries in this case.
>
> In respondent's view, the above-mentioned persons' presentations at the Hearing cannot be considered as evidence, but rather their statements should be considered as claimant's own assertions.
>
> The respondents hereby submit their protest and objection to the claimant's presentation of said persons as witnesses."

The American lawyers had been surprised and worried. The Chairman of the arbitral tribunal had a civil law background. If he refused to hear the two key witnesses, how could the Americans prove their case?

Moreover, if a Neutralian arbitrator were inclined not to accept parties as witnesses, who would be considered to be a party or so closely related to a party as to be unacceptable as a witness? For example, the two lawyers wondered whether the following would be considered unacceptable as witnesses: (i) the President of Hightech, who is not a shareholder of that company; (ii) the President of Steelco, who is a shareholder of that company; (iii) other high executives of the two companies some of whom own stock, and some of whom do not; (iv) an engineer of Hightech who was employed by it at the time the System was designed, but who now works for another company; (v) an engineer of Steelco who was employed when the air conditioning was installed, but who has now retired and receives a pension from Steelco; (vi) a paid consultant to Steelco who has never been its employee; (vii) the janitor at Steelco who happened to be present when the room became too hot allegedly causing the System to burn out.

In this case, executives of Steelco and Hightech were the only individuals who had direct knowledge of certain important events. If they could not be witnesses, how would the arbitral tribunal be informed of facts that only they knew?

QUESTION 32

Would the arbitral tribunal accept parties as witnesses?

ANSWERS TO QUESTION 32

MR. HOELLERING

The arbitral tribunal would permit parties to testify. Even though such testimony may not be competent in a civil trial in every jurisdiction,[72] it is well-established in US arbitration law and practice that conformity to the legal rules of evidence is not necessary. The weight given by the arbitral tribunal to the testimony of interested persons will depend on the credibility of the witnesses.

MR. HUNTER

Yes, certainly. The weight given to the evidence of the parties (or other persons having a direct interest in the outcome) will be assessed according to the effectiveness with which that evidence may be tested. The unsworn written statement of a party may be treated by the tribunal with some reservation, particularly if it is directly contradicted by evidence of weight presented by the other party. On the other hand, oral evidence given on oath by a party, duly tested by cross-examination, or a probative examination by the members of the tribunal may be accorded considerable weight. English arbitrators tend to place great importance on the impression they receive from hearing the oral evidence of the parties themselves.

MR. JARVIN

The practice prevailing in most civil law systems is that no person is refused an appearance before the arbitrators to state what he knows. A party can be heard, even if not as a witness.

In court proceedings the importance of deciding who is to be heard as witness and who is to be heard as a party relates to the swearing of an oath which only a witness may do. This distinction is of less interest in arbitration where the persons to be heard are – as a rule – not sworn.

The different approach to a party as compared to a witness remains, however, when it comes to assessing the person's statement. The arbitrators, informed of the person's relationship to the party and his interest in the outcome of the case, will keep this in mind and give weight to his statement accordingly. In some civil law countries the arbitrator reminds the person to be heard of his "moral duty" to speak the truth, whereas in others not even a reminder is given.

National variations do exist however. The German-tradition arbitrators will be reluctant to hear a managing director of a company or chief executive officer (*Vorstand* in an *Aktiengesellschaft* and *Geschäftsführer* in a *Gesellschaft mit beschränkter Haftung*) since he will be considered too close to the quality of the party. As a last resort however, where other means have been exhausted, a managing director or chief executive officer may be heard.

In Italy, diverging views exist as to whether a party can and should swear as a witness.[73]

In theory, it is possible in many countries to have a witness sworn and heard by a court of law where the arbitrators do not want to or cannot swear him in the arbitration. In practice it is very rarely used if at all.

---

72. Under both the Federal Rules of Evidence, Rule 601, and New York Rules of Evidence, Civ. Prac. Law 4512, however, virtually every person is competent to testify, regardless of their possible interest in the case.

73. Prof. Edoardo F. Ricci, Report to Fourth ICC Seminar on East–West Arbitration to be held in Varna, Bulgaria, October 1986.

PROF. LEBEDEV

These Questions touch upon an important aspect of the law of evidence of the country of arbitration, by which, apparently, the arbitrators will be guided in this particular case. Answering these Questions, therefore, in a most general way, it might be noted first of all that according to this law, on the one hand, no evidence can have a predetermined force and, hence, all evidence should be evaluated in its totality. On the other hand, "explanations of the parties" and "testimony of witnesses" are both recognized as "means of proving", although classified as two separate types thereof. As far as legal persons are concerned, information given by their officers, who are to be considered as "organs" of companies, i.e., authorized by their constitutions, statutes, etc., to bind a company (presumably, for example, the presidents of Steelco and Hightech) should be treated as "explanations of the parties", i.e., the named companies.

Although explanations of the parties are admitted as evidence, including information about the circumstances of the case presented by the above-mentioned officers in oral or written form, they require very careful examination, comparison with other evidence, etc., because of obvious legal interest of those officers in the outcome of the case.

Under any circumstances, the award cannot be based only on the explanations of the party without further proof.

Other individuals, who are not the "organs" of the company, including high executives aware of certain circumstances relevant for the case, may be heard as witnesses. A special relationship of the witness with the party, e.g., an official or even a family relationship, presupposing in the circumstances that the witness is interested, is not considered as being in and of itself a ground to challenge the witness, although this relationship also will require very careful examination of testimony, all-round evaluation in the light of every other evidence, etc.

PROF. EL-HAKIM

We already pointed out (Question 27) that a party may be heard to answer questions put by the tribunal *in his capacity as a party, not as a witness*. It is, therefore, excluded in such cases that parties be sworn, even if the procedure takes place before a judicial court. A party can only be sworn when taking a "decisive" oath at the demand of the other party or a "suppletory oath" administered by the tribunal for insufficient evidence in cases provided for by the law. Nothing, in the Arab countries, prevents the arbitrators from receiving such an oath.

MRS. OYEKUNLE

Yes, the arbitral tribunal would accept parties as witnesses. It is specifically provided by Section 8(a) of the Arbitration Act Laws of the Federation of Nigeria and Lagos that –

> "The arbitrators or umpire acting under a submission shall, *unless the submission expresses a contrary intention, have power to administer oaths to or take the affirmations of the parties* and witnesses appearing".

MR. SIQUEIROS
Under Latin American laws parties can not be witnesses.

The arbitral tribunal can receive information from the parties as to the facts of which they have direct knowledge through the *prueba confesional*, which is the equivalent of a request for admission, i.e., written statements of facts concerning the case which are submitted to an adverse party and that party is required to admit or deny.

Note

For a discussion of a practical solution to the problem of admissibility of testimony by parties in an arbitral tribunal that includes both civil and common law arbitrators *see* M. Straus, "The Practice of the Iran-United States Claims Tribunal in Receiving Evidence from Parties and from Experts: Questions 32–34 and 38–39", Communication to Working Group I (copies available from Department of International Commercial Arbitration of the T.M.C. Asser Institute, The Hague, The Netherlands).

QUESTION 33

If a party cannot be a witness, who is considered to be a party or so closely related to a party as to be unacceptable as a witness?

ANSWERS TO QUESTION 33

MR. HOELLERING
This question is not relevant to United States practice because interested persons may give evidence.

MR. HUNTER
Not applicable where Neutralia is England. But the understanding of the present Rapporteur is that executive officers of a corporate party to the dispute would generally be considered to be interested parties.

MR. JARVIN
See the answer to Question 32.

PROF. EL-HAKIM
Close relatives or legal representatives or agents of the parties cannot be heard as witnesses. This applies to attorneys, company managers, sale agents, etc. Persons having an indirect interest in the dispute (such as partners or shareholders in the company involved, guarantor of a party) also cannot be heard as witnesses. Government employees must also be authorized by the competent Authority to disclose secret information relating to their function. Other persons subject to

professional secrecy (e.g., lawyers, doctors or agents) must be authorized by their clients or principles to disclose secret professional information.

QUESTION 34

If a party cannot be a witness, what procedure, if any, can be used so that the arbitral tribunal can receive information from such individuals as to facts of which they have direct knowledge?

ANSWERS TO QUESTION 34

MR. HOELLERING
This question is not relevant to United States practice because interested persons may give evidence.

MR. HUNTER
Not applicable in England.

MR. JARVIN
The individual can be heard as a party, i.e., state what he knows in front of the tribunal and be questioned by the arbitrators and the counsel in the same way as a witness.

The arbitrators have no coercive measures to force a person to give information to the tribunal and if a person refuses to appear, the arbitrators have a choice between asking a court to order the hearing of the individual (where this possibility exists) or take the person's refusal into account when weighing the overall evidence.

K. Written Statements by Witnesses

HYPOTHETICAL CASE

The Rules provide that evidence of witnesses may be presented orally at a hearing or in the form of written statements signed by them ("affidavits"). (Art. 25(2), (4) and (5)) The Lawyers of Steelco and Hightech each had a number of questions concerning this for which they needed the answers as they prepared their cases.

QUESTION 35

Are written statements of fact by witnesses welcome?

ANSWERS TO QUESTION 35

MR. HOELLERING
In the United States, arbitral tribunals generally prefer live testimony of

witnesses. Live testimony permits the tribunal, and the opposing party, to observe and question the witness first-hand. This is particularly true with regard to significant and controverted testimony.[74] In an international case, this preference for live testimony may be offset by an arbitral tribunal which, by reason of the legal orientation or nationality of its members, will place greater emphasis on written, rather than oral, proceedings. The parties also may agree to place greater reliance on written factual statements in order to reduce the length of oral hearings.

Arbitrators will receive and consider evidence in affidavit form, however, and will give it such weight as deemed appropriate, after consideration of any objection to its admission.

MR. HUNTER

Yes. Normally an English arbitrator would give little weight to the unsworn written testimony of a partisan witness, presented by one party. (The position would be different in the case of an independent witness approached by the tribunal itself with a request for a written statement of fact.) However, most arbitrators would welcome the opportunity to see in advance, in writing, the evidence that will be given by a witness orally at the hearing.

Sometimes the written statement may be taken as the "evidence in chief" ("direct evidence") of the witness, so that the oral part of his evidence may start with cross-examination, and be followed by re-examination ("re-direct"), and examination by members of the tribunal.

One advantage in submitting written statements of evidence of witnesses in advance of the hearing is that the opposing party will sometimes indicate that he does not challenge the testimony. This then makes it unnecessary for the witness concerned to attend at the hearing, with consequential savings of hearing time and expense.

MR. JARVIN

It would depend on the nature of the question and the facts to be proven. Technical or otherwise complex facts may be better presented in writing. The arbitrator would then be in a better position to put questions to the witness at the hearing and to follow the cross-examination by the counsel (where permitted).

Generally speaking, though, the arbitrator prefers live testimony and does not expect to receive advance knowledge of what the witness is going to say. Affidavits are not welcome in replacement of oral witness statements unless there are very good reasons for not having the witness come to the hearing. Less weight will generally speaking be given to affidavits under any circumstances.

PROF. LEBEDEV

Although in the practice of civil procedure in the Soviet courts, only the oral testimony of a witness is admitted, arbitrators may hardly a priori reject the

74. This differs somewhat from arbitration practice outside the United States, and may be costly in terms of time. *See* Goekjian, *The Conduct of International Arbitration*, note 32 *supra* at 422; Holtzmann, "What an Arbitrator Can Do . . .," note 43 *supra*.

testimony of a witness presented in written form, especially when the parties agreed on the admissability of such testimony by adopting the UNCITRAL Rules (Art. 25(5)).

PROF. EL-HAKIM
Yes, but they will not have the value of a testimony without being sworn before the tribunal, to enable both parties to put questions to the witnesses.

PROF. MICHIDA
In Japan, written statements of fact by witnesses are not welcome because of the lack of opportunity to question the witness.

MR. SIQUEIROS
No, generally speaking "affidavits" are not submitted in arbitral proceedings. Witnesses normally appear before the tribunal in the company of the party who offers their testimony; those who do not voluntarily appear may be summoned by subpoena. Elderly people or those witnesses that are ill may render their testimony at home in the presence of both parties. High officials of the government may render testimony through written statements addressed to the tribunal.

In matters of commercial procedure, the examination of witnesses shall always be effected by written interrogatories, while in processes of "civil" nature, the evidence may be taken orally.

Witnesses, when rendering a testimony, do not have to be sworn. However, they must testify to tell the truth and admit before the court that they are knowledgeable of the legal sanctions which may be imposed upon those who give false testimony.

QUESTION 36

If written statements of a witness are presented, should the witness also be present at the hearing, if possible, to answer questions?

ANSWERS TO QUESTION 36

MR. HOELLERING
Written statements are frequently utilized in international arbitration cases whenever a witness cannot be present at the hearings, and to reduce the costs of transporting witnesses and expedite the oral hearings. The primary objection to the use of affidavits is that such written statements cannot be cross-examined. Therefore, the presence of the witness at the hearings would overcome this objection. On certain aspects of the case, the tribunal may also prefer the live testimony over the written statements. Production of the live witness in addition to written testimony, however, runs counter to the cost-reduction advantages of

admissibility of written testimony, depending, of course, on the location and proximity of the witness to the hearings. Therefore, a balance must be struck between the two, in the interests of just and economical dispute resolution. A sensible approach would be to encourage written testimony, but have witnesses available for cross-examination on key points, or to clarify written statements and to answer questions on points not fully covered by the written testimony.

Counsel for Hightech and Steelco will want to consider carefully the nature of the evidence presented in written and oral form. The more significant and controversial the evidence, the better it will be to produce the witness at the hearings. At times, counsel will reach agreement on which witnesses are to appear, and when they will appear. The arbitral tribunal itself may also request the presence of a particular witness for examination.

MR. HUNTER
Unless the opposing party accepts the evidence as submitted in written form, it would be normal for the witness to appear for examination. See the answer to Question 35.

MR. JARVIN
Yes.

PROF. LEBEDEV
In light of the practice mentioned in connection with Question 35, it should be recommended to a party, considering written testimony of a witness as having great importance, to ensure the appearance of that witness at the hearing. It cannot be excluded, however, that, depending on the nature of the testimony, the arbitrators may require a witness to appear at their own initiative or at the request of the other party (Art. 24(3) of the UNCITRAL Rules).

PROF. EL-HAKIM
Yes.

PROF. MICHIDA
In Japanese practice, if a witness can be present, his written statement is not presented. Dual presentations (i.e., written and oral), burden witnesses and parties. The oral statement in the hearing (with the opportunity to cross-examine) is the most important element in the fact-finding process.

HYPOTHETICAL CASE K. cont.

Both lawyers had questions in their minds concerning the formalities with which they should comply if they were to submit sworn written statements of witnesses. They wondered whether the statements should be sworn to in accordance with the applicable formal procedures at the place where signed, and whether there were any authentications or other formalities that a Neutralian arbitrator would expect (e.g., "notarial act," "apostille," "consular certificate").

QUESTION 37

Should written statements by witnesses be sworn to? If so, what formalities, if any, should be observed in connection with the oath?

ANSWERS TO QUESTION 37

MR. HOELLERING

Written statements by witnesses should be sworn to as to their veracity. Such statements are presented in the form of an affidavit, in which a notary acknowledges the authenticity of the signature.

MR. HUNTER

A party may elect (or be required by the tribunal) to present the written testimony of witnesses in sworn form. This would normally be in the form of an "affidavit". The witness signs the statement, and then swears (in appropriate terms, depending on the deponent's faith) that the document displays his signature and that its contents are true.

The "jurat" clause for an affidavit is in the following form:

SWORN by the above-named Deponent)
at [address]) [signature of
this day of 19) deponent]
before me)

[signature of person administering oath]

The person administering the oath (who must be duly empowered under the Solicitors Act 1974, s. 81) should not be a solicitor with the firm representing the party on whose behalf the affidavit is to be submitted.

A false declaration on oath renders the deponent liable to criminal penalties for "perjury".

However, in practice, arbitrators tend to give very little additional weight to sworn statements of partisan witnesses, by comparison with simple signed statements.

The real factor affecting the weight given to the personal testimony of witnesses depends on the extent to which their evidence is tested by oral examination.

MR. JARVIN

Using sworn written statements is generally not the practice in international arbitration under civil law systems.

A party might have evidence taken with state court assistance and present a witness statement made in court (where available). Such statement will be sworn in the same way as a witness statement made in a litigation before the court.

PROF. LEBEDEV

Since there are no provisions in this regard in the law of the country of arbitration, the presiding arbitrator will be guided, as far as written statements are concerned, mostly by Article 25(5) of the UNCITRAL Rules, the only requirement of which is to have such written statements of the witnesses "signed by them". Nevertheless, the authenticity of the signature should be, of course, certified, at least in the manner adopted in the country where the signature was made.

PROF. EL-HAKIM
We already pointed out that written statements by witnesses must be sworn before the arbitral tribunal or a judicial court to be accepted as testimonial evidence. When sworn before a notary public (where no question could be put to the witness by the parties), they must be followed by such examination. If not sworn, they may only be accepted as circumstantial evidence ("presumption").

PROF. MICHIDA
It is reported that in the United States, the written statements of witnesses should be sworn to as to their veracity by a notarized affidavit.

However, in Great Britain, it is reported, although a party has the option to do this, arbitrators tend to give very little additional weight to sworn statements of partisan witnesses, in comparison to simple signed statements, because the real test abides in the oral examination. In civil law, sworn statements are not required.

In Japanese practice, a witness may be unavailable to give an oral statement because he might, in a maritime case, for example, be stationed abroad. Under such circumstances, his written statement may be presented, but the arbitrator cannot require the statement to be under oath. As the UNCITRAL Rules provide in Article 25(5), it will be "signed," or otherwise bear his name with seal or chop.

The Japanese Code of Civil Procedure expressly provides that an arbitrator cannot require a witness or expert to make statements under oath (Sect. 795(2)). Japanese law distinguishes between court proceedings, where witness oaths are required, and arbitration. Arbitration is a method of private dispute adjudication, based on the parties' consent. Prohibiting the oath reduces the formalities in arbitration proceedings and tends to enhance the amicable nature of the hearing. Moreover, if, in practice, witnesses are not prosecuted for perjury because of discrepancies between their testimony and the facts, requiring sworn statements is not very likely to deter false testimony.

L. Experts

HYPOTHETICAL CASE

The decision of several aspects of the case between Steelco and Hightech will require specialized technical evidence. For example: (i) Was the failure of the System to perform due to failures of design or manufacture by Hightech, or to burnouts caused by improper air conditioning? (ii) Were the correct air-conditioning specifications provided by Hightech, and were they as complete as industry custom required? (iii) Did the course of training provided by Hightech to Steelco's employees meet the standards generally recognized in the industry? (iv) What financial valuation principles should be applied in determining the amount of profits lost by Steelco because the System was not available on time? If the arbitral tribunal decides to hear the issues of patent validity and infringement, other highly technical questions will be involved.

QUESTION 38

Would the arbitral tribunal appoint its own experts, or rely on experts presented by the parties?

ANSWERS TO QUESTION 38

MR. HOELLERING

It is customary for arbitral tribunals to rely on experts presented by the parties. In a case such as the hypothetical case, both Hightech and Steelco will want to present their own experts to testify on their behalf. Opposing counsel, in turn, would want an opportunity to cross-examine the other party's expert, so as to impeach his testimony and rebut any negative inference which may be drawn from any expert report. Should the parties' expert testimony prove inconclusive or confusing to the arbitrators, the tribunal may appoint its own experts, if so authorized by the applicable rules or by agreement of the parties.[75] This "neutral" expert would then either assist the tribunal with a report on outstanding technical matters, or give testimony thereon. Both parties thereafter would be given the opportunity to interrogate the expert with regard to his findings at the hearing.[76]

When arbitration is conducted under its auspices, the AAA will assist the arbitrators and the parties in the appointment of neutral experts. One possible approach is for the parties to submit a list of mutually agreeable experts to the AAA for transmission to the arbitral tribunal. The arbitral tribunal would then make a selection from that list. A second method is for the AAA to submit a list of proposed experts drawn from its panel. The tribunal would then make its selection from the AAA list. A third way would be for the arbitrators, who themselves know the field, to pick an expert on their own. Whatever the way, the tribunal normally will seek the parties' concurrence to the selection and role of the neutral expert.

MR. HUNTER

It could be either, or both. In general, English arbitrators prefer the adversarial approach; that is to say, they would listen to the evidence of experts presented by

75. The tribunal is expressly granted such authority under Art. 27 of the UNCITRAL Rules. Under AAA Commercial Arbitration Rules sect. 31, such power, while not expressly stated, is implied. As a practical matter, however, use of experts appointed by the tribunal is not customary. This may be due to the high level of expertise typical of panel members in international arbitrations conducted under AAA auspices.

76. Stein and Wotman, *International Commercial Arbitration in the 1980's*, note 5 on page 154 *infra* at 1716–17.

the parties, which is subject to questioning by the members of the tribunal and cross-examination.

There is, however, a growing appreciation that an arbitrator who has little or no expertise in the subject matter of a dispute involving complex technical issues can get little assistance even from skilled cross-examinations of opposing technical experts of high standing.

Where a tribunal takes this view, it will appoint an expert to assist. It has this power under the general law of England, and it is given expressly by Article 27 of the UNCITRAL Rules. The UNCITRAL Rules (Art. 27(4)) also reflect the general position in English arbitration law that, even where the tribunal invokes the assistance of an expert, the parties themselves may still present expert witnesses to testify on the points at issue.

MR. JARVIN

It would appoint its own experts.[77] As regards experts, all the civil law countries I have examined permit the arbitrator to appoint an expert on his own initiative and for his own information.[78] The expert's opinion must be made available to the parties and the expert prepared to answer questions from the parties.

However, since the costs of an expert are borne by the parties, there are limits to what an arbitrator can order. If, therefore, the parties refuse to pay the advance required for an expertise, the arbitrator will draw his conclusions from such behaviour.

On the other hand, if the parties want to present their own experts, the arbitrator would accept this. In complex cases, there may be experts appointed by the party and the arbitrator. The expert appointed by the arbitrator may be of great assistance to evaluate the statements of the party-appointed experts.

PROF. LEBEDEV

It is submitted that in accordance with the usual practice in the country of arbitration, at least the presiding arbitrator will be inclined to call for the report of expert(s) appointed by the arbitral tribunal itself in accordance with Article 27 of the UNCITRAL Rules, especially on technical questions.

PROF. EL-HAKIM

Under Egyptian and Syrian laws on evidence (Arts. 136 and 139 respectively) the tribunal must confirm the appointment of the experts agreed on by the parties. Failing such agreement, it is up to the arbitrators to appoint one or three experts.

PROF. MICHIDA

In Japanese practice, arbitral tribunals usually rely on experts presented by the parties. By doing so, the amicable nature of dispute settlement is preserved. However, in maritime cases, where special problems affecting highly technical

---

77. ICC Court of Arbitration Rules, Art. 14(2) stipulates: "The arbitrator may appoint one or more experts, define their Terms of Reference, receive their reports and/or hear them in person."

78. *Switzerland*, Yearbook Commercial Arbitration, Vol. III, 1978, p. 193; *France*, Yearbook 1981, p. 14; *Germany*, Yearbook 1979, p. 70; *Sweden*, Yearbook 1978, p. 170; *Austria*, Yearbook 1979, p. 32.

issues have been involved and qualified experts on these issues were well known to the arbitrators, tribunals have appointed their own experts.

DR. SZURSKI

The arbitral tribunal will generally be inclined to appoint an expert whom both parties will recognize as impartial and properly qualified to evaluate the technical questions of the dispute. It is only in case of lack of agreement between the parties in this respect that the arbitral tribunal will not hesitate to appoint an expert based exclusively on the tribunal's own choice.

Also while preparing the questions to be answered by the expert, the arbitral tribunal will normally take into consideration the suggestions made by the parties. It may even be expected that any suggestion of a party in this respect will be taken into consideration by the arbitral tribunal, unless the tribunal finds the suggestion completely irrelevant.

Note

For a discussion of the recent practice of the Iran–United States Claims Tribunal concerning its appointments of experts, *see*, M. Straus, cited in *Note* following Question 32 *supra*.

QUESTION 39

If the arbitral tribunal were to appoint its own experts, would it request the parties to submit suggestions for the experts' terms of reference? Would the arbitral tribunal submit its proposed terms of reference to the parties for comment before giving them to the experts? Would it solicit comments on the names of experts before appointing them?

ANSWERS TO QUESTION 39

MR. HOELLERING

As noted above, if the arbitrators consider it necessary to appoint an expert, it is customary for them to seek the agreement of the parties with regard to the precise functions of such experts. Under the UNCITRAL Rules, the costs of such experts are allocable in the award, and thus will be borne by the parties.[79] Whether the tribunal would first request the parties to submit suggestions, or would take the initiative to propose its own terms of reference will depend on the preference of the tribunal in the context of the arbitral proceedings. In either case, the tribunal will consult the parties regarding the scope of the role and testimony to be provided by the neutral expert.

79. *See* Art. 38(c).

MR. HUNTER
The way in which a particular tribunal would proceed would vary according to the circumstances. However, under Article 27(1) of the UNCITRAL Rules, the tribunal must determine the "specific issues" on which the expert is to submit his report.

In practice, the present Rapporteur considers that the tribunal would first ask the parties to submit suggestions for the terms of reference of the expert; then draw up terms of reference in draft form, taking into account its own requirements as well as the views of the parties; and then submit those terms of reference to the parties in draft form for their comments.

There is no general practice as to the method of selection of an expert. The present Rapporteur doubts that many English arbitrators would consult the parties *before* making the appointment. However, they would certainly listen carefully to any objection that might be made subsequently.

MR. JARVIN
Answer to the first two questions: Yes.
Answer to the third: Probably yes, but no practice can be established.

PROF. LEBEDEV
It is quite possible that, taking into account the complexity of technical questions, the arbitral tribunal would first ask the parties to give their views concerning the terms of reference for the expert and, very likely, offer them an opportunity to prepare the draft of such terms themselves.

Likewise, the arbitral tribunal most probably will ask the parties to give their opinion in regard of its own draft of the terms of reference, prepared on the basis of the parties' suggestions, including the joint ones (since in the end an expert should present a report on specific issues "to be determined by the tribunal" – Art. 27(1) of the UNCITRAL Rules). Such procedure has undoubted advantages. Certainly, the time factor should be taken into regard when following it; however, this factor may not be of practical importance if the question of terms of reference can be settled – subject to sufficient preliminary preparations – in the course of pre-hearing conference (Sect. E) or in the course of the first hearing of the case.

The tribunal may wish to discuss the names of experts with the parties. It would hardly appoint an expert to whom both parties objected.

M. Order of Proceedings at the Hearing

HYPOTHETICAL CASE

The lawyers of Steelco and Hightech both expected that hearings would be held at which each side would present (i) oral testimony of witnesses and other evidence, and (ii) oral arguments on factual and legal issues. While the Rules provide for hearings for "presentation of evidence by witnesses, including expert witnesses, or for oral argument," they do not specify how, or in what sequence, the parties should present their cases at the hearings. (Art. 15(2)) The two

the parties should present their cases at the hearings. (Art. 15(2)) The two lawyers knew that customary practice relating to the pattern of hearings varies in different legal systems. For example, they knew that in some legal systems it is usual for each side to present an opening oral statement, describing the claim or defense, outlining the facts and how it intends to prove them, and giving a brief view of its legal arguments, whereas in other systems it is customary for each side to present evidence of witnesses, and for the lawyers to present oral arguments only after the witnesses of both sides have been heard; elsewhere the claimant presents its evidence and oral argument, and then the defendant does likewise. In some systems, closing statements, in which each party summarizes its case, are customary; elsewhere that is uncommon. In some systems, the practice is for there to be three rounds in the hearing, with claimant usually speaking last: i.e., presentation of the claimant's case, followed by presentation of the respondent's case, followed by claimant's reply (with rejoinder for the respondent permitted only as to new material introduced by claimant in its reply). In other systems four rounds are typical, with the respondent always giving its rejoinder to claimant's reply, and thus speaking last. Both lawyers wondered which party speaks last. They knew that in customary common law procedures, the claimant speaks last, in recognition of the fact that he has the burden of proof. They were also aware that those who have a civil law background, however, are accustomed to having the respondent speak last, a practice designed to balance the fact that the claimant had the opportunity to speak first. They were confident that both systems could yield just results. They did not dare to take one method or the other for granted, but knew they should find out which procedure the arbitral tribunal intended to use, so that they could properly plan their presentations.

QUESTION 40

What is the customary pattern and sequence of proceedings at arbitral hearings?

ANSWERS TO QUESTION 40

MR. HOELLERING

Each side will first make a brief opening statement. In a complex international case such as the hypothetical dispute, it is customary for the opening statement to be preceded by a pre-hearing brief, which may be summarized orally by counsel before the tribunal. Thus, as claimant, Steelco's statement would be submitted first, and the respondent's (Hightech) statement would follow.

Steelco and Hightech each then presents its direct case through oral testimony of witnesses and by means of documentary and other physical evidence. Opposing counsel has the right to cross-examine, and to object to evidence prior to its submission to the tribunal.[80] Again, the claimant would go first, and the

80. As with a failure to hear material evidence, a failure by the tribunal to permit cross-examination may result in vacatur of the award. *See* Holtzmann, *The Basic Principles of Presenting Evidence*, note 30 *supra*.

respondent would follow. As already noted, strict rules of evidence do not apply in the proceedings, unless othewise agreed by the parties. On occasion, the tribunal will permit redirect and recross; i.e., the recall of a witness for further direct testimony and cross-examination.

The case is concluded with closing statements by each party. These usually are oral, but may be supplemented by post-hearing briefs. The respondent, in this case Hightech, usually gives its closing statement first, followed by the claimant (Steelco), who has the last word due to the fact that the claimant bears the burden of proof.

While the above-outlined procedure represents the normal course of events in arbitral hearings, it should be noted that the arbitral tribunal has broad discretion to vary the order of the proceedings to suit the exigencies of the circumstances.[81]

MR. HUNTER

Court hearings in England follow the classic English adversarial pattern. The plaintiff's counsel "opens" the case on the assumption that the judge (or jury) has no prior knowledge of the case. He explains the facts, reads the documents and presents his analysis of the facts in the context of the relevant legal principles, citing authorities and arguing questions of interpretations of the law as necessary. He will have given the judge and his opponent in advance a list of authorities to which he intends to refer. He then "calls" the plaintiff's witnesses, who are cross-examined and re-examined. The defendant's counsel then presents his client's witnesses and makes his closing statement followed by the plaintiff's counsel's closing statements. The judge may allow replies and rejoinders if new points arise. The justification for the plaintiff having the first and last word is that he has to discharge the burden of proof. The oral hearing, once started, usually proceeds continuously, day by day, until it is concluded. (This stems from the system of jury trial where, once a jury was empanelled, it would be impracticable to allow the jurors to disperse and try to re-assemble them at a later date.)

There is no reason why English arbitration hearings should follow the same pattern. Indeed there is every reason why they should not. First, the arbitrators (assuming that they have done their duty) will have read the written statements submitted prior to the hearing in accordance with Articles 18, 19, 22 and 24 of the UNCITRAL Rules. Secondly, it may often be more efficient to make several small "bites at the apple", disposing of and clarifying various aspects of the case piecemeal, rather than having a single long hearing (which is in any event impracticable in this case of an international arbitration tribunal composed of distinguished and busy arbitrators of different nationalities).

Thus, there is no *customary* pattern. It differs according to the viewpoints of individual arbitrators, always subject to what the parties may agree. If the arbitrator is a retired judge, or senior lawyer whose practice is mainly in the domestic arena, or if the parties are represented by lawyers whose procedural

81. *See generally* Stein and Wotman, *International Commercial Arbitration in the 1980's*, note 5 on page 154 *infra* at 1715.

experience is mainly in the domestic courts, the proceedings at the hearing may tend to follow the general lines of English court procedure.

Many experienced English arbitrators, however, prefer to hear all the evidence from both parties first, leaving the main oral statements (containing arguments of the parties both on the facts and the legal principles) to the end.

The general practice of the present Rapporteur (but this varies from case to case) is to invite the party's representatives each to start with a ten minute address giving a general over-view of their contentions of fact and law and the evidence to be presented in support. Then, all the evidence of both parties is heard; generally the claimant's witnesses first, but sometimes on an "agenda" basis. For example, in the present hypothetical case it might be convenient to hear first all the evidence, from each side, in connection with the issue concerning the validity of the patent and then, later, all the evidence concerning the adequacy of the air-conditioning system. Finally, the parties' oral statements are heard, starting with the claimant and finishing with the respondent, with successive replies and rejoinders being permitted as necessary. This practice is based on the philosophy that it is more useful to hear the arguments *after* all the evidence of fact has been admitted.

MR. JARVIN

After previous exchange of briefs, oral hearings take place for the hearing of witnesses and experts. The hearings end with oral arguments of both sides on factual and legal issues. Often post-hearing briefs are submitted.

Below are three examples taken from ICC awards describing the procedure used in each case:

1. "In its letter of September 23, 1982 . . . B.V. filed its claims and requested the Secretariat of the Court of Arbitration of the International Chamber of Commerce to appoint an arbitrator. In its letter of October 29, 1982 to the Secretariat of the Court of Arbitration . . . S.A. filed a counterclaim against the. . . .

   "The Court of Arbitration nominated . . . as sole arbitrator and decided that the arbitration had to be held in Brussels, Belgium. The arbitrator proceeded with the arbitration in Brussels and according to the Arbitration Rules of the International Chamber of Commerce. He submitted several drafts of the Terms of Reference to the parties for signature. At a meeting between the parties and the arbitrator in Brussels on September 16, 1983 both parties agreed on and signed the Terms of Reference which constitute the basis for the present arbitral proceedings.

   "Both parties have submitted their arguments to the arbitrator in several letters and briefs, copies of which were sent to the other party. A hearing took place in Brussels on March 13, 1984. In its letter of May 25, 1984 the arbitrator requested additional information, which was given by the parties. Moreover, the letter of May 25, 1984 stated that the arbitrator would render an award on the basis of the evidence submitted unless one of the parties requested a new hearing. Neither party asked for a hearing. The arbitrator deems the submitted evidence satisfactory to render an interim award to decide most of the points in dispute between the parties and to nominate a chartered accountant to examine . . .'s books as indicated in the present interim award. When the accountant shall have submitted his report to the arbitrator, the final award shall be rendered."

2. "At a second hearing held in Zurich on January 20, 1984, both parties' counsel had the opportunity to present their case in oral pleadings. At this meeting draft pleading notes, as well as a memorandum, with annexes on quantification of demurrages were handed over by counsel for the claimant to the arbitrator and the respondent's counsel. Both parties then filed a post-hearing memorial. The claimant filed its post-hearing memorial on February 8, 1984; the respondent filed its respective one on February 9, 1984 and on February 10, 1984 filed copies of the authorities on Swiss law referred to in it. In its post-hearing memorial, the claimant amended its claims up to US$341,276.74 by introducing a new method of calculating the demurrages costs."

3. "On July 21, 1981, the Claimant initiated arbitration with the ICC Secretariat claiming damages because of the unilateral termination, by the Respondent, of a contract signed on August 4, 1980. In their response, dated October 20, 1981, the Respondents urged that the claim be denied. On January 13, 1982, the Claimant supplemented its claim in a reply memorandum.

   "The Tribunal was initially composed of the following members: Mrs. . . ., appointed by the Claimant; Dr. . . . appointed by the Respondents; and Mr. . . ., appointed by the two arbitrators chosen by the parties. In the course of the proceeding, Dr. . . . resigned for health reasons and was replaced, at the Respondents' request, by Mr. . . . . This appointment was confirmed by the Court of Arbitration at its session of July 5, 1983. As per the Terms of Reference, the actions of the Tribunal in which the replaced arbitrator had participated were upheld so that the arbitration could proceed.

   "The Terms of Reference were signed by all parties on December 31, 1982, and transmitted to the Court's Secretariat on April 13, 1983. On January 27, 1983, the Respondents submitted a 'Note en Délibéré.' On the grounds that it was filed without having been solicited and after the signing of the Terms of Reference, the Claimant contested its admissibility in a rejoinder memorandum dated March 22, 1983, which it submitted at the start of the hearing in Paris the next day. The Tribunal admitted both the 'Note en Délibéré', and the rejoinder, as part of the case file, reserving the parties' right to submit further briefs.

   "The first hearing was held in Paris on March 23 and 24, 1983, the minutes of which were signed by the members of the arbitral Tribunal and the parties' representatives. These minutes confirmed the arbitral Tribunal's jurisdiction, the authority of the arbitrators to decide as *amiables compositeurs*, and the application of French law. The hearings were completed on December 8 and 9, 1983, during a hearing in Paris.

   "After the first hearing the parties, pursuant to an order of the Tribunal, submitted various briefs: the Respondents on May 31, 1983, and the Claimant on July 13, 1983 (with a supplementary brief dated August 23, 1983). There followed on September 20, 1983, a reply to Claimant's supplementary brief (of August 23, 1983), and on September 29, 1983, a memorandum in which the Claimant again contested the statements of Respondents' counsel at the oral hearing.

   "In conformity with their wishes, the parties were allowed to supplement their oral pleadings of December 8 and 9 with 'Notes en Délibéré' which were submitted by the Claimant on December 30, 1983, and by the Respondents on January 20, 1984. The parties also submitted a statement of their legal expenses incurred in connection with the proceedings.

   "During the proceeding, the Chairman issued three orders on behalf of the Tribunal, with which the parties agreed to comply.

"Deliberations commenced on January 20, 1984. The time for the rendition of the award was extended by the Court of Arbitration at its sessions of February 28 and June 12, 1984. The arbitrators convened on August 30 and 31, 1984, for their final deliberations and to render this award. The arbitrators, having duly considered all facts and contentions presented by the parties at the hearings and in their briefs, declared themselves sufficiently informed to render this award."

PROF. LEBEDEV

From the standpoint of existing practice it may be assumed that the hearings will be opened by brief statements of the parties describing their positions, first on the part of the claimant and then the defendant. In the second stage and in the same sequence, the parties may be invited to state their positions in detail (to present written evidence, testimony of witnesses and of expert-witnesses, legal arguments, etc.) on the principal issues in dispute following a certain order set up by the tribunal, for example: presence and nature of defects in the System; true causes of the defects; state of the air-conditioning equipment; training by the defendant of the claimant's employees in operating this equipment; problems connected with the patents (if they were considered as "arbitrable" – Question 31); damages under the principal claim and the counterclaim, etc. In the third stage (if the parties wish so, the arbitrators may decide to have this stage before the second one) the expert appointed by the arbitrators would be heard and the parties would have the opportunity to examine him (Art. 27(4) of the UNCITRAL Rules). At the end, the parties, first the claimant and after him the defendant, would have the opportunity to make their closing statements and, thereafter, the arbitral tribunal in accordance with Article 29(1) of the UNCITRAL Rules "may declare the hearings closed".

DR. SZURSKI

The sequence of the proceedings at arbitral hearings conducted by a Polish arbitrator will be most probably modelled on the one practised in the Court of Arbitration at the Polish Chamber of Foreign Trade.

The hearings will be started by checking the powers of attorney of the legal representatives of the parties and afterwards by a question of the presiding arbitrator as to whether the parties have any procedural motions which it is important to decide upon beforehand (e.g., motions re: the challenge of an arbitrator, the modification of the claim, the withdrawal of the claim or a part of it, etc.).

Since it is not customary to prepare terms of reference, the next step in the proceedings will comprise a short introduction by the presiding arbitrator on the facts and character of the dispute and quite probably on questions or issues to be clarified during the hearing. After the introduction, the representatives of the parties will be given a possibility to make remarks, clarifications or additions as regards the state of the case as reported by the presiding arbitrator. Afterwards the members of the arbitral tribunal, i.e., first, the presiding arbitrators appointed by the parties will put questions to the representatives of the parties to clarify any doubts or uncertainty they may have with regard to the statements and facts submitted by the parties in the exchange of documents and writings.

This stage being over, the arbitral tribunal will request the representatives of the parties to present briefly their positions in respect to particular points of the dispute – first the claimant, then the defendant.

In the next stage there will be the hearing of evidence presented by each party in an order established by the arbitral tribunal (e.g., as in the example, given in the Report of Prof. Lebedev). The expert will be heard after hearing the witnesses. At the end, explanations of parties may take place.

Closing oral statements by representatives of the parties with the presentation of legal arguments will take place in the same order as previous statements: first the claimant, then the defendant. It is not excluded that the representatives of the parties will submit to the arbitral tribunal written summaries or even the whole texts of their oral closing statements with the legal argumentation.

QUESTION 41

Is it customary to hold hearings on successive days until all parties have completed the presentation of their cases? If not, are there any customary points at which adjournments are taken?

ANSWERS TO QUESTION 41

MR. HOELLERING

It is quite customary and preferable in international cases to hold hearings on consecutive days, if at all possible. Such a schedule usually makes it easier for the arbitral tribunal, the parties and the witnesses to schedule their time in advance, and may reduce costs in terms of travel, etc.[82]

Where successive days for the arbitration hearings are not possible, the tribunal may either allocate a sequence of dates for particular phases of the arbitration during the pre-hearing conference, or adjourn the hearings after completion of testimony of a witness or series of witnesses.

MR. HUNTER

In general, see the answer to Question 40. Most English arbitrators would try to complete the hearing of the substantive issues in one continuous session, day after day. There are no particular points at which adjournments are customarily taken (although at the close of the evidence, the parties' lawyers might ask for a brief pause to enable them to prepare the presentation of their closing submissions).

However, the present Rapporteur considers that, in a long and complex case, it may well be more practical, and more efficient, to take several "bites at the apple". This results in the tribunal being able to start its examination of the substance of the case earlier (because it will be easier to find mutually convenient dates for, say, a three or four day hearing than one which is expected to last several weeks). It also means that substantive issues may be taken on an

82. The AAA's Supplementary Procedures for International Arbitration specifically provide in Rule 5 that "the AAA will attempt to schedule consecutive hearings to reduce the need for unnecessary travel. . . .' Most parties prefer consecutive days of hearings. *See* Coulson, *Survey*, note 3 *supra*.

"agenda" basis as described under Question 40, and a determination of some issues may make others irrelevant. Sometimes this can be done, with care not to prejudice the appearance of impartiality, by the tribunal giving the parties an indication that they have reached provisional conclusions on certain issues ("Showing his hand" – see Mustill and Boyd, The Law and Practice of Commercial Arbitration in England, London 1982, at page 219).

In general, the present Rapporteur considers that the overall hearing time is likely to be less if arbitration hearings are conducted in this way, and (because the hearings will start much sooner) there is no reason to think that the total timespan of the arbitration, from commencement until the final award, will be greater.

MR. JARVIN

Yes. Where it is not possible to have hearings on successive days until all parties have completed their presentations, as is sometimes the case in complex international cases, adjournments are taken at times scheduled in advance, usually in relation to a particular claim or issue.

In large construction disputes (30% of all ICC cases in 1984 were construction disputes), where the number of claims and counterclaims is often considerable, it is rather the rule to schedule hearings on a number of different dates with shorter or longer intervals between each hearing. This makes it easier to plan the intervention of different witnesses. Also the arbitrators prefer then to decide the case by making separate, partial awards disposing of various claims and counterclaims that can be decided separately without influencing the hearing of other claims and counterclaims. (It is questionable whether this salami-method is the most efficient one when looking at the overall time spent on the case before reaching a final award, but this is another matter that should not be discussed under this question.)

PROF. LEBEDEV

Usually the hearings are held on successive working days (sometimes on Saturdays and even on Sundays) without adjournment unless there are good reasons for it.

PROF. MICHIDA

Although they are both English-speaking common law countries (as distinguished from the civil law countries), Great Britain and the United States, it is reported, express opposite preferences.

Japanese practice is generally in line with the British preference, taking several "bites at the apple" and enabling an earlier start of the hearing. This is not always the case, however. For example, in a maritime case, a ship's officers may be on board and unable to attend several hearings. Japanese practice accommodates such special requirements of the parties which will vary with the circumstances of each case.

DR. SZURSKI
As regards the question of adjournments of the hearing, the position of a Polish arbitrator will be most probably similar to that presented in the Report of Mr. Hunter.

N. Presentation of Oral Evidence

HYPOTHETICAL CASE

The Rules provide that the arbitral tribunal is free to determine the manner in which witnesses are examined. (Art. 25(4)) The Steelco and Hightech lawyers had a number of questions concerning Neutralian practice with respect to witnesses.

QUESTION 42

Is it customary for witnesses to make an oath or affirmation that they will speak the truth? If so, are there any customary formalities?

ANSWERS TO QUESTION 42

MR. HOELLERING
It is customary for the tribunal to require witnesses to testify under oath or affirmation. The oath is usually administered by the stenographic reporter, who is always a notary public, or by the presiding arbitrator.[83]

MR. HUNTER
a. It depends on the wishes of the parties, or of the tribunal. In ordinary commercial arbitration, there is a tendency not to have the witnesses give sworn oral testimony unless credibility is specifically in issue. However, if one party asks that a particular witness should give his testimony on oath, the tribunal will usually agree. If one witness is to be put on oath, then usually they are all sworn.

b. An arbitrator is expressly empowered to administer an oath (Arbitration Act 1950, s. 12(3)). If the witnesses are to be sworn, it should be done in a proper form, which is governed by the Oaths Act 1978 and is as follows:

1. For a Christian, to hold the New Testament in his uplifted hand and to say "I swear by Almighty God that the evidence I shall give shall be the truth, the whole truth, and nothing but the truth".

83. Many arbitration statutes grant the arbitrators express authority to administer oaths. *See, for example*, N.Y. Civ. Prac. Law sect. 7505; Uniform Arbitration Act sect. 7(a). *See also* AAA Commercial Arbitration Rules sect. 27. The AAA's *Guide for Commercial Arbitrators* suggests the following language: "Do you solemnly swear that the evidence you are about to give in this arbitration will be the truth, the whole truth, and nothing but the truth?"

2. For a Jew, the same words, but holding the Old Testament.
3. For persons of other religions, the oath may be administered in such form and with such ceremony as he declares to be binding on his conscience.
4. For persons of no religion, or any person who objects to being sworn, a solemn "affirmation" may be made. This is done by saying the following:

> "I do solemnly, sincerely and truly declare and affirm that the evidence that I shall give shall be the truth, the whole truth, and nothing but the truth".

In any of these cases the words may be either repeated after the arbitrator, or read from a card. A witness who gives untrue evidence having been sworn in proper form commits the criminal offence of "perjury" and may be prosecuted.

Oaths may also be administered to interpreters in the same manner, using the following words:

"... that I will and faithfully interpret and true explanation give of all such matters and things as shall be required of me according to the best of my skill and understanding".

MR. JARVIN

Witnesses do not swear, but may be reminded by the arbitrators of their duty to speak the truth.

In some civil law systems a court of law can be asked to administer a witness hearing under oath. However, arbitrators are not empowered to hear witnesses on oath and the question of perjury could not normally arise.

PROF. LEBEDEV

The existing practice in the country of arbitration does not require a witness to make an oath, affirmation, etc., before the arbitrators, since in the absence of any express legal sanctions for the breach of it, the obligation of a witness to tell the truth in the arbitration proceedings is considered mainly as a moral obligation.

PROF. EL-HAKIM

There is no provision in Arab Codes forbidding arbitrators to receive oaths. The Jordanian law on arbitration explicitly requires the oath (Art. 9(3)); the Lebanese Code of Procedure excludes it (Art. 779(2)). It is only when a witness fails to appear or refuses to answer that the arbitral tribunal must refer to the President of the court which had jurisdiction originally over the dispute to condemn him to the respective fine (Art. 779(1), Lebanese Code of Procedure; Art. 506, Egyptian Code; Art. 526, Syrian Code; Art. 9(1), Jordanian law on arbitration).

PROF. MICHIDA

Japanese practice and law are already described in the comment on *Question 37*.

DR. SZURSKI

To supplement the statement made by Prof. Lebedev, which applies also to arbitrations in Poland, it should be added that, nevertheless, an affirmation that a witness will speak the truth, done according to the formula provided for in the Code of Civil Procedure, is sometimes practised in international commercial arbitrations in Poland in order to underline the value of the testimony of the witness.

It happens particularly in complex cases where the testimony of a witness is of particular importance for the decision of arbitrators.

The arbitral tribunal will also be inclined to require the affirmation in cases when such affirmation is requested by one or both parties.

In any case, the arbitral tribunal will always inform the witnesses of his obligation to tell the truth or even warn him of the possible responsibility for false testimony.

QUESTION 43*

Is it customary for the arbitral tribunal to call a witness it desires to hear, if the parties do not do so?

ANSWERS TO QUESTION 43

MR. HOELLERING

Occasionally, the arbitral tribunal may call a witness whom the parties did not present, although this practice is not followed frequently. The tribunal would do so only where it deems the testimony of such witnesses significant and necessary to the determination of an issue in dispute. While the UNCITRAL Rules contain no specific provision on this point, the AAA Rules are somewhat more explicit, providing that parties may offer such testimony as they desire and shall produce such additional evidence as the arbitrators deem necessary to an understanding and determination of the dispute.[84]

MR. HUNTER

More usually, the tribunal will indicate to a party that it wishes to hear evidence on a particular point or issue. It will then be for that party to arrange for a witness to be present, or to make an application to the court for an order that a witness should give evidence in accordance with the Arbitration Act 1950, Section 12(6)(d). (This can only be effective if the witness is in England.) Exceptionally, the tribunal may wish to hear the evidence of a particular individual, in order to assist its determination of an issue of fact. It would be possible for the tribunal to make an application to the court under Section 12(6)(d). However, this is rarely done (it has not occurred in any case in which the present Rapporteur has been involved).

In general the tribunal will normally leave it for the parties to decide how to discharge their respective burdens of proof in relation to disputed issues of fact. If a party fails to present adequate testimony, the tribunal will normally simply

* This question is not intended to refer to experts, a matter covered by Question 38.

84. AAA Commercial Arbitration Rules, sect. 31.

make a finding against that party on the particular issue, rather than itself take the initiative to assist the party concerned in discharging the burden of proof.

The tribunal may often require the *parties* to appear before it for the purpose of giving oral testimony. Apart from the relevant provisions of the UNCITRAL Rules, the Arbitration Act 1950 Section 12(1) provides as follows:

> "Unless a contrary intention is expressed therein, every arbitration agreement shall, where such a provision is applicable to the reference, be deemed to contain a provision that the parties to the reference, and all persons claiming through them respectively, shall, subject to any legal objection, submit to be examined by the arbitrator or umpire, on oath or affirmation, in relation to the matters in dispute, and shall, subject as aforesaid, produce before the arbitrator or umpire all documents within their possession or power respectively which may be required or called for, and do all other things which during the proceedings on the reference the arbitrator or umpire may require."

The tribunal has no direct power to compel the attendance of witnesses other than the parties. It may, however, make an application to the court under the Arbitration Act 1950 Section 12(6)(d).

MR. JARVIN

This is a most unusual situation. There is no practice to refer to.

PROF. LEBEDEV

The right of the arbitrators at their own initiative to raise a question of calling a witness named by one of the parties (who presented, for example, only written testimony – see Question 36) or not mentioned by any party, is, in our opinion, undoubted as from the standpoint of practice existing in the country of arbitration as well as from the point of view of the UNCITRAL Rules (Art. 24(3)).

It has to be borne in mind, however, that a call of a witness, as a general rule (see Question 26), cannot be enforced.

PROF. EL-HAKIM

Certainly not. It is up to the parties to submit their evidence. The arbitral tribunal can only call a witness (and must do so) if this is requested by either party and if such evidence is acceptable under the law applicable to the case.

QUESTION 44**

Is it customary for the arbitral tribunal to refuse to hear any witness? If so, for what reasons?

ANSWERS TO QUESTION 44

** This question is not intended to refer to testimony by parties, a matter covered by Questions 32 and 33.

MR. HOELLERING

It is rare for the arbitral tribunal to refuse to hear a witness. If, however, it is satisfied, on the basis of the record of the proceeding, that the testimony of the witness would not add anything to its understanding of the case, or would unnecessarily prolong the hearing, the tribunal may refuse to hear it.

Arbitrators will consider carefully the relevance and materiality of the evidence to the party's case before refusing to hear testimony. This is because a failure to hear such evidence is ground for vacatur of the resulting award.[85]

MR. HUNTER

It is rare for a tribunal to refuse to hear a witness presented by a party. It could do so, on the grounds that the evidence that the witness will give is irrelevant, or that the arbitrators do not consider that the particular individual can give any convincing evidence on the point at issue. However, a tribunal is usually conscious of the requirement that a party must be given a full and proper opportunity to present its case. The refusal to hear a witness presented by a party involves the risk of the award being set aside on a subsequent application to the court under the Arbitration Act 1950, Section 23.

More realistically, the point usually arises where a party wishes to call a large number of expert witnesses on one particular issue. In such a case, the tribunal may indicate to the parties that it wishes to limit the number of expert witnesses to be called to a specific number on each side.

MR. JARVIN

When the arbitrator thinks that nothing essential for the outcome of the case could be proven by hearing the witness, he would refuse to hear him. But this Rapporteur cannot state that it would be customary to do so in ICC cases under civil law rules; there are no indications available to support the thesis that it would be customary, nor not customary for that matter.

PROF. LEBEDEV

In practice, the arbitral tribunal most probably will not refuse to hear a witness, suggested by any party, except for some absolutely clear reasons. For example, it may be supposed that the subject upon which a witness will give his testimony and which should be communicated according to Article 25(2) of the UNCITRAL Rules by the party intending to call a witness, may be considered by the arbitrators as irrelevant and immaterial for the case (Art. 25(6)), and the eventual delay caused by calling such a witness as unjustified.

PROF. EL-HAKIM

The arbitral tribunal can only refuse to hear a witness if, under the law applicable to the case, testimonial evidence is excluded, if a specific witness cannot be heard or if the fact to be proved by witnesses is not relevant.

85. 9 U.S.C. sect. 12.

QUESTION 45

Should questions be put to a witness mainly by the lawyer who presents the witness, or by the arbitrators?

ANSWERS TO QUESTION 45

MR. HOELLERING

The lawyer responsible for preparation and presentation of his client's case mainly will question any witness he presents. The tendency and preference is for parties to "bring the case to the arbitrator," presenting such evidence and arguments as they deem pertinent. If the arbitral tribunal feels that important questions need to be answered, however, they may put such questions to a witness, since, from the outset, they have been provided with information about each party's case. It is thus to be expected that the tribunal, as it considers appropriate, will actively participate in the proceedings.

MR. HUNTER

Questions are put mainly by the lawyers representing the parties. However, any member of the tribunal may ask questions at any stage of the examination of a witness. It is normal for arbitrators who have made lists of specific questions they wish to put to a witness to wait until the end of the examination by the parties. It is not infrequent for an arbitrator to interrupt the examination of a witness by one of the parties' lawyers in order to seek clarification or amplification of what the witness is saying.

MR. JARVIN

Both methods are practised, and more often, it seems, a combination of the two where the lawyer calling the witness starts the examination and the arbitrator fills in with questions that he did not find were already answered.

PROF. LEBEDEV

In the light of the practice existing in the country of arbitration, the presiding arbitrator is most likely to be inclined to invite the witness to tell those facts which are known to him in regard of the subject, as communicated by the party, upon which he is to give his testimony (Art. 25(2) of the UNCITRAL Rules). After that, questions may be asked by the lawyer, who called the witness, as well as by the arbitrators.

PROF. EL-HAKIM

The questions will be put by the arbitrators either on their own initiative or at the request of a party or its lawyer.

DR. SZURSKI

In contradiction to the practice of arbitral tribunals in the US as reported by Mr. Hoellering, a Polish presiding arbitrator will first request a witness to tell the facts known to him as regards the case for which the witness has been called and, thereafter, the presiding arbitrator and other arbitrators will ask supplementary questions, so as to clarify all doubts and points arbitrators find important. Afterwards, the parties will be given the possibility to ask further questions – if any – first, the party who called the witness, then the other party. The arbitrators will be allowed to put complementary questions at all times. In other words, the initiative for the clarification of all doubts and points important to the proper understanding of the case lies in the hands of the arbitral tribunal and not with the parties' lawyers as in the US or England.

QUESTION 46

If questions are put mainly by lawyers, to what extent do the arbitrators also ask questions?

ANSWERS TO QUESTION 46

MR. HOELLERING

Most experienced arbitrators will permit the parties to develop the facts in their own way. They, therefore, will ask questions or call for the production of additional evidence only where required to clarify a point or to gain evidence in an area not addressed by the parties.

There are those who suggest that arbitrators should decide cases only on the basis of evidence presented by the parties. Such suggestions are largely offered by litigators accustomed to the procedures of the courtroom. The prevalent view and prevailing practice, however, is for tribunals to take a more active role in management of the case, by asking questions whenever there is a need to clarify testimony, or for further information. This facilitates the fact-finding process and expedition of the hearings.

MR. HUNTER

This depends on the habits of individual arbitrators. Some prefer to remain silent. The main reasons for this course are (a) to avoid prolonging the hearing unnecessarily and (b) to avoid any risk of being accused subsequently of misconducting the proceedings by showing some form of bias (silence is safety in this respect).

However, probably the majority of English arbitrators are unable to resist the temptation of joining in the examination of a witness, by at least asking a few questions. Where the parties are not represented by skilled lawyers, it may actually be necessary for the arbitrator to intervene in order to ensure that the witness has covered all the relevant points on which he is able to give evidence on the points in issue.

However, where the parties are well represented, it would be rare for such intervention by the arbitrator to be necessary. His questions would normally be for the purpose of clarifying in his own mind precisely what a witness is intending to convey.

MR. JARVIN
See my answer to Question 45.

PROF. LEBEDEV
In addition to what has been said in connection with Question 45, it should be emphasized that according to the usual practice the arbitrators are free to ask a witness any questions at their discretion.

QUESTION 47

When party-appointed arbitrators have questions for a witness, do they usually request the Chairman to put the questions, or do they address the witness directly?

ANSWERS TO QUESTION 47

MR. HOELLERING
The arbitrators serving on the tribunal usually have equal authority. Customarily, party-appointees tend to address questions to a witness directly, rather than requesting the Chairman to put the questions to the witness.

MR. HUNTER
Party-appointed arbitrators would normally address questions to witnesses directly. As a matter of courtesy, they would normally ask the permission of the Chairman to intervene at a particular point in the examination, if the arbitrator does not wish to reserve his questions for the point at which the Chairman will specifically invite his colleagues to address questions to the witness.

MR. JARVIN
They address the witness directly. However, out of courtesy they would probably have agreed in advance with the Chairman that this is an appropriate way of proceeding.

PROF. LEBEDEV
The most typical procedure would be when the arbitrator, having asked the permission of the Chairman, puts his questions directly to the witness.

QUESTION 48

After the lawyer who presents a witness completes his questions, would the opposing lawyer have an opportunity to put questions to the witness (i.e., "cross-examination")? Should the opposing lawyer address the witness directly? Or should he request the Chairman to put his questions?

ANSWERS TO QUESTION 48

MR. HOELLERING

It is traditional for the opposing lawyer to have an opportunity to cross-examine a witness presented by his adversary. Every witness who presents oral testimony at the hearings is subject to cross-examination.

The objectives of cross-examination are clarifications of facts raised on direct examination; correction of misstatements; placement of facts in true perspective; reconciliation of apparent contradictions; and testing of the reliability and credibility of the witness. In order to accomplish these objectives, the lawyer will address the witness directly during cross-examination.

MR. HUNTER

Yes. The order of examination would normally be as follows:

a. "examination-in-chief" by the lawyer representing the party calling the witness;
b. "cross-examination" by the opposing party's lawyer;
c. "re-examination" limited to points raised in the cross-examination, thus excluding the giving of fresh evidence at this stage, by the lawyer representing the party calling the witness.

The questions would be put directly to the witness by the lawyers. Any requirement that questions should be addressed to the witness through the Chairman would be regarded as an unsatisfactory method of testing the evidence being given.

MR. JARVIN

There are great differences in civil law systems in respect to cross-examination. No general answer on the practice can, therefore, be offered. Whereas cross-examination is unknown in German and Austrian arbitration practice, and it can take place in France only if both parties agree to it, it may be ordered by the arbitrators in Switzerland also in the case where parties do not agree. In Sweden it is common practice for cross-examination to be held and the Swedish procedure is in this respect closer to common law procedure than other civil law procedures.[86]

PROF. LEBEDEV

Although "cross-examination" as such is not used in the country of arbitration, the lawyer of the opposing party certainly has the right to put his questions to the witness. It is unlikely that the presiding arbitrator would object to questioning of the witness directly by the lawyer with consent and under the control of the arbitral tribunal.

---

86. *Germany*, Yearbook Commercial Arbitration, Vol. IV, 1978, p. 70; *Austria*, Yearbook 1979, p. 32; *France*, Yearbook 1981, p. 14; *Switzerland*, Yearbook 1978, p. 193; *Sweden*, Yearbook 1978. p. 169: "Witnesses will nowadays normally be examined by the parties or their representatives in the manner used in the common law jurisdictions, i.e., by examination-in-chief, cross-examination and re-examination."

PROF. EL-HAKIM
The opposing lawyer must certainly be entitled to put questions to the witness, as long as they are relevant, to safeguard equality between the parties (*principe du contradictoire*). But he can only put questions through the Chairman.

QUESTION 49

When a lawyer puts questions to a witness, is it considered improper to phrase the questions in a way that suggests the answer to be given (i.e., "leading" questions)? Is there a distinction in this connection between questioning a witness the lawyer presented and cross-examining a witness presented by the other side?

ANSWERS TO QUESTION 49

MR. HOELLERING
Because formal rules of evidence do not strictly apply in arbitration, leading questions may be permitted upon the direct examination of a witness. It is recognized, however, that testimony is more effective when the witness relates facts from knowledge. Questions from counsel may be useful in emphasizing the points being made, or in keeping witnesses "on the track." If too many leading questions are asked of the witness, opposing counsel is likely to object. The tribunal may then suggest that counsel permit the witness to testify from his own knowledge.

The situation is somewhat different with regard to cross-examination. As stated above, one of its purposes is to test the reliability and credibility of the witness. Given this objective, the arbitral tribunal is likely to accord counsel greater latitude during cross-examination and freely permit the use of leading questions. Because the tribunal ultimately determines the weight to be accorded any testimony, leading questions are not likely to cause a problem.

MR. HUNTER
This refers to what is known as "leading questions". The general rule in English court proceedings is that a lawyer calling a witness must not "lead" that witness into giving his testimony in a particular way by addressing questions in a form which suggests the answer to be given. In court proceedings, if a lawyer asks questions in this way in examination-in-chief, the opposing party's lawyer would raise an objection.

In arbitration proceedings, the strict rules of evidence do not necessarily apply. However, it would generally be regarded as unsatisfactory to "lead" a witness. An arbitrator who permitted a witness to be led in examination-in-chief, notwithstanding an objection by the opposing party's lawyer, and then relied heavily on that evidence when making his award, would risk an attack on the award under the Arbitration Act 1950, Section 23 on the basis that the proceedings had been misconducted.

It is perfectly in order for a lawyer to try to "lead" a witness in cross-examination. Indeed, most of the questions will be put to the witness in a manner in which the cross-examiner is attempting to get the witness to agree with a proposition being put to him. So the answer to the second part of the question is "yes".

MR. JARVIN

It is proper for a lawyer to put leading questions.

PROF. LEBEDEV

The question itself is phrased "in a way that suggests the answer to be given". It is submitted that on the basis of Article 25(4) of the UNCITRAL Rules, the arbitral tribunal most probably will reject obviously "leading" questions of the lawyer, whether put to a witness through the Chairman or directly, although, of course, evaluation of the question very often depends on subjective perceptions.

PROF. EL-HAKIM

Leading questions are excluded in principle, without distinction between the parties.

DR. SZURSKI

The arbitral tribunal under the chairmanship of a Polish arbitrator will most probably not allow leading questions to be put to a witness by any party's lawyer.

QUESTION 50

When a lawyer puts a question to a witness, is it appropriate for opposing counsel to interrupt to object to the question on the ground that it is irrelevant, repetitive, unclear or otherwise improper?

ANSWERS TO QUESTION 50

MR. HOELLERING

Since arbitration is intended to be an informal procedure, it is not appropriate for a party's attorney to frequently interrupt opposing counsel during the questioning of a witness. Too many objections tend to disrupt the hearing and are not favored by the arbitrators.

However, relaxing the application of legal rules of evidence in arbitration does not mean that lawyers are foreclosed from referring to them. For example, pointing out the likelihood that hearsay evidence may be erroneous will warn the tribunal not to place too much reliance on it. Objections may be made by counsel to exclude a particular question, to modify the form or manner of questioning, to change momentum, or to reassure a witness who is testifying on cross-examination. It is up to the tribunal to ensure that objections are kept within reasonable bounds.

MR. HUNTER

A lawyer will be aware that constant interruptions by him when his opponent is examining a witness will irritate the arbitrators, and he will normally try to keep his interruptions to a minimum. He will therefore not usually object to irrelevant or repetitive questions being put. On the other hand, where a lawyer examining a witness seems to be trying to gain an advantage over the witness by asking unclear questions, or if the questions are in some way offensive or otherwise improper, then an objection will be made and a ruling will be asked from the tribunal.

MR. JARVIN

Yes. But if a lawyer interrupts the witness too much and disturbs the course of the witness examination he risks irritating the arbitrators. It is up to the arbitrator to decide whether he accepts interruptions or not.

PROF. LEBEDEV

Except for some extraordinary situations, the presiding arbitrator, based on the usual practice in the country of arbitration, will most probably assume that the general rule about the determination of relevance, materiality, etc. of the evidence by the arbitral tribunal itself (Art. 25(6) of the UNCITRAL Rules), is applicable also to the testimony of a witness, including the stage of examination of a witness (Art. 25(4)). There is no "presumption" of acceptance of relevance, etc. by the opposing counsel.

DR. SZURSKI

As a rule, interruptions or raising objections by the opposing counsel to questions put to a witness by a party's lawyer on the ground that they are irrelevant, repetitive, unclear or otherwise improper, will not be treated by the arbitral tribunal as appropriate. The presiding arbitrator, himself, will normally decide on the admissibility or relevance of questions put to a witness by a lawyer and will restrict or cut off a testimony which he considers irrelevant, repetitive or otherwise improper.

QUESTION 51

Is it customary for the arbitrators to interrupt when questions are asked that they consider irrelevant, repetitive, unclear or otherwise inappropriate?

ANSWERS TO QUESTION 51

MR. HOELLERING

It is not customary for arbitrators to interrupt such questions. As previously noted, such objections generally are made by opposing counsel. The arbitral tribunal will strive to conduct the hearing in a way calculated to bring about an expeditious, economical, and just determination of the dispute, however. To this end, the panel may well caution the parties against inappropriate, repetitive and cumulative testimony, and may restrict or cut off such testimony when persistently offered.

MR. HUNTER

By contrast with the answer to Question 50, English arbitrators will sometimes interrupt if they consider the questions put to a witness are irrelevant, repetitive, unclear or otherwise inappropriate. The purpose of this is to avoid unnecessarily prolonging the hearing, and also to avoid the issues being confused by the introduction of irrelevant material.

However, interruptions of this kind are normally made rather delicately. It would be unusual for an arbitrator to assert dogmatically that a line of questioning was irrelevant and to refuse to permit the examining lawyer to proceed. This would carry a risk of an attack under the Arbitration Act 1950, Section 23 at a subsequent stage, on the grounds that the proceedings had been misconducted by the refusal of the arbitrator to allow the party a full and proper opportunity to present his case. Normally, therefore, an arbitrator will interrupt gently and ask the examining lawyer to explain why the particular line of questioning is relevant. The examining lawyer will normally take the hint and, realizing that he is irritating the tribunal, abandon the particular line of questions.

MR. JARVIN

Civil law trained arbitrators are used to taking an active role in the proceedings and would not hesitate to interrupt irrelevant and other questions as indicated. The arbitrator has a responsibility to manage the arbitration in the most efficient manner avoiding unnecessary prolongation of hearings and that the issues are confused by inappropriate questions.

PROF. LEBEDEV

The answer as given in connection with Question 50 suggests, in our opinion, a positive answer to Question 51.

PROF. MICHIDA

It is reported that in civil law countries and the Soviet Union, arbitrators would not hesitate to interrupt. On the other hand, in the United States, it is reported, arbitrators do not customarily interrupt such questioning.

Japanese practice parallels the practice in the United States. Arbitrators may sometimes request witnesses to testify succinctly, but they do not interrupt testimony. This is in line with the amicable texture of the Japanese arbitration process.

HYPOTHETICAL CASE *N*. cont.

The Rules permit, but do not require, the arbitral tribunal to exclude witnesses from the hearing when they are not giving testimony. (Art. 15(1), Art. 25(4))

QUESTION 52

Is it customary for the arbitral tribunal to permit a witness to be present in the hearing room only when he is giving testimony?

ANSWERS TO QUESTION 52

MR. HOELLERING

Ordinarily, all parties and their witnesses attend the oral hearings. The tribunal has the power to require the exclusion of any witness, other than a party or other essential person, during the testimony of any other witness. Exclusion of a witness occurs mostly if the opposing party so requests, or if the arbitral tribunal deems it appropriate in certain situations, in order to safeguard the credibility of the testimony to be offered. It is not the general practice for the tribunal, on its own initiative, to permit witnesses to be present only when giving testimony, however.

MR. HUNTER

There is no specific rule, and the practice of arbitrators varies. In general, the main guideline is that witnesses are only excluded when there is a good reason to do so. This is probably based on a general notion of courtesy, in that usually a witness (not being a party, who would be entitled to be present throughout the hearing) has come voluntarily to assist the parties and the tribunal in its task, and that it would be discourteous to make them wait outside for long periods until their turn came to give evidence. However, in some cases either the parties, or one of them, or the tribunal itself, might consider that a particular witness should not have the opportunity to listen to the evidence of other witnesses before he gives his own evidence, in case this may affect the way in which he gives his own evidence.

Normally, there is no obligation to a witness being present after he has completed his testimony.

MR. JARVIN

The answer is uncertain as no practice can be established. The answer, however, is probably yes.

PROF. LEBEDEV

According to the usual practice, it is considered improper for a witness who has not given his testimony to be present at the hearing of the case on the merits.

PROF. EL-HAKIM

A witness cannot be present in the hearing room before he is heard because he may be influenced by what he hears there. After the hearing, he may be present only if he has to confront other witnesses. Otherwise, the secrecy of arbitration does not authorize the presence of witnesses in the hearings.

PROF. MICHIDA

The answers from the civil law countries and the Soviet Union tend to affirm the presence of a witness only during his testimony, and the reports from Great Britain and the United States generally disclose more permissive practices.

In Japan, since the order of hearings, and their dates and time, are set by the tribunal (there are Rules governing these matters), a witness will be in the hearing room only during his testimony. However, if it is difficult to fix the exact time for the testimony of a non-party witness in certain cases, e.g., a maritime case, it is deemed inappropriate to make him wait for a long time outside the hearing room. Even in such cases, consideration will be given to Article 25(4) of the UNCITRAL Rules, which provides that an arbitral tribunal "may require the retirement of any witness."

DR. SZURSKI

Unlike the practice in the US as reported by Mr. Hoellering and similar to the practice in the USSR, the Polish presiding arbitrator will normally not permit a witness who has not given his testimony to be present at the hearing on the merits.

After having completed his testimony the witness will be normally allowed to remain in the hearing room if he so wishes. Sometimes the arbitral tribunal itself may ask the witness to remain in the hearing room for the purpose of confrontation with other witnesses.

Note

For a study of practices in various civil and common law national courts concerning oral evidence, *see* P. R. Meurs-Gerken, "Étude Comparative de la Preuve Orale", Association Internationale des Jeunes Avocats, *International Arbitration Gazette*, No. 8, February 1986, Copenhagen. (Copies of the English and French versions are available from the Department of International Commercial Arbitration of the T.M.C. Asser Institute, The Hague, The Netherlands.) While this study reflects practices in court ligitation, it is of value in understanding approaches that may be taken by arbitrators who are influenced by methods with which they are familiar in their national courts.

O. Presentation of Oral Argument

HYPOTHETICAL CASE

The lawyers for Steelco and Hightech had a number of questions concerning customary practice with respect to presentation at the hearing of their oral arguments on issues of fact and law.

QUESTION 53

In the course of oral argument on the facts, is it permissible to present further documentary evidence other than in rebuttal? (*See also* Question 21.)

ANSWERS TO QUESTION 53

MR. HOELLERING

Although not customary, it is permissible for a party to present further documentary evidence other than in rebuttal during oral argument. While the UNCITRAL Rules encourage the parties to come forward with all documentary evidence at the outset of the proceedings, it would be inappropriate for the tribunal to reject documentary evidence which is material and relevant to the resolution of the dispute, even when introduced during oral argument. In fact, a refusal to accept such additional documentary evidence may provide a basis for vacatur of the award.[87]

MR. HUNTER

As stated previously, "trial by ambush" is to be discouraged in the context of international commercial arbitration. An English arbitrator will not formally admit new documentary evidence during the course of the hearing unless the opposing party had no objection. On the other hand, where fresh evidence which is clearly of great value had come to light at a late stage, whether the party producing it had a reasonable excuse or not, the tribunal would prefer to find a way of receiving that evidence if it is plainly going to be of assistance to it in determining the issues. If the tribunal decided to admit such fresh documentary evidence, then the opposing party would be given a full and proper opportunity to respond to it. If this involved an adjournment of the hearing, or any other form of additional expense, the tribunal would be likely to penalize the party producing the fresh evidence by making an appropriate order as to costs unless the party concerned had a reasonable excuse.

MR. JARVIN

Yes, provided the other party can be given an opportunity to consider such evidence and present his point of view before the end of the arguments.

Presenting fresh evidence at this stage may have cost implications and the arbitrator may decide to penalize the party coming forward with new evidence when deciding on the apportionment of the costs of the arbitration.

PROF. LEBEDEV

As in the light of the customary practice in the country of arbitration, as well as in the light of Article 15(1), providing for the opportunity for each of the parties "at any stage of the proceedings" to present his case, the arbitral tribunal is unlikely to refuse to accept additional evidence presented by the party before the hearings are "closed" (Art. 29).

---

87. 9 U.S.C. sect. 10(c). *See also Cofinco, Inc.* v. *Bakrie & Bros., N.V.*, 395 F.Supp. 613 (S.D.N.Y. 1975).

Such a situation may occur when, for example, the time limit for presenting additional evidence has been agreed upon or set forth (see Question 21) and one of the parties, having had the opportunity to present the evidence within this time limit, did not do so and, on the contrary, presented it at a later date, for example, at the end of the hearings when it becomes necessary to adjourn the hearings, etc. Here, the arbitral tribunal is, evidently, entitled to take into account the unjustified delay and expenses caused by the late presentation in the "apportionment" of the arbitration costs between the parties (Art. 40 of the UNCITRAL Rules).

QUESTION 54

If pre-hearing briefs have been submitted, could the lawyers during their oral arguments on legal issues, other than in rebuttal, cite further laws, court decisions, arbitral awards (such as those reported in the *Yearbook Commercial Arbitration*) and legal literature that were not referred to in the pre-hearing briefs?

ANSWERS TO QUESTION 54

MR. HOELLERING

Even though pre-hearing briefs were submitted, it would be unusual for the arbitral tribunal to preclude counsel from raising additional legal arguments, and to cite further laws, court decisions, arbitral awards and legal literature that were not previously referred to. It is possible that, during the course of the proceedings, a party may be surprised by the testimony of the other side, and need time to research and respond to the material presented. Since one of the mandates of arbitration is to give the parties due process in terms of presenting their case and reaching a just result, a preclusion of such authority would not be favored.

MR. HUNTER

As stated previously, an English arbitrator would not be familiar with the pre-hearing brief system. However, he would think it very odd if the oral argument was limited to matters already submitted or cited in the written statements submitted by the parties. He would expect the lawyers to develop their arguments in detail at the hearing, and to cite specific passages from relevant authoritative sources. In advance of the hearing, the lawyers should give the tribunal, and to each other, a list of the authorities they intend to cite so as to avoid the risk of unnecessary delays being caused by requests for adjournments so that the other party can find books in which the material to be cited appears.

MR. JARVIN

If the oral arguments on legal issues are aimed at explaining more fully what has been stated in pre-hearing briefs, further references to support such statements will be allowed.

If, on the other hand, new elements are introduced by citing further laws, court decisions and awards, the other party must have a chance to consider these and supply new arguments.

It is unlikely that an arbitrator would not permit the presentation of further arguments.

Post-hearing memoranda tend to become more and more frequent (*note de délibéré*).

PROF. LEBEDEV

It seems that the answer to this question should be, in general, the same as the answer to Question 53.

HYPOTHETICAL CASE O. cont.

The lawyer for Steelco was aware that in some legal systems it is the usual practice at the hearing for the lawyers on both sides immediately following their oral arguments to submit to the arbitrators a written summary of those arguments (i.e., *note de plaidoirie*). In other legal systems, however, presentation of such a document for the first time at a hearing would be seen as unusual and, perhaps, improper.

QUESTION 55

Is it customary for the lawyers of each party to submit at the hearing a written summary of their arguments? If so, at what stage of the hearing is this done? What does such a summary customarily include?

ANSWERS TO QUESTION 55

MR. HOELLERING

It is customary for counsel, either prior to or at the beginning of the hearings, to submit a written brief summarizing their arguments. The summary would recite the factual contentions and legal arguments to be proven in the arbitral proceedings.

In this case, Hightech would submit a statement alleging that it met all of its contractual obligations, that the contract was terminated wrongfully, and include an outline of the requisite proof of its case. Steelco, on the other hand, would present facts tending to prove that Hightech's performance was insufficient under the contract, as well as outline its evidence regarding the poor design of the computer and air-conditioning systems.

MR. HUNTER

Yes, this is quite frequently done, either at the suggestion of the lawyers for the parties, or at the request of the tribunal. The summaries would be provided either just before the lawyers make their respective closing submissions or at the end of the oral hearing, but would certainly be done after all the evidence had been concluded. Such a summary would usually be very short, and merely indicate in headline form the propositions of fact that the party relies on following the evidence that had been given, and may ask the tribunal to make specific findings of fact. They would also include a list of the propositions of law relied upon, with references to authorities (limited, of course, to authorities which have already been introduced; it would not be acceptable to produce a list of new authorities at the end of the hearing).

MR. JARVIN
Probably not, but the answer is uncertain.

PROF. LEBEDEV
Although such practice is not customary in the country of arbitration, there are hardly any grounds for the arbitral tribunal to refuse to accept a written document from the lawyer, where the arguments stated in the course of the oral hearings are summarized.

PROF. EL-HAKIM
Yes. Such a summary is usually presented at the hearing or in the following days, as agreed on between the parties or decided by the arbitral tribunal. Such a summary is supposed to sum up the pleadings and relate to both the facts and the arguments. But it should not contain new claims or evidence which was not notified previously to the other party to enable it to discuss it and reply to it.

P. Verbatim Records and Minutes of the Hearing

HYPOTHETICAL CASE

The Rules provide that the arbitral tribunal is free to make arrangements for a "record of the hearing" if it considers that necessary in the circumstances of the case, but it is not required to do so. Nor is there any explanation in the Rules concerning the form of "record" that might be made. (Art. 25(3))

QUESTION 56

Is it customary for the arbitral tribunal to make arrangements for a record of the hearing in a case such as this? If so, are stenographic transcripts used or tape recordings?

ANSWERS TO QUESTION 56

MR. HOELLERING
In arbitration cases such as our hypothetical case, arrangements for a record of the hearing are invariably made, either at the request of the parties or of the arbitral tribunal. Usually, a stenographic record is taken by a certified court

stenographer. Tape recordings are rarely used, because they are not deemed fully reliable and may be subject to damage or abuse.

MR. HUNTER

This is mainly a question of expense relative to the size of the case and the other costs of the arbitration. The cost of a full "daily" transcript of the oral proceedings in England would (in 1985) be approximately £500 per day. ("Daily" means that the parties have the transcript for a particular day in their hands on the evening of the day in question, or at the latest early the following morning.) The cost of a transcript produced subsequent to the hearing is somewhat less, but it is still expensive. In the case of the size of *Steelco* v. *Hightech*, it is probable that the *evidence* would be transcribed, but not the arguments. In cases where there are three-member tribunals, which are clearly going to involve deliberations which may take place sometime after the conclusion of the hearings, arbitrators find it helpful to have an accurate record of the evidence that has been given.

Where a verbatim record is being transcribed, it is not usual to rely solely on tape recordings. Experience shows that these are very difficult to transcribe accurately, and it is often difficult to identify precisely who is speaking at any given time. Normally, a stenographic service is used, but most firms of stenographers now use tape recordings as a "back up" to their own shorthand or mechanically taken notes.

MR. JARVIN

No, in the majority of cases; but probably yes in a case of a certain complexity like this. If a record of the hearing is arranged, it would be done by stenographic transcripts more often than by tape recordings, and would record the evidence but not parties' arguments.

If the arbitrator does not make arrangements on his own initiative for a record of the hearing, a party may ask him to do so and the arbitrator would adhere to such a request.

PROF. LEBEDEV

In the light of customary practice in the country of arbitration, verbatim records (most often by stenography) of the oral hearings in the course of the proceedings of the case are made only when both parties request it (see also Art. 25(3) of the UNCITRAL Rules).

DR. SZURSKI

It is not customary to use stenographic transcripts or tape recordings in arbitrations in Poland. However, on request of the parties, stenographic transcriptions can be arranged.

On the other hand, it is customary to prepare minutes of each hearing session. Minutes are normally made by the recording-secretary of the arbitral tribunal. First of all, statements by the representatives of the parties which are important for the evaluation of the case, as well as for the conduct of the proceedings are recorded in the minutes. The minutes also reflect all decisions of the arbitral tribunal made during the hearing.

Very often the most important statements which are to be recorded in the minutes are dictated by the presiding arbitrator so as to avoid any mistake in the formulation.

When important statements are recorded in the minutes they are read aloud by the recording-secretary of the tribunal for their confirmation by the party who made the statement.

The minutes are normally signed by the recording-secretary and all members of the arbitral tribunal.

In case the minutes reflect a settlement agreement made at the hearing, they are signed also by the representatives of the parties.

HYPOTHETICAL CASE P. cont.

The lawyers for Steelco and Hightech had heard that in some legal systems it is the practice of the Chairman or secretary of the arbitral tribunal to prepare minutes of the hearing, often at the close of each session.

QUESTION 57

Is it customary for the Chairman or secretary to prepare minutes of each session? What is included in the minutes and how detailed are they? Do they summarize evidence and arguments? Are they submitted to the parties for comment? Are they signed? If so, by whom?

ANSWERS TO QUESTION 57

MR. HOELLERING

It is not customary for minutes of each hearing session to be prepared. Where a stenographic record of the proceedings is taken, copies of the record are provided to the tribunal and all parties, and can be delivered within a short time after the hearings, if desired. Such records, except for off-the-record discussions, are verbatim transcripts and contain all evidentiary references and arguments. The parties always have an opportunity to correct any errors in the stenographic record.

In AAA administered cases, a brief record of hearing is completed by the tribunal chairman or tribunal administrator. It includes the case docket number, the identity of the parties, the names of the arbitrators, the time when the hearing commenced, a listing of each documentary exhibit, the name and address of each witness, and a note as to any special stipulations and arrangements, such as filing of briefs or additional evidence. The record of hearing is signed either by the presiding arbitrator or by the AAA administrator. These records do not summarize evidence and arguments and are not submitted to parties for comment. Rather, they constitute a part of the arbitration case file.

A similar record may be kept by the presiding arbitrator in non-AAA cases.

MR. HUNTER

A minute would normally be prepared by the Chairman (or registrar or secretary) recording procedural rulings or decisions of the tribunal, unless they are in any event going to be reproduced in a verbatim transcript. The Chairman will normally be responsible for producing a record of the administrative decisions taken at preliminary meetings. This record might be submitted to the parties in draft form for comment, depending on whether the tribunal considered it necessary. The record would normally be signed by all the arbitrators, although sometimes the parties or the arbitrators themselves might authorize the Chairman to sign them alone. This rather depends on the status and importance of the matters recorded in the minutes.

It would not be normal practice for minutes to be taken of the substantive hearings, summarizing arguments or evidence. If there is no verbatim transcript of the evidence, the arbitrators would be expected to make their own personal notes for use in the deliberations of the tribunal at a later stage.

MR. JARVIN

First question: Yes.

Second question: Not extensive, they would merely record prodecural events and rulings by the arbitrators.

Third question: No, the minutes would not contain arguments or evidence.

Fourth question: No, they are not submitted to the parties for comment.

Fifth question: Yes, they are signed, always by the Chairman, most often also by the co-arbitrators in addition to the Chairman, and sometimes also by the parties.

It is customary in ICC arbitration that the award contains a description of the procedure, indicating when and where hearings were held, who was present, what witnesses were heard, when notifications were posted and received, etc. The minutes from each session are of great help in establishing this history of the proceedings and offer a means of proof of what took place; the minutes sometimes will be indispensable as proof in a setting aside action against the arbitration award.

PROF. LEBEDEV

It may be considered customary practice in the country of arbitration to prepare minutes, where legal and factual arguments of the parties, including testimony of the witnesses, expert-witnesses, experts, appointed by the arbitral tribunal, etc., are briefly noted. As a rule, minutes are prepared by the secretary (see Question 5) and then are checked and signed by all arbitrators. When there is proper request, minutes may be given to the parties, who, of course, may comment on them.

Q. Post-Hearing Briefs

HYPOTHETICAL CASE

The Rules contain no specific provisions concerning submission of briefs by the parties after the hearing. The power of the arbitral tribunal either to allow or exclude post-hearing briefs arises from the rule that permits the arbitrators to decide what further written statements will be allowed (Art. 22) as well as from the general rule empowering arbitrators to determine procedures (Art. 15). The Steelco and Hightech lawyers were uncertain about Neutralian practice in this connection.

QUESTION 58

Is it customary for the arbitral tribunal to permit post-hearing briefs in a case such as this? If so, would they usually be required to be submitted simultaneously by both parties?

ANSWERS TO QUESTION 58

MR. HOELLERING
The submission of post-hearing briefs is customary, and is quite common in a substantial international case which has consumed several days of hearings. The manner in which they are filed will vary, depending on the issues that still need to be addressed. The arbitral tribunal and parties may conclude that they will be filed simultaneously, or the order of filing may be plaintiff, respondent, plaintiff. Whatever the approach adopted, they would be mutually exchanged among the parties.

In UNCITRAL cases administered by the AAA, the transmittal of post-hearing briefs to the tribunal is handled by the Association.

MR. HUNTER
It would not be customary for post-hearing briefs to be submitted. Exceptionally, the tribunal might ask the parties, or one of them, to submit additional material which it considered necessary for the determination of the issues. If such material were to be produced by one party, then it would be supplied to the other party who would have an opportunity to comment on it.

Normally, an English arbitrator would expect to proceed to make the award as soon as practicable after the hearing was closed, without any further material or argument being presented by the parties.

MR. JARVIN
It is not customary, but it is becoming more frequent.

The arbitrator has a duty to proceed as quickly as possible with the making of the award, and would not wait for parties' suggestions to submit post-hearing briefs.

PROF. LEBEDEV

In the light of the usual practice in the country of arbitration, submission of any briefs after the hearings may be allowed only if both parties agree. In our opinion, the same conclusion may be made on the basis of Article 29(1), according to which the arbitral tribunal declares the hearings closed if the parties, being asked whether there are further submissions or proof, confirm that "there are none".

PROF. MICHIDA

The answers from Great Britain and the civil law countries are negative, and the answer from the United States is affirmative.

Japanese practice is in line with that of the United States. Rule 32 of the Japan Commercial Arbitration Association and Section 20 of the Rules of The Japan Shipping Exchange, Inc. provide for the re-opening of proceedings "by its decision" or "if the Board deems it necessary."

R. Costs

HYPOTHETICAL CASE

The Rules require that the tribunal fix the costs of the winner's expenses for legal representation, but provide the arbitrators with some discretion in determining what amount is reasonable and in apportioning those costs among the parties in appropriate circumstances. (Art. 38(e); Art. 40(2)) The question of the amount of the winner's legal fees that might be awarded is a matter of more than passing interest to the lawyers of Steelco and Hightech.

QUESTION 59

How does the arbitral tribunal determine the amount to be awarded for the winner's costs for legal representation?

ANSWERS TO QUESTION 59

MR. HOELLERING

Awards in large international cases will provide for the payment of the costs of legal representation wherever the arbitral tribunal is granted such authority either by the contract, the applicable arbitration rules, or by express agreement of the parties.[88]

In order for the tribunal to determine the amount to be awarded, where such fees are allowed, counsel for the parties will need to present to the arbitrators information establishing the reasonableness of the legal costs sought, such as hours spent, hourly rates charged, etc.

88. Art. 38 of the UNCITRAL Rules specifically provide for payment of legal fees. Absent agreement of the parties, attorney's fees are not awardable under US law. *See* note 20 *supra*.

MR. HUNTER

It would be customary for the tribunal to award that the winner should receive at least a contribution towards his legal costs and other expenses in relation to the arbitration. There is a provision in the Arbitration Act 1950 which provides that either the tribunal or the High Court may "tax" (this being a technical term having nothing to do with the collection of revenue by the government) the costs of a party. This is the Arbitration Act 1950, Section 18(1) which states:

> "1. Unless a contrary intention is expressed therein, every arbitration agreement shall be deemed to include a provision that the costs of the reference and award shall be in the discretion of the arbitrator or umpire, who may direct to and by whom and in what manner those costs or any part thereof shall be paid, and may tax or settle the amount of costs to be so paid or any part thereof, and may award costs to be paid as between solicitor and client.
> 2. Any costs directed by an award to be paid shall, unless the award otherwise directs, be taxable in the High Court.
> . . . ."

The word "tax" in this context is a reference to a particular scale adopted in the High Court under which so-called "necessary" costs of the winning party are recoverable from the loser in a court action. Such costs are normally ordered on what is known technically as a "party and party" basis. This method of assessing the costs to be paid by the loser under the Arbitration Act 1950, Section 18(1) is frequently adopted by arbitrators in *domestic* arbitrations, but it is not necessarily applicable in the case of international arbitrations.

In the case of international arbitrations, an English arbitrator would probably make some general estimate of what he considers the "reasonable" legal costs and other expenses of the winning party, based on supporting evidence provided by that party. There is a tendency in ICC arbitrations for arbitrators to leave each party to bear its own costs – particularly where neither side has had a total victory, as is so often the case.

MR. JARVIN

In many cases the arbitrators do not debate or decide on the legal costs of the parties otherwise than by stating that each side shall bear its own legal costs. This applies particularly where both parties win in part or lose in part.

In other cases the arbitrator makes an estimate of what is reasonable to award the winning party considering all the circumstances.

PROF. LEBEDEV

The practice in regard of the expenses for legal representation in the country of arbitration is not uniform, being dependent on the applicable rules of arbitration procedure: while under one set of rules (FTAC) such expenses are paid by each party himself, the other (MAC) provides that the unsuccessful party may be obliged to bear the expenses of the winning party within the limit of 5% of the satisfied or dismissed part of the claim.

It follows from the UNCITRAL Rules that the arbitral tribunal has wide discretion in regard of these expenses (which "were claimed during the arbitral proceedings, and only to the extent that the arbitral tribunal determines that the amount of such costs is reasonable" (Article 38(e)); "taking into account the circumstances of the case", the arbitral tribunal may order that these expenses *a.* are to be borne in full by the winning party, or *b.* are to be paid in full by the losing party, or, *c.* are to be partially paid by the losing party, "if it determines that apportionment is reasonable" (Art. 40(2)).

Taking into account that we are dealing with *ad hoc* arbitration, it may be certainly expected that the presiding arbitrator would be inclined to determine that a losing party should bear (at least in part) these expenses, although other determinations, of course, cannot be excluded, as in any situation where discretion can be exercised.

PROF. MICHIDA

The answers from Great Britain and the United States state that it is customary to award the winner costs for legal representation, and the report from the Soviet Union inclines to give the same award. On the other hand, in the civil law countries, in many cases, each side bears its own legal costs.

In Japan, in maritime cases, where a basic goal is to start the proceeding quickly, and legal representation is not required, costs for legal representation are not awarded. In commercial cases, they have been awarded in one case in the light of all the circumstances and where a party made a special request, but, generally, legal representation fees are not awarded.

This general practice in Japan is further evidence of the Japanese conception of arbitration as a method of amicable settlement between the parties, and not necessarily to be fought via lawyers.

MRS. OYEKUNLE

Section 16 of Arbitration Act Laws of the Federation of Nigeria and Lagos provides that:

> "Any order made under the Act may be made on such terms as to costs, or otherwise, as the authority making the order thinks just".

In view of the discretionary power in awarding costs given to the arbitral tribunal by law, there is no standard practice on the award of arbitration costs. The arbitral tribunal would decide on how to apportion costs taking into consideration the circumstances of the case, the evidence adduced and any other determination that may be deemed necessary.

DR. SZURSKI

Under the Rules of the Court of Arbitration at the Polish Chamber of Foreign Trade, lawyers' fees are not awarded by arbitral tribunals.

It is most probable that Polish arbitrators would normally stick to this principle also in *ad hoc* arbitrations unless the parties in their arbitration agreement explicitly provide otherwise.

However, even lacking such explicit agreement, one cannot exclude that in a case where one party wins the dispute totally or almost totally, an *ad hoc* arbitral tribunal will award a reasonable amount to be paid by a losing party as compensation for the costs of legal representation of the winner. The arbitrators will decide at their discretion what is reasonable on the basis of the bill presented by the winning party and of the circumstances of the case.

S. Awards

HYPOTHETICAL CASE

The Rules provide that the arbitral tribunal shall state the reasons upon which the award is based, unless the parties otherwise agree. (Art. 32(3)) The Rules, however, contain no provision either authorizing or excluding an arbitrator from writing a dissenting opinion, or from writing a concurring opinion agreeing with the conclusion of the award but differing with the reasons stated by the majority.

QUESTION 60

Is it customary for an arbitrator to write a dissenting or a concurring opinion? If so, are such opinions usually attached to the award if promptly submitted, or are they filed separately?

ANSWERS TO QUESTION 60

MR. HOELLERING
The filing of a dissenting or concurring opinion is entirely up to the arbitrator. However, it is not usual for arbitrators to write dissenting or concurring opinions in most cases. If an arbitrator dissents, the award usually will so indicate in clear terms.

In those cases in which such an opinion is filed, it customarily is attached to the award when it is transmitted to the parties, provided that it does not unduly delay the award.

It would be quite unusual for an award to be accompanied by a concurring opinion, absent some special circumstances.

MR. HUNTER
"Separate" opinions concurring with a unanimous award are very rarely given by English arbitrators. Most English arbitrators who find themselves in a minority, and refuse to sign a majority award, like to justify their position by explaining why they have not agreed with the other two arbitrators. They would normally, therefore, write a dissenting opinion, which might be quite short. If it is available in time, it would normally be sent to the parties with the majority award. (ICC practice however discourages this method of proceeding.)

Even where the Chairman (or the majority) refuses to send a copy of the dissenting opinion to the parties with the award, there is nothing to prevent the dissenting arbitrator from sending them his dissenting opinion separately.

MR. JARVIN

First question: No.

Second question: Yes, they are usually submitted to the Court of Arbitration simultaneously with the award.

The question, thereafter, arises whether the dissenting opinion should be notified to the parties or not. The system is different in different civil law systems and to communicate the dissenting opinion is, in some countries, seen as a violation of the arbitrator's right to confidentiality of deliberation. The dissenting opinion is then communicated to the parties only where the parties, or failing them the arbitrators, consent to such communication.

The ICC Court of Arbitration reviews dissenting opinions but does not express any opinion on their form and content and does not approve or disapprove them.

PROF. LEBEDEV

According to the customary practice in the country of arbitration, any member of the arbitral tribunal, who does not agree in whole or in part with the award made by majority of votes, is entitled to state his dissenting opinion. The dissenting opinion is not, however, attached to the award, but is filed as a separate document with the materials of the case. There are, however, no obstacles for the arbitrator, who has a dissenting opinion, to indicate this fact while signing the award, instead of refusal to sign (Art. 32(4) of the UNCITRAL Rules).

PROF. EL-HAKIM

In most Arab Codes of Procedure (Art. 790(5), Lebanese Code of Procedure; Art. 509, Egyptian Code; Art. 527, Syrian Code), arbitral awards must state the grounds of the decision, unless the arbitrators are *amiables compositeurs*. As before the courts, dissenting opinions are frequent. They aim at establishing why the decision of the majority is not shared by the dissenting arbitrator and help, therefore, in establishing a possible violation of public policy or any other reason for the annulment of the award (if authorized in the country where it is sought) or the refusal of a leave for enforcement (exequatur).

This is why it has to mention its legal grounds like the award itself.

Even if dissenting opinions are not notified to the parties with the arbitral award, they are part of the file and a true copy thereof must, therefore, be delivered to the parties upon their request like any other document of the file.

Confidentiality of deliberation has nothing do with that formality since the arbitrator has explicitly stated that he is dissenting and has mentioned in writing the reasons for his disapproval. The writing of that opinion would be useless if it is not notified to the parties who request it. Discussing the grounds of the decision guarantees that the award is legal and fair; otherwise, it should not be implemented.

PROF. MICHIDA

It is reported that in Great Britain most minority arbitrators refuse to sign the award, but in the civil law countries the answer is "no" and in the United States it is not usual. The answer from Japanese practice is "no".

DR. SZURSKI

Writing a dissenting opinion is sometimes practised by Polish arbitrators acting within the Court of Arbitration at the Polish Chamber of Foreign Trade.

Dissenting opinions are not attached to awards but are kept in the files of the Court and are delivered to a party only on request.

Arbitrators submitting dissenting opinions sign the award adding before the signature *c.v.s.* (*cum voto separato*).

In *ad hoc* arbitrations, dissenting opinions if any are most likely to be attached to the award or even included in its text.

T. Role of Arbitrators in Settlement

HYPOTHETICAL CASE

At various times during the arbitration proceeding, some of the arbitrators believed that the case could be settled by agreement of the parties. The Rules provide that the arbitrators may record a settlement as an award on agreed terms, but contain no guidelines as to whether arbitrators should appropriately have any role in bringing about a settlement. (Art. 34(1)) The party-appointed arbitrators from Metalia and Machinia were unfamiliar with Neutralian practice in this regard.

QUESTION 61

Is it appropriate for the arbitral tribunal to suggest generally to the parties that they discuss the possibility of settling the case?

ANSWERS TO QUESTION 61

MR. HOELLERING

It is appropriate and within an arbitral tribunal's discretion, at a propitious time during an arbitral proceeding, to suggest to the parties that they discuss settlement. There have been occasions when well-timed suggestions, based on insights gained by the arbitrators during the presentation of the case, have resulted in resolution of a dispute without the need for further proceedings which are costly in time and money.[89]

89. The American Arbitration Association, in addition to administering arbitrations, provides a full range of alternative dispute resolution services. If parties so desired, they could pursue settlement negotiations with the aid of a mediator, or explore their case via the minitrial. A hybrid process, called "med-arb," is sometimes employed wherein mediation or conciliation is first attempted. If unsuccessful, the parties proceed to final, binding arbitration. A majority of respondents to the Coulson survey indicated that they would be willing to engage in pre-arbitration conciliation efforts. *See* Coulson, *Survey*, note 3 *supra*.

MR. HUNTER

There is no objection for the tribunal to suggest generally to the parties that, for reasons of expense and so forth, they should consider making a settlement. However, all communications between the tribunal and the parties should be on an "equality" basis. It would therefore be wholly inappropriate for the tribunal, or any individual member of the tribunal, to suggest to one of the parties that it would be in his interests to negotiate a settlement.

In particular, it would be considered improper for a party-appointed arbitrator to indicate to the party who nominated him that the case is going badly for that party, and that he should try to reach a settlement in order to avoid an adverse award.

MR. JARVIN

Yes. Such suggestions shall be made to both parties. But the arbitrator should use his *Fingerspitzengefühl*, and abstain from making suggestions where it is clear that either the parties have tried a settlement and failed or where the parties are determined to go ahead with the arbitration and do not want to lose time on a conciliation. A suggestion to settle the case must never be a mandatory step of an arbitration, but it may be a useful help where the conditions are favourable.

PROF. LEBEDEV

Under the customary practice in the country of arbitration, such a suggestion, though not inadmissible, would seem unlikely.

DR. SZURSKI

It is even to a certain extent customary for arbitral tribunals, acting within the framework of the Court of Arbitration at the Polish Chamber of Foreign Trade, to suggest to the parties to discuss the possibility of a settlement, particularly when it would lead to the avoidance of lengthy and costly proceedings and where the circumstances of the case favour an amicable settlement of the dispute. Such custom has its source in the clear provision of the Rules of the said Court (the 1970 Rules, Art. 27(4)) which defines the right of the presiding arbitrator to induce the parties to an amicable settlement at any stage of the arbitral proceedings.

Polish arbitrators, normally, will be in full agreement with the majority of Rapporteurs that it is not appropriate for arbitrators to participate in settlement negotiations.

On the other hand, on mutual request of the parties, a settlement formula is sometimes suggested by arbitrators acting within the framework of the Court of Arbitration at the Polish Chamber of Foreign Trade. It is, however, always expressed without prejudice to the position the arbitral tribunal may take in the award and is done particularly in cases when in the eyes of the arbitrators further prolongation of the proceedings it is not really sensible from the economical point of view.

The present commentator shares the view that, as a rule, an arbitral tribunal should not suggest a settlement formula unless, when requested by the parties, it sees a ground to suggest the settlement on a purely commercial basis: fifty-fifty.

Any other formula of settlement expressed by the arbitral tribunal, when not accepted by the parties, may negatively influence the further course of the proceedings, at least from the psychological point of view.

QUESTION 62

Is it appropriate for the arbitral tribunal to suggest to the parties a possible formula for settlement? Would this be appropriate if both parties requested the arbitrators to do so?

ANSWERS TO QUESTION 62

MR. HOELLERING

It would be inappropriate for the arbitrators to specifically suggest a formula for settlement of the case. On the other hand, it would be permissible for the tribunal to make such a suggestion if both parties so requested. In such a case it would be advisable, however, for the arbitrators to comply with such a request only if the parties agreed in advance that the non-acceptance of the suggestion for settlement did not impair the acceptability of the tribunal to continue with the arbitration proceeding and determination of the dispute. This situation seldom arises, due to the investment in time and money in the arbitral proceedings.[90]

MR. HUNTER

In general, the tribunal should only propose specific terms of settlement to the parties if the parties have requested the tribunal to do so. Otherwise, it would be an excess of authority.

The view of the present Rapporteur is that it is difficult, and dangerous, for the tribunal to try to act simultaneously, or in parallel, as conciliators and as arbitrators. The standard of conduct required for these two separate functions is materially different. Where the parties agree during the course of the arbitration that the arbitrators should try to act as conciliators, if this fails and the matter has to proceed as an arbitration, then the individual arbitrators may have acted in a way which disqualifies them from achieving the degree of independence and impartiality required for the making of a valid award.

MR. JARVIN

First question: No. But the arbitrators might ask the parties if they would like them to work out a formula. If the parties agree to that, it would be appropriate for the arbitrators to suggest a possible formula for settlement.

Second question: Yes.

90. *See* American Bar Association and American Arbitration Association, *Code of Ethics for Arbitrators in Commercial Disputes*.

PROF. LEBEDEV

It seems that except for some special situations (for example, when the parties themselves in essence have determined the principal elements of the compromise and when, therefore, it is highly possible that the case will be so ended), the presiding arbitrator is most likely to abstain from suggesting any formula to the parties, even if both of them agreed to that.

PROF. MICHIDA

It is reported that in the United States and the civil law countries, it would be inappropriate unless both parties so requested; and that in the Soviet Union, the arbitrator would not suggest any formula even when both parties request one, unless the parties have compromised on the principal elements of the dispute and successful compromise is highly likely. In Great Britain, the general practice is that if both parties so request, it is permissible. However, the Rapporteur expresses his view that it is difficult and dangerous for the tribunal to try to act simultaneously, or in parallel, as conciliators and as arbitrators.

Japanese practice is different on this question. Section 21 of The Rules of The Japan Shipping Exchange, Inc. emphasizes the amicable nature of arbitration in Sub-Section (1) and affirms the proposal of a settlement on the Board's initiative in Sub-Section (2) as follows:

> "Section 21. (Mediation)
> (1) The parties do not lose their respective rights to settle the dispute amicably even after the application for arbitration has been filed.
> (2) The Board may, at any stage of the arbitration proceedings, mediate between the parties for the whole or a part of the dispute."

It is in these respects that the present commentator finds convincing manifestations of the amicable texture of Japanese arbitration.

QUESTION 63

Is it appropriate for arbitrators to participate in settlement discussions with the parties? Would this be appropriate if both parties requested the arbitrators to do so?

ANSWERS TO QUESTION 63

MR. HOELLERING

It is not appropriate for the arbitrators to participate in settlement discussions. Given the nature of such negotiations, it is unlikely that the arbitrators would continue to enjoy the confidence of the parties if such discussions failed. Since this would mean that the entire case would require rearbitration, it seldom occurs that arbitrators participate in such settlement discussions unless the parties stipulate in advance that notwithstanding any such failure, the authority of the arbitrators would remain unimpaired. Such a stipulation would be extremely rare.

MR. HUNTER

See the answer to Question 62. On the one hand, the arbitrators should in principle do whatever the parties jointly agree that they should do. On the other hand, if the tribunal (or, even worse, any individual members of it) confer privately with the parties separately to discuss possible settlement terms, it is difficult to envisage how they could then resume the function of an arbitrator if the settlement discussions fail.

In the view of the present Rapporteur, it would in any case be wholly inappropriate for the tribunal (or individual members of it) to participate in settlement discussions unless *both* parties specifically request them to do so.

MR. JARVIN

First question: No.

Second question: Yes, and a request from both parties would be a condition for such participation.

PROF. LEBEDEV

The answer to this question is most likely to be negative, rather than positive.

QUESTION 64

What should the arbitral tribunal do if a party during a hearing starts to disclose the details of settlement discussions that have been held?

ANSWERS TO QUESTION 64

MR. HOELLERING

If a party were to disclose the details of prior settlement negotiations, it is customary for the tribunal to promptly cut off any further discussion on the matter. The details of settlement discussions traditionally are deemed confidential and not admissible as evidence in adversary proceedings. This is due to the strong public policy favoring free settlement discussions between disputing parties. Moreover, such evidence is deemed irrelevant and is thus excludable.[91]

MR. HUNTER

This depends on the basis of the settlement discussions which have taken place. If they have been on a "without prejudice" basis, it is improper for even the existence of the settlement discussions to be disclosed to the tribunal, let alone the substance of what has been discussed. The proper course would be for the tribunal to intervene immediately and to stop the party from revealing details of any settlement discussions, and then to ask the opposing party whether he has

91. Rule 408 of the Federal Rules of Evidence reflect this policy. The notes of the Advisory Committee indicate that such evidence is deemed inadmissible as irrelevant and contrary to the public policy encouraging settlement. *See also Quillen* v. *Board of Education*, 115 N.Y.S.2d 122, 126 (Supp. Ct., N.Y.Cty. 1952); Fed. Rules Civ. Proc. Rule 68; N.Y. Civ. Prac. Law R. 3221, which provides that offers to compromise "shall not be made known. . . ." *See also Code of Ethics*, note 90 *supra*.

any objection to the revelation of these details on the grounds that the discussions were on a "without prejudice" basis.

MR. JARVIN

The arbitral tribunal should stop him and ask the parties what they agreed regarding the disclosure of details of settlement discussions.

PROF. LEBEDEV

If the parties (without participation of the arbitrators) discussed between themselves the possibilities for a settlement, which was not achieved, and then one of the parties starts to disclose the details of such discussions, the arbitral court would, primarily, take into account the attitude thereto of the other party.

If the latter objects, the tribunal would have to ask the first party not to make any references to the content of the above-mentioned discussions.

IV. GENERAL COMMENTS OF RAPPORTEURS AND COMMENTATORS

Arbitration Practice in the United States as Applied to the Hypothetical Case

Michael F. Hoellering

International commercial arbitration is enjoying ever-growing acceptance as a forum for the resolution of transnational business disputes. It allows parties, when making the contract, to select the appropriate procedures for resolution of disputes which may arise over the course of dealings with a great degree of specificity, and provides them with an opportunity to structure their arbitration arrangements so as to avoid any nation's unfamiliar rules of law and court system.

Although arbitration generally follows the same pattern worldwide, there is variety and distinction among the many jurisdictions, arbitral institutions and arbitral procedural rules, of which the practitioner must be aware. Some of these differences have developed due to the underlying legal framework of the host nation chosen as the situs of arbitration. Many other variables are introduced through the agreement of the parties or the practice of the arbitral tribunal.

A most important and significant aspect of US arbitration law and practice is the enormous flexibility of the arbitration process. The focus is on party autonomy – the parties are free to mutually agree to tailor the process of arbitration in the manner that best suits their requirements, either when drafting the arbitration agreement, or during the course of the proceedings themselves.

Although the answers to the questions, so thoughtfully prepared for our discussion by our colleagues Howard M. Holtzmann and Giorgio Bernini, represent an overview of the conduct of international commercial arbitration in the United States, one must always bear in mind the flexibility of the arbitral process. In virtually every case, the particular facts, legal issues, parties and arbitrators will influence the conduct of the arbitration so as to produce a result most satisfactory to the situation. This is the beauty of arbitration.

United States public policy is extremely supportive of arbitration as an alternative to judicial dispute resolution. This is evidenced by the legislation favoring arbitration as an enforceable method for resolving both existing and future disputes, and by decisions from both federal and state courts. Both the law and the courts recognize the contractual aspect of arbitration and respect the freedom of the parties to shape the process to their needs. The role of the courts in general is one of assistance supportive of the arbitral process and not one of interference with it. In addition, arbitration is deemed a quasi-judicial proceeding. Arbitrators are granted almost plenary power to conduct arbitrations and resolve disputes without judicial interference,[1] and are protected in the performance of their duties by an umbrella of immunity.[2]

The encouragement of arbitration is especially evident in the field of international arbitration. The United States has ratified the 1958 Convention on the Recognition and Enforcement of Foreign Arbitral Awards,[3] as well as a number of other international treaties favoring arbitration.[4] In a number of important decisions, the courts have evidenced significant hospitality toward international arbitration and distinguished domestic law in favor of a broader, more "truly international" approach.[5]

In my answers to the Questions of the Hypothetical Case, my aim was to point up the customary practice in international arbitration as it is conducted in the United States. The UNCITRAL Arbitration Rules, chosen by the hypothetical disputants, address many practical aspects of the conduct of the arbitration. Where they do not expressly control the proceedings, however, I have in many instances referred to the rules of the American Arbitration Association, as they not only address these "grey areas" in many cases, but also reflect the custom and practice of arbitration in the United States generally.

In answering the questions based on the hypothetical case involving Steelco and Hightech, it was assumed that the applicable procedural law of the arbitral locale, Neutralia, is identical to that of the United States. It was further assumed that the Neutralian Arbitration Association, named as administering authority under the UNCITRAL Rules by the parties, is similar in all respects to the American Arbitration Association.

---

1. *See generally* Hoellering, *Remedies in Arbitration*, 20 *Forum* 516 (ABA Tort & Insurance Practice Section, Spring 1985); "Conduct of Hearings: the Arbitrator's Authority," AAA *Lawyers' Arbitration Letter* Vol. 5, No. 4 (Dec. 1981).
2. *See* "Immunity and the Arbitration Process," AAA *Lawyers' Arbitration Letter* Vol. 7, No. 1 (Mar. 1983).
3. [1958] 330 U.N.T.S. 38. The US acceded to the Convention in 1970. 3 U.S.T. 2517.
4. *See* von Mehren, "Outline of Applicable Treaties," in AAA, *A Short Course on International Commercial Arbitration* (1981); Aksen, "The Case for Bilateral Investment Treaties," in Southwestern Legal Foundation, *Private Investors Abroad – Problems and Solutions Abroad* (1981 Matthew Bender); Gudgeon, "Arbitration Provisions of US Bilateral Investment Treaties," in American Society of International Law (Rubin & Nelson, ed.) *International Investment Disputes: Avoidance and Settlement* (1985 West Publ. Co.); Broches, "Bilateral Investment Protection Treaties and Arbitration of Investment Disputes," in *Art of Arbitration, Liber Amicorum P. Sanders* (1982 Kluwer, Netherlands).
5. *See Scherk* v. *Alberto-Culver Co.*, 417 U.S. 506 (1974); *Mitsubishi Motors Corp.* v. *Soler Chrysler-Plymouth Inc.* — US —, 105 S.Ct. 3346 (1985); cases cited in Aksen, *International Arbitration Received Favorably in US.*, *N.Y.L.J.*, Nov. 5, 1976, p. 1, col. 1. *See also* McClendon, *Alternative Methods of Dispute Settlement*, 17 *Houston L.Rev.* 979, 988 (1980); Stein and Wotman, *International Commercial Arbitration in the 1980's: A Comparison of the Major Arbitral Systems and Rules*, 38 *Bus. Lawyer* 1685, 1687–88 (Aug. 1983).

Hypothetical Case Study
Steelco v. *Hightech*
(Neutralia = England)

J. Martin H. Hunter

My answers to the Hypothetical Case assume that the arbitration takes place in England, that the London Court of International Arbitration is the "Neutralian Arbitration Association" (the appointing authority designated in the arbitration clause) and that the presiding arbitrator is English.

It was not the purpose of this Report to fatigue the reader with an exposition of the virtues of England as a forum for international arbitration, but it is nonetheless appropriate to make some general comments about arbitration in England. English arbitration is possibly the most misunderstood of all arbitral systems. How often does one hear people confusing arbitration procedure with court procedure? How many people still think that "discovery" of documents is mandatory in an English arbitration? In fact, an arbitrator has discretion (under the Arbitration Act 1950, Section 12(1)) to order the production of as few or as many documents as he wishes. Even this discretion may be limited by the agreement of the parties. It is true that a party may apply to the court (under Sect. 12(6) of that Act) for an order for full "discovery" of all relevant documents (whether a party wishes to rely on them or not); but it seems inconceivable that the court would exercise its power to make such an order in *international* arbitration where the arbitrator himself evidently does not consider that this would be helpful for his determination of the issues.

Another misconception relates to the extent of court intervention in the arbitral process. The English courts are certainly "interventionist" by comparison with, for example, the position in Belgium under its new law governing international arbitration. This may be good or bad, depending upon the eye of the beholder. But there is little, if any, difference in practice between the philosophies of court intervention in England, Switzerland and France, whether that intervention is in the supportive or supervisory mode. (See Goldman, "The Complementary Roles of Judges and Arbitrators in Ensuring that International Arbitration is Effective", in *60 Years On, A Look at the Future*, p. 257).

Party autonomy is as much the most significant element of arbitration procedure in England as it is anywhere else in the world. With very few limitations the parties may agree on whatever procedure they wish to follow; or they may agree that the procedure should be determined by the arbitral tribunal, which is normally the position if they have incorporated an established set of arbitration rules.

Where the parties have chosen to arbitrate their disputes under a set of arbitration rules, in the present Hypothetical Case the UNCITRAL Rules, an arbitration held in England will still be subject to the relevant provisions of English law. It is not possible to hold a so-called "de-localized" arbitration on English soil. This is one of the few limitations on party autonomy (another example is that the parties could not validly agree that the tribunal should commit a criminal act).

Arbitration in England is governed primarily by three Acts of Parliament; the Arbitration Acts of 1950, 1975 and 1979. The 1950 Act establishes the basic framework within which arbitration, whether international or domestic, may exist within the law, and sets out the main supportive and supervisory role of the courts in relation to the conduct of arbitral proceedings. The 1975 Act simply gave legislative effect to the provisions of the New York Convention of 1958. The primary purpose of the 1979 Act was to abolish the notorious and much abused "case stated" procedure for appealing to the courts on questions of law.

Within this legislative framework, the practice of arbitration is controlled by the law as interpreted and established by decisions of the courts. All matters relating to arbitration are referred to the Commercial Court, which is presided over by a small number of judges with relevant background and experience. In relatively recent times, the opinions of academics and authors have also become an important influence in the development of the way in which practitioners, whether arbitrators or lawyers representing parties, approach their work. *The Law and Practice of Commercial Arbitration in England*, London 1982, by Mustill and Boyd, and the latest edition of *Russell on the Law of Arbitration*, 20th edition, London 1982, are now routinely quoted to arbitrators during the course of arbitral proceedings to establish points of practice.

However, it must be emphasized that the *practice* of arbitration in England, particularly in the international field, depends on the attitudes of individual arbitrators and the customs and usages of particular sectors of commerce. Unless the parties have reached a specific agreement, or unless an implied agreement takes effect by custom in a particular type of arbitration, the arbitrator has almost total discretion as to how he will conduct the proceedings. This accords with modern international opinion (evidenced, for example, by the UNCITRAL Model Law), even if some English lawyers might prefer a more old-fashioned approach to the effect that arbitral proceedings should be in line with court procedure and strictly controlled by the courts.

The *law* of England itself therefore gives little, if any, guidance as to how the questions raised in the Hypothetical Case should be answered. Since the UNCITRAL Rules also permit a substantial flexibility to the arbitral tribunal as regards procedure, a wide variety of answers to the questions raised in the Hypothetical Case might be obtained from individual English practitioners.

Answers to the Questions of the Hypothetical Case in a Typical Civil Law Country

Sigvard Jarvin

I have been asked to prepare answers to the Questions of the Hypothetical Case that reflect civil law practice based on observations of those cases decided under the ICC Rules that are conducted under civil law. "Practice" has been defined to mean those elements of arbitral procedure that arbitrators have discretion to determine because they are not specified in the national law governing the arbitration or in the arbitration rules agreed to by the parties.

ICC arbitration can and does take place anywhere in the world. Whereas in 1984 not more than 55% of all the parties had a West European origin, West European sites are the most frequently chosen places of arbitration. Western Europe was the situs in more than 86% of the cases in 1984, and looking closer at European sites those in a civil law system predominate. As you will see from the table below, the parties themselves have agreed on the place of arbitration themselves in most cases ("confirmed" by the Court of the ICC) and the ICC Court has fixed the place to a small extent only ("fixed" by the Court). This corresponds to a general trend in present ICC arbitration practice where parties more often agree on the place rather than leave it to the Court to decide. In 1984 parties made their own choice of place of arbitration in 81% of all cases and the Court consequently had to fix it in the remaining 19% of cases only.

TABLE I *Place of ICC Arbitration in 1984, some examples*

SWITZERLAND	75 (68 confirmed – 7 fixed by the Court)
FRANCE	58 (52 confirmed – 6 fixed by the Court)
UK	14 (11 confirmed – 3 fixed by the Court)
AUSTRIA	9 (4 confirmed – 5 fixed by the Court)
GERMANY (Federal)	5 (5 confirmed by the Court)
NETHERLANDS	5 (3 confirmed – 2 fixed by the Court)
SWEDEN	4 (3 confirmed – 1 fixed by the Court)
BELGIUM	3 (1 confirmed – 2 fixed by the Court)
GREECE	3 (3 fixed by the Court)
LIECHTENSTEIN	1 (1 fixed by the Court)
USA	6 (5 confirmed – 1 fixed by the Court)
CANADA	None

(Note: The statistics for 1985 were not available when this Report was written.)

It is superfluous to state that in most civil law systems the parties and the arbitrators have complete or next to complete freedom to agree on the general procedure to be followed. This is one of the key attractions of international arbitration over state court procedures.[1] Where provisions exist they aim at assuring a fair trial by stipulating rules of a fundamental character.[2]

---

1. *Switzerland* "Whilst the parties are free to choose how they wish to organize the Arbitration Proceedings, there are nevertheless some fundamental rules which apply to any arbitration held in Switzerland". (*International Arbitration in Switzerland*, published by the Swiss Arbitration Association, 1984, p. 15).

"According to Concordat Art. 24 the arbitral rules of procedure shall be determined by the agreement between the parties, or in the absence of such agreement, by the decision of the arbitral tribunal" (*ICCA Yearbook*, 1978, p. 192, cited below as "*Yearbook*").

France "The rules applicable to the procedure in international cases are those chosen by the parties wherever the place of arbitration.

If parties and/or the arbitrators have themselves devised the rules applicable to the proceedings without a reference to any national law those rules have to be respected". (*Yearbook*, 1981, p. 13).

Germany "To a large extent German law allows the parties to arrange the arbitral procedure as they deem appropriate. The arbitrators are obliged to observe the arrangements of the parties". (*Yearbook*, 1979, p. 70).

Sweden "The Arbitration Act contains very few procedural rules, and most of the rules laid down are excludable. It is for the parties to determine the procedural rules to be followed". (U. Nordenson, Former Justice of the Supreme Court of Sweden, in *Swedish and International Arbitration*, *Yearbook of Stockholm Chamber of Commerce*, 1984, p. 9).

"The Arbitration Act gives a specific rule as to the mode of commencing the proceedings (notice of arbitration). The Arbitration Act further directs that the chairman must be appointed if there are several arbitrators. There are also provisions as to evidence, the award and the time for making an award". (*Yearbook*, 1978, p. 169).

Austria "(The Code of Civil Procedure) leaves the parties and the arbitrators the greatest possible flexibility". (*A Guide to Commercial Arbitration in Austria*, published by Federal Economic Chamber, Vienna, 1983).

2. *Switzerland* "The purpose of (these fundamental rules) is to ensure the fairness of the proceedings and to ensure that general principles of due process will be abided by, such as giving a party the right to challenge an Arbitrator for certain specified reasons.

"Swiss law further provides that each party must be allowed to state its case, be given access to every document submitted to the Arbitrators, that no party may be denied the right to attend the hearings of the Arbitral Tribunal and that counsel can also attend. Similarly, the Concordat provides that all the arbitrators must participate in the decisions of the arbitration panel and that the reasons for the award be given unless the parties expressly waive this right. Also, the award must be dated and signed (at least by a majority of arbitrators)". (*International Arbitration in Switzerland*, p. 15).

France "Whatever freedom the parties and the arbitrators may have, French principles of international public policy should nevertheless be respected, otherwise the award might be aside by a French judge. Concerning proceedings, those principles may be restricted to two basic ideas: the principle of equality between the parties and the possibility for each party to present its views on every point in dispute". (*Yearbook*, 1982, p. 10).

Germany "A basic principle of the arbitral procedure is that the arbitrators should not deny a party the possibility to present his case (rechtliches Gehör' (*Yearbook*, 1979, p. 70).

Sweden "The arbitrators are enjoined to deal with the case in an impartial, practical and speedy manner. It follows from this and more particularly from Section 14 of the Arbitration Act that the arbitrators should hear both parties". (*Yearbook*, 1978, p. 169).

"Beyond (Section 14) and except for certain provisions regarding evidence and the rendering of the award itself the Act keeps silent on procedural matters" (Justice Nordenson in *Swedish and International Arbitration* 1984, p. 9).

Austria Code of Civil Procedure, Art. 587 makes it obligatory for the arbitrators to hear the parties before making an award. This is stated to mean that the parties are given the opportunity to present their case. (*A Guide to Commercial Arbitration in Austria*, Vienna 1983, p. 18).

In those cases where nothing particular has been agreed on the arbitration procedure, one notes similarities and differences in various civil law countries. The procedure applicable in ordinary court proceedings then applies, wholly or in part, or by analogy. However the application of ordinary procedural rules is often less strict in an international arbitration. The prevailing pattern is to have a written exchange of pleadings in an introductory stage whereafter oral hearings take place. Although the arbitrators are entitled to decide a case on the basis of written documents alone, thus without hearing the parties, little use seems to be made of this possibility in practice.[3]

Based on the statistics it can be stated that the arbitrator in the majority of ICC arbitrations enjoys the freedom to decide the procedure and thus to exercise discretion. The answers given to the questions of the hypothetical case reflect how the arbitrators' discretion is used in typical cases. Since the discretionary power of the arbitrator is often not complete and changes from one civil law country to another, as the above brief survey highlighting a few aspects will have shown, the answers to the Questions of the Hypothetical Case can only be approximative indicating the "average" practice.

3. *Switzerland* "According to the Concordat Art. 24 the Federal Act on Federal Civil Procedure of December 4, 1947 shall be applicable by analogy. It is common to have first an exchange of written pleadings. Oral hearings are not necessary unless the parties desire or the arbitrators decide so. It is also possible for the arbitrators to decide only on written evidence without hearing the parties in person, although in practice this will be rather rare". (*Yearbook*, 1978, p. 192).

Germany "As a general rule, arbitrators will follow the ordinary court procedure in an informal way". (*Yearbook*, 1979, p. 70).

Sweden "A pattern is the one employed in the Swedish courts of first instance: the claimant's request would then contain proper points of claim, and the respondent will plead to these orally at the first meeting before the arbitrators. However, the parties will, more often, exchange written pleadings once or twice before the main hearing.

"A purely written type of procedure is accepted by the statute (Sect. 14), provided the parties are both given a proper chance of presenting their cases. But normally the arbitrators will not be allowed to refuse an oral hearing if either party requests one". (*Yearbook*, 1978, p. 169).

"Generally speaking, arbitral tribunals dealing with international commercial disputes leave more room for the proceedings to be carried out in terms of written submissions that is customary in court proceedings. It is current practice that the claimant party is requested by the tribunal to submit – unless he has done so in connection with his demand for arbitration – within a specified period of time – which may vary, depending on the size and complexity of the dispute, between a couple of weeks and a few months – a written memorial, stating the claims raised, the grounds upon which they are based, both in facts and law, and the relief sought". (Justice Nordenson in *Swedish and International Arbitration 1984*, p. 10).

Answers to the Questions of the Hypothetical Case from the Viewpoint of an Arbitration in the Soviet Union

Sergei N. Lebedev

The structure of this Report has been predetermined by the basic report under the above theme of the Congress, submitted by H. Holtzmann and G. Bernini: "The Hypothetical Case for Use in Comparative Study of Arbitration Practice in Various Legal Systems".

In this context the hypothetical case suggesting a number of questions which may arise in connection with the above arbitration, calls a responding Rapporteur to answer such questions relying on practices which prevail in his legal system, for the present report it thus being the Soviet legal system.

A reservation seems appropriate to be made that the answers presented in this Report reflect purely personal opinion of the author: it is quite probable, that many respective questions in specific arbitrations, depending on circumstances of a case and the individual arbitrators involved, might well be resolved in a different manner.

Firstly, when speaking of "practice", the Rapporteur has in mind the practices which, within his knowledcge, have been formed under the impact of laws relating to and rules of procedure of institutional arbitration bodies existing in the USSR, i.e., the Foreign Trade Arbitration Commission (FTAC and the Maritime Arbitration Commission (MAC) at the USSR Chamber of Commerce and Industry, whereas in our "hypothetical case" we deal with *ad hoc* arbitration to be governed by its own rules of procedure, i.e., the UNCITRAL Arbitration Rules, having international genesis.

Secondly, and perhaps most importantly, the questions under consideration relate, to a great extent at least, to such elements of the arbitration proceedings which, as noted in the basic report itself, "are not controlled by applicable procedural laws or by parties' agreed Arbitration Rules" and hence may frequently be resolved by a free discretion of the arbitrators hearing a particular case. Such freedom is explicitly provided for in Article 15(1) of the UNCITRAL Arbitration Rules, by virtue of which "Subject to these Rules, the arbitral tribunal may conduct the arbitration in such manner as it considers appropriate . . .". In our view, this principle, generally quite natural for arbitration, allows for effectively adapting arbitral proceedings to the needs and peculiarities of a specific case which is particularly important in international cases, involving parties from different countries, moreover so where arbitration is held in a third country. At the same time the above principle necessarily presupposes a possible diversity in resolving the matters left to a free discretion of arbitrators appointed for each specific case. It is believed however that in most instances such eventual differences would not cause serious difficulties, unexpected "surprises" for the parties, etc., since the relevant matters, which are really significant, may well be settled at the very initial stage of the proceedings by accord with both parties or at least by taking into account their reasonable suggestions. From this point of view the list of problems raised in the basic report, although not exhaustive of course, appears to be a useful "guide" for the practice of international commercial arbitration.

Thirdly, while orientating ourselves to the practice in the country of arbitration, speaking of traditions or preferences of the third arbitrator (Chairman) from that country etc., it is necessary to remember that under Article 31 of the UNCITRAL Arbitration Rules, when there are three arbitrators, all matters, including of course those of procedure, are finally decided "by a majority of the arbitrators". Hence, it is impossible to exclude that in matters not mandatorily regulated in the applicable law or in the UNCITRAL Rules, there well may be a departure from the "customary practice" in the country of arbitration, particularly when the other members of the arbitral tribunal, apart from the Chairman, are nationals of the countries having, with regard to the matter involved, similar practices, differing from that of the country of arbitration. In fact, however, for various reasons, often more psychological than legal, both or least one of the other two arbitrators may well be expected to choose to follow the practice customary for and preferred by the Chairman, thus making it the controlling one, even in the above situation.

Fourthly, while it seems clear that the parties are free to agree on any point of procedure (Art. 11 of the UNCITRAL Rules) this does not mean that the arbitrator having accepted the mission, becomes their meek servant or a kind of *instrumentum vocalis*. The Rules themselves envisage the arbitrator's resignation (Art. 13(1)), which well may happen in particular if a rule agreed by the parties *after* the arbitrator has been appointed appears to be irrational, unreasonable or otherwise unacceptable to him. So, it would be important that both propositions be kept in mind in the course of arbitral proceedings.

Civil Law Practice with Respect to Arab Countries

Jacques El-Hakim

1. The following comments aim at completing the report submitted by Mr. Sigvard Jarvin on civil law practice with respect to Arab countries. The legal system of the latter is mainly inspired by French Law, either directly or through Egyptian or Lebanese Codes which were often taken as a model in most Arab countries. This is why most of the comments stated in Mr. Jarvin's report generally apply to Arab countries. It is only when the practice of those countries differ from what is stated in that report that the appropriate correction or addition is hereinafter made.
2. A basic feature in most Arab countries is the impact on arbitration of the laws of procedure applicable to judicial courts. Most arbitrations involve a government agency or a public sector organization or company and, as consequence, many arbitrators are court judges or government employees – sometimes in the same corporate body party to arbitration (as long as the other party does not object to their appointment). Such parties and arbitrators are naturally inclined to apply the basic laws of procedure applicable before the judicial courts because:

    a. They are familiar therewith.
    b. Legal provisions or rules of institutional arbitration are rather scarce. Most local arbitrators have no knowledge of other rules or of case law on arbitration.
    c. Most Arab countries are formalist and wish to have explicit written rules to abide thereby.
    d. Courts are very jealous of their authority and although most judges like to act as arbitrators, they are inclined to stick to the basic laws of procedure when granting leave for enforcement (exequatur) of arbitral awards or examining any issue relating to arbitration.

3. It was hardly possible, in my comments, to give a precise idea of what is going on in every Arab or Middle-Eastern country, due to their different legal systems, political regimes and social situations. We therefore tried to describe the predominant general practice of most of these countries, bearing in mind that our statements cannot be absolute and may vary considerably in a particular situation or in a specific country.
4. Some of the comments might seem somewhat blunt. They only aim at describing the real situation, frankness being always the best means of communication between people.

The Amicable Texture of Japanese Arbitration

Shinishiro Michida

These comments discuss Japanese practices that may apply to the questions raised in the hypothetical arbitration between Steelco Corporation (Steelco) and Hightech Corporation (Hightech), and that differ from those described in the Reports on a typical civil law country by Sigvard Jarvin, Great Britain by J. Martin Hunter, the Soviet Union by Sergei N. Lebedev and the United States by Michael F. Hoellering.

There are numerous differences between Japanese practices and those in the civil law countries, Great Britain, the Soviet Union or the United States. Because it is impossible to report on all of them within the space limitations, I concentrated on those I regard as most significant.

In making this selection, I have been guided by the old proverb that "one must not lose sight of the forest for the trees." Most of the comments therefore focus on "the forest," that is, they stress the overall character and spirit of Japanese arbitration – what I have chosen to designate as the "amicable texture" of Japanese arbitration rules and practices.

Practice of Arbitration in the African Region

Tinuade Oyekunle

The purpose of this commentary is to reflect practice in arbitration in the African region as may be applicable to the facts of the hypothetical case which Rapporteurs from four main regions of the world have reported on.

The practice of arbitration in the African region varies depending on whether the law of the particular place of arbitration is based mainly on the civil law or common law system.

Practice in the civil law system has been clearly reported on by Mr. Sigvard Jarvin and I am reliably informed that arbitral procedure in most French speaking African countries are similar to those ably reported on by him.

Nigerian law is based mainly on the common law system and the native cum customary law of the land, but the legislation with reference to arbitration is set out in the Arbitration Act Cap 13 Laws of the Federal Republic of Nigeria and Lagos 1958, which has its origins in the old pre-1979 Arbitration Act of England.[1]

The Nigerian Arbitration Act of 1958 still retains the infamous case-stated principle thereby allowing for references to the court. Section 15 of the Act specifically provides that "any arbitrator or umpire may *at any stage of the proceedings* under a reference, and shall, if so directed by the court or judge state in the form of a special case for the opinion of the court any question of law arising in the course of the reference".

This case-stated procedure is not looked at with favour by foreign entrepreneurs who have commercial dealing with the State and the people. Recently in most cases, parties (foreign and national) provide for specific arbitration clauses in their contracts. Reference to application of the ICC Rules, Rules of London Court of Arbitration or the UNCITRAL Rules are now in use in many contracts. The Nigerian Arbitration Association is aware of the modern trend in arbitration and is making efforts to educate the people to adopt flexible rules. The Association is also optimistic that the Government, in the course of the present law reform, will update the 1958 Arbitration Law which is out dated in many respects.

The comments in this paper reflect the practices that are likely to be adopted bearing in mind the circumstances of the case and the law applicable if the place of arbitration is in Nigeria. The comments are the personal opinion of the commentator.

1. Arbitration Act (Cap 13) Laws of the Federation of Nigeria and Lagos 1958 Sect. 8(b). Arbitration Law (Cap 10) Laws of the Lagos State of Nigeria 1973 Sect. 8(b).

Comments on Latin America

José Luis Siqueiros

I. THE PRACTICE OF INTERNATIONAL COMMERCIAL ARBITRATION IN LATIN AMERICA

Most of the Latin American nations obtained their political independence from Spain in the first or second decade of the nineteenth century. However, in most cases the greatest part of the Spanish legislation governing civil and commercial law in the old colonies, remained in force.

Along with the old Spanish rules the Latin American legislatures imported from Europe the concept of peaceful settlement of disputes by third party arbitrators. Hence, the use of arbitration to resolve commercial controversies gradually grew into the commercial codes and the codes of civil procedure in all of the Latin American nations. When the Spanish law and the Portuguese legislation (in the case of Brazil) ceased to be applicable, the new legal enactments maintained the old principles and the ancient tradition of allowing the parties to submit judicial cases to amicable settlement by arbitration.

Most of the Codes of Civil Procedure enacted during the second half of the nineteenth century regulated arbitration, allowing that civil and commercial matters, with few exceptions, be settled through an arbitral compromise and the award rendered in accordance to the rules of law or in equity. In these latter cases, the arbitrators were bound by few legal provisions and enjoyed an ample discretion in the conduct of the proceedings. They were also permitted to decide the issues *ex aequo et bono*.

At the VIIth International Conference of American States Meeting held in Montevideo, Uruguay, 1933, a resolution was adopted to establish an interamerican system on arbitration; such systems should not be developed between governments but rather between trade and commercial organizations operating in the different nations. The Conference recommended the respective Chambers of Commerce to draw up and sign a Convention of International Arbitration, similar to the Convention signed in 1916 between the Bolsa de Comercio of Buenos Aires and the United States Chamber of Commerce. Several standards in matters of procedure were laid for this latter purpose. An agency, i.e., the Inter-American Commercial Arbitration Commission came into being. The Commission started functioning in 1934 but its activity languished for three decades until it became strengthened and restructured in 1968. Since then, the IACAC has been acting in a dynamic and productive fashion. The Commission has National Sections in each of the Latin American countries as well as in the United States. Each National Section appoints a delegate to the Commission. The latter, has enacted its rules of procedure adopting these approved by UNCITRAL, including its own fee schedule. It provides a facility for processing demands for arbitration, has a current listing of arbitrators and makes available expertise for conducting the proceedings in the site selected by the parties. The Commission has carried an extensive program of study and education in the realm of arbitration, including the publication of a quarterly newsletter. The Mexican National Section sponsors a school for the training of arbitrators and through the Academy of International Commercial Arbitration (ADACI) has organized nine Symposia for the discussion and updating of matters connected with this subject. The IACAC has received encouragement and financial support from the Organization of American States and from the Inter-American Development Bank. It has set up an efficient relationship with other arbitration centers throughout the world such as the International Arbitration World Trade, the Japan Arbitration Association, the Indian Arbitration Council and the Foreign Trade Arbitration Commission in the USSR.

II. INTERNATIONAL TREATIES

Given the pragmatic realities of the commercial arbitration systems in each of the countries of the Western Hemisphere and recognizing the need to harmonize the existing differences in the local laws and practices, efforts have been made to regulate these matters within international treaties. These endeavours have partially succeeded at the regional and sub-regional areas of the Continent. Almost all of the Latin American countries are bound to one or more international instruments. However, some of these treaties or conventions which were entered into at the late part of the nineteenth century or during the first decades of the twentieth, have become obsolete and superseded by more general and modern instruments like the United Nations Convention of 1958 and the Inter-American Convention of Panama signed in 1975.

For the Latin countries, the principal treaties in the matter of international commercial arbitration are the following:

a. Treaty on International Procedural Law, signed in Montevideo, Uruguay, in 1889 and the similar instrument signed at the same city in 1940. The 1889 treaty was ratified by Argentina, Bolivia, Panama, Peru, Uruguay and Colombia. The second treaty was ratified by Argentina, Paraguay and Uruguay.
b. The Bolivian Convention of the Enforcement of Foreign Awards, signed at Caracas, Venezuela in 1911. This Convention was ratified by Bolivia, Colombia, Ecuador, Peru and Venezuela.
c. The Convention on Private International Law (Bustamante Code), signed at La Habana, in 1928. The Code was ratified by Bolivia, Brazil, Costa Rica, Chile, Cuba, Dominican Republic, El Salvador, Ecuador, Guatemala, Haiti, Honduras, Nicaragua, Panama, Peru and Venezuela.
d. The United Nations Convention on the Recognition and Enforcement and Foreign Arbitral Awards, signed at New York in 1958. This Convention

has been ratified or acceded to by Chile, Colombia, Cuba, Ecuador, Guatemala, Mexico, Panama and Uruguay. Haiti, Trinidad and Tobago and the United States of America are also parties to this Convention in the Western Hemisphere.

e. The Inter-American Convention on International Commercial Arbitration, signed in Panama in 1975. The following Latin American countries have ratified the instrument: Costa Rica, Chile, El Salvador, Honduras, Mexico, Panama, Paraguay, Uruguay and Venezuela.

III. HYPOTHETICAL CASE

1. General Comments

A hypothetical case has been presented by Judge Holtzmann and Professor Bernini to illustrate the various procedural approaches followed in many parts of the world in conducting an international commercial arbitration. The case provides the facts for a comparative examination of typical practices, i.e., elements of procedure that arbitrators have discretion to determine, assuming that such elements are not specified in the national law governing the arbitration or in the arbitration rules agreed by the parties. For this hypothetical case it has been assumed that the parties have agreed upon the UNCITRAL Arbitration Rules, which leave wide areas of procedure for determination by the arbitrators.

Under such premises, the Rapporteurs have answered the sixty-four questions of practice which may arise in arbitrating the contemplated dispute judging from their own experience in different areas of the world. Unfortunately, such premises are not yet present in Latin America. The limited experience obtained in this area is mostly reflected in *domestic* arbitration, for *international* arbitration practice is virtually non-existent. It is true that due to a greater influx of foreign investment, transfer of technology and international contracts, the inclusion of the arbitration clause in the contractual instruments is becoming gradually accepted as a tool to resolve disputes arising between the parties.

However, Latin American Codes of Commerce and Civil Procedure do not specifically deal with international commercial arbitration, although domestic arbitration provisions have been interpreted as applying to the international sphere. There is only one country in the area (Ecuador) that has enacted a specific law on commercial arbitration administered by arbitral institutions (national or international); in the rest of the Latin American countries arbitration is governed by the Codes of Commerce and the Codes of Civil Procedure. Generally speaking, commercial arbitration is on an *ad hoc* basis.

From such factual and legal background it follows that the resort to the UNCITRAL Rules or for that matter to any other rules of procedure auspiced by international arbitration centers is seldom used. However, in those cases where the parties have accepted to arbitrate future disputes in accordance with the rules of procedure of the Inter-American Commercial Arbitration Commission (in the absence of express agreement between the parties) the UNCITRAL Rules will apply.

2. Different Legal Systems in Latin America

There is a widely spread misconception about uniformity in the Latin American legal systems. Without denying the common juridical heritage referred to in the Introduction of the Comments, there are broad differences in the legislation and judicial interpretation of each of the countries of the region in matters affecting arbitration. Aside from the fact that some of the nations are unitary states and others are formed as federal republics, there are a great number of legal divergencies in matters of substance and procedure. Such diversity has been a fertile field for conventions on private international law. However, the process of harmonization and codification has followed a trend toward international agreements on conflict laws rather than reaching legal uniformity. Therefore, although one finds similar patterns in matters related to arbitral procedures in the twenty countries of the region, there are also striking differences arising out of each nation's historical and political experience. While some countries like Brazil and Peru still maintain in their legal thinking that arbitration is a process of judicial nature rather than a contractual one, others, like Chile, Mexico and Panama have shown a more liberal opening to international commercial arbitration. Whereas some of the countries have preferred to accede to regional or sub-regional agreements on this matter, others have expressed their preference to be linked to more universal treaties. Hence, comments on arbitration practices in Latin American can not be defined as *typical* on the area. The remarks on some of the questions posed on the hypothetical case must be construed in the light of the scarce experience obtained in those countries where international arbitration is gradually taking root.

Comments on "Comparative Arbitration Practice" as presented in Four Reports

Tadeusz Szurski

I. The previous comments do not relate to detailed arbitration practice in the whole CMEA region but are rather limited to arbitration practice which may be expected in arbitrations held in Poland.

The comments are based on arbitration practice which may be expected on the part of arbitrators acting within the frame of the Court of Arbitration at the Polish Chamber of Foreign Trade. Such practice can be considered to a certain extent as representative for Polish arbitrators' practice, since arbitrators from the panel of the Court of Arbitration at the Polish Chamber of Foreign Trade most often act also as arbitrators in *ad hoc* arbitrations organized in the Polish People's Republic. Of course the reservation should be made that the approach of individual arbitrators may well be quite divergent, particularly depending on the circumstances of a case.

The present commentator does not expect that arbitration practice in other CMEA countries than Poland will deviate to a great extent from the Polish arbitrators' practice or from that as described in the Report of Professor Lebedev. The reservation of possible deviations should be made, however.

II. Arbitration as a way of settlement of disputes is very widely used in the international commercial relations of economic organizations of countries belonging to the Council of Mutual Economic Assistance. According to the Moscow Convention 1972, arbitration is the exclusive way of settlement of disputes in mutual relations between these organizations.

Arbitration practice in the CMEA Countries as regards the sphere of international commercial relations is based on the laws and regulations concerning arbitration. In this regard one has to distinguish:

a. general laws on arbitration, and – more important for international commercial relations –
b. arbitration rules of permanent arbitral institutions at Chambers of Commerce in these countries.

In most CMEA countries, general rules on arbitration are contained in the Codes of Civil Procedure. It is only in Czechoslovakia and GDR that there are special legislative acts relating to arbitration in international trade.

The general law on arbitration applies first of all to arbitrations *ad hoc* which, however, in most CMEA countries take place rather seldom.

Almost all arbitration disputes held in countries belonging to the Council of

Mutual Economic Assistance are decided by courts of arbitration or arbitration commissions attached to the Chambers of Commerce in these countries. With the exception of the Maritime Arbitration Commission at the USSR Chamber of Commerce and Industry, which Commission has its own, original Rules of Arbitration, the activities of all these courts or commissions are subject to the rules which are based on CMEA Uniform Arbitration Rules, and as such are similar to one another. As one of the most essential differences among these Rules, one can mention that some of them, namely these of Hungarian and Romanian arbitration courts, provide for the supplementary application of civil procedure laws. Similar provisions do not exist in the Arbitration Rules of arbitration courts or commissions in other countries.[1]

For deciding economic disputes between organizations of the CMEA Countries, the Moscow Convention 1972 provides for the rule of exclusive competence of the arbitration court or commission in the country of the defendant party, unless the parties explicitly agree that the dispute will be settled in the court or arbitration or arbitration commission at the Chamber of Commerce of another member country of the Moscow Convention 1972.

In Poland, beside the Court of Arbitration at the Polish Chamber of Foreign Trade, which has, by far, the predominant share of general practice in the sphere of international trade, there are three other, more specialized, courts of arbitration, all with the seat in Gydnia, namely

- The International Court of Arbitration for Marine and Inland Navigation,
- The Court of Arbitration of the Cotton Association,
- The Court of Arbitration at the Gdynia Wool Federation,

all having their own arbitration rules.

The Court of Arbitration at the Polish Chamber of Foreign Trade consists of approximately 80 arbitrators, the 5 members of the Presidium and the Secretariat, all arbitrators being of Polish nationality.

Beside the Rules of 1975 based on CMEA Uniform Arbitration Rules, which Rules apply in Poland exclusively to arbitrations based on the Moscow Convention 1972,[2] the Court of Arbitration at the Polish Chamber of Foreign Trade has still two other separate sets of Rules, namely:

1. The Rules of 1970, which, being of general application, in international commercial relations, apply first of all to disputes in which the competence of that Court arises out of an arbitration agreement; in other words – to disputes where at least one of the parties does not come from a country belonging to the Moscow Convention 1972. On the other hand these Rules also supplement the above-mentioned Rules of 1975 in points, where the latter contain no regulation.

1. However, such provision is also contained in the Rules of the Court of Arbitration of the Cotton Association in Gdynia and of the Court of Arbitration at the Gdynia Wool Federation, as mentioned hereunder.

2. For information about the Moscow Convention 1972 and CMEA Uniform Arbitration Rules see: Prof. Heinz Strohbach: "General Introduction" in *Yearbook Commercial Arbitration*, Vol I (1976) p. 4 and *International Handbook on Commercial Arbitration*, Supp. V, May 1986.

2. Rules for *ad hoc* arbitrations administered by the Court of Arbitration at the Polish Chamber of Foreign Trade (of 1985). These Rules can be accepted in arbitration agreements (arbitration clauses included) by the parties from any country, to constitute the basis for settlement of disputes by *ad hoc* arbitral tribunals taking place in Poland.[3]

Subject to modifications, if introduced by the parties, the Rules assure for *ad hoc* arbitrations taking place in Poland, all necessary administrative services by the Secretariat of the Court of Arbitration at the Polish Chamber of Foreign Trade as well as the services of the President of that Court to act as the appointing authority. In case the parties do not agree otherwise, the Rules provide that the UNCITRAL Arbitration Rules shall apply to the arbitral proceedings.

Mention should be made that these Rules can apply to any *ad hoc* arbitral tribunal independent of the nationality of the arbitrators.

My comments relate only to those questions where the practice in the commentator's country is different from that described in all the Reports or as to which special information or emphasis seems to be useful for outsiders who arbitrate in Poland.

The way of presentation is similar to that as in the Reports. Although the replies (like the questions) may relate to the hypothetical case prepared by Judge H. M. Holtzmann and Prof. G. Bernini, they have been presented in a way as to show the practice or understanding which may be expected to be encountered in any arbitration when the country of arbitration will be the commentator's country and Polish arbitrators will have a decisive influence on the procedure.

V. CONCLUSION BY JUDGE HOLTZMANN AND PROFESSOR BERNINI

The answers to the questions of the hypothetical case given by the distinguished Rapporteurs and Commentators and in the written communications and oral interventions by the participants in the Working Group make a unique contribution to facilitating the conduct of international commercial arbitration. This comparative analysis indicates that there has been a gradual internationalization of practice, that traditionally sharp lines of division between legal systems are yielding to a process of harmonization, that there are now more basic similarities than differences, and – most importantly – that all systems share the mutual goal of achieving worldwide arbitral justice.

3. Section 2 of these Rules contains a recommended arbitration clause providing for their application.

List of Written Communications to Working Group I

William M. Barron, Esq.,
"Court Ordered Consolidation of Arbitration Proceedings in the United States" Stanton P. Belland
"Arbitration under Civil Law Concepts"
Giuseppe Mirabelli
"Answers to the Questions of the Hypothetical Case from the Point of View of an Arbitration in Italy"
Giorgio Recchia
"Answers to the Questions of the Hypothetical Case from the Point of View of an Arbitration at the Italian Arbitration Association"
Guilio Rosauer
"Judgments Rendered by Italian Courts, in the Light of the New York Convention, on Arbitration Agreements by Reference"
Michele Savarese
"Communication Submitted to the VIIIth International Arbitration Congress, New York City – May 6–9, 1986"
Peter F. Schlosser
"Right and Remedy in Common Law Arbitration and in German Arbitration Law"
D. C. Singhania
"International Commercial Arbitration. Indian Law and Procedure"
Michael Straus
"The Practice of the Iran–US Claims Tribunal in Receiving Evidence from Parties and from Experts: Questions 32–34 and 38–39"
S. C. Nirwani
"International Arbitration Movement. Comparative Arbitration System and Public Policy"

List of Oral Interventions to Working Group I

Questions 1–5

John W. Combs (Canada)
Charles Poncet (Switzerland)
Gino Lörcher (FR Germany)
Peter Hafter (Switzerland)
John Tackaberry (UK)
Lateef Adegbite (Nigeria)
Satya Kar Roy (India)
John Christmann (Canada)
Khalil Malouf (Greece)
Cedric Barclay (UK)
P. G. Lim (Malaysia)

Questions 6–13

Pierre Bellet (France)
J. C. Seth (India)

Questions 14–16

Paul Mitsem (Norway)
Peter Hafter (Switzerland)
Peter Schlosser (FR Germany)
J. Sorton Jones (USA)

Questions 17–19

John W. Combs (Canada)
Charles Molineaux (USA)
Cedric Barclay (UK)
Jean Thieffry (France)

Questions 20–27

Jean Thieffry (France)
E. Neil McKelvey (Canada)
Menno Aden (FR Germany)
James Carter (USA)
Giovanni Ughi (Italy)
Jan Ramberg (Sweden)
Teruo Doi (Japan)
Ljubomir Popov (Bulgaria)

Questions 28–31

Paul Mitsem (Norway)
Peter Hafter (Switzerland)
Peter Schlosser (FR Germany)
J. Sorton Jones (USA)

Questions 32–34

Paul Mitsem (Norway)
Paul Meurs-Gerken (Denmark)
Mauro Rubino-Sammartano (Italy)
Gerold Herrmann (Austria)
Michael Straus (USA)
Cedric Barclay (UK)
Giovanni Ughi (Italy)
Gerhardt Bubnik (Czechoslovakia)
Anghelos Foustoucos (Greece)
Gerald Geddes (UK)
Mauro Ferrante (Italy)
Lauren D. Rachlin (USA)

Questions 35–39

Sheldon L. Berens (USA)
Michael Straus (USA)
Laurie Slade (UK)
Michael Marks Cohen (USA)
Charles Beach (USA)
Giorgio Recchia (Italy)

Questions 40–43

None

Questions 44–48

Menno Aden (FR Germany)
Giovanni Ughi (Italy)
Khalil Malouf (Greece)

Questions 49–52

John Christmann (Canada)
Paul Meurs-Gerken (Denmark)

Gino Lörcher (FR Germany)
Peter Hafter (Switzerland)
Jean Pierre Thevenard (France)

Questions 53–57

Paul Mitsem (Norway)
Teruo Doi (Japan)
Jan Ramberg (Sweden)
Menno Aden (FR Germany)
Sheldon L. Berens (USA)

Questions 58–60

Michael Tupman (USA)
Gerhardt Bubnik (Czechoslovakia)
John Tackaberry (UK)
Giorgio Recchia (Italy)
Michael Marks Cohen (USA)
Cedric Barclay (UK)
Mauro Ferrante (Italy)

Question 61–63

Mauro Ferrante (Italy)
Gino Lörcher (FR Germany)
Teruo Doi (Japan)
Paul Mitsem (Norway)
Paul Meurs-Gerken (Denmark)
Richard Meade (France)
J. C. Seth (India)
Cedric Barclay (UK)

Reports
Working Group II
Public Policy in Arbitration

Public Policy and Arbitrability

*Karl-Heinz Böckstiegel**

TABLE OF CONTENTS

* President, Iran–US Claims Tribunal, The Hague, The Netherlands; Holder of the Chair of International Business Law, University of Cologne, FR Germany.

I. SCOPE AND CONCEPT

1. The Issue

Public policy in the context of international arbitration is normally considered from the basis of the New York Convention where it may be a defence against enforcement once the arbitral award is rendered. Thus the issue appears only at the very end of the arbitral procedure. Public policy in relation to arbitrability, however, – although it may still be a defence against enforcement – concerns the very beginning and basis of the arbitration, namely the arbitration agreement or arbitration clause.

Party autonomy and the specific rights of the parties derived therefrom to choose arbitration instead of national courts to settle their commercial disputes are the well known conditions for international commercial arbitration. This is true in spite of the fact that certain specific arbitration procedures are due not to the individual choice of the contractual parties, but to a decision of their respective states, examples being the Iran-United States Claims Tribunal and perhaps also the obligatory jurisdiction of the foreign trade arbitration institutions of the socialist countries for their internal foreign trade disputes. Such exceptions do not concern us in our context, and, therefore, it can be said that the traditional and still today normal international commercial arbitration is not possible without the agreement of the parties. If, therefore, the jurisdiction of the arbitrators can only go as far as the parties by agreement have authorized them, one has to add immediately, that this jurisdiction can also go only as far as the parties *can* authorize them. Limits of party autonomy thereby become limits for the jurisdiction of the arbitrators. The lack of arbitrability is such a limit, and public policy is a specific qualification of that limit.

This placement of our topic in the framework of international commercial arbitration raises both theoretical and practical issues of a more general nature: The relevance of national and regional concepts and laws for international arbitration and the possibility of developing independent international standards are the basic legal policy issues involved. The temptation for national judges to insist on too many of their national standards[1] to the detriment of the advantages of international arbitration and the function of being a net for obvious *ultra vires* conduct of arbitrators are the major practical issues involved.

As this Rapporteur has been asked to report on "Public Policy and Arbitrability", he understands this to be a mandate not to deal either with public policy or arbitrability as such, but only to deal with the limited relevance of both concepts which is characterized by their relation to each other. This paper will therefore concentrate on those aspects of public policy which relate to arbitrability and those aspects of arbitrability which are claimed to be part of public policy.

Nevertheless, to have a common ground of consideration and argumentation, it seems necessary to outline briefly the concepts of public policy and of

1. *See*: Fouchard, *L'Arbitrage Commercial International*, Paris 1965, 354; Bartos, *Internationale Handelsschiedsgerichtsbarkeit*, Frankfurt, 1984, 49.

arbitrability, before the relation between them and its consequences are discussed.

2. *Public Policy*

Right from the outset it should be noted that public policy – the term is used here interchangeably with the term *ordre public*[2] – plays a much greater role in the theory of arbitration than in practice. As a last resort against the application of agreements, rules and awards which otherwise would have to be respected, its abstract role is indeed a fundamental one from the viewpoint of the respective legal system. Although in every state or other community with a separate legal system the codified and uncodified law reflects the basic convictions and values of that community, those responsible for the legal system in the community feel that even the correct application of the law, especially if its conflict of law rules lead to the application of rules created by foreign communities, may hurt standards "so sacrosanct as to require [their] maintenance at all costs and without exception"[3] or, since the notion of public policy in private international law is not always identical to that in the field of arbitration,[4] if a court feels that enforcement of the arbitral award "would violate the forum state's most basic notions of morality and justice."[5]

This description, in addition to the absolutely exceptional character of the principle,[6] indicates the relativity of the very concept of public policy:

First of all, public policy is dependent on the judgment of the respective legal community. What is considered to be part of public policy in one state may not be seen as a fundamental standard in another state with a different economic, political, religious or social, and therefore, legal system. In regard to our topic, what may be considered as an absolutely exclusive domain of national courts in some Latin American countries may be left to party autonomy and arbitration – if the parties so wish – in Western European countries. From this perspective it is also easier to view the widely discussed concept of an "international public

---

2. The interchangeable use of the terms is common practice today though, at the outset and for a long period, "ordre public" was used as a more general term while "public policy" was more used in connection with specific applications of the principle. *See*: Husserl, "Public Policy and Ordre Public", Va.L.Rev 25 (1938) 37; Lloyd, *Public Policy – A Comparative Study in English and French Law*, London 1953; Lagarde, *Recherches sur l'ordre public en droit international privé*, Paris 1959; von Heymann, *Der ordre public in der privaten Schiedsgerichtsbarkeit*, Bielefeld 1969.

3. Cheshire and North, Private International Law, 9th ed., 149f.

4. Stressed *e.g.* by Kornblum, "Grenzfragen des Ordre Public in der privaten Schiedsgerichtsbarkeit", KTS 1968, 143, 155, 157.

5. US Supreme Court 508 F 2d, 974. Or, in the words of the Swiss Supreme Federal Court: ". . . *il faut qu'il s'agisse de la violation des principes fondamentaux de l'ordre juridique suisse, qui heurte de façon intolérable le sentiment du droit*". BGE 96 I 391, Sem.jud. 1971, 247.

6. That public policy can only be applied in absolutely exceptional cases, is also a long and unchanged tradition of the German legal system, started by the Reichsgericht in 1905 (RGZ 60, 296, 300), kept to the very end of that Supreme Court (RGZ 138, 214, 216) and continued by its successor, The Federal Court of Justice (BGHZ 22, 162, 167), although a wider application of *ordre public* has been suggested by some (Kornblum, *op. cit.*, 149; Sachse, "Die Anfechtbarkeit der Schiedssprüche wegen Verletzung des materiellen Rechts", Gruchot 71, 1931, 574, 579).

policy". Insofar as there is a regional or international community or legal system, only its common denominators in values and standards can be the basis for its eventual public policy, and they may obviously differ from those of the individual member states.

A second relativity is introduced by the time factor. The values and standards of communities are not stable, they change and develop. So does public policy since it is derived therefrom. Thus, with regard to arbitration, national public policies have changed over the years, influenced by a number of factors such as national developments in the political and legal system, the involvement of the national economy in international trade, political decisions such as the promotion of foreign investment, or international developments such as the coming into force of the New York Convention, the growing acceptance of arbitration by other states, the growing infrastructure and legal security of international arbitration which has made it more difficult for states to adopt or keep a negative approach to arbitration if they wanted to participate in international trade and investment to the benefit of their countries. Although sometimes concepts of public policy were widened leading to greater restrictions in arbitrability as in certain Islamic countries some years ago,[7] the general trend is clearly that public policy limits to international arbitration in general and to arbitrability in particular have been reduced considerably. The growing acceptance of the doctrine of separability with regard to arbitration clauses in contracts has contributed its share to that development.[8]

If we look not at the trend of development, but at the present point in time, a similar conclusion is possible: in the modern practice of courts and arbitral tribunals, public policy does not seem to be a major obstacle to international arbitration in general and to arbitrability in particular.[9]

At least that can be said for international as distinct from national arbitration. For international arbitration with which this report is only concerned, two aspects, which ought to be distinguished although this is not always done, lead to specific considerations in our context.[10]

First, national public policy may be more liberal regarding arbitration on international contracts than on contracts in internal national relations, since national standards restricting arbitrability have, either due to express reference[11]

7. *See* Böckstiegel (ed.), *Vertragspraxis und Streiterledigung im Wirtschaftsverkehr mit arabischen Staaten*, Vol. 2 of the series of the German Institute of Arbitration, Köln 1981, 61, 95 (Krüger), 101 (Dilger). On the other hand, more recently ratifications of the New York Convention (Kuwait) and changes in the national law (Saudi Arabia) seem to reverse the trend.

8. This has rightly been stressed by Lew in his paper on "Determination of Arbitrators' Jurisdiction and the Public Policy Limitations on that Jurisdiction" to the 1985 Opening Conference of the London School of International Arbitration published in Lew, ed., *Contemporary Problems in International Arbitration*, London 1986, 73.

9. The same experience is reported by Holtzmann in *ICC Court of Arbitration 60th Anniversary*, Paris 1984, 364.

10. *See* in our context: Bartos, *Internationale Handelsschiedsgerichtsbarkei* 43, 51, 54, 60, 66, 71; van den Berg *The New York Arbitration Convention of 1958*, Deventer 1981, 360.

11. *E.g.*, Art. 1502(5) of the new French International Arbitration Law of 1981. On the change brought about thereby, *see* Mezger, in Böckstiegel (ed.), *Schiedsgerichtsbarkeit in Frankreich*, Vol. 3 of the series of the German Institute of Arbitration, Köln 1983, 58.

or due to interpretation by courts,[12] not been applied to international contracts.

And secondly, there is – of course – the growing recognition of a truly "international" public policy. Since a separate report of my esteemed colleague and friend Pierre Lalive will deal with this topic at this conference, there is no need to discuss it here in any detail. But it must be noted that also with regard to arbitrability, this notion of international public policy – insofar as it can be considered as existing not only *de lege ferenda* but *de lege lata* – is relevant and, in fact, further reduces the limits of public policy to arbitration agreements. In this respect, the Emperor does not have "the same old clothes".[12a]

3. *Objective Arbitrability and Capacity as Subjective Arbitrability*

As said before, it cannot be the purpose of this paper to deal generally with arbitrability as such, its regulation in national laws and the different methodological approaches found there.[13] It should be noted in our context, however, that the traditional notions of arbitrability and capacity, as well as the dogmatic distinction between both, may need some reconsideration. The seemingly clear dividing line between both is that "arbitrability" answers the question *what* can be arbitrated and that "capacity" answers the question *who* can arbitrate. Although it may satisfy the desire for dogmatic clarity to consider and treat both as different animals, dogmatic distinctions can, however, only be accepted as a reason for differences in the application of law if they are found to reflect different functions in the law. It is doubtful, however, whether this is so in all cases between arbitrability and capacity. The final effect for the arbitration agreement and for the arbitration procedure is identical: the arbitration agreement is invalid and the arbitrators lack jurisdiction if either one of the two is missing. In regulating arbitrability on the one hand and capacity on the other hand, different means are employed to regulate the same question, namely whether arbitration is to be an accepted method of dispute settlement or not. If the term "arbitrability" is seen as answering that question, also regulating what is commonly understood as "capacity" is in fact a regulation of arbitrability by subjective criteria, namely by criteria connected with the parties in arbitration. And even if one wishes to stick to the traditional restricted concept of "arbitrability" as excluding such subjective criteria, one will have to admit that such objective arbitrability and capacity supplement each other, and that a realistic answer to the basic questions at stake, whether the arbitral agreement is valid and whether arbitration is admissable, can only be given if both aspects are

12. *E.g.*: In France: *Trésor public* c. *Galakis*, JCP 1966, 14 798. In the United States: *Scherk* v. *Alberto Culver Co.*, 417 US 506 (1974); *Mitsubishi* v. *Soler*, 53 LW 5069 (1985).

12a. *See* the opposite conclusion by Corr with regard to modern choice of law and public policy in University of Miami Law Review 39 (1985) 647.

13. *See also* the introduction to Section III (2) of this paper. For a more general presentation on arbitrability, a comparative presentation of national laws and an analysis of methodology, *see, e.g.* Charpentier, *L'arbitrabilité des differends internationaux*, Paris, 1967; Sareika, *Die Gültigkeit von Schiedsgerichtsvereinbarungen nach kanadischem und deutschem Recht*, 1975, 100, 130; Schlosser, *Das Recht der internationalen privaten Schiedsgerichtsbarkeit*, Tübingen 1975, 274; van den Berg, *The New York Arbitration Convention of 1958*, 368; von Hülsen, *Die Gültigkeit von internationalen Schiedsvereinbarungen*, 1973, 117.

examined. And the same connection is relevant for the legislator. If he wishes to prohibit arbitration for certain categories of disputes, he may employ either objective or subjective criteria. And although these two types of criteria may not always be available interchangeably, e.g., for the protection of minors one can only use subjective criteria and for the exclusion of certain antitrust matters only objective criteria may be available, they are used by legislators and considered in the practice of international arbitration in connection with each other. A most important example is the submission to arbitration by states and state institutions which makes up a growing portion of international commercial arbitration in general and, e.g., more than one quarter of the disputes submitted to ICC arbitration. As will be seen later when this paper deals with this category of disputes in more detail, legislators, national courts and international arbitrators by no means simply apply conflict of law and substantive rules on capacity to those disputes, but rather a mixture of subjective and objective criteria to answer the question whether international commercial arbitration is admissable or limited by public policy.

In order to receive a complete picture of the impact of public policy on arbitrability and in order to avoid misleading conclusions on the admissability of arbitration, it is therefore suggested that in our context the subjective criteria connected with arbitrability cannot be excluded. Although this may mean a widening of a traditional dogmatic concept, it should be noted that the consequences for our field of international commercial arbitration are not dramatic, because most limitations of capacity such as those for minors or other natural persons incapable of disposing have no practical relevance in this field. On the other hand, for those areas where, in fact, public policy is relevant for admissibility of international commercial arbitration, it is considered necessary to deal with arbitrability based both on objective and subjective criteria.

Therefore, in order to see public policy and arbitrability in their full context, it must be seen that public policy can lead to limitations or lack of arbitrability in two ways.[14] Most commonly one will think in this context of certain fields of law or kinds of disputes which by their subject matter are excluded from arbitration and reserved for state courts such as certain antitrust matters. In this category, what is lacking, may be called "objective arbitrability". For, there is a second category where not the object of the dispute, but the subject involved leads to the same effect, namely that the dispute cannot be settled by arbitration. In the context of international commercial arbitration that concerns us here, this "subjective arbitrability" or "capacity" to submit to arbitration may be lacking especially for states or certain state institutions on the basis of national laws.

Both with regard to objective and to subjective arbitrability the exclusion of arbitration as a means for settling disputes may be considered of such fundamental importance that it becomes part of public policy of the applicable law.

Less perhaps in the theory, but certainly in the practice of legislators and

14. For the same twofold approach *see e.g.*: in French law Motulsky, *Etudes et Notes sur l'Arbitrage*, Paris 1965, 54, 60; Lew's Report on capacity and the arbitration involving an Ethiopian city corporation, *Applicable Law in International Commercial Arbitration*, Dobbs Ferry 1978, 548.

courts, arbitrability and its limitations are strongly influenced by the extent of control of arbitral awards by courts. If legislators or courts feel that certain factual or legal aspects of commercial contractual relationships involve a public interest and should, therefore, not be left entirely to the disposal of private parties and their arbitration, in order to achieve the necessary influence of the state, they can either exclude arbitrability or provide for control of awards by state courts. From the legal policy consideration at stake, both methods, furthermore, are not necessarily alternatives, but are in a relationship to each other[15] to the effect that a more liberal approach to arbitrability may induce a less liberal approach to control of awards. As will be seen later in this paper, e.g., with regard to European Community or national antitrust law – this relationship has come into play more and more.

4. Relation between Public Policy and Arbitrability

In the context of the New York Convention it seems to be generally accepted that arbitrability forms part of the general concept of public policy and that, therefore, Article V(2)(a), which mentions objective arbitrability separately from public policy which is mentioned in Article V(2)(b), can be deemed to be superfluous.[16] Although it may be true that it is for historical reasons that the Convention mentions them in separate sections,[17] the distinction as such does not seem superfluous to me. Legal rules restricting arbitrability need not necessarily be part of public policy. It may well be that such restrictions, be they incorporated in the private or public law of a state, only have to be applied by arbitrators or courts if they form part of the law applicable to the dispute, but need not be considered as being so fundamental that they are part of the public policy of the state with the effect of having to be applied even if another law is applicable to the dispute. Thus, although rules limiting arbitrability will always be meant as mandatory rules not subject to change by party autonomy, it is important to note, since this is not always seen, that mandatory rules are not necessarily identical with public policy rules. Public policy requires further additional qualifications.

Every public policy rule is mandatory, but not every mandatory rule forms part of public policy.[18] This distinction may also become relevant with regard to arbitrability. And indeed, some of the restrictive interpretations of public policy

15. Already stressed by Schlosser, *Das Recht der internationalen privaten Schiedsgerichtsbarkeit*, 274.
16. Sanders, "The New York Convention", in *International Commercial Arbitration* Vol. II, The Hague 1960, 293, 323; Klein, Revue Suisse de Jurisprudence 57 (1961) 229, 249; Schwab, *Schiedsgerichtsbarkeit*, 3rd ed., Munich 1979, 427; van den Berg, *op. cit.* 360.
17. The distinction appeared in the Geneva Convention of 1927, The ICC Draft Convention of 1953 and the ECOSOC Draft Convention of 1955 and was kept by the New York Convention without discussion in spite of an objection raised by the French delegate (UN Doc.E/CONF.26/SR.11).
18. In the same sense: Bartos, *op. cit.* 70; Bertheau, *Das New Yorker Abkommen vom 10. Juni 1958 über die Anerkennung und Vollstreckung ausländischer Schiedssprüche*, Diss. Zürich Winterthur 1965, 62; Köhn KTS 1956, 138; Roth, *Der Vorbehalt des Ordre Public gegenüber fremden gerichtlichen Entscheidungen*, 1967, 176. Regarding the relevance of mandatory national law for international arbitration *see also* Böckstiegel "The Relevance of National Arbitration Law for Arbitrations under the UNCITRAL Rules" Journal of International Arbitration 1 (1984) 229.

by arbitral tribunals and courts that we find in regard to certain concrete categories of arbitrability limits mentioned later in this paper, can only be understood on the basis of this distinction, as denying public policy qualification to what are, no doubt, mandatory legal rules. In Austrian law this distinction has been codified. Until 1983, Article 595(6) ZPO permitted a challenge against every domestic arbitral award in breach of mandatory law, while for foreign awards the New York Convention was applicable with the test of public policy.[19] In the new Federal Law of 2 February 1983, Article 595(6) permits setting aside not on the basis of any mandatory rule, but only if the award "infringes mandatory provisions of the law, the application of which cannot be set aside by a choice of law of the parties . . . ," a change intended to generally exclude those mandatory rules which are not part of public policy.[19a]

To avoid further misunderstanding, attention should also be drawn to the distinction between public policy and public law. In most national legal systems public law will typically be mandatory, but, by no means, also thereby automatically part of public policy. This is especially obvious for more technical rules of public law which do not reflect fundamental principles, but are only mandatory for reasons of legal efficiency.

5. *Applicable Law*

Agreement on the conclusion that there is disagreement seems to be the only common denominator that one can find between arbitrators, courts and publicists regarding the question which is the applicable law on arbitrability.[20] Although a detailed evaluation is not possible within the limits of this paper, at least a short summary of the state of law and practice seems necessary.

Objective arbitrability is considered to be subject to the law found applicable either to the arbitration agreement,[21] or to the main contract,[22] or to both,[23] or to the procedure of arbitration,[24] or to the subject-matter in question.[25] Subjective arbitrability is normally found to be subject to the law of the respective party, but sometimes also to international legal principles.[25a]

---

19. Fashing, *Schiedsgericht und Schiedsverfahren im österreichischen und im internationalen Recht*, Vienna 1973, 153.

19a. Art. 595(6) includes a reference to Art. 35 of the International Private Law Act, which permits choice of law, but subject to limits thereof such as those of Art. 6 (Public Policy) of the same Act. *See also* Melis, *A Guide to Commercial Arbitration in Austria*, Vienna, 2nd ed. 1983, p. 25.

20. For a general presentation *see* Lew, *Applicable Law in International Commercial Arbitration*, 531, 557, 560.

21. *See, e.g.*, Goldman, *Recueil des Cours* 1963 II 468.

22. *See, e.g.*, Batiffol, *Annuaire de l'Institut de droit international* 1952 I 489.

23. *See, e.g.*, Mezger, Rabels Z 29 (1965) 289.

24. *See, e.g.*, Sanders, NTIR 1956, 220.

25. *See, e.g.*, Lalive, *Recueil des Cours* 1967 I 602.

25a. *See* Lew, *op. cit.* 548, and *Benteler* v. *Belgian State*, Arbitration Award of 18 Nov. 1983, French original in Journal des Tribunaux, Brussels 1984, 230, English translation in Journal of International Arbitration 1984, 184.

Insofar as international arbitration conventions are applicable, we do receive some guidance.

The Geneva Convention for the Execution of Foreign Arbitral Awards of 1927 provides in Article 1(2) that, in order for the award to be recognized, the submission to arbitration must be valid under the law applicable thereto (a) and the subject matter must be capable of settlement by arbitration under the law of the enforcement state (b). Thus a test of arbitrability seems to be required on the basis of both laws.[26]

The New York Convention of 1958,[27] in Article V(1)(a), requires validity of the arbitration agreement "under the law to which the parties have subjected it or, failing any indication thereon, under the law of the country where the award was made" and in Article V(2)(a) permits refusal of recognition and enforcement, if "the subject matter of the differences is not capable of settlement by arbitration under the law of that country", i.e., the law of the enforcement state. Article V(2)(b) also makes the law of the enforcement state applicable to the test of public policy.[28]

The Geneva European Convention on International Commercial Arbitration of 1961, which of course has a wider scope than only recognition and enforcement of awards, contains a more detailed and sophisticated codification. It provides in Article VI(2):

> "In taking a decision concerning the existence or the validity of an arbitration agreement, courts of Contracting States shall examine the validity of an arbitration agreement with reference to the capacity of the parties, under the law applicable to them, and with reference to other questions
> (a) under the law to which the parties have subjected their arbitration agreement;
> (b) failing any indication thereon, under the law of the country in which the award is to be made;
> (c) failing any indication as to the law to which the parties have subjected the agreement, and where at the time when the question is raised in court the country in which the award is to be made cannot be determined, under the competent law by virtue of the rules of conflict of the court seized of the dispute.
> The courts may also refuse recognition of the arbitration agreement if under the law of their country the dispute is not capable of settlement by arbitration."

Finally, for arbitration practice, it is suggested that the arbitrator not restrict himself to merely finding out what is the technically applicable law for him on the basis of the will of the parties, arbitration rules and conflict of law rules. Beyond this legal obligation to apply the law thus found, the arbitrator has at least a moral obligation to give the parties an award which can be expected to stand, both in case of setting aside procedures and in case of enforcement procedures, before national courts. The arbitrator should therefore make every effort possible

---

26. Greminger, *Die Genfer Abkommen von 1923 und 1927, über die internationale private Schiedsgerichtbarkeit*, Winterthur 1957, 55.

27. Regarding the law applicable to arbitrability in this most important convention *see* further: van den Berg, *op. cit.* 369 with further references.

28. Regarding this double test *see e.g.*: Schwab, *Schiedsgerichtsbarkeit*, 342.

to find out and respect also mandatory or at least public policy rules of countries where such court procedures might be expected.

II. PROCEDURAL EFFECTS OF PUBLIC POLICY LIMITS TO ARBITRABILITY

Public policy cannot be examined except in relation to the forum. What is contrary to public policy for the national courts of one country, may be acceptable to those of another country. And for arbitral tribunals, public policy may play a different role altogether. It is, therefore, necessary to outline at least briefly which fora will have to deal with public policy limitations of arbitrability in which procedural contexts.

1. Refusal of Jurisdiction by Arbitral Tribunal

Most of the time it is usual that the defence of public policy limits to arbitrability will be initially raised before the arbitral tribunal. The respondent party will object to the arbitrators' jurisdiction by claiming that the arbitral agreement is void because of lack of objective or subjective arbitrability. The arbitrators will have to deal with this objection as a preliminary procedural question. If they find it valid, they will refuse to continue with the arbitration procedure either by an order or award. Otherwise, they may either issue a separate procedural decision accepting their jurisdiction or simply continue in the arbitration procedure and then issue a formal decision on their jurisdiction in their final award.

In this context, the arbitrators' *Kompetenz-Kompetenz*, i.e., their authority to decide on their own jurisdiction, has been questioned. Indeed, it can be argued that, since the arbitrators' authority can solely be derived from the arbitration agreement of the parties, if that arbitration agreement is void due to lack of objective or subjective arbitrability, there is no longer any basis for any decision of the arbitrators. The doctrine of "separability", which has been discussed as dealing with this difficulty,[29] does not seem to be relevant: it can only establish the competence of the arbitrators if the entire contract is void and thereby also the arbitration clause. In our context, however, the situation is different, since a lack of arbitrability is a direct defect of the arbitration clause. Even on the basis of separability, one could, therefore, only conclude that the rest of the contract remains unaffected and valid, exactly the opposite situation to the one where that doctrine establishes an unaffected jurisdiction of the arbitrators. It is, therefore, rather for practical reasons and respect for the will of the parties, if, nevertheless, one accepts also the *Kompetenz-Kompetenz* of the arbitrators on arbitrability.

Similar problems arise with the solution – often found in contractual practice – of establishing the *Kompetenz-Kompetenz* of the arbitrators by an express provision

---

29. Lew in his paper to the 1985 Opening Conference for the London School of International Arbitration, published in Lew, ed., *Contemporary Problems in International Arbitration*, 75.

in an *ad hoc* arbitration clause or in the rules of arbitration institutions. Article 8(3) of the ICC Arbitration Rules provides the most commonly used example:

> "Should one of the parties raise one or more pleas concerning the existence or validity of the agreement to arbitrate, and should the Court be satisfied of the *prima facie* existence of such an agreement, the Court may, without prejudice to the admissibility or merits of the plea or pleas, decide that the arbitration shall proceed. In such a case any decision as to the arbitrator's jurisdiction shall be taken by the arbitrator himself."

First of all, this clause clarifies the competence between the ICC Court of Arbitration and the arbitrator to the effect that the latter decides on his own competence. If the plea of a party concerns arbitrability, it may still be agreed that such a clause cannot establish the competence of the arbitrators since, just like the arbitration clause itself, also such an express authorization clause cannot be valid if arbitrability is lacking, because the parties in such a case do not have the legal power to authorize the arbitrators. On the other hand, if a party, after signing an arbitration clause and even accepting such an express authorization clause, then raises the defence of non-arbitrability, this may well be rejected by the arbitrators as a *venire contra factum proprium* or by similar legal argument. The question whether in such a case non-arbitrability should be even considered as a part of public policy, can only be relevant under two possible conditions: either the public policy must be part of the law to be applied by the arbitrators, or it must be part of the law to be applied in an annulment procedure or enforcement procedure by national courts so that the procedural effects discussed hereafter come into play.

2. *Acceptance of a Claim by National Courts in Spite of Arbitration Agreement*

A public policy limitation of arbitrability may also be the reason for the decision of one of the parties to submit its claim directly to the national courts in spite of an arbitration clause. Then this national court will accept jurisdiction over the claim and overrule the defence raised by the other party on the basis of an arbitration agreement, if the public policy of the law of the state to which the court belongs excludes arbitrability for the claim in question.

In this context, however, it may be of importance that the contract or the arbitration are international in character, because state courts may apply different standards for those. For, as already mentioned above under I., national public policy, either in codified law or in interpretation by the courts, may have different and more liberal standards of arbitrability in regard to international contracts and disputes.

3. *Decision by Court on Invalidity of the Arbitration Agreement*

In some countries, such as the United Kingdom,[30] a party claiming that the

30. *See* Mustill and Boyd, *The Law and Practice of Commercial Arbitration in England*, London 1982, 514.

arbitration agreement is void because of public policy limitations of arbitrability may apply for a declaratory decision by the national courts to that effect. A party may choose to do so in order to clarify a dispute on this issue with the other contractual party on the procedure for dispute settlement, or to prepare for a court dispute on this issue in another country, be it in view of a setting aside or an enforcement procedure.

Vice versa, in some countries, such as the United States,[31] if one contractual party refuses to participate in an arbitration procedure on the ground of an alleged public policy limitation of arbitrability, the other party may apply to the courts for a decision ordering that party to submit to arbitration.

4. Setting Aside of Arbitral Award

While the criteria and chances are quite different, all national legal systems provide for some kind of annulment procedure against arbitration awards. And although the growing acceptance of arbitration has led to a reduction of the possible grounds for such a procedure to few and very basic faults, in most countries, public policy limitations of arbitrability are generally accepted in national laws as a ground for the setting aside of arbitral awards. The best illustration of this common denominator is the Model Law on International Commercial Arbitration elaborated by the United Nations Commission on International Trade Law (UNCITRAL). Article 34(2) of the Model Law provides:

> "An arbitral award may be set aside by the Court specified in article 6, only if
> (a) the party making the application furnishes proof that:
> (i) a party to the arbitration agreement referred to in article 7 was under some incapacity, or the said agreement is not valid under the law to which the parties have subjected it or, failing any indication thereon, under the law of this State; . . .
> (b) the Court finds that:
> (i) the subject-matter of the dispute is not capable of settlement by arbitration under the law of this State; or
> (ii) the award is in conflict with the public policy of this State."

Thus – as this Rapporteur knows from his own participation in this UNCITRAL work[32] – the Model Law purposely uses a wording nearly identical to that contained in the New York Convention in Article V as a ground for refusal of recognition and enforcement of arbitral awards. For the sake of conformity and consistency in this important matter, one has accepted that a certain duplication also appears in the Model Law: lack of objective arbitrability is covered by paragraph (b)(i), but may also fall under the second alternative of (a)(i) as well as under (b)(ii). Lack of subjective arbitrability is covered by (a)(i), but may also fall under the second alternative of (a)(i) as well as under (b)(ii), if public policy is involved.

31. US Arbitration Act of 1925, Section 4.
32. This Rapporteur presented the International Law Association in the UNCITRAL working group.

5. *Refusal of Recognition and Enforcement of Arbitral Awards*

Finally, public policy limitations of arbitrability may have the procedural effect that, on application of a party, national courts refuse the recognition and enforcement of the arbitral award.

Such a refusal was provided for in the Geneva Convention of 1927 (Art. 1(2)(e)). However, today, and in our context of international commercial arbitration, the most important source of law for this effect is the New York Convention on the Recognition and Enforcement of Foreign Arbitral Awards of 1958. This is so both in view of the great number of states that have ratified the Convention and also because on no other aspect of our topic do we have such a body of court decisions and literature. This, and especially the most comprehensive reporting and collection of court decisions and commentaries in the *Yearbooks Commercial Arbitration*[33] make it impossible, but also unnecessary, to go into details in this limited frame of this paper.

Article V of the New York Convention provides a wording almost identical to that cited above from Article 34 of the Model Law, so that it does not seem necessary to remind the reader thereof. Lack of objective or subjective arbitrability and, especially, if forming part of public policy, may fall under the alternatives mentioned in Article V(1)(a), (2)(a) and (2)(b). Nevertheless – in comparison with Article 34 of the Model Law – a slightly different scope of applicability of the same wording may result from the fact that the New York Convention, by its very title dealing with "foreign arbitral awards", defines them in its Article 1 quite differently from the Model Law which, by its title, deals with "international commercial arbitration" and then provides in its Article 1 a definition of which arbitration is "international". The definition of "international" was long disputed in the UNCITRAL work and also in its final version differs widely from the New York Convention. The Rapporteur, although tempted to do so, will not go into the details of these differences except to point out that this difference in the scope of applicability will also have its relevance for the interpretation of Article 36 of the Model Law which provides the grounds for refusing recognition or enforcement under the Model Law in language almost identical to Article V of the New York Convention.

As far as the New York Convention is concerned, courts and authors have concluded that, in view of its applicability only to "foreign" arbitral awards, both limitations of arbitrability and public policy should be interpreted in a more restrictive sense than they might be in regard to domestic awards, thus accepting arbitration in cases which would have been considered non-arbitrable had they been domestic ones. Though this resumée is beyond doubt, the method of arguing and the denomination – especially whether one accepts a separate "international" public policy – is found to differ widely. A detailed analysis would go beyond the limited function of this paper.

33. *See* for further references the Consolidated Table of Court Decisions and Commentaries on the New York Convention in the most recent *Yearbook Commercial Arbitration* Vol. X (1985) p. XXVI. In addition reference may be made to: van den Berg, *op. cit.*, and Gaja, *International Commercial Arbitration – New York Convention*, New York 1978–1980.

III. AREAS WITH LIMITATIONS OF ARBITRABILITY

1. Regulation in International Instruments

We have already seen that international instruments – such as the Geneva Protocol and the New York Convention – may include references to limitations of arbitrability and public policy and provide for certain consequences where they apply to an arbitration agreement or an award. When we now try to describe major areas with such limitations, before one gets to national law, an obvious question is whether in international conventions or other instruments we find provisions to the effect that certain areas are not arbitrable.

As neither the Geneva Protocol or Geneva Conventions nor the New York Convention contain such provisions, suggestions have been made to amend the latter by a list of non-arbitral subject matters for each member state or even by such a list generally valid for all member states as an annex or a new convention.[34] But these suggestions have never been taken up, and rightly so, because it seems indeed unrealistic that one could achieve a well defined workable list to deal with the wide variety of different situations occurring and acceptable by all or most member states in spite of all the differences found in different national systems.

It is therefore only in a few exceptional cases that we find some guidance in international instruments.

a. European Community

The Treaties creating the European Communities (EC) as well as regulations issued by its organs contain a number of provisions with direct applicability to individuals and enterprises in the member states and their contracts. When such contracts contain arbitration clauses, the question arises to what extent the arbitrators may – or perhaps even must – decide the matter. One will have to distinguish different aspects of the question.

On the one hand, there can be no doubt that, if the arbitrator has jurisdiction, EC law may be part of the law to be applied by the arbitrator, just as he applies a national law which he finds applicable and relevant, be it part of private law or of public law. He will of course only have to apply those parts of EC law that do not only create obligations of the member states in public international law, but have direct effect on the parties and their contracts either due to the direct legislative power of the Economic Community or due to their indirect incorporation into the national law by the states (Art. 189 EEC Treaty).

But prior thereto arbitrability has to be established, and it is there that problems arise. Although these problems were widely discussed, they were not solved by a resolution adopted in Rotterdam 1966 by a majority at the 2nd ICCA arbitration conference. The resolution said:

34. Nestor, Report to UNCITRAL, *UNCITRAL Yearbook* Vol. III (1972) p. 193, 244 (UN Doc. A/CN. 9/64 paragraph 172). See also the comments by Chavanne at the ICCA Interim Meeting in Vienna 1976, in: *Schiedsgerichtsbarkeit und Gewerblicher Rechtsschutz*, (Arbitration and Transfers of Patents, Know How, Trademarks and Similar Rights for Promoting International Industrial Cooperation) Vienna 1976, 17.

"... Subject to the exclusive jurisdiction granted to the Community authorities, it falls to the arbitrators seized of disputes involving community law, to verify their authority and to decide on the merits of Community public policy under the control of the appropriate authorities."[35]

The discussion[36] has continued after that resolution and it would not be fair to the disputants to say that a clear solution has yet emerged. Arbitration practice as well, limited as it is, has not been consistent. Some arbitrators have refused arbitrability and thereby their own jurisdiction right at the outset,[37] others have fully examined questions of EC law and awarded on the merits of the case.[38] A worldwide ICCA Congress outside Europe does not appear to be the right forum nor does this paper offer the frame to continue in detail discussions on issues of EC law. But at least a few comments may be permitted in the context of our topic.

There is a good reason to approach the issues of arbitrability and public policy in EC law similarly as in national law.[39] First, those parts of EC law that can become relevant in international commercial arbitration are of a type we also find in national laws; in fact, they often replace or supplement national law. This is especially true for the most debated area, namely EC antitrust law (Art. 85 EEC Treaty and regulations issued on that basis). And second, for disputes in international commercial arbitration, the alternative jurisdiction to that of the arbitrators and the forum for the procedural effects mentioned above in Section II of this paper is not the European Court of Justice, but national courts, and these will apply their own understanding of public policy which indeed differs between courts of different states, as the above-mentioned discussion as well as this paper show. Such national differences can be accepted from the viewpoint of EC law as long as procedures rest at the disposal of the parties to get a final decision by those organs of the EC, be it the Commission or the European Court of Justice, which the Treaty equips with an exclusive competence on certain issues, e.g., decision on the non-application of Article 85(1) pursuant to Article 85(3) by the Commission or final decisions on the validity and interpretation of Acts of EEC organs pursuant to Article 177 by the European Court of Justice. It should be added that arbitral tribunals are not considered to be eligible for referring questions of EC law to the European Court of Justice under Article 177.[40]

35. Revue de l'Arbitrage 1966 (Spécial), 62.

36. For further references to court decisions and literature *see e.g.*: Cohn, AWD 1966, 432; "Review of the decision of the European Court of Justice 30.6.1966", AWD 1966, 431; Goldman, *Droit commercial européen*, Paris 1970, 352; von Hülsen , RabelsZ 35 (1971) 151; Lew, *op. cit.* 335; Kovar, "Droit communautaire de la concurrence et arbitage", in *Le droit des relations économique internationales, Etudes offertes à Berthold Goldman*, Paris, 109; Mok/Johannes, "Schiedsgerichsbarkeit und EWG-Vertrag", AWD 1965, 181 and further in AWD 1966, 125; Robert, *L'Arbitrage – droit interne – droit international privé*, 5th ed. Paris 1982, 348; Schlosser, *op. cit.* 289; von Wartburg, "Commercial Arbitration and Antitrust Matters in the European Economic Community", Arbitration Journal 21 (1966) 65.

37. Award of 22 July 1964 of a Dutch arbitral tribunal, Arbitrale Rechtspraak No. 524, p. 240 (French in Rev. Arb. 1965, 28).

38. ICC Arbitral Award of 21 Sept. 1966 in Case 1397, reported by Thompson and Derains in Clunet 101 (1974) 878.

39. Similarly: Schlosser, *op. cit.* 292.

40. *Nordsee Nordstern* v. *Mond Nordstern and Busse*, European Court of Justice, Case 102/81, 23 March 1982, ECR 1095.

On the other hand, there remains a substantial area of arbitrability of EC law. The doctrine of separability is also applicable here and therefore the alleged invalidity of a contract due to substantive provisions of EC law such as Article 85(1) does not automatically invalidate the arbitration clause and the jurisdiction of the arbitrators based thereon. The arbitrator thus retains jurisdiction on the validity of the contract and the claim based on it. He, e.g., may decide that the contract is valid either on the basis of Article 85(1) or of a block exemption issued by the Commission pursuant to Article 85(3), since both are part of the applicable law for him. But he may not put himself in the place of the Commission and decide that an exemption would be justified pursuant to paragraph (3), since that is a decision exclusively reserved to the Commission for which there is no arbitrability. However, if and after an arbitrator finds a contract void in application of Article 85(1), a party is not stopped from still applying to the Commission for an exemption pursuant to Article 85(3).

Finally, since a losing party may either apply for setting aside of the award or resist enforcement on the grounds of public policy, even where public policy does not limit arbitrability, since many substantive provisions of EC law, including Article 85, may be considered as either part of the national public policy of the member states[41] or of a separate *ordre public communautaire*, the arbitrator must be extremely careful in respecting EC law and aware that his award runs a greater risk of being successfully challenged if EC law is involved.[42] This may seem a bad compromise solution. But it is the solution coming closest to the intention of the parties who after all by their arbitration clause chose that method of dispute settlement.

b. Other treaties

There are not many other instruments of public international law which provide for a limitation of arbitrability.

One may think of the Convention on the Settlement of Investment Disputes between States and Nationals of other States of 1965 creating ICSID which provides an indirect limitation of arbitrability under that Convention by describing in Article 25(1) the kinds of disputes under the jurisdiction of the Centre. But thereby other ways and machineries of arbitration are not excluded.

Even in Latin America, under the influence of the Calvo Doctrine, traditionally a difficult area for arbitration, while national law mostly does contain certain restrictions, the only international instrument with such restrictions is the Andean Pact between Bolivia, Columbia, Ecuador, Peru, and Venezuela. Its statute provides that all contracts on investments and transfer of technology require registration and authorization by the national authorities and that contractual clauses are inadmissable which withdraw disputes from the

41. This has *e.g.* been recognized by the German Federal Court of Justice, BGH 27.2.1969, ZZP 1971, 203 and BGH 31.5.1972, ZZP 1973, 215.

42. Similarly: Lew, *op. cit.* 342; *Russell on the Law of Arbitration* seems to accept arbitrability, but finds it necessary to inform the Commission (19th ed. 1979, 417).

jurisdicción y competencia nacionales of the host country.[43] This regulation is interpreted to exclude the arbitrability of such contracts by international arbitral tribunals, while it will depend on the national law of the member state whether the arbitrability of such contracts before domestic arbitral tribunals is permitted or not.[44]

The regulation on arbitrability by the 1981 Accords of Algiers between Iran and the United States is of a quite different sort. They provide for exclusive jurisdiction of the Iran–United States Claims Tribunal in The Hague for all claims of nationals of one of the two states against the other state and any counterclaim which arises out of the same contract, transaction or occurrence, if such claims and counterclaims were outstanding on the date of the Accords.[45] The only exception mentioned are contractual clauses specifically providing for the sole jurisdiction of Iranian courts.[46] Thus, by *argumentum a contrario* it must be and has been concluded by the Tribunal that arbitration clauses – a number of such contracts, e.g., provided for ICC arbitration – were overruled by the Accords.[47] This, of course, is not a complete exclusion of arbitrability, but rather a substitution of the chosen arbitration machinery by another.

2. *Regulation in National Laws*

While international regulation of arbitrability is rare, all national legal systems provide for the exclusion of arbitrability with regard to some areas of disputes, often giving such limitations the additional qualification of public policy. The basic consideration behind such regulations is that, in the judgment of the legislator – or sometimes only the courts – of that state, certain subject matters involve so much of a public interest (objective arbitrability) or certain groups of parties in a dispute require so much protection (subjective arbitrability, capacity) that only the courts – sometimes special courts for that area – should have jurisdiction. The implementation methods differ widely between national laws. While, e.g., in Germany one starts from the question of what matters are excluded from private disposition and settlement,[48] French law uses public policy

43. Art. 51(I) of the Statute. Regarding the interpretation *see* Parra-Aranguren, *Codificación del derecho internacional privado en America*, Caracas 1982, 368.

44. Samtleben, RIW 1984, 604.

45. Claims Settlement Declaration Art. II.

46. *Ibid.*

47. *See, e.g.*, Award of 5 Nov. 1982 ITL 8–293–FT (part III) in *Stone and Webster Overseas Group, Inc. and National Petrochemical Company et al.*, 1 Iran–USCTR 274, 279; Award of 13 April 1984 No. 123–283–3 p. 5 in *General Dynamics Corporation et al.* and *The Islamic Republic of Iran et al.* Both Awards considered ICC arbitration clauses as overruled.

48. *See, e.g.*: von Hülsen, *Die Gültigkeit von internationalen Schiedsvereinbarungen*, 121; Schlosser, *op. cit.* 275. In general there is a trend of liberalization in German law, especially by a restricted application of public policy; *see* the most recent analysis by Bartos, *op. cit.* 61, 73 (with further references).

as the central device;[49] English[50] and US[51] law courts as well as publicists take a more pragmatic area by area approach.

For some areas, the exclusion of arbitrability is so obvious that there is no need to go into them and that no one would think of trying to have them arbitrated. Thus, e.g., objective arbitrability is lacking for matters of criminal law and subjective arbitrability is lacking for minors. If this paper now deals with some specific areas where arbitrability is found to be limited, it only takes up those that are of major relevance in the context of international commercial arbitration. In doing so, one reservation must be made: within the limited frame of this paper, no detailed description is possible of the exact legal situation in any particular country. National laws differ widely in their limitations of arbitrability, even where they provide limitations for the same subject matter or group of persons or institutions. What can be done here is only an attempt to draw some common denominators or general characteristics and trends.

a. Antitrust law

The classic area with limited arbitrability, and at the same time one of the most difficult ones, is antitrust law.

Above, in Section III(1)(a) of this paper, we saw that the antitrust law of the European Community, although not entirely excluded from the jurisdiction of arbitrators, is subject to important limitations of arbitrability. With regard to national antitrust law, the basic issue is the same, but the solutions by national legislators and courts differ as their antitrust laws differ.

In some countries we find an express codification on the arbitrability of antitrust matters. An illustration is Section 91 of the German Antitrust Act (GWB). It provides that arbitration agreements or clauses with regard to future disputes on contracts covered by the GWB are void, unless they grant each party the right to start court proceedings instead of arbitration in any given case. This still leaves a wide range of arbitrability on antitrust matters.[52] Arbitration agreements on disputes that already have arisen are binding without the option to go to the courts. And even arbitration agreements on future disputes establish full jurisdiction of the arbitrators if neither party objects; objections in practice will not be and have not been frequent, because they would damage a party's reputation as not sticking to the rules of the game of its branch or industry. With regard to international arbitration, it has been rightly argued[53] that the above restriction of Section 91 does not apply at all to arbitrations covered by the

49. *See, e.g.*: Robert, *L'Arbitrage – droit interne – droit international privé*, 5th ed. 21; Motulsky, *Etudes et Notes sur l'Arbitrage*, 60, 62. On *ordre public international* in Art. 1502 Nr. 5 of the new French International Arbitration Law of 1981 see Mezger, in Böckstiegel (ed.), *Schiedsgerichtsbarkeit* in *Frankreich*.

50. *See, e.g.* Mustill and Boyd, *The Law and Practice of Commercial Arbitration in England*, 117; Russell-Walton, 20th ed.

51. *See, e.g.*: Domke, *The Law and Practice of Commercial Arbitration*, Chicago 1968 with Supplement, Section 12 and American Jurisprudence, Arbitration Section 54.

52. *See*, similarly, Schlosser, *Entwicklungstendenzen in Recht und Praxis der internationalen privaten Schiedsgerichtsbarkeit*, Karlsruhe 1976, 63.

53. Mezger, RabelsZ 29 (1965) 244; Greminger, *Die Genfer Abkommen von 1923 und 1927 über die internationale private Schiedsgerichtsbarkeit*, 9.

Geneva Protocol of 1923 and Convention of 1927, the New York Convention of 1958 or the Geneva Convention of 1961 on arbitration, since these – although not all as clearly as Article 1(1) of the Geneva Protocol of 1923 – do not permit a distinction on arbitrability of future disputes on the one hand and already existing disputes on the other. Furthermore Section 91 GWB contains a separate sentence on export cartels which is interpreted to grant general arbitrability for all such contracts which do not affect the German market. Finally, it should be added that Section 98(II) GWB generally excludes from the applicability of the GWB and thereby also from all limitations of arbitrability all contracts that do not have effects on the German market. The other side of the coin to this wide range of arbitrability in German law is the far reaching control by courts. The Federal Court of Justice has continuously interpreted major rules of antitrust law and the principles of state control thereon to be part of German public policy.[54] Therefore, if a losing party challenges an arbitral award in a setting aside or enforcement procedure by claiming breach of antitrust law, the courts will mostly examine the substance of this objection both factually and legally.

In most countries there is no such express codification on the arbitrability of antitrust matters. The most important example – both in view of the preeminent position of the US in world trade and of the strong influence of US antitrust law on the law of other states – is offered by the law of the United States. It is also presented here in some detail because most recently we have had to register a rather fundamental change in that country. In the United States traditionally the courts have drawn their conclusions from the function and primacy of antitrust law. The traditional position as it still stands at present for domestic arbitration in the United States may perhaps be best illustrated by the summary of the *American Safety* Doctrine[55] given for the non-arbitrability of antitrust matters in the 1983 decision of the US Court of Appeals for the First Circuit in *Mitsubishi Motors Corporation* v. *Soler Chrysler-Plymouth Inc.* where the court said:[56]

> "The reasoning is fourfold: (1) governance of the realm of antitrust law, so vital to the successful functioning of a free economy, is delegated by statute to both government and private parties, the latter being given special incentive to supplement efforts of the former, the work of both being equally the grist of judicial decisions, 391 F.2d at 826; (2) the strong possibility that contracts which generate antitrust disputes may be contracts of adhesion militates against automatic forum determination by contract, id. at 827; (3) antitrust issues are – an understatement – 'prone to be complicated, and the evidence extensive and diverse', id., and, we may add, the economic data subject to rigorous analysis dictated by a growing and increasingly sophisticated jurisprudence, with the subject correspondingly ill-adapted to strength of the arbitral process, i.e., expedition, minimal requirements of written rationale, simplicity, resort to basic concepts of common sense and simple equity; and (4) the notion, suggestive of the proposition that issues of war and peace are too important to be vested in the generals, that decisions as to antitrust regulation of business are too important to be lodged in arbitrators chosen

54. *See, e.g.*, BGHZ 46, 365, 367; BGH 31.5.1972 in Straatmann-Ulmer, *Handelsrechtliche Schiedsgerichtspraxis* A4a Nr.12.
55. *American Safety*, 391 F.2d. 821, pp. 826–827.
56. 723 F.2d. 155 (1983), p. 162.

from the business community that has had no experience with or exposure to our law and values".

The decision of the Court of Appeal then goes on to extend these considerations made in regard to domestic contracts also to apply to international ones[57] and stresses the public policy character of the Sherman Act.[58] But when the case went to the United States Supreme Court, in a widely followed procedure in which the American Arbitration Association and the ICC filed *amicus curiae* briefs urging the arbitrability of antitrust claims arising out of an international commercial relationship, by its decision of 2 July 1985[59] the Supreme Court largely adopted the approach urged in the Association's brief and reversed the decision of the Court of Appeal. Some sections of the decision, when the Supreme Court examines the above four major arguments raised by the Court of Appeal, give rise to speculation as to whether for domestic arbitration a reconsideration is also on its way.[60] But with regard to international arbitration, the decision rather clearly stated the arbitrability of antitrust matters. After confirming the well known decisions in *Scherk* v. *Alberto-Culver Co.*[61] and *The Bremen* v. *Zapata Off-Shore Co.*,[62] the Supreme Court extended that liberal approach in international arbitrability to antitrust matters:

> "*The Bremen* and *Scherk* establish a strong presumption in favor of enforcement of freely negotiated contractual choice-of-forum provisions. Here, as in *Scherk*, that presumption is reinforced by the emphatic federal policy in favor of arbitral dispute resolution. And at least since this Nation's accession in 1970 to the (New York) Convention . . . and the implementation of the Convention in the same year by amendment of the federal Arbitration Act, that federal policy applies with special force in the field of international commerce. Thus we must weigh the concerns of *American Safety* (for non-arbitrability of antitrust matters) against a strong belief in the efficacy of arbitral procedures for the resolution of international commercial disputes and an equal commitment to the enforcement of freely negotiated choice-of-forum clauses".[63]

Then, in going through the four major ingredients of the American Safety doctrine as confirmed by the Court of Appeal, the Supreme Court finds none of them requiring a non-arbitrability of antitrust matters in international commercial arbitration and then concludes that the agreement to arbitrate must also be honored in these matters.

Finally, it is interesting to note that, in its reasoning for arbitrability, the decision uses a similar argument as we have seen it by the German Federal Court of Justice in quite a different legal environment. The Supreme Court says:

57. *Ibid*, at p. 163.
58. *Ibid*, at p. 163–166.
59. Section 4, 53 LW 5069.
60. The Supreme Court even starts out on that examination in saying: "At the outset, we confess to some skepticism of certain aspects of the American Safety doctrine" (p. 5074).
61. 417 US 506 (1974).
62. 407 US 1, 15 (1972).
63. *Ibid*, p. 5074.

"Having permitted the arbitration to go forward, the national courts of the United States will have the opportunity at the award enforcement stage to ensure that the legitimate interest in the enforcement of the antitrust laws has been addressed. The (New York) Convention reserves to each signatory country the right to refuse enforcement of an award where the 'recognition or enforcement of the award would be contrary to the public policy of that country'. . . . While the efficacy of the arbitral process requires that substantive review at the award-enforcement stage remain minimal, it would not require intrusive inquiry to ascertain that the tribunal took cognizance of the antitrust claims and actually decided them".[64]

Although it is not possible, in the limits of this paper, to go into details of arbitrability on antitrust matters in more national laws,[65] the two illustrations of one national system of codification on arbitrability and one, where the courts have developed the standards, as well as what we were able to indicate on EC law, and finally as well the resolution of the 1966 Rotterdam ICCA Conference, all seem to indicate a trend to the effect that, on the one hand, international arbitrability on antitrust matters is more widely accepted, but, as the other side of the coin, awards will face intensive scrutiny by courts in view of the public policy character of major antitrust regulations.

b. Industrial and intellectual property

Another area where limitations of arbitrability are found are disputes on the validity of industrial and intellectual property rights (patents, trademarks, etc.) This topic was the central object of discussion from different national and legal backgrounds at the 1976 ICCA Interim Meeting[66] so that it seems more appropriate here not to repeat a general resumée of the state of law and practice, but to offer some additional comments.

The basic philosophy behind this exclusion is similar to other such areas. Since such rights are established by acts of state in a specific procedure established by each state – or by a group of states as in the case of the European patent – a dispute settlement procedure in which this state is not involved and in which "only" competing enterprises quarrel about the validity of the property right cannot decide with finality. The state which grants the right has also the authority to determine the procedure in which the validity of the right is decided in case of a dispute.

Many states make this clear by express codification establishing an exclusive jurisdiction of the courts or even of special courts on the validity of such rights.[67] But even in countries without such express codification one will normally come to a similar conclusion.[68] A generally binding decision declaring such property rights null and void cannot, therefore, be issued by arbitration, but only by the

64. *Ibid*, p. 5076.
65. *See*, *e.g.*, with further references: von Hülsen, RabelsZ 35 (1971) 132; Kronstein, *Das Recht der Internationalen Kartelle*, 1967, 214.
66. Proceedings ICCA: *Schiedsgerichtsbarkeit und gewerblicher Rechtsschutz*, Vienna 1976.
67. This is *e.g.*, the situation in German law. Regarding the consequences for arbitrability *see*: Schlosser, *op. cit.* 318.
68. For the situation in Anglo-American Countries see: Henderson, in *Proceedings* ICCA, Vienna 1976; *op. cit.* 24.

state authorities or courts, as has been confirmed with regard to trademarks by the Italian Supreme Court in 1978.[69]

But the situation is not quite the same as in antitrust law. There it is exactly the form of cooperation between two or more enterprises which the state wants to control and to restrict, and therefore the state cannot leave the final settlement of disputes thereon to the parties since these parties, vis-à-vis the state, may have a common interest to reduce competition between them, while this common interest runs contrary to the public interest and the interest of third competitors to keep the market forces working. In the case of industrial and intellectual property rights on the other hand we find the opposite situation. For these rights are primarily granted in the interest and for the protection of the holder of such rights, giving him certain privileges in the market to the exclusion of other competitors. If he wishes to dispose of these privileges, he may do so as is done, e.g., in licence agreements. If he can even dispose of the substance of these rights, there is no reason why he could not as well "only" dispose of procedural privileges connected with them. If, therefore, he signs an arbitration clause with another participant in the market, it is difficult to see a relevant public interest why – between those parties to the arbitration agreement – there could not be a final settlement of the dispute on the validity of the right. While such an arbitral award could be binding *inter partes*, it will of course not be binding for the state authorities who have registered the right nor for third competitors because they neither signed the arbitration agreement nor participated in the arbitration procedure. As far as the arbitrators are concerned, it will have to depend on the circumstances of the case whether they choose to interrupt the arbitration procedure in order to get a generally binding decision on the validity of the right from the competent state authorities or courts, or whether they choose to decide on the matter themselves. If, in the latter case, the decision taken in the arbitral award is found to be in conflict with a decision taken at a later stage – e.g., because a third competitor started litigation there – by the competent state authorities or state courts, the result may be that the party that lost in the arbitration procedure – in view of its signing the arbitration agreement – is precluded from relying on the differing court decision in relation to the party that won the arbitration. Even in countries where the exclusive jurisdiction of state courts is established by mandatory law, it is difficult to see a public interest so important that it should be considered as part of public policy, to exclude arbitrability.[70]

We may, therefore, well have cases in this area where mandatory limitations of arbitrability, nevertheless, do not reach the qualification of public policy. With regard to the procedural effect this means that the recognition and enforcement of such an arbitral award could not be refused on the basis of Article V(2)(b) of the New York Convention. Whether a refusal would nevertheless be possible on the basis of Article V(1)(a) or Article V(2)(a) would depend on the circumstances of each case.

---

69. Corte di Cassazione 12 May 1977 in *Scherk* v. *Grandes Marques*, *Yearbook Commercial Arbitration* IV (1979) 289.

70. This conclusion seems to be in line with the reasoning of the Italian Supreme Court mentioned above when it held that the arbitration could proceed on the contractual rights and claims based on the trademarks.

c. Restrictions of foreign trade, exchange and security transactions

Although similar considerations as in antitrust law could be applied, it seems that generally very few cases have had to be decided in practice where foreign trade or foreign exchange restrictions were claimed to exclude arbitrability. Of course, such restrictions are often relevant in international arbitration procedures when one of the parties tries to excuse its non-fulfilment or late fulfilment of deliveries or payments by such restrictions. But then this issue forms part of the merits of the case, and the arbitrators have to decide whether such restrictions are part of the applicable law, or should be applied as part of public law even if the applicable law of the contract is another national law, or should be recognized as a valid excuse under legal formulas like impossibility or *force majeure*.

While these are most important questions for the practice and theory of international commercial arbitration,[71] they have to be seen quite distinct from the issue of arbitrability that concerns us here. They only arise once the arbitrability is established.

There are, however, cases where the defence of public policy was considered against enforcement of awards in this area.

An example with regard to foreign trade restrictions is a case of 1983 before the High Court of Bombay.[72] There, respondent parties, who in spite of an arbitration agreement had not appointed an arbitrator and had not appeared before the arbitration, later contested enforcement of the arbitral award with the argument that the export permit for the delivery ordered had been cancelled and, therefore, the enforcement of the award would be contrary to Indian public policy. The judge did not accept that contention and used an argument of indirect relevance to the question of arbitrability:

> "In the first instance it was open for the respondents to raise this contention before the arbitrator. The contention . . . was open for consideration before the arbitrator. The mere fact that the respondent did not choose to appear before the arbitrator is not sufficient to enable them to claim that this Court should exercise the appellate jurisdiction over the award passed by the arbitrator . . .".

From this it is obvious that the judge took the arbitrability of the matter for granted, since it was exactly the possibility to raise the defence before the arbitrators that made him refuse the contention of public policy.

An example with regard to foreign exchange restrictions[73] is a case recently decided by the Court of Appeal of Perugia, Italy.[74] In that case the Italian Supreme Court had already earlier refused to give a preliminary ruling on the question of jurisdiction pending the arbitral proceedings in New York, as requested by one party who contended that the arbitration clause was void since the future award would be inoperative not being enforceable in Italy due to Italian currency regulations. When later the same contention was raised against

71. *See, e.g.*: Böckstiegel, "The Relevance of National Arbitration Law for Arbitrations under the UNCITRAL Rules", Journal of International Arbitration 1 (1984) 223.
72. Decision of 29 January 1983, *Yearbook Commercial Arbitration* IX (1984) 411.
73. *See also*: L G Mannheim 1.4.1953, NJW 1953, 1436.
74. Decision of 17 November 1981, *Yearbook Commercial Arbitration* X (1985) 458.

enforcement of the award, the court rejected it in pointing out, *inter alia*, that the arbitrators were competent to decide on the validity of the arbitration clause, that there was no breach of public policy, and that enforcement should be granted under the New York Convention. French courts have been less liberal on the arbitrability of foreign exchange restrictions.[75]

With regard to restrictions of security transactions, it may suffice here to briefly draw the reader's attention again to the famous decision of the US Supreme Court in *Scherk* v. *Alberto-Culver Co.*,[76] since that case as well as its implications for arbitrability and public policy in international commercial arbitration have been widely reported and commented.[77] As is well known, the Supreme Court held that, while disputes arising out of the securities transactions are not arbitrable if the contract is domestic, they are arbitrable if it is international. This is considered one of the leading cases on the distinction between domestic and international public policy. The line of reasoning developed in that decision of 1974 has then been confirmed and extended to antitrust matters by the Supreme Court decision of 1985 reported above under III (2)(e). A recent decision of the German Federal Court of Justice of 1984 could be an indication that German courts might be insisting on their exclusive jurisdiction in similar cases.[78]

d. Bribery and corruption

There has been reason recently to resume the discussion in international arbitration circles on the arbitrability – and public policy restrictions thereon – of claims connected with bribery and corruption.

It was my predecessor in my present function at The Hague who contributed as early as 1963 important considerations on this matter and on the notion of international public policy in general. In his award[79] as sole arbitrator in an ICC arbitration, Judge Lagergren had to deal with a claim for a "commission" for a contract obtained by a British Corporation in Argentina based on an earlier agreement according to which the claimant was to receive 10% of the value of the contract while it seemed clear to the arbitrator that a major portion thereof was to be used to bribe employees of the then Argentine government. Although both parties submitted their dispute to arbitration and were content that the arbitrator decide on the merits, Judge Lagergren considered himself in a position *ex officio* to decline arbitrability.

He first expressed the view that one could not contest that "contracts which seriously violate *bonos mores* or international public policy are invalid or at least unenforceable and that they cannot be sanctioned by courts or arbitrators. This principle is especially apt for use before international arbitration tribunals that

75. As a summary see the report by Boulbes, "La violation de l'ordre public, moyen de validité de compromis d'arbitrage et de la sentence arbitrale", JCP La Semaine Juridique, 1962, 1676.
76. 417 US 506 (1974).
77. *See, e.g.*: van den Berg, *op. cit.* 362; Holtzmann in *60 Years On, A Look at the Future*, Paris 1984, 364.
78. Decision of 12 March 1984, IPRax 1985, 216, which, however, concerned a forum clause, not an arbitration clause. *See also* note by Roth, IPRax 1985, 198.
79. ICC Award of 15 January 1963 in case 1110.

lack a 'law of the forum' in the ordinary sense of the term." This is a most interesting comment insofar as it speaks of "international public policy" not in the most commonly used sense that a national public policy might have to use different standards for international contracts than for domestic ones, but in the sense of a truly international public policy for international arbitrations as no doubt my colleague Pierre Lalive will consider it in detail in his paper to this conference.

With regard to the specified issue of bribery, Judge Lagergren came to a conclusion on arbitrability which – to my knowledge of unpublished arbitration practice – has not been shared by some other arbitrators, although for obvious reasons very few of such cases are submitted to arbitration at all. Faced with the argument and accepting that, even if part of the "commission" was to be used for bribes, other parts were a compensation for "other important and quite irreproachable functions" performed by the claimant, his award found:

> "Although these commissions were not to be used exclusively for bribes, a very substantial part of them must have been intended for such use. Whether one is taking the point of view of good government or that of commercial ethics, it is impossible to close one's eyes to the probable destination of amounts of this magnitude, and to the destructive effect thereof on the business pattern with consequent impairment of industrial progress. Such corruption is an international evil; it is contrary to good morals and to an international public policy common to the community of nations. . . . Thus jurisdiction must be declined in this case. It follows from the foregoing, that in concluding that I have no jurisdiction, guidance has been sought from general principles denying arbitrators to entertain disputes of this nature rather than from any national rules on arbitrability. Parties who ally themselves in an enterprise of the present nature must realize that they have forfeited any right to ask for the assistance of the machinery ofjustice (national courts or arbitral tribunals) in setting their disputes."

Twenty years later, another sole arbitrator in an ICC arbitration was faced with the same issue in a similar case. This award[80] illustrated that, although the basic rejection of bribery had not changed, the procedural consequences drawn therefrom might be different:

> *"Pourtant, la présente sentence . . . ne peut non plus suivre l'arbitre Lagergren lorsqu'il arrive à la conclusion qu'une prétention tirée d'un accord violant les bonnes moeurs et/ou l'ordre public ne peut pas être jugée ni par un tribunal étatique ni par un tribunal arbitral. La clause arbitrale doit être considerée indépendamment du contrat dont elle fait partie (cf. l'article V§ 3 de la Convention européenne du 21 avril 1961 . . .) Ell n'est pas affectée par une nullité frappant les autres stipulations entre les parties."*

On the basis of the now dominating doctrine of separability, therefore, the arbitrator accepted to have jurisdiction in this case, but then dismissed the respective claim for a commission in the procedure on the merits, since it was based on a contractual clause which was null and void. Like my colleague Goldman,[81] Kosheri and Leboulanger also seem to favour this new approach and

80. ICC Award of 1982 in case 3916.
81. In *60 Years On, A Look at the Future*, 272.

rightly point out in that context that denying arbitrability leaves the contract in suspense, while this new approach goes a step further and is more rigid, since "l'arbitre transforme la moralité qui doit régner dans la conduite des affaires en règle matérielle d'application immédiate",[82] an approach similar to that taken in a recent decision of the German Federal Supreme Court of Justice.[82a] This is in line with the function of the arbitrator stressed by Mbaye,[83] in view of the dangers of corruption especially in developing countries, "as an element of the service of international justice, one of the facets of which is the attack on corruption".

e. Certain disputes with states and state institutions

One area of subjective arbitrability or capacity has played a major role in international commercial arbitration and must therefore be taken up here: the limitation found in many national laws that the state or certain state institutions may not at all or only under certain conditions submit to arbitration. Although this Rapporteur, both in his arbitration practice[84] and in his publications,[85] has been dealing with arbitrations involving states and state institutions in great detail, he will resist the temptation to use much of the reader's time on an extensive presentation of this area of limitations. But in view of the steadily growing number of arbitrations – e.g., they form by now more than 25% of all ICC arbitration cases – at least a short summary of the legal situation seems necessary within the limited framework of this paper.

The basic idea behind the restrictions on the capacity of the state and its institutions to submit to arbitration is normally that these entities should solve their disputes before courts of the same state and that commercial arbitration is "too private" to be accepted also by such state parties.

To many of the questions arising from those restrictions, a definite answer will very much depend on the respective national law, the wording, background and context of the restriction, as well as on the specific factual and legal circumstances of a given case. Are such restrictions a mere question of capacity of a party or also of objective arbitrability? What is the applicable law? What relevance do such restrictions have, if either the procedural law and/or the substantive law applied by the arbitrator is another national law or even international law? Are the restrictions meant to apply not only to domestic but also to international contracts and arbitrations? Even if the restriction is found to be applicable, may the state party, in view of its signing the arbitration agreement, be barred from

82. "L'arbitrage face à la corruption et aux trafics d'influence", Rev.Arb. 1984, 18.

82a. BGH 8.5.1985 in RIW 1985, 653.

83. In *ICC Court of Arbitration 60th Anniversary*, 297.

84. *See, e.g.*: Award of 18 November 1983 in the Ad Hoc Arbitration *Benteler* v. *Belgian State*, Journal des Tribunaux (Brussels) 1984, 230, English translation in Journal of International Arbitration I (1984) 184.

85. *See, e.g.*: Böckstiegel, "The Legal Rules Applicable in International Commercial Arbitration Involving States or State-Controlled Enterprises", in *60 Years On, A Look at the Future*, 117; Böckstiegel, *Arbitration and State Enterprises, Survey of the National and International State of Law and Practice*, Deventer (Netherlands) 1984; Böckstiegel, *Der Staat als Vertragspartner ausländischer Privatunternehmen*, Frankfurt 1971.

relying on the restriction under legal principles such as *bona fide*, *venire contra factum proprium*, abuse of rights, estoppel or international public policy?[86]

Raising those questions illustrates already why few generalizations are possible. The situation is further complicated by the fact that closer examination shows in many countries the practice to be not identical to the written law, either because the state entities involved in international commerce and investment disregard their own restrictions or because courts interpret these restrictions as not applying to international arbitration or at least certain areas thereof.

For European states, in addition to such considerations of national law and practice, the Geneva Arbitration Convention of 1961 may come into play, since its Article II expressly provides for the right of legal persons of public law to resort to arbitration, but also permits a declaration of limitation of that principle for ratifying states.

If, subject to the above reservations that a definite evaluation can only be made case by case, one ventures to some sort of resumée on the basis of the material available in this area, one might first of all point out that most state parties nowadays, once they have signed an arbitration agreement, will honor it in case of a dispute, submit to and participate in the arbitration, and in fact accept the award even if they lose. Where state parties, in spite of their signing the arbitration agreement, have raised the objection of non-arbitrability based on their national law before the arbitrators, these have in general tended to reject this defence by applying one or more of the arguments raised in the above collection of questions.

In view of the express permission in the Geneva Convention of 1961 and of the widespread and growing practice of state parties to accept arbitration, it is hard to imagine that national law restrictions on their subjective arbitrability are considered so important as to be part of international public policy. On the other hand, it cannot be excluded that national courts refuse enforcement of awards against state institutions or at least states themselves. But, although the unfortunate decision of the US District Court in *Liamco* v. *Libya*[87] denied arbitrability in the sense of Article V(2)(a) of the New York Convention, the refusal would be effected normally by granting them immunity.[88] Here, on the one hand, the signing of the arbitration agreement may be considered as a waiver by the state or the doctrine of restrictive immunity may bar such a defence. But even if the court accepts arbitrability, it may still happen that a court – should it in principle consider the state as eligible for immunity in this case – refuses enforcement, since a possible waiver of immunity seen in the arbitration agreement may not necessarily be interpreted to be also a waiver with regard to enforcement.[89]

86. *See, e.g.*: Ad Hoc Arbitration Award of 18 November 1983 in *Benteler* v. *Belgian State*, *op. cit.*
87. Decision of 18 January 1980, 482 Fed. Supp. (1980) 1175 and *Yearbook Commercial Arbitration* VI (1981) 248.
88. *See further, e.g.*: Böckstiegel, in *60 Years On, A Look at the Future*, 145.
89. Böckstiegel, *op. cit.* at 147.

IV CONCLUSIONS

A resumée on this topic is both frustrating and encouraging. The deeper one studies the practice and theory, the more one realizes the great variety of issues, of nuances, of basic and technical solutions in different countries, of nomenclature in different writings. They make it clear that in regard to a topic as fundamental to states as public policy, national laws are bound to dominate for a long time to come and international codification of what are non-arbitral matters has little chance. On the other hand, the study illustrates that similar results are often reached in many different ways, that the liberalization of international arbitration progresses also in this field, especially by acceptance of specific public policy standards for arbitration if it is international, and that thereby the practical relevance of the topic is decreasing, although there must be a net for obvious *ultra vires* conduct of arbitrators.

The leitmotiv should also here be: as much state involvement as necessary, but as little as possible.

V ANNEX SUMMARIES ON NATIONAL LAWS

The size of this Annex, comprising national summaries on 48 countries, made it impossible to have it printed and included as part of this Report. The documentation was produced under the guidance of Prof. Böckstiegel by Beate Maiwald, assistant to the Chair of International Business Law at the University of Cologne. Copies of the Annex may be ordered from:

Department of International Commercial Arbitration
T.M.C. Asser Institute
P.O. Box 30461
2500 GL The Hague
The Netherlands
Telex 34273 asser nl
Tel. (0)70 630900

A small charge will be made to cover the cost of the photocopying and postage.

Public Policy and Arbitral Procedure

*Stephen M. Schwebel**
and
*Susan G. Lahne**

TABLE OF CONTENTS

I INTRODUCTION

To speak of public policy, those mandatory norms that comprise a State's "most basic notions of morality and justice,"[1] as it relates solely to arbitral procedure may at first seem obscure and narrow, as the relationship between the two topics is not immediately self-evident. On reflection, however, the subject reveals its interest and importance, particularly once procedure is understood to

---

* Judge of the International Court of Justice.
** Associate Attorney at Covington & Burling, Washington, D.C.
1. *Parsons & Whittemore Overseas Co., Inc.* v. *Société Générale de l'Industrie du Papier*, 508 F.2d 969, 974 (1974), *see Yearbook Commercial Arbitration* Vol. I (1976) at 205 (USA No. 7).

encompass the entire process of arbitration, the underlying structure that causes arbitration to be viewed as part of a legal system. States are impelled, in order to protect their "fundamental norms of procedural fairness,"[2] to exert control over the process of arbitration. At the very least, if the form and the underlying process by which an arbitral award was created do not meet all potentially applicable domestic procedural requirements, there will be confusion over where and to what extent the award will be enforceable, particularly if it involves transnational commerce.

The domestic mandatory norms applicable to procedure, including those specifically related to arbitral procedure, differ from State to State. The need to control and limit the arbitral process thus may conflict with certain needs of international commerce, such as the principle of party autonomy and the desire for certainty of enforcement of arbitral awards. In this way, as has been the case in other areas, public policy has been a limiting principle in efforts to unify and simplify the laws governing international commercial arbitration. This Report is concerned with the extent to which protection of these fundamental norms limits parties' (and arbitrators') freedom to shape the structure of the arbitral process, notwithstanding the "international" quality of the underlying commercial relationship or the parties' own preference as to rules and forum. This Report is intended to survey the cases that have dealt thus far with this conflict. To what extent can the goal of ensuring transnationally the enforcement of arbitral awards be reconciled with States' needs to protect domestic conceptions of procedural regularity and States' wishes to control the process of arbitration, either when conducted on the State's own soil or when brought to it at a post-award stage for review? To what extent can there be said to be uniform principles transnationally within the "public policy" that limits the shaping of arbitral procedure?

The number of cases in which these issues have been discussed is not very large. Reliance upon public policy in public international law judgments is rare.[3] Reliance upon public policy in national judgments is far more frequent, not only because there are so many more national than international judgments, but also because national public policy has a well-established tradition, while the concept that there may exist an "international public policy" is of extremely recent

2. Park, "The Influence of National Legal Systems on International Commercial Arbitration: Recent Developments in English Arbitration Law", in *Resolving Transnational Disputes Through International Arbitration* 87 (1984).

3. The outstanding example is found in International Court of Justice, *Case concerning the Application of the Convention of 1902 governing the Guardianship of Infants (Netherlands* v. *Sweden), Judgment of 28 November 1959, ICJ Reports 1958* at 55, particularly in the Separate Opinion of Judge Sir Hersch Lauterpacht at 79. *See also* Permanent Court of International Justice, *Serbian and Brazilian Loans* cases, 1929, Series A, No. 20/21 at 12. 46. The pertinent point in the *Convention of 1902* case was the relationship of Swedish public policy to Sweden's treaty obligations. In the *Serbian and Brazilian Loans* cases, the Court also spoke of public policy in national terms, of "cases concerning public policy, a conception the definition of which in any particular country is largely dependent on the opinion prevailing at any given time in such country itself."

vintage.[4] Nonetheless, the cases dealing with procedure are still, all in all, few. Sir Michael John Mustill has recently written that in the last sixty years English courts "have never found it necessary to ask themselves whether the conduct of an arbitration is subject to rules of public policy. . . ."[5]

These relatively few cases have been comprehensively collected in the ten volumes of the *Yearbook Commercial Arbitration* (hereinafter "*Yearbook*") available at this writing, and a number of them have been the subject of comment by Judge Howard M. Holtzmann,[6] by Dr. Albert Jan van den Berg in his excellent book on *The New York Arbitration Convention of 1958* (1981), and by others. The "public policy" defences to enforcement of a foreign arbitral award found in the New York Arbitration Convention of 1958 are a helpful guide to the analysis contained in this Report. Article V of the New York Convention provides in pertinent part:

> "1. Recognition and enforcement of the award may be refused, at the request of the party against whom it is invoked, only if that party furnishes to the competent authority where the recognition and enforcement is sought, proof that:
>
> . . .
>
> "(*b*) The party against whom the award is invoked was not given proper notice of the appointment of the arbitrator or of the arbitration proceedings or was otherwise unable to present his case; or
>
> . . .
>
> "(*d*) The composition of the arbitral authority or the arbitral procedure was not in accordance with the agreement of the parties, or, failing such agreement, was not in accordance with the law of the country where the arbitration took place; or
>
> "(*e*) The award has not yet become binding on the parties, or has been set aside or suspended by a competent authority of the country in which, or under the law of which, that award was made.
>
> "2. Recognition and enforcement of an arbitral award may also be refused if the competent authority in the country where recognition and enforcement is sought finds that:
>
> "(*a*) The subject matter of the difference is not capable of settlement by arbitration under the law of that country; or
>
> "(*b*) The recognition or enforcement of the award would be contrary to the public policy of that country."

It will be observed that only Article V(2)(*b*) expressly refers to public policy, and it does so in terms of "the public policy of that country" (e.g., the country where enforcement is sought). However, other provisions of Article V implicate public policy as it affects procedure, particularly, but not exclusively, paragraphs (1)(*b*) and (1)(*d*). Paragraph (1)(*e*) provides that the procedural actions taken by the State in which the award was rendered and the procedural status of the award within that State will be given effect. Paragraph (2)(*a*), of course, concerns arbitrability, which is beyond the scope of this Report. These individual

---

4. Jenks, in *The Prospects of International Adjudication* (1964), has a substantial chapter on "The Concept of International Public Policy," which examines public policy in international law and in a number of systems of municipal law.

5 Mustill, "Transnational Arbitration and English Law", *Current Legal Problems 1984*, p. 134.

6. Holtzmann, "Commentary" in *60 Years On, A Look at the Future* 361 (1984).

provisions are particular specifications of the public policy of which Article V(2)(*b*) is the more general, residual repository.[7]

Dr Julian D. M. Lew, in *Applicable Law in International Commercial Arbitration* (1978), summarizes the relevance of national public policy to international commercial arbitration as follows:

> "The relevance of national public policy on international commercial arbitration may be felt in two situations. First: where, despite the existence of an agreement to submit to arbitration, one party institutes court proceedings. Whether those proceedings should be stayed pending arbitration will depend on the validity of the arbitration agreement. For this purpose, a court will consider whether national public policy legislation denies one of the parties the right to submit to arbitration or has reserved for the exclusive jurisdiction of its national courts' [sic] disputes of that particular nature.
> "Second: where a national court is requested to enforce a foreign arbitration award. Here for the purposes of recognition and enforcement, the court must again consider the right of the parties to submit to arbitration and the arbitrability of the subject-matter of the dispute. Furthermore, a court may not give effect to a foreign award if the procedure followed in the arbitration proceedings or the award *per se* violate the fundamental public policies of the forum."

(*Ibid.* at 556.) This Report will focus on the latter aspect of Dr Lew's analysis: the instances in which a State's court must decide whether to give effect to an international commercial arbitral award where the procedure followed in the arbitration proceedings has been attacked as violative of that State's (or another State's) public policy. In terms used within the United States, these attacks could be viewed as claims that the arbitral procedures employed do not provide "due process of law,"[8] which in the United States of America is under constitutional protection and therefore part of that State's mandatory norms.

The general conclusions to be drawn from this survey are on the whole encouraging for the future of international commercial arbitration. While occasionally having to grapple with the outer limits of permissible procedures and arbitrators' conduct, national courts generally have upheld international

---

7. On the relationship between Article V(1)(*b*) and Article V(2)(*b*) of the New York Convention, Dr. van den Berg writes:

> "According to Article V(2)(*b*) a court may refuse enforcement on its own motion if 'The recognition or enforcement of the award would be contrary to the public policy of that country.' As due process is generally conceived as pertaining to public policy, the question is raised whether the specific provision of Article V(1)(*b*) concerning due process would have the effect of excluding due process from Article V(2)(*b*), which concerns public policy in general. This question is important because if due process were only covered by Article V(1)(*b*), a court would not be allowed to refuse enforcement of the award on its own motion if it finds that an award is tainted by a serious violation of due process; it could refuse enforcement only if the respondent asserts it. In practice it will make little difference as a respondent will be eager to point out that a violation of due process has occurred; in none of the reported cases has a court refused enforcement on its own motion on account of a violation of due process. It may make a difference in the case where the respondent declines to appear before the court in the enforcement proceedings, but that happens rarely at this stage."

(*op. cit.* at 299). Dr. van den Berg further reasons that Article V(1)(*d*) must "be deemed to be limited by the fundamental requirements of due process" and, thus, that Article V(2)(*b*) acts as a corrective of Article V(1)(*d*). *Ibid.* at 301.

8. Procedural due process in American constitutional analysis connotes the fundamental guarantees of procedural form and regularity of the Federal Constitution. *See* US Constitution Amend. V.

arbitral awards involving commerce, finding that public policy requires only a basic minimum of procedural protection, especially when international commercial affairs are concerned. That eminent student and practitioner of the international arbitral process, Judge Holtzmann, concludes:

> "Faced, as we are, with the potential problems of public policy defenses in international arbitration cases, it is encouraging to be able to report that the defense is succeeding less and less in modern courts. Courts are increasingly recognizing that narrow, nationalistic grounds of public policy that might be properly applicable in domestic cases are inappropriate in international cases."[9]

He quotes Professor Pieter Sanders, the distinguished President of this Council, as follows:

> "More and more we see a distinction between domestic public policy (*ordre public interne*) and international public policy (*ordre public international*) gaining ground. The notion of the latter is more restricted than the former. International public policy, according to a generally accepted doctrine is confined to violation of really fundamental conceptions of legal order in the country concerned. For the sake of international commercial arbitration the distinction between domestic and international public policy is of great importance."[10]

This is equally true in the area of procedure. As Professor Delaume has summarized,

> "[C]ases have shown that the defense of public policy is usually of limited importance, except in cases of alleged lack of due process. Even then, however, the courts show little sympathy for claimants who, after having been given an opportunity to appear and defend, elect not to participate in the process and subsequently plead lack of due process as a bar to the recognition of awards against them."[11]

For ease of reference, I will survey the available cases in what might be called a chronological fashion (as viewed from the point of view of the party to an arbitration): the appointment and incompatibilities of the arbitrator or arbitrators; the proceedings; and the award.

II. APPOINTMENT AND INCOMPATIBILITIES OF ARBITRATORS

In many systems of law, the parties' freedom to select arbitrators is limited by the public policy that their impartiality must be assured.[12] Thus, prospective arbitrators often must disclose any circumstances that may prejudice their

---

9. "Commentary", in *60 Years On, A Look at the Future* 364 (1984).
10. *Ibid.*
11. Delaume, "Court Intervention in Arbitral Proceedings", in *Resolving Transnational Disputes Through International Arbitration* 222 (1984).
12. *But see, e.g.*, Goldring & Skapinker, "National Report Australia" 6 in *International Handbook on Commercial Arbitration* (1984).

impartiality, and they are subject to challenge on ground of partiality. *See, e.g.*, Melis, "National Report Austria" 7 in *International Handbook on Commercial Arbitration* (1984) (hereinafter "*Handbook*") ("A general ground for challenging an arbitrator is 'if there is sufficient reason to doubt his impartiality.'"); Stalev, National Report Bulgarian People's Republic 6 in *Handbook* (Sect. 4(4) of the BCCI Rules provides that the arbitrators must be independent and impartial (like judges) in the performance of their functions."). Attacks on the ground of partiality could lead a court to refuse enforcement of an award on the grounds of public policy. The UNCITRAL Arbitration Rules illustrate these principles in providing that "the appointing authority shall have regard to such considerations as are likely to secure the appointment of an independent and impartial arbitrator . . . ." (Art. 6(4).)

Article 9 of the UNCITRAL Rules specifies that:

> "A prospective arbitrator shall disclose to those who approach him in connexion with his possible appointment any circumstances likely to give rise to justifiable doubts as to his impartiality or independence. An arbitrator, once appointed or chosen, shall disclose such circumstances to the parties unless they have already been informed by him of these circumstances."

Article 10(1) provides:

> "1. Any arbitrator may be challenged if circumstances exist that give rise to justifiable doubts as to the arbitrator's impartiality or independence."

The extent to which impartiality must be protected, and the required degree of impartiality, differ from State to State. A not infrequent basis for challenge has been the existence of some form of relationship between the party appointing the arbitrator and the arbitrator himself. As a general matter, however, courts have been reluctant to accept evidence of some prior or post-arbitration relationship as sufficiently harmful of independence to warrant not enforcing the award, particularly when the dispute involves elements of international commerce.

For example, in *Denis Coakley Ltd.* v. *Sté. Michel Reverdy*, a judgment of 23 July 1981 of the Court of Appeal of Reims (Civil Chamber), *see Yearbook* Vol. IX (1984) at 400 (France No. 6), an award was attacked for bias under Article V(2)(*b*) of the New York Convention on the basis that, subsequent to rendering the award, an arbitrator had acted as counsel for one of the parties when the award was on appeal before an appeal board constituted under the Arbitration Rules of the Grain and Feed Association. The French Court rejected the attack and upheld the award, noting that under Article V(2)(*b*), "the public policy governing the enforcement of foreign arbitral awards is not domestic public policy, but the public policy of international law of the State where the decision is invoked." (*Ibid.* at 401.) Because the arbitration panel on which the arbitrator had served "was definitively no longer competent (*functus officio*)" at the time he acted as counsel for the party, and because "such a manner of proceeding is in conformity with English law adopted by the parties," the award rendered by the appeal arbitration board did not violate "the French concept of international public policy or due process." (*Ibid.*) This judgment is in line with the current

French legislative distinction drawn in the treatment of international arbitration as compared to domestic arbitration. *See* French Code of Civil Procedure, Book IV, Arts. 1442–1507.

Some American cases also illustrate this point. In domestic arbitrations in the United States, the Supreme Court of the United States in *Commonwealth Coatings Corp.* v. *Continental Casualty Co.*, 393 US 145, 89 S. Ct. 337 (1986), had set a very rigorous requirement in domestic arbitrations regarding prior relationships between arbitrators and parties. The Court there vacated an award[13] because the arbitrator had been engaged and paid at an earlier time as a consultant by the party who had appointed him, and the arbitrator had failed to dislose these facts to the other party. No actual bias or misconduct in the arbitration could be shown. The opinion states that "any tribunal permitted by law to try cases and controversies not only must be unbiased but also must avoid even the appearance of bias." (*Ibid.* at 340.)

Despite this stringent domestic requirement, mere proof of some minor prior relationship has not resulted in lack of enforcement of international arbitral awards. For example, in *Fertilizer Corp. of India* v. *I.D.I. Management, Inc.*, 517 F. Supp. 948 (1981), *subsequent opinion denying motion to reconsider*, 530 F. Supp. 542 (SD Ohio 1982), *see Yearbook* Vol. VIII (1983) at 419 (USA No. 41), the American Federal District Court rejected a claim of partiality based on the party-appointed arbitrator's having previously served on two occasions as counsel for the party in other arbitrations. Relying on the reasoning of *Scherk* v. *Alberto-Culver Co.*, 417 US 506 (1974), *see Yearbook* Vol. I (1976) at 203 (USA No. 4), and *Parsons & Whittemore*, *supra* n.1, leading public policy cases described elsewhere in the proceedings of this Congress, the court held that "[t]he stronger public policy . . . is that which favors arbitration, both international and domestic . . . ." (*Ibid.*, 517 F. Supp. at 955). The crucial factor, the Court reasoned, was that no actual bias had been shown.[14]

Similar results were reached in three other US cases, *Andros Compania Maritima S.A.* v. *Marc Rich & Co. A.G.*, 579 F.2d 691 (2d Cir. 1978), *see Yearbook* Vol. VII (1982) at 373 (USA No. 34); *Imperial Ethiopian Govt.* v. *Baruch-Foster Corp.*, 535 F.2d 334 (5th Cir. 1976), *see Yearbook* Vol. II (1977) at 252 (USA No. 10); and *Transmarine Seaways Corp.* v. *Marc Rich & Co. A.G.*, 480 F.Supp. 352 (SDNY 1979), *see Yearbook* Vol. VI (1981) at 244 (USA No. 30). In *Andros Compania*,[15] the fact that one of three arbitrators in a maritime arbitration did not disclose that he had "a close personal and professional relationship" with the person who was broker and agent for one of the parties did not warrant vacation of the award because the information was

13. The Court applied the standards of the Federal Arbitration Act, 9 USC sect. 10, which require proof of "evident partiality" before an award can be vacated.

14. *See also International Produce, Inc.* v. *A/S Rosshavet*, 638 F.2d 548 (2d Cir. 1981). Although concerning an arbitration conducted in New York under the Rules of the Society of Maritime Arbitrators, this case demonstrated similar concerns about the disruption to commercial relations that would result in applying such a stringent standard of lack of connection.

15. The Court in this case declined to rule whether the dispute was governed by the Federal Arbitration Act or the New York Convention, holding that the result would be identical under Article V(2)(*b*) of the Convention because it is "no more liberal than 9 USC para. 10 on the matter of vacating awards, and . . . we find none of appellant's contentions adequate under section 10." 579 F.2d at 699 n.11.

common knowledge, easily discoverable, and did not demonstrate a sufficiently close business relationship to justify any suspicions of bias. In *Imperial Ethiopian Govt.*, decided under the New York Convention, the Federal Circuit Court dismissed out of hand a belatedly raised claim of bias based on an arbitrator's having served previously as a member of a commission in charge of drafting a civil code for Ethiopia (which was one of the parties to the arbitration). The Court noted the United States' policy of encouraging recognition and enforcement of foreign arbitral awards under the Convention and ruled that the bias claim "never achieved any more dignity than that of a conclusory statement in an unverified answer." (535 F.2d at 337.) The challenger had failed to meet his burden of proof under Article V(1)(*b*) of the New York Convention. Finally, in *Transmarine Seaways*, also decided under the Convention, the Federal District Court rejected a bias claim based on the fact that the law firm to which one of three arbitrators belonged had previously represented another company that had brought an unrelated claim against the challenging party. Because the relationship between the arbitrator and the party who had appointed him was not a "direct financial or professional" one (480 F. Supp. at 357), it was "far too tenuous a relationship to require the disqualification of an experienced and respected maritime arbitrator." (*Ibid.* at 358.)

Implicit in these cases is the assumption that actual partiality is unacceptable. In the only international case found involving a claim of partial action, however, the court also found grounds for granting enforcement. In *Sidarma Societá Italiana di Armamento* v. *Holt Marine Indus., Inc.*, 515 F. Supp. 1302 (SDNY 1981), an American case involving a maritime arbitration, one of three arbitrators had issued a dissent to the award, asserting that the two majority arbitrators had improperly refused to "pierce the corporate veil"[16] to find a party liable "solely because their 'personal business considerations caused them to overlook the use of the corporate form to intentionally avoid proper liability.'" (515 F. Supp. at 1305.) The United States Federal District Court, applying the "evident partiality" standard of 9 USC, paragraph 10(*b*), noted that "the most the Court finds plaintiff can fairly allege is that the majority arbitrators permitted their commercial business interests to influence their determination." (*Ibid.* at 1307.) The Court declined to vacate the award, reasoning that "it would not be in the interests of an industry such as the maritime industry, in which arbitration is frequently used as a means of dispute resolution, to require that arbitrators abstain from giving any consideration to the effect their decision might have on the industry generally." (*Ibid.*) Only a showing of "direct and definite partiality" would require vacating the award. (*Ibid*).

By way of interesting contrast to the general enforcement of arbitral awards stands a case between a Danish buyer and an FR German seller, which resulted in the judgment of 10 June 1976 of the Cologne *Oberlandesgericht*, Federal Republic of Germany, *see Yearbook* Vol. IV (1979) at 258 (FR Germany No. 14). This case involved a challenge to the procedures adopted by the Copenhagen Arbitration

16. This is an American law concept under which the corporate entity may not be recognized and liability may be imposed on the shareholders of a corporation where certain improper action has been found. *See* H. Henn & J. Alexander, *Laws of Corporations* §146 (1983).

Committee for Grain and Feed Stuff Trade. Those procedures provided that the president of the Committee would select the arbitrators to act on a specific case from a publicly available list, but the parties would not be informed of the identity of the specific arbitrators selected. The resulting award would be signed only by the president. The German Court of Appeal refused recognition under the New York Convention to an award given under these procedures, holding that recognition "would have been against the public order of the FR of Germany." (*Ibid.* at 260.)[17] Because the impartiality of arbitrators was a "fundamental principle of both FR Germany and international legal order," and because the right to challenge for partiality "has a fundamental meaning for a fair arbitral procedure, the exclusion of this right constitutes a violation of the German public order." (*Ibid.*) The *Yearbook* quotes the German Court's explanation of this holding:

> "The institution of challenge can be effective only if the parties have the possibility of knowing the names of the judges or arbitrators who take part in the decision of the dispute in question. Only if this condition is fulfilled, can it be investigated whether the judge or arbitrator who takes part is partial and can his participation be prevented. In international law also, great importance is attached to the disclosure of the names of arbitrators: in the New York Convention (Art. V, para. 1 under b) as well as in the European Convention (Art. IX, para. 1, under b), the lack of notification of the appointment of the arbitrators is mentioned expressly as a ground for refusal of recognition and enforcement."

(*Yearbook* Vol. IV (1979) at 260). That a challenge could be brought against persons included in the generally available list was not sufficient; nor was it sufficient that the party seeking enforcement could prove that no persons connected with him had acted as arbitrator. This case demonstrates what might be considered an outer limit to the procedural possibilities in structuring an arbitration.

Another issue of impartiality has arisen out of the practice of limiting the list of available arbitrators by nationality to a specified State. On several occasions, the claim that arbitrators chosen solely from such a limited list must lack independence has been rejected. In *Billerbeck Cie* v. *Bergbau-Handel GmbH*, a judgment of 3 May 1967 of the Swiss Federal Tribunal, *see Yearbook* Vol. I (1976) at 200 (Switzerland No. 3), involving the Eastern European arbitration courts, the Swiss Court observed that "what really matters is whether in a specific case the arbitral tribunal behaved in a partial way." (*Ibid.*) The parties' knowing selection of such a forum has further been considered critical. In a judgment of 6 March 1969 between a Czechoslovak firm and German respondents, *see Yearbook* Vol. II (1977) at 235 (FR Germany No. 5), involving the Czechoslovak Chamber of Commerce, the Hamburg Court noted that selection of that arbitral forum, and therefore its requirement that only Czechoslovak arbitrators be

17. The Court also held that Articles IV(1)(*a*) and V(1)(*b*) of the Convention had not been complied with because the enforcing party had submitted only an incomplete copy of the award, lacking the names of the arbitrators, and because the respondent had never been given adequate notice of the appointment of the arbitrators.

selected, had been voluntary. No principle of public policy was found violated. Similarly, the Austrian Supreme Court reasoned, in its judgment of 11 June 1969, *see Yearbook* Vol. II (1977) at 232 (Austria No. 3), that: "It is not a violation of the Austrian public policy to recognize an award made by an arbitral tribunal to which the parties have subjected themselves in conformity with their agreement." (*Ibid.*)

In the not-infrequent situation of a party's defaulting and refusing to appoint an arbitrator, if the party-appointed arbitrator acts as sole arbitrator, as permitted under English law, he may be elsewhere subject to attack for partiality. Although virtually every State permits arbitration by a sole arbitrator, the impartiality of a decision by the party-appointed arbitrator acting alone may be questioned. In three Italian cases reported in the *Yearbooks*, the awards were enforced under the Convention, although such a procedure would have been impermissible within the enforcing State. *See S. A. Pando Compania Naviera* v. *S.a.S. Filmo*, judgment of 21 May 1976, *Yearbook* Vol. III (1978) at 277 (Italy No. 16); *Efxinos Shipping Co. Ltd.* v. *Rawi Shipping Lines Ltd.*, judgment of 2 May 1980, *Yearbook* Vol. VIII (1983) at 381 (Italy No. 51); and *Rocco Giuseppe e Figli s.n.c.* v. *Federal Commerce and Navigation Ltd.*, judgment of 15 December 1982, Sez. I, *Yearbook* Vol. X (1985) at 464 (Italy No. 72). In these decisions, the fact that such a proceeding was permitted under English law, which was the arbitration law selected by the parties, justified enforcement even though Italian law would not permit a party-appointed arbitrator to act alone. Distinguishing between its domestic public policy and its international public policy, the Italian courts found no violation of Italian public order. The opinions note that English law provides an additional safeguard against partiality in the extensiveness of its court supervision of the appointment process. *See also* a judgment of 10 February 1984 of the Supreme Court of Spain, *Yearbook* Vol. X (1985) at 493 (Spain No. 5) (sole arbitrator acting under English law; award enforced); and a judgment of 11 February 1981 of the Spanish *Tribunal Superior*, *Yearbook* Vol. VII (1982) at 356 (Spain No. 1) (same).

In a third case, *Bucher-Guyer S.A.* v. *Meiki Co. Ltd.*, a judgment of 17 March 1976, *Yearbook* Vol. V (1980) at 220 (Switzerland No. 2), the Swiss Federal Tribunal held that Article 10 of the Swiss Arbitration Concordat, which requires the appointment of three arbitrators unless the parties have agreed upon a different uneven number, did not form part of the Concordat's mandatory procedural rules. Therefore, where the parties to an arbitration agreement had specified both that ICC Rules and the procedural law of Geneva were to govern the arbitration, the ICC's decision to appoint a single arbitrator of its own choosing over one party's objection was found acceptable.

A recent case of interest is ICC arbitral award 3526/RP, *Cementation International Ltd* v. *Republique Islamique d'Iran.* The contract between a British company and the Iranian Ministry of Health provided that differences arising thereunder would be settled by conciliation or arbitration of the International Chamber of Commerce by a tribunal of three arbitrators. Each of the parties was to designate an arbitrator and the third was to be named by the Director-General of the World Health Organization. The arbitral tribunal was to sit in Geneva, and the law of Iran was to apply to all aspects of the contract. The company named its arbitrator; Iran did not; and the Court of Arbitration of the ICC designated a Swiss arbitrator in lieu of that defaulted appointment. The Director-General of WHO declined to nominate the third arbitrator, whereupon the ICC decided that the arbitral clause of the contract contained a lacuna to be filled by the terms of Article 2(4) of the ICC Rules,[18] and appointed as president of the tribunal Professor Böckstiegel. The tribunal so constituted met and held that it was properly constituted. In the course of the proceedings, Iran challenged the validity of the designation of the arbitrators, alleging, *inter alia*, that the composition of the tribunal did not conform to the contract or to provisions of the Constitution of Iran, which had been promulgated after the contract had entered into force. After an award in favor of the company was made, Iran brought an action in the Court of Justice of the Canton of Geneva, maintaining that the award was null. The Swiss Court, while noting that the contract provided that it was to be governed by the law of Iran – a provision that it interpreted as embracing arbitral procedure – nevertheless held that the parties had submitted to the ICC Rules. The Court concluded that, having regard to the parties' adoption of the ICC Rules, a subsequently adopted constitutional provision of one of the parties could not enable it to escape from a freely accepted bilateral contract. Admittedly, the ICC Rules did not contemplate an appointing authority's declining to appoint. But in accepting the ICC Rules, the parties to a contract were deemed to have accepted the ICC's choice of arbitrators, which, having regard to the powers set out in the Rules, the ICC was entitled to make. On this and other grounds, the action seeking to have the award nullified was rejected. The Swiss Federal Tribunal upheld this judgment on 18 April 1984.

This case is of interest in more than one respect. Presumably a constitutional provision of Iran regarding the composition of arbitral tribunals to which Iranian State agencies may submit is a matter of the public policy of Iran, but that public policy was given effect neither by the arbitration tribunal nor by Swiss courts. At the same time, the Swiss courts treated a substitute recourse by the ICC, even where its Rules did not foresee an appointing authority declining to make an appointment, as in accordance with due process. This ruling once more conduces towards the effectiveness of international arbitral commitments and arbitrations undertaken thereunder.

However, an order of 20 December 1984 of the Port Said Court of First Instance cuts the other way. It ordered the stay of ICC arbitral proceedings to take place in Egypt on the ground that the contract's provision for arbitration was "at variance with the established judiciary rules in the Arab Republic of Egypt which require the two parties' agreement on the name of the arbitrator . . . ." (*Rolaco Holdings S.A. and Casino Palace Port Said* v. *The Mohafazat of Port Said and Suez Canal*

18. Art. 2(4) provides:

"Where the dispute is to be referred to three arbitrators, each party shall nominate in the Request for Arbitration and the Answer thereto respectively one arbitrator for confirmation by the Court. Such person shall be independent of the party nominating him. If a party fails to nominate an arbitrator, the appointment shall be made by the Court. The third arbitrator, who will act as chairman of the arbitral tribunal, shall be appointed by the Court, unless the parties have provided that the arbitrators nominated by them shall agree on the third arbitrator within a fixed time limit. In such a case the Court shall confirm the appointment of such third arbitrator. Should the two arbitrators fail, within the time limit fixed by the parties or the Court, to reach agreement on the third arbitrator, he shall be appointed by the Court."

Authority, ICC Document 410/6618). Whether these conflicting positions will ultimately be reconciled in such a way as to enhance enforcement of the obligation to arbitrate and facilitate the arbitral process can only be hoped.

III. CONDUCT OF THE ARBITRAL PROCEEDINGS

Professor Berthold Goldman has rightly observed that:

> "the details of mandatory public policy requirements concerning the arbitral hearing and related procedures . . . are so obvious. They lay down that each party's right to present its case and to discuss the position of the other party must be respected . . . these two requirements are not identical, since the first implies that every party must have the opportunity to develop fully its claims and arguments in defence, whilst the second ordains that no question shall be decided by the arbitrator until each party has been afforded the opportunity of discussing it."[19]

Because the fundamental public policy requirements for the conduct of arbitral proceedings are so obvious, cases in which such questions have arisen are neither many nor controversial. The shared, general principles of "international due process" in this sphere are (a) equal treatment of the parties, (b) fair notice (both of the appointment of arbitrators and the conduct of proceedings) and (c) fair opportunity to present a case. The UNCITRAL Model Law on International Commercial Arbitration, for instance, provides, in mandatory terms, that: "[t]he parties shall be treated with equality and each party shall be given a full opportunity of presenting his case." (Art. 18.) Article 24(2) further states that "[t]he parties shall be given sufficient advance notice of any hearing and of any meeting of the arbitral tribunal for the purpose of inspection of goods, other property or documents," and Article 23(3) requires that "[a]ll statements, documents or other information supplied to the arbitral tribunal by one party shall be communicated to the other party." Requirements of this nature are found in virtually every State's arbitration statutes. *See, e.g.*, Melis, National Report Austria 8–9 in *Handbook*:

> "As regards arbitral procedure, a fundamental provision in the CCP is Article 587, para. 1, which states that before making the award, the arbitrators shall hear the parties and examine the facts on which the dispute is based. . . . The law intends only to secure that the parties are given the opportunity to present their case."

The National Report France equally states that:

> "the principle of equality between the parties must be respected, and no decision should be made on the basis of facts or evidences on which the parties or one of them had no chance to comment. . . ."

(Derains, National Report France 15 in *Handbook*; *see also ibid.* at 16 (same principles applicable to international arbitration).)

---

19. *60 Years On, loc. cit.*, at 267.

Within the framework of these fundamental policies, the guiding principle has nonetheless been liberal enforcement of foreign arbitral awards. Thus, cases in which arbitral procedures are found deficient are rare; variations in the methods of implementing the general principles are tolerated; and enforcement of awards is denied, on public policy grounds, only for egregious departure from the due process of law.

1. Fair Notice

The initial step of any arbitration is notification of commencement. In many systems, a party's notice of appointment of its arbitrator serves this function; under some rules (such as the UNCITRAL Arbitration Rules, Art. 3), a separate notice of arbitration is required. In either case, the other party's receipt of such a notification is crucial to its being bound by any subsequent award; particularly when a party defaults and refuses to participate in the arbitration, it is likely to argue against enforcement on the basis of inadequate notice. That sufficient notice is an element of international public policy is shown by the reasoning of the following cases. What is also shown is that in the international context courts will look to the substance of whether notice was actually received, rather than to whether the technical service requirements of its domestic law were met.

Courts in Spain, Italy, and Mexico, for example, have rejected the simple argument that an award should not be enforced because it was made in the absence of a party who had refused to participate in the arbitration. In its judgment of 10 February 1984, *see Yearbook* Vol. X (1985) at 493 (Spain No. 5), the Spanish Supreme Court enforced a foreign award and declined to apply its domestic law, which refused enforcement to foreign default judgments. Under the Convention, the Court held, "proper notice of the appointment of the arbitrator and of the arbitration proceedings, and that it [the party] be otherwise enabled to present its case" are the only requirements for enforcement. (*Ibid.* at 495.) Of similar import was the Spanish judgment of 11 February 1981, *see Yearbook* Vol VII (1982) at 356 (Spain No. 1), enforcing an award rendered by a sole arbitrator in the face of the other party's default. The court reasoned that because the defaulting party had actually received all notifications punctually it could have presented its defence, had it so chosen. *See also* the Spanish Supreme Court judgment, had it so chosen. *See also* the Spanish Supreme Court judgment of 24 March 1982, *Yearbook* Vol. VIII (1983) at 408 (Spain No. 3); and its judgment of 8 October 1981, *Yearbook* Vol VIII (1983) at 406 (Spain No. 2) (same reasoning). In a contrary ruling, however, the same Court refused to enforce another award and held that the notice of appointment given to the other party, although actually received, was insufficient where it lacked technical detail, such as points in dispute, dates of hearings, or dates for submitting a defence. *Holargos Shipping Corporation* v. *Hierros Ardes S.A.*, judgment of 3 March 1982, *Yearbook* Vol. IX (1984) at 435 (Spain No. 4). Though these cases may not be wholly reconcilable on the issue of the extent to which notice must be detailed (Spain No. 4 may well be an aberration), they coincide on the basic principle that a defaulting party with notice will be bound by the ensuing award.

Italian cases have focused also on whether actual notice was received; if it was, enforcement is summarily granted. *See Intercommerce, Sofia* v. *Menaguale Eugenio*, judgment of 24 September 1973, *Yearbook* Vol. I (1976) at 192 (Italy No. 9); *S.a.S. Wieland K.G.* v. *Società Industriale Meridionale*, judgment of 19 May 1976, *Yearbook* Vol. V (1980) at 266 (Italy No. 34); *G.A. Pap-KG Holzgrosshandlung* v. *Ditta Giovanni G. Pecoraro*, judgment of 13 February 1978, *Yearbook* Vol. VI (1981) at 228 (Italy No. 36); *Brüder Groessing* v. *Franco Vacchelli*, judgment of 13 October 1981, *Yearbook* Vol. VIII (1979) at 390 (Italy No. 55); *Vacchelli Franco* v. *Brüder Groessing*, judgment of 19 January 1984, *Yearbook* Vol. X (1983) at 475 (Italy No. 78, affirming Italy No. 55).

In two cases, the Mexican courts have held that compliance with specific Mexican service requirements was unnecessary for enforcement of a foreign arbitral award, as long as actual notice was received. In the judgment of 24 February 1977, the Eighteenth Civil Court of First Instance for the Federal District of Mexico, *Yearbook* Vol. IV (1979), at 301 (Mexico No. 1), the petitioner had served its notice of arbitration by mail in accordance with ICC procedures. This method, however, violated Mexican law, which requires initial personal service. The Court held that the parties, by agreeing to arbitration, had waived the service formalities of Mexican law, which were not part of Mexican public policy.

Similarly, in its judgment of 1 August 1977, the Court of Appeals (Fifth Chamber) for the Federal District of Mexico, *see Yearbook* Vol. IV (1979) at 301 (Mexico No. 2), the Court reversed a trial court's refusal to enforce an award, holding that service by mail in accordance with procedures of the American Arbitration Association did not violate Mexican public policy, especially since actual notice to the other party had been clearly proved. *See also* the German judgment of 11 January 1978, *Yearbook* Vol. IV (1979) at 262–264 (FR Germany No. 16) (full and timely notice provided; defaulting party held bound by award); the Bremen judgment of 8 June 1967, *Yearbook* Vol. II (1977) at 234 (FR Germany No. 3) (*ex parte* award enforced where party duly notified and of own accord failed to participate); *European Grain & Shipping Ltd* v. *Seth Oil Mills Ltd.*, judgment of 29 January 1983, High Court of Bombay, *Yearbook* Vol. IX (1984) at 411 (India No. 9) (actual notice); *Niroshi Nishi* v. *Compagnia di navigazione et commercio*, judgment of 14 March 1963, Court of Appeal, Tokyo, *Yearbook* Vol. I (1976) at 194 (Japan No. 1) ("There was no question of violation of public order since the Japanese party was duly informed about the arbitration and it was entirely due to his own attitude that the award was made *ex parte*").

In an interesting case, *Corporación Salvadorena de Calzado, S.A.* v. *Injection Footwear Corp.*, 533 F. Supp. 290 (S.D. Fla. 1982), the United States Federal District Court found a "due process" violation in the service methods adopted by a party who had commenced an arbitration in El Salvador and sought to enforce a resulting default judgment under Florida State law. The initial notice of arbitration had been sent in the form of a letter rogatory from an El Salvador Court, but it was delivered to the other party only by certified mail from an attaché in the American Embassy, rather than being served through a US Court. The court-appointed arbitrators conducted *ex parte* proceedings in El Salvador without making any effort to notify the American party, who did not participate, and the resulting award was confirmed by a default judgment of the El Salvador court; the only attempt to notify the American party of the effort to confirm was through posting on a judicial bulletin board in El Salvador. The Federal District Court held that El Salvador law on service of process had been violated and that US Federal and State guarantees of due process also had been violated:

> "The notice procedures employed here are defective, in terms of due process, in that they were not reasonably calculated to apprise the Defendant that proceedings had been instituted against him and to afford Defendant the opportunity to defend, as to both the commencement of arbitration and the subsequent attempt to reduce the arbitral award to judgment."

(533 F. Supp. at 298.)

The court recognized that parties surrender some of their traditional procedural safeguards in agreeing to arbitration, but it held that "Defendant nevertheless did not agree to surrender certain due process rights, including the orderly process of commencing arbitration through notice procedures required under the law of El Salvador." (*Ibid.* at 298–99.)

2. *Time Limits*

A series of cases have dealt with objections raised to arbitrators' setting relatively short time limits, often shorter than those provided by municipal law. These challenges have been uniformly unsuccessful and the courts have found no public policy violations, holding the shorter time periods adequate given the nature of the arbitral process. *See* the Basel judgment of 3 June 1971, *Yearbook* Vol. IV (1979) at 309, 310–11 (Switzerland No. 5); the Naples judgment of 20 February 1975, *ibid.* Vol. IV at 275 (Italy No. 21); the Italian Court of Cassation judgment of 20 January 1977, *ibid.* Vol. IV at 279 (Italy No. 23); the Milan judgment of 3 May 1977, *ibid.* Vol. IV at 284 (Italy No. 27); *Société Italo-Belge pour le Commerce et l'Industrie* v. *S.p.a. I.G.O.R.*, judgment of 27 December 1980, *Yearbook* Vol. VIII (1983) at 383 (Italy No. 52); and the Hamburg judgment of 27 July 1978, *Yearbook* Vol. IV (1979) at 266 (FR Germany No. 18). The crucial test in these cases seems to be whether the time limit or notice period in fact precluded the objecting party from appointing his arbitrators, preparing his defence, or appearing at a hearing. *See Danaos Shipping Co.* v. *Fratelli Variola S.p.A.*, judgment of 28 January 1982, *Yearbook* Vol. IX (1984) at 425 (Italy No. 59). These cases are well within the general perception that international commerce requires enforcement of arbitral awards unless egregious errors have been committed.

3. *Handling of Evidence*

Two significant cases demonstrate the outer permissible limits to the handling of evidence in an arbitration. The first, the Hamburg judgment of 3 April 1975, *Yearbook* Vol. II (1977) at 241 (FR Germany No. 11), involved an arbitration between a German and an American firm. A single arbitrator had decided the issue in favor of the American firm, as was proper under the rules selected, without oral hearings and on the basis of submitted documents. Among the documents relied on was a letter from the American firm, which the arbitrator had failed to forward, before decision, to the German firm. In addition, the arbitrator had given no weight to a contradicting letter submitted by a German Ministry on behalf of the German firm. The Hamburg Court of Appeal denied enforcement of the award, holding that this conduct of the arbitrator had violated German public policy. Relying on previous French and Swiss decisions, the Court acknowledged that a distinction must be made between domestic and international public policy. The actions of this arbitrator, however, presented the "extreme case," "where a party had not been able to present his case in an arbitration abroad," that violated "basic principles of the German legal order." (*Yearbook* Vol. II at 241.) "The arbitrator . . . had not only violated the principles of a fair hearing, but the award was made without giving an opportunity to the German firm F to obtain knowledge of the letter the other party had submitted. Moreover, the arbitrator had not paid any attention to the letter of the German Ministry. . . ." (*Ibid.*) Enforcement must be refused, the Court established, "as soon as it cannot be excluded that a hearing (of the German firm F) could have led to a more favorable decision (for the German firm F)." (*Ibid.*)

In *Totem Marine Tug & Barge, Inc.* v. *North American Towing, Inc.*, 607 F.2d 649 (5th Cir. 1979), a maritime dispute arising in the United States, reliance on *ex parte* evidence was similarly found to violate due process.[20] After the close of the arbitration proceedings, the three arbitrators had discovered that each had different calculations for the earnings of the vessel, a figure around which damages were to be calculated. One arbitrator proceeded to contact one party to ascertain this figure, without notifying the other party of the request, and the award was calculated based on the *ex parte* information. In addition to finding the panel's decision beyond the scope of its mandate, the United States Federal Circuit Court held the procedural actions improper. Noting that "all parties in an arbitration proceeding are entitled to notice and an opportunity to be heard," 607 F.2d at 651, the Court concluded that "the ex parte receipt of evidence . . . constituted misbehavior by the arbitrators prejudicial to Totem's rights in violation of 9 USC para. 10(c)." (*Ibid.*, at 653.)

Where the errors are not prejudicial, courts turn a permissive eye on arbitrators' handling of evidence. There is great reluctance to overrule decisions on whether to hold hearings or hear certain witnesses. For example, in *Parsons & Whittemore Overseas Co., Inc.* v. *Société Générale de l'Industrie du Papier*, 508 F.2d 969 (2d Cir. 1974), *see Yearbook* Vol. I (1976) at 205 (USA No. 7), the United States Court of Appeals dismissed, *inter alia*, the claim that the arbitrators in an ICC arbitration had violated due process by refusing to delay proceedings to accommodate the speaking schedule of a witness. The court reasoned that Article

20. Although this case was decided under the United States Federal Arbitration Act, 9 USC, paras. 10, 11, it seems likely that the same standard would be applied under the Convention. *See also Chevron Transport Corp.* v. *Astro Vencedor Compania Naviera*, 300 F. Supp. 179 (SDNY 1969) (failure of maritime arbitrators to make one party's evidence available to other party, where party could show prejudice, held grounds for vacating award).

V(1)(*b*) of the New York Convention "essentially sanctions the application of the forum state's standards of due process." (508 F.2d at 975.) Moreover, "inability to produce one's witnesses before an arbitral tribunal is a risk inherent in an agreement to submit to arbitration" and "the logistical problems of scheduling hearing dates convenient to parties, counsel and arbitrators scattered about the globe argues against deviating from an initially mutually agreeable time plan unless a scheduling change is truly unavoidable." (*Ibid.*) The circumstances showed no such necessity, and therefore the arbitrators' action was within their discretion. A similar approach was taken in *Petroleum Transport, Ltd.* v. *Yacimiento Petroliferos Fiscales*, 419 F. Supp. 1233 (SDNY 1976), a maritime arbitration case, in which the United States District Court approved the arbitrators' decision not to hear an additional witness, proposed after the close of evidence-taking but before the award had been released, and set a modest standard for reviewing evidentiary decisions: "Barring a clear showing of abuse of discretion, the court will not vacate an award based on improper evidence or the lack of proper evidence." (419 F. Supp. at 1235.) *See also Compagnie de Saint Gobain-Pont à Mousson* v. *Fertilizer Corporation of India, Ltd.*, judgment of 15 May 1970, and of 10 May 1971, *Yearbook* Vol. I (1976) at 184 (France No. 1) (claim that party in ICC arbitration was not allowed to present case because arbitrator had refused to hear argument on specific issue or to hold a new hearing of witnesses after certain documents submitted, rejected; no violation of rules of public order); *Laminoirs-Trefileries-Cableries de Lens, S.A.* v. *Southwire Co.*, 484 F. Supp. 1063 (ND Ga. 1980), *see Yearbook* Vol. VI (1981) at 247 (arbitrators' decision in ICC arbitration to limit cross-examination approved as "not clearly an abuse of discretion" and not a denial of a fair hearing); judgment of 17 September 1976, Canton of Geneva, *Yearbook* Vol. IV (1979) at 311 (Switzerland No. 6) (arbitrators' consultation *ex parte* of expert on uncontroverted question held proper and no violation of public policy).

A final, somewhat singular case, *Biotronik Mess-und Therapiegeraete GmbH & Co.* v. *Medford Medical Instrument Co.*, 415 F. Supp. 133 (DNJ 1976), *see Yearbook* Vol. II (1977) at 250 (USA No. 8), involved a claim that a party to an ICC arbitration had committed fraud by failing to present to the tribunal relevant evidence favorable to the other party, who had defaulted in the arbitration. The United States Federal District Court rejected the claim, holding that "a party cannot complain about the non-production of evidence when it failed to offer such evidence itself." (415 F. Supp. at 138.) The Court also noted the "'pro-enforcement bias informing the Convention'" (quoting *Parsons & Whittemore, supra*) and emphasized that "in international commercial arbitration considerations of international reciprocity furnish an additional reason to construe defenses narrowly." (*Ibid.* at 139). Further rejecting the party's argument that it had been unable to present its case because its contract rights and liabilities had not matured at the time of the arbitration, the Court held that, under Article V(1)(*b*) of the New York Convention "the primary elements of due process are notice of the proceedings and the opportunity to be heard thereon." (*Ibid.* at 140.) As long as these had been provided, the defaulting party had to bear the consequences of its voluntary decision not to participate.

4. *Bankruptcy*

In *Fotochrome, Inc.* v. *Copal Co., Ltd.*, 517 F.2d 512 (2d Cir. 1975), *see Yearbook* Vol. I (1976) at 202 (USA No. 3), the United States Federal Court of Appeals reconciled a conflict between US bankruptcy law and the conduct of a foreign arbitration, holding that the filing of a Chapter XI petition in bankruptcy did not render invalid pending foreign arbitration proceedings. The subsequent arbitration award, reached after the party filing for bankruptcy had withdrawn from the arbitration, was held binding on the parties, although the prevailing party would be required to seek a judgment in a US court based on the award before it could be filed as a claim in bankruptcy. This case is relevant to the general topic of the conduct of proceedings because the Court recognized that in some cases bankruptcy laws could implicate US public policy and require that arbitral proceedings be halted or set aside; to deny a party the right to resort effectively to bankruptcy could give rise to a true conflict that US courts could not ignore. The Court's resolution of the issue in this case represented a compromise, but one that explicitly recognized the importance of fostering effective international commercial arbitration. The Court would not permit a party who had voluntarily agreed to arbitration to abort those proceedings by filing for bankruptcy. (*See ibid.* at 516.)

IV. THE AWARD

Certain procedural issues emerge as relevant to the issuance of the arbitral award, both as to its form and its content. The major element of procedure underlying these issues seems to be a guarantee that an award not be flagrantly and abusively contrary to the law that governs it. Although this principle crosses the line from procedure to substance, it is so closely related to the procedural process and to the relationship between courts and arbitration that it is useful to consider here.

In the United States, the concept that arbitrators face a limiting standard of review was enunciated in the case of *Wilko* v. *Swan*, 346 US 427, 436 (1953), where, in discussing the limited review that courts may exercise over arbitral awards, the Court stated:

> "Power to vacate an award is limited. While it may be true, as the Court of Appeals thought, that a failure of the arbitrators to decide in accordance with the provisions of the Securities Act would 'constitute grounds for vacating the award pursuant to section 10 of the Federal Arbitration Act,' that failure would need to be made clearly to appear. In unrestricted submissions, such as the present margin agreements envisage, *the interpretations of the law by the arbitrators in contrast to manifest disregard* are not subject in the federal courts to judicial review for error in interpretation." (Footnotes omitted; emphasis added).

The implication of this analysis was that arbitrators' interpretations of the law that do amount to "manifest disregard" will be subject to judicial review.

1. *Manifest Disregard of Law*

This notion of "manifest disregard of law" as a limit to an arbitrator's decision-making powers is considered in a number of countries to form part of public policy, although the standard of review in an international context remains at a relatively permissive level.

For example, in *Sidarma Societá Italiana di Armamento SPA* v. *Holt Marine Indus., Inc.*, 515 F. Supp. 1302 (SDNY 1981), discussed also *supra*, the United States Federal District Court rejected a claim of manifest disregard of law,[21] stating that "to vacate an arbitration award for manifest disregard of law there must be 'something beyond and different from a mere error in the law or failure on the part of the arbitrators to understand or apply the law' [citations omitted] . . . Plaintiff has not demonstrated, as it must, that the majority arbitrators deliberately disregarded what they knew to be the law in order to reach the result they did." (515 F. Supp. at 1308–9.)

In contrast, in *Sea Dragon, Inc.* v. *Gebr. van Weelde Scheepvaartkantoor B.V.*, 574 F. Supp. 367 (SDNY 1983), the United States Federal District Court, reviewing a maritime arbitration, affirmed that "ordinarily, an award may not be set aside because of the arbitrators' error in interpreting the laws. . . . Arbitration awards are regarded with extreme deference and arbitrators need not state the rationale behind their decision. . . . Extensive judicial review of arbitration awards would frustrate the basic purposes of arbitration, which is [sic] to dispose of disputes quickly and avoid the expense and delay of extended court proceedings." (574 F. Supp. at 371.) Nevertheless, the Court found that the award in question was indeed contrary to public policy and in manifest disregard of law because it knowingly ordered the non-prevailing party to violate a Dutch court order. On that ground, the American court vacated the award.

In other countries, a similarly modest standard of review is applied. In its judgment of 18 November 1982 in *Norsolor S.A.* v. *Pabalk Ticaret Ltd.*, *see Yearbook* Vol. IX (1984) at 159 (Austria No. 1), the Austrian Supreme Court found no infringement of mandatory provisions of substantive law in a decision of an ICC arbitral tribunal sitting in Vienna to apply an "international *lex mercatoria*," and award damages on the basis of equity, rather than to apply national conflict-of-law rules, as indicated by the ICC Rules. The Supreme Court reversed a lower court's holding that the arbitrators had violated public policy by so exceeding their mandate, holding that in applying *lex mercatoria* and the principle of good faith the tribunal had merely "applied a principle inherent in the private law systems which in no way is contradictory to strict legal regulations of the countries here concerned." (*Ibid.* at 160.) The Court also held that the arbitral tribunal's overstepping of a simple rule concerning the duration of the proceedings would not be regarded as a ground for nullifying the award. *See* discussion by Dr. Werner Melis, *ibid.* at 161–63.

Some limits on decision-making do nonetheless exist. In its judgment of 20 June 1978, *see Yearbook* Vol. V (1980) at 260 (FR Germany No. 19), a German

21. *See also Revere Copper & Brass, Inc.* v. *OPIC*, 628 F.2d 81 (DDC 1980); *A/S Siljestad* v. *Hideca Trading, Inc.*, 541 F. Supp. 58 (SDNY 1981).

Court refused to enforce a RUCIP arbitration award, essentially holding that the arbitrators had failed to consider the evidence and to rule on the preliminary issue of whether an arbitration agreement had been made. The Court stated:

> "Assuming even that the examination is admissible, then the arbitral award still cannot be enforced on grounds as to substance, because it is contrary to German public order (Art. V, para. 2, of the Convention).
>
> "The arbitral tribunal ... has committed serious procedural violations. Notwithstanding the objections of the respondent that no arbitration agreement had been concluded, it has omitted the necessary examination as to whether there existed valid arbitration agreements at all. The sales confirmations produced by the claimant in the arbitration only constitute proof that they were signed by him. They are not evidence that the arbitration agreement was concluded. As it appears from the reasoning of the award, the arbitral tribunal has not examined the question whether and how in each of the 200 transactions a valid arbitration agreement had been concluded. It has merely dealt with the interpretation of the sales confirmations.
>
> "A further serious procedural violation is that the arbitral tribunal has only considered the 200 transactions in their totality, without distinguishing between the legal aspects of each of the 200 cases.
>
> "Finally, it is inadmissible to deal with the competence of the arbitral tribunal in Hamburg without making the preliminary inquiry whether the competence of the arbitral tribunal is already lacking because of the time limits contained in Art. 10, para. 2, of the RUCIP Arbitration Rules."

(*Ibid.* at 261–62.)

2. *Lack of Reasons in Award*

In the United States, an arbitrator is not required to give reasons in his award. *See* Holtzmann, National Report United States in *Yearbook* Vol. IX (1984) IX at 62. This is also the case in England. *See* Steyn, National Report England 21, in *Handbook*. This is not so in many states. *See* Derains, National Report France 20, in *Handbook*; *see also* UNCITRAL Arbitration Rules, Article 31(3); UNCITRAL Model Law on International Commercial Arbitration, Article 31(2). Cases have arisen in some jurisdictions over enforcement of awards that do not give reasons. The result uniformly has been enforcement of the award if the jurisdiction where the award was made permitted such a practice.

In *S.A. Tradax Export* v. *S.p.a. Carapelli*, judgment of 22 October 1976, *see Yearbook* Vol. III (1978) at 279 (Italy No. 18), the Court of Appeals of Florence, enforcing an arbitration award under the Rules of the Grain and Feed Trade Association (London) that contained no reasons, noted that English law permits awards without reasons and that the New York Convention itself does not require reasons, and concluded that "what is fundamental in Italian law of procedure cannot be imposed upon foreign legislatures or judicial authorities." (*Ibid.* at 280.) Similarly, in its judgment of 8 October 1977, *see Yearbook* Vol. IV at 289 (Italy No. 29), the same Court enforced an arbitration award of the American Arbitration Association despite a lack of reasons, stating that "the fact that the reasoning constitutes a principle of the Italian Constitution is not important because what is fundamental in Italian law of procedure may not be considered as such by foreign legislative and judicial authorities." (*Ibid.* at 292.) *See also Efxinos Shipping Co. Ltd.* v. *Rawi Shipping Lines Ltd.*, judgment of 2 May 1980 of the Court of Appeal of Genoa, *Yearbook* Vol. VIII (1983) at 381, 383 (Italy No. 51): "it appears to be no longer contrary to Italian public policy to recognize a foreign award which does not contain reasons, provided that the parties have agreed in advance that reasons shall not be given." The French decision in *Denis Coakley Ltd.* v. *Sté. Michel Reverdy*, judgment of 23 July 1981, *see Yearbook* Vol. IX (1984) at 400 (France No. 6), discussed also *supra*, came to the same conclusion with regard to an English (GAFTA) award; and of similar import and reasoning were the judgment of a Hamburg Court of 27 July 1978, *see Yearbook* Vol. IV (1979) at 266–68 (FR Germany No. 18), and the judgment of 29 January 1983, in *European Grain & Shipping Ltd.* v. *Seth Oil Mills Ltd.*, High Court of Bombay, *see Yearbook* Vol. IX (1984) at 411, 414 (India No. 9).

3. *Form of Award*

As the preceding discussion infers, technical details of form are unlikely to affect the enforceability of an award. In the judgment of 26 April 1973, *see Yearbook* Vol. IV (1979) at 305 (Netherlands No. 3), the opponent to enforcement alleged that the arbitrators had failed to date the award (and that therefore it had never become binding). The Hague Court held that sufficient proof had been submitted on the date of signing and that such dating is not a mandatory requirement of Dutch law. And in the noted *Götaverken* case, *AB Götaverken* v. *General National Maritime Transport Company, Libya*, judgment of 13 August 1979, *see Yearbook* Vol. VI (1981) at 237, 238, 240 (Sweden No. 1), the Swedish Supreme Court affirmed its Court of Appeals holding that an arbitrator's alleged failure to participate in some minor supplemental decision and to sign the award did not violate Swedish public policy.

A third case, *Sonatrach* v. *Shaheen Natural Resources*, 585 F. Supp. 57 (SDNY 1983), *see Yearbook* Vol. X (1985) at 540 (USA No. 58), although principally an arbitrability case, involved some minor procedural details, including a claim that failure to issue the award within the time limit imposed under ICC Rules precluded enforcement. This argument was rejected, the Court holding that the party had failed to object at the proper time to the extension of time in which to issue the award.

V. CONCLUSION

This brief survey of the cases pertinent to public policy and arbitral procedure reveals that, although the basic elements of procedural regularity are commonly shared goals among the international community, when they are in conflict with the perceived needs of a thriving international commerce, they will be observed only in their most basic requirements. The elements of domestic due process, it seems, are in the process of being reformulated into an "international public policy" that will foster the free flow of goods and services and enhance arbitration and the arbitral process.

Public Policy and the Law Applicable to the Dispute in International Arbitration*

*Yves Derains***

TABLE OF CONTENTS

I. INTRODUCTION

1. In domestic law, public policy forms a set of rules that parties may not contract out of.[1] In private international law, public policy known as "international public policy" enables the judge to exclude the foreign law that

* Translation of the original French version of the Report.

** Past Secretary General, Court of Arbitration of the International Chamber of Commerce; Lawyer; member of ICCA.

1. *Cf.*, *e.g.*, Article 6 of the French Civil Code: "laws relating to public policy and morals cannot be contracted out of by means of special agreements".

would otherwise be applicable when it infringes on social or legal concepts considered to be essential in his legal system.[2] In this connection it is known as "overriding public policy". Private international law also contains concepts of "mandatory rules" sometimes described more accurately as "public policy" or "laws of immediate application". These are laws "whose observation is essential for safeguarding the political, social and economic organization of the country".[3] They are basically aimed at domestic relations, but do in fact govern all legal relationships entering into their field of application, even if these contain a foreign element. Consequently, public policy does not just operate to oust the law that would normally be applicable, but to exclude the application of foreign laws in a predetermined field in any circumstances.

2. There is no doubt that public policy in the various accepted senses of the term can affect the solutions given by an international arbitrator to the merits of the case. We shall content ourselves with setting out a number of examples, all derived from the practice of international arbitration.

a. A contract for the sale of a ship concluded between a Norwegian shipbuilding firm and a Peruvian shipowner governed by French law, provided for arbitration in Paris. The contract included a clause restricting the seller's liability for latent defects to a period of one year from the date of delivery of the ship.

Under French case law, such a clause restricting the seller's liability is void when the seller is a seller by profession, which was the case here. Did the arbitrators have to declare that this clause was void on the basis of French law, or to the contrary, rule that it was valid on the grounds that in arbitration the will of the parties should prevail over the law applicable to the contract?

b. A Swiss bank granted a loan in US dollars to a Portuguese company. The loan agreement was subject to English law and provided for arbitration in Zurich.

The Portuguese company did not repay the funds lent to it, claiming that it had obtained the necessary authorization for the transfer from the Portuguese exchange control authorities.

Should or could the arbitrators take account of the Portuguese mandatory rule raised as a defence despite the fact that the contract was subject to English law?

c. Two firms, one Italian, the other German concluded a contract subject to Swiss law and fixing Geneva as the place of arbitration. This contract was contrary to the competition provisions under the Treaty of Rome, which are

2. *Cf.* H. Batiffol and P. Lagarde, *Droit International Privé* (Paris 1981) vol. 1, no. 354.
3. *Cf.* Ph. Francescakis, Répertoire Dalloz de Droit International (Rep. D. Dr. Int.), V "Conflits de lois, principes généraux", no. 124 and no. 137.

mandatory rules in both German and Italian law. What should the arbitrators do in such a situation?

3. In the above examples, public policy can affect the solution given to the merits of the case on two different grounds:

- as the domestic public policy of the *lex contractus* (first example)
- as mandatory rule (second and third examples).

I shall discuss this division in the second and third parts of this report.

I have not dealt with the question of "overriding public policy" since it is too closely linked to the subject of "truly international public policy" which is the subject of Professor Pierre Lalive's report.

However, it seemed essential to deal briefly with the position of arbitrators in international commercial arbitrations when called to make a ruling on the law applicable to the merits of the case[4] in the first part of my report. Indeed, the specific solutions given by arbitrators when faced with public policy in its various guises, result from the uniqueness of that position.

II. THE INTERNATIONAL ARBITRATOR AND THE LAW APPLICABLE TO THE MERITS OF THE CASE

4. The main characteristic of the position of the international arbitrator called upon to decide on the merits of the case is his discretion (*1*). In using that discretion, the arbitrator seeks to find an answer to the legitimate expectations of the parties (*2*).

1. The Arbitrator's Discretion

5. Most often, the arbitrator's discretion in determining the law applicable to the merits of the case is implied. This results from the fact that when enforcement proceedings are required to make an arbitral award effective, the judge's review does not generally relate to the application of one law rather than another to the

4. The subject is only dealt with here to facilitate the problems proper to public policy. For a more complete summary of the problem, see, in particular: J. D. M. Lew, *Applicable Law in International Commercial Arbitration* (Dobbs Ferry 1978); B. Goldman, "Les conflits de lois dans l'arbitrage international de droit privé", in *Recueil des Cours* 1963 II, Académie de Droit International (Leiden 1964) vol. 109, pp. 347 *et seq.*; P. Lalive, "Les règles de conflits de lois appliquées au fond du litige par l'arbitre international siégeant en Suisse", Revue de l'arbitrage (Rev. Arb.) (1976) p. 155; Y. Derains. "Possible Conflict of Laws and the Rules Applicable to the Substance of the Dispute", P. Sanders, ed., ICCA's Congress Series No. 2, *UNCITRAL's Project for a Model Law on International Commercial Arbitration* (Deventer 1984) p. 169, Y. Derains, "Attente légitime des parties et droit applicable au fond en matière d'arbitrage commercial international", Travaux du Comité français de Droit international privé (1985).

merits of the case. This is taught by comparative law.[5] The contents of the law applied by the arbitrator may happen, of course, to violate the international public policy of the country where enforcement of the award is sought, and that incompatibility may be grounds for refusing enforcement. But in such a case it is not the choice of law that is in question, but its solutions on the merits. Thus, for example, an award ordering a party to pay interest may not be enforced in Saudi Arabia. But it is irrelevant whether it is dependent on German, English, French or any other law. The cause of the refusal of enforcement is the fact that it provides a solution contrary to the notion of public policy as defined by the Islamic Sharī'a rather than the choice of one law rather than another.

6. The New York Convention of 10 June 1958 on the Recognition and Enforcement of Foreign Arbitration Awards also impliedly confirms the arbitrator's discretion in this field.

In its list of grounds for refusal to enforce awards, Article V of the Convention does not refer at all to the question of the law applicable to the merits of the case.

7. Some more recent legislative texts expressly recognize the arbitrator's discretion. First of all, Article VII(1) of the Geneva Convention of 21 April 1961 on International Commercial Arbitration is worded as follows:

> "The parties shall be free to determine, by agreement, the law to be applied by the arbitrators to the substance of the dispute. Failing any indication by the parties as to the applicable law, the arbitrators shall apply the proper law under the rule of conflict that the arbitrators deem applicable. In both cases the arbitrators shall take account of the terms of the contract and trade usages."

Ever since 1981, the French New Code of Civil Procedure has provided in its Article 1496:

> "The arbitrator shall decide the dispute according to the rules of law chosen by the parties, in the absence of such a choice he shall decide according to the rules which he deems appropriate.
>
> In all cases, he shall take into account trade usages".

The 1984 Djibouti Code on International Arbitration contains in its Article 12 a provision in similar terms:

> "The parties are free to determine the rules of law which the arbitrators shall apply to the substance of the dispute. Failing agreement by the parties, the arbitrators shall apply the rules of law which they consider appropriate.
>
> In all cases, the arbitrators shall take into account contractual provisions and shall apply international trade usages".

5. *Cf.* Ph. Fouchard, *L'Arbitrage Commercial International* (Paris 1965) no. 562. The application of a law that is improper under the conflict rules of the judge ruling on the enforcement is analyzed as an error of law that could only be ratified by a review of the merits of the case, which is nowadays forbidden everywhere.

8. Lastly, the United Nations Commission on International Trade Law (UNCITRAL) in its Model Law adopted on 21 June 1985 provides in its Article 28:

"(1) The arbitral tribunal shall decide the dispute in accordance with such rules of law as are chosen by the parties as applicable to the substance of the dispute. Any designation of the law or legal system of a given state shall be construed, unless otherwise expressed, as directly referring to the substantive law of that state and not to its conflict of laws rules.
(2) Failing any designation by the parties, the arbitral tribunal shall apply the law determined by the conflict of laws rules which it considers applicable.
(3) The arbitral tribunal shall decide *ex aequo et bono* or as *amiable compositeur* only if the parties have expressly authorized it to do so.
(4) In all cases, the arbitral tribunal shall decide in accordance with the terms of the contract and shall take into account the usages of the trade applicable to the transaction."

9. Thus, the arbitrator's discretion with regard to determining the law applicable to the merits of the case is recognized by national laws and the most important international conventions, whether expressly or impliedly. This discretion is only actually limited by the express designation of the applicable law by the parties, or indirectly when the parties are subject to the rules of national arbitration institutions which in common with the arbitration centres of the CMEA countries[6] ask arbitrators to follow the conflict of laws rules of the headquarters of the institution. It should be noted in this connection that international arbitration rules on the other hand confirm the arbitrator's discretion to determine the applicable law. Two examples of this are:

Article 13(3) of the Rules of the ICC Court of Arbitration:

> "The parties shall be free to determine the law to be applied by the arbitrator to the merits of the dispute. In the absence of any indication by the parties as to the applicable law, the arbitrator shall apply the law designated as the proper law by the rule of conflict which he deems appropriate."

Article 33(1) of the UNCITRAL Arbitration Rules:

> "The arbitral tribunal shall apply the law designated by the parties as applicable to the substance of the dispute. Failing such designation by the parties, the arbitral tribunal shall apply the law determined by the conflict of laws rules which it considers applicable."

10. Whatever the circumstances, the consequence of the arbitrator's discretion to determine the law applicable to the merits of the case is that he has no *lex fori* in

6. *Cf.* J. D. M. Lew, *op. cit.*, no. 224.

the private international law sense of the term.[7] Consequently, his position is fundamentally different from that of the national judge faced with a conflict of laws problem.

In the most widely accepted concept of the conflict of laws rules, that is to say, the bilateralist theory, the *lex fori* enables the judge to characterize the legal question involved, supplies him with the connecting factors, plays a part in the sphere of public policy and in fraudulent evasion of the law. Furthermore, would any of the problems raised in private international law with regard to foreign law – its status, its method of proof – have any meaning if there were no *lex fori* and no foreign laws? Because of the lack of a *lex fori*, it is extremely difficult to approach the problem of the applicable law in arbitration cases in the same way as this is usually done where national courts are concerned.

For the international arbitrator there are at least two major consequences of the absence of a *lex fori*:

- The first is that the concept of competent law is meaningless; there is no law that he has to apply *a priori*. The law chosen by the parties is certainly an exception in this respect, but this is the consequence of the application of a rule proper to international arbitration and not the result of the operation of any particular *lex fori*.
- The second, particularly highlighted by B. Goldman, is that there is no foreign law in international arbitration[8] in the sense of a rule that is not part of the legal system of the authority responsible for resolving the dispute. All national laws have the same value and none of them has a privileged status. This has important consequences not only at the level of the proof of the contents of the applicable law, but also with regard to the coming into operation of the so-called "overriding public policy". The international arbitrator does not have to ensure that concepts that are purely national are respected.

11. Since there is no established system of conflict of laws and they do not have to take questions of competent law and foreign law into account, international arbitrators are bound to determine the law applicable to the merits of the case on the basis of quite different precepts from national courts.

2. The Legitimate Expectations of the Parties

12. It has been noted[9] that with the exception of certain cases where they decided to place themselves within the framework of a national conflict of laws system,

7. *Cf.*, in particular, ICC award no. 1512 of 1971, Journal du Droit International (Clunet) (1974) p. 904, Y. Derains "Jurisprudencia Arbitral de la Camara de Comercio Internacional" (Jurisprudencia Arbitral) p. 87, *Yearbook Commercial Arbitration* (Yearbook) Vol. V (Deventer 1980) p. 174, which states "the international arbitrator has no *lex fori* from which he can borrow rules of conflict of laws."

8. *Cf.* B. Goldman, *op. cit.*, p. 443.

9. *Cf.* P. Lalive, *loc. cit.*, p. 185 *et seq.*

arbitrators most often look for the law applicable to the merits of the case on the basis of one of the three following methods:

- cumulative application of conflict of laws systems concerned with the dispute;
- recourse to general principles of private international law;
- *voie directe*.

Under the first of the above methods, the arbitrator considers the conflict of laws rules of the various national legal systems connected to the disputes submitted to him one by one. If these rules, whose contents are nearly always different, converge towards one single domestic law, the arbitrator declares that this is the applicable law.[10]

Under the second method, the arbitrator refers to a conflict of laws rule which is widely accepted internationally.

And lastly, under the third system, the "direct method", the arbitrator, without concerning himself about referring to one particular system of conflict of laws, decides that the contract must be subject to the law of a certain country in view of its nature and characteristics.

13. It would be going too far to claim that these three methods are the only ones that arbitrators refer to, but they are so frequently adopted that any other approach can be classified as in the minority.[11] Generally, they lead to the application of a national law, but they may also sometimes lead to the application of a-national rules, which for the convenience of this report can be grouped together under the term *lex mercatoria*.[12]

However, whatever the outcome, and despite their differences in form, the common denominator of these methods is the fact that they result in the selection of the law whose application best corresponds to the parties' legitimate expectations. This is clearly the case with the cumulative application of the conflict of laws systems connected with the case, and recourse to general principles of private international law. Both methods select a law that a community to which the parties belong agrees to recognize as applicable, whether this is a limited community as in the first case, or the international community as in the second. The concern to respond to the parties legitimate expectations is also present when the arbitrators have recourse to the "direct method". The outcome of their analysis of the contract demonstrates to the parties that they could not legitimately expect the arbitrators to apply any law other than the one finally chosen.

In consequence, all these approaches have an underlying common basis – a concern for justification – to show the parties that the decision taken by the

10. For more details, see Y. Derains, "L'application cumulative par l'arbitre des systèmes de conflit de lois intéressées au litige", Rev. Arb. (1972) p. 93.
11. *Cf.* Y. Derains, Possible Conflict of Laws, *supra* n. 4, p. 178.
12. *Cf.* B. Goldman, "Frontière du droit et lex mercatoria", *Archives de philosophie du droit* (Paris 1964); "La lex mercatoria dans les contrats et l'arbitrage international: réalité et perspectives", Clunet (1979) p. 475.

arbitrators is the only one they could inevitably have expected from the competent arbitrators chosen by them.

This has in fact been very well expressed by Arthur Taylor Von Mehren in the following terms: "Their approach (the arbitrators) can and should be more in terms of what the parties' expectations or understanding were or would have been, had they addressed the issue".[13]

14. Thus, the concern to apply the law that best responds to the parties' legitimate expectations seems to be the central pivot round which the international arbitrator's actions revolve when he has to determine which legal rules he will apply to resolving the dispute. What is understood by the expression "the legitimate expectations of the parties"?

Negatively one might say that "the legitimate expectations of the parties" are not to be confused with "the will of the parties".

This is so, first of all, because the problems of determining the law applicable to the merits of the case arise mainly in cases where the will of the parties has not been expressed. For example, there seems unquestionably to be a lack of will expressed by the parties in a case where in the course of their pre-contractual negotiations the parties had held diametrically opposed points of view on the question of the applicable law, and that was why they did not specify such a law in their contract.

Next, the express or implied choice by the parties of the law applicable to the merits of the case does not preclude the possibility in some cases for it to be legitimate to expect the arbitrator to take account of the operation of a rule that the parties had not specified as applying to the contract, or indeed had deliberately excluded from it. Here, of course, I am referring to mandatory rules.

15. As a matter of fact, arbitrators seek to show the parties that they cannot, from the basis of the position that they are in when the arbitral procedure commences, expect the arbitrator to come to any decision as to the proper law other than the one actually rendered. Any other expectation would not be legitimate.

16. Having described the general position of the arbitrator who has to determine the law applicable to the merits of the case, I shall go on to consider the particular problems presented by the interplay of public policy in its various guises.

III. THE DOMESTIC PUBLIC POLICY OF THE *LEX CONTRACTUS*

17. To assist us in our considerations, it will be useful to refer again to the example set out above (No. 2a).

A contract for the sale of a ship concluded between a Norwegian shipbuilding firm and a Peruvian shipowner governed by French law, provided for arbitration

13. *Cf.* A. T. van Mehren, "To what Extent is International Arbitration Autonomous?" in Ph. Fouchard, Ph. Kahn, and A. Lyon-Caen, eds., *Le droit des relations économiques internationales, Études offertes à Berthold Goldman* (Paris 1982) p. 227.

in Paris. The contract included a clause restricting the seller's liability for latent defects to a period of one year from the date of delivery of the ship.

Under French case law, such a clause restricting the seller's liability is void when the seller is a seller by profession, which was the case here.

This is a case involving the intervention of domestic public policy which is a set of rules within a given legal system which parties cannot contract out of.

Are arbitrators in international commercial disputes bound to ensure that such domestic public policy is respected, or to give preference to the will of the parties by giving effect to the clause they included in their contract, despite the fact that it was void under French law, which was applicable to the contract?

18. It would appear that a distinction has to be drawn between two hypotheses:

- The applicable law was chosen by the parties;
- The applicable law is determined by the arbitrator.

The international commercial arbitrator is in a special position when faced by a two-fold problem of this sort.[14] The special features of his position can be more clearly understood when they are contrasted with the position of the national judge (*1*).

1. The National Judge and the Public Policy of the Lex Contractus

19. This is one of the questions that the subjectivists and objectivists – people holding two completely different viewpoints on private international contract law – have been discussing for many years.[15] These two different concepts result from differing analyses of the private international law rule – nowadays accepted by all legal systems – whereby parties have complete discretion in designating the law applicable to the contract, at least so far as the merits are concerned.

20. The subjectivist theory is that no law is recognized as having the power to govern an international contract unless the parties have decided that it is to do so. There are two consequences of this: firstly, the application of a law to an international contract is always based on the will of the parties, in the sense that if that will has not been expressed or was actually non-existent the judge has to establish what the parties would have decided if they had considered the question of the law applicable to their contract. Secondly, the law applicable to the international contract has no mandatory effect except insofar as the will of the parties has given it that effect.[16] This is the system known as "the incorporation" of the law into the contract[17] whereby the law is part of the contract and therefore

14. For more details, *cf.* Y. Derains, "Attente legitime des parties", *supra* n. 4, no. 23.

15. *Cf.*, in particular, H. Batiffol, "Subjectivisme et objectivisme dans le droit international privé des contrats", *Mélanges offerts à Jacques Maury*. p. 39 *et seq.*

16. *Cf.* P. Mayer, Droit International Privé (Paris, 1977) p. 545.

17. *Cf.* on this point, H. Batiffol and P. Lagarde, *op. cit.*, (1983) vol. 2, no. 571.

has no greater or lesser value than its other provisions. As has been pointed out,[18] this concept enables the parties:

- to choose a law which has no link with their situation;
- to exclude future provisions of the applicable law;
- to make the contract subject to no law – the so-called "law-free contract" theory;
- to choose certain provisions from a law and exclude others.

In the example set out above, the judge might, therefore, consider that by including a clause restricting the seller's liability in their contract the parties validly excluded the French public policy rule that makes such a clause void when the seller is a seller by profession. Such a conclusion has long-established origins in doctrine since Savigny took the view that provisions in the law declared applicable by the parties which render the contract void should not be taken into account.[19]

21. The objectivist theory is that an international contract is of necessity governed by a law. This law is determined by the judge on the basis of various objective criteria: place of conclusion of the contract, place of performance, etc. It may, for example, be a matter of applying one single criterion (e.g., in the case of a sale, the location of the seller's main establishment), or of looking at each case separately and weighing up the different criteria in each case and their relative importance in relation to the center of gravity of the contract. The will of the parties, whether express or implied, then features as an objective criterion which is a particularly important determining factor. Mr. Batiffol in the theory of the "localization" of the contract has judiciously charted the role played by the will of the parties. He has specified that the applicable law is not simply a stipulation, but is applicable like a law with all the consequences that that entails.[20] These consequencs all flow from the fact that the applicable law, whether or not chosen by the parties, is not an integral part of the contract, but governs it. So it is not at all surprising that in the example put forward here it can make the contract or one of its clauses void. The judge should therefore take the view that the clause restricting the seller's liability is void by virtue of the French public policy rule since the parties "localized" the contract under the French legal system.

22. For some time, case law in different countries has been veering between the subjectivist and objectivist theories, although purely subjectivist theories have remained in the minority. One example is a decision of the French Cour de Cassation in 1910 regarding a charter party made expressly subject to the law of New York containing a clause prohibited by that law that excluded the shipowner's liability. The Cour de Cassation did not sanction the Cour d'Appel

---

18. *Cf.* H. Batiffol and P. Lagarde, *op. cit.*, (1983) vol. 2, no. 571; P. Mayer, *op. cit.*, p. 545.
19. F. C. von Savigny, *System des heutigen römischen Rechts*, VIII §374.
20. *Cf.*, *inter alia*, H. Batiffol, "Subjectivisme et objectivisme dans le droit international privé des contrats", *loc. cit.*, p. 53.

for having considered that the parties "only intended anything not expressly provided for in the charter party to be subject to New York law".[21] However, the most extreme consequences of the subjectivist approach rapidly ceased to be followed. To refer again to French case law, in 1980 the current legal position was expressed in a decision of the Cour de Cassation that acknowledged that judges of the merits of the case are empowered "to interpret the common intention of the parties as to the 'localization' of the contract and deduce from this the applicable law".[22] Consequently the contract was governed by the applicable law, which implied that the judge should cancel contractual provisions contrary to the public policy of that law.[23]

23. This would seem to be the prevailing view in comparative law, even if the doctrinal analyses on which it is based are not always identical. An indication of this can be found in Article 3.1 of the Rome Convention of 19 June 1980 which provides that "the contract shall be governed by the law chosen by the parties". Whatever its geographical field of application, this Convention expresses a certain state of international thinking on the law applicable to contractual obligations. But, although this Convention sanctions the parties' right to choose the law applicable to the contract, and, as such is subjectivist in its approach, it specifies that that law governs the contract. It is not incorporated in it, and the classic consequences of subjectivism are thus avoided.

In this connection, it has been called "moderate subjectivism".[24] When the parties have not chosen the law governing the contract, it will be up to the judge to determine it on the basis of a number of criteria. But in every case such a step will result in the designation of laws governing the contract, which may as a result make some of its clauses void on the grounds of public policy, or even make it wholly void.

24. From the above comments – which although rather long are essential as background to the analysis of the position of the international arbitrator – it can be concluded that as far as the judge is concerned, because of the failure of the pure subjectivist doctrine to be admitted under the law in force, the contract is subject to the proper law, whether this law was chosen by the parties or determined by the judge in the absence of such choice. This is probably one of the effects of the bilateralist concept of the conflict of laws rule whereby the world's legislative jurisdictions are divided up. For the judge, there is always a law proper to a contract, and once that law has been determined by the conflict of laws rules, the contract is subject to that law, whatever the role played by the will of the parties in bringing it into play. Therefore, the public policy rules of that law must

21. *Cf.* Cass. Civ., 5 Dec. 1910, American Trading Co., Sirey (S) (1911) 1.129, note Lyon-Caen; Revue critique de droit international privé (Rev. Cr. dr. int. prv.) (1911) p. 395; Clunet (1912) p. 1156. *Cf.* also in the same terms, req. 19 Oct. 1938, Rev. cr. dr. int. prv., no. 935, p. 127.
22. Cass. Civ. 25 March 1980, Rev. cr. dr. int. prv. (1980) p. 576, note H. Batiffol, Clunet (1980) p. 650, note Ph. Kahn.
23. French case law provides examples of contracts or clauses in contracts made void by the law chosen by the parties, *cf.* Cass. Civ. 28 June 1966, Rev. cr. dr. int. prv. (1967) p. 334, note H. Batiffol.
24. P. Mayer, *op. cit.*, p. 549 *et seq.*

be applied by the judge even if that leads him to call into question the parties' contractual agreement.[25]

In the example put forward, it would therefore, seem that because of a public policy rule of French law which is applicable to the contract, a national judge would cancel the clause in the contract restricting the seller's liability.

What would the international arbitrator do in the situation?

2. *The International Arbitrator and the Public Policy of the* Lex Contractus

25. A distinction has to be drawn between cases where the law of the contract has been chosen by the parties (a.) and those where this law is determined by the arbitrator (b.).

a. *The* lex contractus *has been chosen by the parties*

26. The arbitrator is bound to apply the law specified by the parties. One award in 1971 in ICC Case No. 1581[26] states this expressly:

> "Whereas the arbitral tribunal derives from the terms of reference the entire scope of its powers and of its competence and that, contrary to a State Court, it is bound by the will of the parties where such parties are unanimous on the question;
>
> Whereas, therefore, notwithstanding that it is surprising in view of principles of private international law to link French law to a matter of which the principal elements are found in Switzerland, the tribunal is bound to declare French law applicable in this case."

Moreover, as we have seen, both international and national legislative texts dealing with the law applicable to the merits of the case in international arbitration have placed the same obligation on the arbitrator.

The 1961 Geneva Convention indicates that "the parties are free to determine the law that the arbitrators must apply to the merits of the case"; this mandatory wording is used again in the Djibouti Code on International Arbitration. The French New Code of Civil Procedure requires the arbitrator to decide the case in accordance with the rules of law chosen by the parties (see No. 7 above). Identical solutions are also found in arbitration rules (*cf.* No. 9 above). The arbitrator does not have to evaluate whether the parties' choice of the applicable law is well-founded; he simply has to respect it. But does this apparently indefeasible respect of the will of the parties mean that he has to put an end to the contractual agreement resulting from the same will on the grounds of the public policy of the chosen law?

27. One is tempted to look for solutions to this conflict in legislative texts or arbitration rules insofar as those referring to the law chosen by the parties and to

25. Obviously the judge might refuse to apply certain public policy provisions of the applicable law because of their content, in the name of his own international public policy, but that is another question.

26. *Cf.* Clunet (1974) p. 887; Jurisprudencia arbitral, p. 70.

the contractual stipulations at one and the same time appear to take a stand on the respective weights of the applicable law and of the contract by recourse to different wording.

The 1961 Geneva Convention, the Djibouti Code and the ICC Arbitration Rules all state in closely similar terms that the arbitrator must apply the law chosen by the parties and take account of the contractual stipulations. It can be deduced from this that the arbitrator must only take account of the contractual stipulations insofar as the law chosen by the parties recognizes that they are valid. Such a deduction presupposes, however, that it is taken as read that the parties had not placed the contractual stipulations in question outside the field of application of the chosen law, or that they did not have the power to do so.

The UNCITRAL Model Law which reproduces in its Article 28(4) the text of Article 33(3) of the UNCITRAL Arbitration Rules appears to confer greater power on the contractual provisions:

> "In all cases the arbitrator shall decide in accordance with the terms of the contract and shall take into account the usages of the trade applicable to the transaction."

Does the arbitrator's obligation to decide in accordance with the contractual stipulations "in all cases" mean that the stipulations must be respected even when the applicable law selected by the parties renders them void? The text does not necessarily go as far as this, for it can be presumed that it is referring to contractual stipulations that are valid under the law governing them. Such a presumption, nevertheless, implies that any conflict between the applicable law and the contractual clauses has been settled in advance in favor of the former, which once again raises the question we were seeking to answer. Thus, an arbitrator will not be able to resolve a possible conflict between a contractual clause and the public policy of the law chosen by the parties by consulting legislative texts and arbitration rules.

In fact, he should be guided only by the will of the parties.

28. As we have seen, the parties' discretion is unrestricted so far as the choice of the applicable law is concerned (*cf.* Nos. 9 and 26). Not only do the parties have the absolute discretion to choose any law that they wish, but they may also exclude the application of any national law by referring to the general principles of law or the *lex mercatoria*,[27] restrict the field of application of the national law selected by combining it with the general principles of law,[28] freeze that law at a given date,[29] etc. They may also very well exclude from the applicable law selected those provisions that would make certain contractual clauses void. However, if this is what they intend, they must specify the fact.

27. *Cf.* B. Goldman, "La lex mercatoria dans les contrats et l'arbitrage international", *loc. cit.*, p. 475.

28. *Cf.* the various examples given by P. Weil, "Principes généraux du droit et contrats d'État", in Études offertes à Berthold Goldman, p. 388 *et seq.*

29. *Cf.* in this connection ICC case no. 3093/3100 where it was held that the law applicable to the contracts is the one that was in force at the moment of the conclusion of the contract, Clunet (1980) p. 251; Jurisprudencia arbitral, p. 255.

29. Thus, a conflict between the wording of the contract and the public policy of the law chosen by the parties must only be resolved by the international arbitrator in the light of the wording of the contractual clauses relating to the applicable law. For example, a clause providing that "for all questions not covered by the contract, Dutch law shall be applicable" obliges the arbitrators to give effect to all the contractual stipulations, even if these would be void by virtue of Dutch public policy. On the other hand, a clause specifying: "this contract is governed by French law" means that there is a direct hierarchical link between French law and the contractual clauses; the parties have decided to have their will put into effect in accordance with French law. A clause that would be void under French public policy would therefore have to be set aside by the arbitrators. In the award rendered in 1980 in ICC Case No. 3380[30] the arbitrators considered that a clause phrased: "this Agreement shall be subject to and constructed in accordance with the laws in Syria meant that "the contract is governed by and should be interpreted in accordance with Syrian law in its entirety without restriction".

Likewise, in 1978, arbitrators in ICC Case No. 2119 held that a clause indicating that a contract was to be "performed and interpreted in accordance with French law" meant that "the contractual provisions were directly applicable insofar as they were not in contravention of the mandatory provisions of French law".[31] Indeed, if a contract has to be performed "in accordance" with a given law, this could not be done in the case of stipulations contrary to the public policy rules of that very law.

30. The actual implications of the wording of certain clauses stipulating the applicable law can be more difficult to determine. For example, faced with a claüse whereby "the arbitration shall take place at The Hague and the arbitrators shall apply Swedish law", can the arbitrators set aside a clause in the contract because it is in breach of Swedish public policy? It would seem that they can, because the apparent will of the parties is that any dispute is to be settled by Swedish law; and the validity of a contractual clause is a dispute like any other. However, there are other interpretations. It is up to the arbitrator, whose task is to interpret the contract, to decide. Likewise, the fact that arbitrators have been granted the powers of *amiables compositeurs* and this is combined with the choice of a particular national law should not be interpreted as authority for excluding the public policy of the *lex contractus*.[32]

31. It is important to underline that so far as the arbitrator is concerned, there is no natural hierarchy between the contract and any particular national law. Quite the contrary, a law is only applied if the parties have chosen it and within the bounds of that will. If the parties have expressly excluded certain rules of that law, the arbitrators may not enforce the application of those rules in the name of

30. *Cf.* Clunet (1981) p. 928; Jurisprudencia arbitral, p. 303; Yearbook, Vol. VII (1982) p. 116.
31. *Cf.* Clunet (1979) p. 997; Jurisprudencia arbitral, p. 242.
32. For a more detailed assessment of the implications, *cf.* E. Loquin, *L'Amiable Composition en Droit Comparé et International* (Paris 1980) p. 268.

public policy of which they are not the guardians. By introducing appropriate clauses into their contract, it is possible that the parties intended to exclude the public provisions of a law which they intended to apply to the rest of the contract.

However, it cannot be held that this is the implied will of the parties on every occasion that a stipulation in the contract is contrary to the public policy of the law chosen by them. It is only by an analysis of the clause whereby the parties designated the applicable law that the arbitrator is able to determine the role that the parties intended to confer on that law and to resolve the conflict between that law and one contractual stipulation or another, or even an entire contract when its validity is in question. In this connection, it should be noted that in practice in concluding contracts preference is given to wording that involves a hierarchical link between the chosen law and the contract, with the chosen law in the dominant position. But the parties may very well alter that hierarchy subsequently by recognizing that a clause that is void by virtue of the public policy of the chosen law is to have effect, either expressly or impliedly by performing it voluntarily. There is nothing to prevent the parties from choosing the applicable law after the conclusion of the contract.[33] Parallel to this, there is nothing to prevent them from restricting the field of application of that law.

32. Therefore, in the example given above, it would seem that the arbitrators should set aside the clause in the contract restricting the seller's liability since it is in breach of a public policy rule of French law – the proper law of the contract – unless it is proved to them that although the parties referred to French law, they wished to exclude that public policy rule.[34]

b. *The* lex contractus *is determined by the arbitrator*

33. If the arbitrator determines the applicable law, where the parties have not specified it, he must apply that law as it stands. It is difficult to see by what right the arbitrator might decide to exclude one provision or another on the grounds that it is contrary to one of the contractual clauses. One can, of course, envisage a case where the arbitrator takes the view that the parties had intended the contract not to be subject to the public policy provision in question, but this would presuppose that the parties' intention on this point was established. This is rather unlikely in a case where the parties have failed to decide on the applicable law.

34. In fact, before determining the applicable law, the arbitrator will draw inferences from any conflict between the wording of the contract and the content of any of the laws that might possibly have a right to be applied. If there is a conflict it is viewed as a negative indication; it is presumed that the parties did not intend their contractual relationship to be governed by a legal system that is unprepared to accept them on their terms. As Mr. Batiffol has pointed out:

---

33. *Cf.* ICC award no. 1434 of 1975, Clunet (1976) p. 978; Jurisprudencia arbitral, p. 145.

34. Obviously, this theory presupposes that the domestic public policy rule also applies to international contracts. Otherwise, the question does not arise. *Cf.* ICC award no. 1434 of 1975, *supra* n. 33.

> "Parties to a contract must be presumed to have the implied intention of choosing a law authorizing the contract rather than one which would nullify it".[35]

To return to the wording of the French New Code of Civil Procedure (Art. 1496) the second law is not "appropriate".

35. Therefore, in the example given above, it can be concluded that if the arbitrator declared French law applicable, he would have to set aside the clause restricting the seller's liability. But more important than this, it seems that the fact that this particular clause was included in the contract should lead him to decide that the contract is not governed by French law since the parties had without any doubt intended their restriction of the seller's liability to have effect.

36. At the end of this consideration limited to the public policy of the *lex contractus*, in principle one can put forward the view that it will most probably be applied by the arbitrator to nullify the contractual stipulation. However, an arbitrator will hesitate to declare that a law excluding one or more clauses is the proper law of the contract. And parties – who have the discretion to make their contract free from the application of any national law – may, provided that they express the fact unambiguously, exclude certain provisions of the applicable law that they do not consider appropriate, even if these provisions are public policy rules.

What is the position of the public policy rules of laws foreign to the *lex contractus*?

IV. MANDATORY RULES

37. Can we not purely and simply state that the international arbitrator does not have to concern himself with the public policy of laws that are foreign to the *lex contractus*? It is tempting to reply in the affirmative, at least when the problems faced by the arbitrator are contractual in nature, that is to say connected with the interpretation, performance, termination, or validity of the contract, etc. Questions of a non-contractual nature – such as capacity, tortious liability, etc. – arise too seldom in arbitration for us to deal with within the necessarily limited context of this report.

Although this approach has the merit of simplicity, it would not, however, take sufficient account of the existence, in addition to public policy in the domestic law sense of the term, of mandatory rules which are too important in the interests of a given national society to enter into competition with foreign laws and whose "field of application is consequently determined basically with regard to their objective".[36]

38. Two of the examples set out above (No. 2 (b.) and (c.)) illustrate the claim of such laws to intervene despite the fact that they do not belong to the *lex contractus*:

35. H. Batiffol, "La loi appropriée au contrat", in Études offertes à B. Goldman, p. 2.
36. Ph. Francescakis, *op. cit.*, nos. 124 and 137.

First example
A Swiss bank granted a loan in US dollars to a Portuguese company. The loan agreement was subject to English law and provided for arbitration in Zurich.

The Portuguese company did not repay the funds lent to it, claiming that it had not obtained the necessary authorization for transfer from the Portuguese exchange control authorities.

Second example
Two firms, one Italian, the other German, concluded a contract subject to Swiss law and fixing Geneva as the place of arbitration. This contract was contrary to the competition law provisions under the Treaty of Rome, which are mandatory rules in both German and Italian law.

In both the above examples, laws foreign to the *lex contractus* claim to affect the contract. Indeed, the field of application of the Portuguese exchange control regulations and the European competition rules does not depend on the choice of the law applicable to a contract. As mandatory rules, their very aim is to disallow parties from excluding them by making their contract subject to a law foreign to the legal system from which they stem, or a judge or arbitrator preventing them from coming into effect by deciding to apply such a foreign law to the contract.

39. When faced with difficulties like this, the national judge has to distinguish between mandatory rules "of the forum" and foreign mandatory rules. The mandatory rules of the forum have a natural priority which the judge has to apply, whatever the proper law of the contract. Therefore, a Portuguese judge would give effect to the Portuguese exchange control regulations, and a German or Italian judge to the rules of the Treaty of Rome. The mandatory rules of the forum by their very existence preclude the operation of the applicable law by virtue of the conflict of laws rule of the *lex fori*.

The question of foreign mandatory rules is more complicated. Should the judge apply them only when they fall within the legal system that its conflict of law rules designate as having jurisdiction, subject to the intervention of overriding international public policy? Does the judge, on the contrary, have to require foreign mandatory rules to be observed in all cases where he considers this is necessary if they are to achieve their objective?[37] To date these questions have not been answered definitively, although the Rome Convention of 19 June 1980 provides useful guidance on this.

40. Since there is no *lex fori* and accompanying distinction between the respective national and foreign laws, the international arbitrator does not go into the question of the application of mandatory rules in the same way as the judge. He takes no account of the distinction between mandatory rules of the forum and foreign mandatory rules. He can only take account of the distinction between mandatory rules of the *lex contractus* (*1*) and mandatory rules of another legal system (*2*).

37. *Cf.* P. Mayer, *op. cit.*, p. 101.

1. *Mandatory Rules of the* Lex Contractus

41. Arbitrators seem to approach the problem of the intervention of mandatory rules of the *lex contractus* differently depending on whether the parties have chosen this law (a.), or whether it is up to the arbitrator to determine it (b.).

a. *The* lex contractus *has been chosen by the parties*

42. As was pointed out above, the arbitrator is bound to apply the law specified by the parties (*cf.* No. 25 *et seq*). Consequently when the parties have chosen a law to apply to their contract, it will be concluded from the outset that the arbitrator has to apply the mandatory rules of that law. Naturally, one may envisage an arbitrator refusing to give effect to a mandatory rule forming part of the law selected by the parties in the name of "truly international public policy", but he would then found his decision on the content of that law rather than on its nature.

43. Thus the problems posed by mandatory rules of the *lex contractus* when it has been chosen by the parties seem to be closely similar to those relating to the domestic public policy of that law. However, they are not entirely similar.

Indeed, as we saw in Nos. 29–31 above, possible conflicts between the contractual stipulations and the domestic public policy of the law chosen by the parties ought to be resolved by discovering what effect the parties intended their stipulated choice of law to have. This is explained by the power that parties have to select the law most appropriate to their needs, to exclude the application of any national law, etc. There is therefore nothing unusual in the parties deciding to restrict the field of application of the chosen law by excluding some of the clauses in their contract from its effect since they would otherwise be void. They could just as well have chosen another law which did not nullify them.

On the other hand, merely discovering the parties' intention as to the effect of their stipulation of the law would not enable the resolution of a conflict between a contractual stipulation and a mandatory rule of the proper law of the contract. A slight alteration to the second example cited above (No. 38) will demonstrate this:

Let us suppose that instead of having chosen Swiss law as the *lex contractus* the parties had chosen German law and specified that their agreement was not subject to European competition law. Would the arbitrator then be able to take the view that he does not have to apply these rules on the grounds that the parties have made their choice of German law only partial by excluding some of its mandatory rules.

The answer is in the negative since the claim of mandatory rules to affect a contractual operation, unlike domestic public policy, is not necessarily dependent on the choice of the *lex contractus*. In the example given above, the European competition law rules are intended to be applied to the contract whether the *lex contractus* chosen by the parties is German law shorn of its policy laws or Swiss law.

The problem thus leads to the question whether the arbitrator has to apply the mandatory rules of a law other than the *lex contractus* when that law was chosen so as to preclude the operation of the mandatory rules in question (*cf. infra* No. 50).

b. *The* lex contractus *is determined by the arbitrator*

44. Unlike the national judge, the arbitrator is not affected by the concept of a particular law with jurisdiction over the contract. Consequently, unless the parties have chosen the *lex contractus* all laws that claim to affect the contract have *a priori* equal right to be applied. Therefore it is not surprising to find that arbitrators decide on the applicability of the mandatory rules directly without asking whether they belong to the *lex contractus*.

An award rendered in ICC Case No. 4123 in 1983 illustrates this type of process.[38] The arbitrator was dealing with a dispute regarding a contract that had to be performed by a party in Korea and another party in the EEC. He considered the question of the application to the contract of Korean mandatory rules and EEC competition law before determining the law applicable to the contract.

> "Here, the Tribunal distinguishes between the (private) law governing the Agreement on the one side, and other rules of (public) law that may be applicable to the Agreement on the other side.
>
> "The parties agree that the Agreement is for an important part to be performed within the territory of the Republic of Korea. Therefore, whatever national private law may govern the Agreement, the latter is likely to affect the domain of Korean (public) law, so that this Tribunal must determine whether Korean law as invoked by the defendant is applicable to the Agreement, even if it does not govern it.
>
> "However, the national public law as invoked by the defendant in this case (antitrust law, price law, fair trade law) is by nature of public order. Usually, the very application of these public laws is based upon considerations of national public policy. It is for this reason that this Arbitral Tribunal is not free directly to apply the Korean public law as invoked by the defendant when such considerations of public policy would be involved to an appreciable extent.
>
> "On the other hand, the Tribunal is empowered to apply national public law insofar as the tribunal is satisfied that in the circumstances of the case pursuant to published jurisprudence of the competent national courts and/or the published and stated policy of the competent national authorities the acts under consideration of the Arbitral Tribunal are deemed null and void and unenforceable as prohibited by any relevant national public law.
>
> "As a consequence of this, the party which in arbitral proceedings appeals to any national public law must prove that this law, indeed, is applicable in the case, and to what extent.
>
> ....
>
> "Since the defendant did not provide sufficient evidence as to the structure of the relevant market and the position of the claimant thereupon, the Tribunal is not satisfied that at the time the claimant was in a dominant position and able to abuse his market power, nor can it see that the technical know-how relating to the manufacture of (the product) on the one side and the supply of the latter raw material on the other side are

38. *Cf.* Yearbook, Vol. X (1985) p. 49.

two independent items causing a tie-in in the sense of Art. 4 of the above Notification (*cf.* preamble and Clause 1 of the Agreement).

"Therefore the tribunal is of the opinion that the defendant did not sufficiently prove his case that Clause 1 and Clause 2 of the Agreement contain tie-in provisions prohibited by Korean public law.

. . . .

"As set out hereabove . . . with respect to national public laws also the rules on competition (Art. 85 *et seq.*) of the Treaty are of public order and part of the public policy of the Community. As far as the possible application of those rules on competition of the Treaty in this arbitral case is concerned, the tribunal refers, mutatis mutandis, to its considerations hereabove. . . .

"Pursuant to Art. 85, para. 2, of the Treaty – which provision is according to the relevant jurisprudence of the competent Court of Justice of the European Communities (CJEC) directly applicable in that any party is entitled to request a national court to ensure the protection of its rights arising out of this Treaty provision – all agreements between undertakings, decisions by associations of undertakings and concerted practices in violation of Art. 85 of the Treaty are prohibited and shall be automatically void.

"If this tribunal finds that the agreement in whole or in part contravenes Art. 85 of the Treaty, the consequence thereof is likely to be that the relevant clauses, if not the Agreement in toto are deemed void and unenforceable.

"With reference to its considerations hereabove, the Tribunal must, therefore, on its own initiative, investigate whether the Agreement comes under the prohibition of Art. 85, para. 1 of the Treaty."

It was only afterwards that the award declared that Korean law was applicable to the contract:

"The Agreement has been executed and performed partly in Italy and partly in Korea. At the time the Agreement was made the parties did not express themselves as to the law that would govern their contractual relationship. Lacking such choice of law by the parties and all further direct points of contract which could be decisive for the determination of the governing law, the Centre of Gravity test, as proposed by the defendant, could indeed be relevant in order to decide this question.

"Notwithstanding the name of the Agreement (Supply and Purchase Agreement) this contract is not just of the nature of a mere supply and purchase contract. Claimant has granted to defendant the right to use their technical know-how relating to the manufacture of (the product), on an exclusive basis in the Republic of Korea. Defendant purchased from Claimant the raw materials required for the production of the product in Korea.

"Taking these special elements of the Agreement into account this Tribunal is satisfied that the Agreement is for a larger part to be performed in Korea and that for that reason Korean private law should prevail as the law governing the Agreement".

The process followed in this award consisted in placing the mandatory rules of the *lex contractus* on the same level as all the mandatory rules liable to claim to be applied to the parties' agreement. The fact that Korean mandatory rules belong to the *lex contractus* did not apparently confer on them any special grounds for being applied.

45. On the other hand, arbitrators may deduce from the fact that a mandatory rule has a claim to be applied to a contract that the law from which that mandatory rule derives is the *lex contractus* as is evidenced by an award rendered in 1982[39] in ICC Case No. 2930:

> "Consequently, the arbitral tribunal observes that the aggregate of the contracts which it has to examine is indisputably closely connected, and even very closely connected, with Yugoslavia and as one single law should be applicable to the entirety of the contractual obligations of the parties, the connection with Yugoslav law prevails without any doubt.
>
> "The arbitral tribunal is even more convinced with this choice in that the Claimants, being under Yugoslav jurisdiction, are subject to the Yugoslav law controlling import and export control (Law of 1972, Federal Official Gazette No. 36 of 1972). This law contains provisions of public law including punitive sanctions; fines according to the 1972 text; and imprisonment, according to the modifications of this law in 1977, the latter not being applicable in this particular case. Consequently, any contract concerning import into Yugoslavia or export from Yugoslavia is subject to the mandatory provisions of this law."

2. *Mandatory Rules Foreign to the* Lex Contractus

46. With regard to mandatory rules foreign to the *lex contractus*, the two examples set out above (*cf.* No. 38) enable us to distinguish between two different cases:

a. The taking into consideration of mandatory rules.
b. The application of mandatory rules.

47. a. In the first example, the Portuguese debtor who claimed that a refusal of authorization for the transfer by the Portuguese exchange control authorities was grounds for his non-payment did not ask the arbitrator to apply the Portuguese mandatory rules that caused this refusal. He merely wanted it to be "taken into consideration"[40] although English law was applicable to the loan agreement. Moreover, it must be admitted that, in any case, the arbitrator would not be able to apply the Portuguese regulations in question by reason of their very nature. All that he has to do is to take its operation into consideration so as to draw legal conclusions under English law, the proper law of the contract.

Situations of this type can be found in decisions in arbitration cases: refusal of the exchange control authorities of the buyer's country to allow the performance of a contract for the sale of oil subject to the law of the seller's country;[41] refusal of consent by the authorities of the place of performance of the contract which was subject to another law.[42] In these examples, it is clear that arbitrators would have had no jurisdiction to apply the public law provisions underlying the

39. *Cf.* Yearbook, Vol. IX (1984) p. 105.
40. On the distinction between application and taking into consideration, *cf.* P. Mayer," Les lois de police étrangères", Clunet (1981) p. 307 *et seq.*
41. ICC case no. 2216, Clunet (1975) p. 917; Jurisprudencia arbitral p. 105.
42. ICC case no. 1782, Clunet (1975) p. 923; Jurisprudencia arbitral, p. 111.

administrative measures whose effects on the performance of the contract they had to evaluate. The question of the applicability of these mandatory rules is not discussed. The effects engendered by them are noted and taken into account in accordance with the *lex contractus*.

47. b. The first example only needs to be slightly amended to take us away from the question of the taking into consideration of the mandatory rules of the *lex contractus* into the field of their applicability. For example, if we were to assume that the Portuguese debtor was no longer claiming that it was impossible to transfer the funds as a result of refusal of authorization by the exchange control authorities, but rather that the loan agreement was void for lack of authorization by the same authorities prior to the loan; the arbitrator would then have to decide whether he could declare a contract subject to English law was void by the application of a Portuguese mandatory rule.

Yet again, the question raised by the second example is the applicability of a mandatory rule foreign to the *lex contractus*. Can a contract subject to Swiss law be declared void by an international arbitrator by virtue of the EEC competition rules?

The ICC award rendered in Case No. 4132 (*cf.* above No. 44) is an actual example of this type of problem. It seems that the question has to be asked in different terms depending whether the parties have or have not chosen the *lex contractus* (*a.* and *b.*).

a. *The parties have chosen the* lex contractus

48. The principle whereby arbitrators are bound to apply the law chosen by the parties (*cf.* No. 26 above) is sometimes all that is needed for them to set aside a mandatory rule foreign to that law. An example of this is the decision by the Court of Arbitration of the Chamber of Foreign Trade of the German Democratic Republic.[43] The arbitrators were called to rule on the validity of a licence agreement concluded between a firm in the GDR and another firm in the GFR. The second firm considered, *inter alia*, that the contract was void as being contrary to the competition law provisions of its own country and to Article 85 of the Treaty of Rome. Stressing that the parties had made the contract subject to the law of the GDR, the arbitrators put forward the following argument:

> "The validity of the agreement must be judged under the law of the GDR designated in the arbitral clause as the law applicable to the agreement.
>
> . . . .
>
> The invalidity of the licence agreement cannot result from Sect. 20 of the Law on Restrictive Trade Practices of the FRG and Sects. 85 *et seq.* of the EEC Treaty. In determining the validity of the licence agreement under GDR law, these provisions must be taken into account only if they would render the performance of the agreement effectively impossible and the invalidity of the agreement would have to be accepted pursuant to Sect. 306 Civil Code (GDR). Such factual impediments for performance have not been proven by the respondent."

43. *Cf.* Yearbook, Vol. IV (1979) p. 197, award of 27 June 1976.

49. However, arbitrators are not usually satisfied with indicating that a mandatory rule is foreign to the *lex contractus* as a reason for not applying it. Indeed, the designation of the *lex contractus* does not necessarily imply that the parties had intended all mandatory rules liable to affect the contract to be excluded. And arbitrators prefer to explain that there are no serious grounds for applying the mandatory rules in question in every respect.

An award rendered in 1982 by the arbitral tribunal of the Amsterdam Grain Trade Association ruling on appeal[44] regarding the applicability of the Austrian exchange control regulations to contracts subject to Dutch law stated as follows:

> "According to Article 16 of the VERNOF conditions Dutch law applies to the contracts concerned here. But even if the conditions had not contained this choice of law, the Dutch law would still have been applicable to the sales contracts according to Dutch private international law, since this concerned the sale FOB Europort of a Dutch product on Dutch standard conditions, which are generally used for this purpose in international trade. Nevertheless appeal-arbitrators could give effect to mandatory provisions of the law of another country if a close link exists between the case and that country; in so deciding, the nature and extent of these provisions must be taken into account as well as the consequences of application or non-application.
>
> Appeal-arbitrators are of the opinion that in the present case the sales contracts do not have such a close link with Austria that the provisions of Austrian currency law should be given effect. The connection with Austria exists exclusively in the fact that the seat of the seller is situated in that country. The product which has been sold is of Dutch origin, the buyer is Dutch, the transactions took place through a FR German broker, the sale took place FOB Europort, with the price expressed in FR German Marks, and, moreover, by telex of November 20, 1980 the seller requested payment of its account with a bank in Germany.
>
> And even if a close connection between the contracts and Austria were to be assumed, the appeal-arbitrators are still of the opinion that no effect should be given to a provision of Austrian currency law which, according to the appellant, would lead to the nullity of the contracts since the seller apparently did not receive authorization in that respect. It is not possible here to accept the nullity which Austrian law apparently prescribes, in the light of the considerable importance to the Netherlands of the preservation of the normal course of legal relations regarding normal international commercial transactions, like the ones concerned here."

This decision, it is true, does not perhaps give a clear indication of the attitude of international commercial arbitrators since the arbitral tribunal seems to have many features of a judge under Netherlands law. One is led to this conclusion by the fact that the tribunal gave Holland's economic interests as an indication that Austrian policy law should in any case be excluded by reason of its content.

If this is the case, its statement that it is not "a priori" impossible to apply policy laws foreign to the *lex contractus* chosen by the parties is perhaps closer to case law precedents of the Dutch Supreme Court[45] than to the practice of international commercial arbitration.

---

44. *Cf.* Yearbook, Vol. VIII (1983) p. 158.

45. *Cf.* Cour de Cassation des Pays-Bas (Court of Cassation of the Netherlands) 13 May 1966, Rev. cr. dr. int. prv. (1967) p. 522.

In this connection an award rendered in ICC Case No. 1512 in 1971[46] appears more significant:

This dispute arose from the non-performance by a Pakistani bank of a guarantee issued in favor of an Indian company which was made expressly subject to Indian law. *Inter alia*, the arbitrator was faced with the question of deciding whether the bank was discharged from its obligations as a result of Pakistani decrees declaring any payment to an Indian party illegal – passed because of hostilities between India and Pakistan which had broken out after the guarantee had been issued. After noting that the question of the extinguishment of the contractual obligations was subject to the proper law the arbitrator added:

> "The question might however be raised of the possible effect, in this respect, of the law of the place of performance (*lex loci solutionis*). It might be raised owing to the reference made by one of the parties, or by both of them, to English and other cases on this point.
>
> "Sitting in Geneva as an international arbitrator acting under the ICC Rules chosen by the Parties, I do not feel bound by these cases as an English judge or arbitrator would feel, however great the respect with which I consider these decisions. Were I sitting in England, moreover, I would be reluctant to decide that illegality supervening under the (foreign *lex loci solutionis*) as such, has any effect when the proper law is a foreign law.
>
> "The prevailing trend of opinion, however, in the absence of any direct authority on this point, seems clearly to favour the negative answer, i.e., that determines the question whether the debtor is discharged by law of his contractual obligation.
>
> "While it may be uncertain whether the foreign law of the place of performance (foreign in relation to the forum) determines this question, on one point, at least, there appears to exist unanimity: where the contract is valid under its proper law and such law is the law of the place of performance. . . . In the present case, the guarantee indicated that the payment should take place in India. The arbitrator is of the opinion that Pakistani law, the law of the place of the debtor's residence, should not intervene".

It should be noted that the arbitrator did not ground his decision on the fundamental inapplicability of the mandatory rule foreign to the *lex contractus* chosen by the parties. He felt it was important to demonstrate that it had no serious right to be applied in view of the nature of the transaction that gave rise to the dispute.

This concern to prove the innate inapplicability of a mandatory rule foreign to the *lex contractus* chosen by the parties is met with even when the parties themselves have stressed that their choice was exclusive. An award rendered at Rotterdam in 1981 by the arbitral tribunal of the Royal Dutch Grain and Feed Association[47] provides an example of this. Once again this involved the applicability of the Austrian exchange control regulations to a contract of sale between a Dutch buyer and an Austrian seller:

> "This assertion of the defendant fails primarily because Austrian law is inapplicable to the present case, the parties having agreed, as noted before, that the contract is exclusively governed by Dutch law.
>
> "But even if the above Austrian law were to be taken into account, the arbitrators fail

46. *Cf.* n. 7.
47. *Cf.* Yearbook, Vol. VII (1982) p. 141.

to understand how it could apply to a transaction which concerns the delivery of goods in the Netherlands to a Dutch buyer. If it were otherwise, international commerce involving an Austrian party would be seriously frustrated, if not made impossible, which cannot be presumed to be the meaning of the Law and the intent of the legislator of Austria – a country which has a well-known reputation in international commerce."

50. The question remains as to the answer that arbitrators ought to reserve for a mandatory rule foreign to the *lex contractus* chosen by the parties when there are serious grounds for applying that law. As I pointed out earlier (*cf.* above, No. 49), the arbitrators might by analyzing the parties' intentions conclude that their choice of law did not exclude the operation of mandatory rules of other legal systems. But would the same rule apply if the parties had expressly stated that this choice was exclusive or if it appeared that by choosing a given law the parties had deliberately decided to take themselves outside the field of operation of certain mandatory rules, e.g., those of the place of performance of the contract?

The second of the examples put forward (No. 38 above) might possibly be used to illustrate a situation of this type.

Indeed, we have to take as a possibility the fact that the German and Italian parties had stipulated that a contract contrary to EEC competition rules was subject to Swiss law with the sole intention of avoiding being penalized for infringing a mandatory rule of the place of performance. They had recourse to arbitration, seeking by this means to reinforce the guarantee apparently given to the choice of the law of a country outside the EEC.

From a theoretical point of view, this question is presented in the same terms as that of the express exclusion by the parties of a mandatory rule of the *lex contractus* chosen by them (*cf.* No. 43 above). In both cases the question is whether an international arbitrator is mandatorily bound to respect the will of the parties as to the choice of rules applying to their contract even at the expense of a deliberate fraud against a national law.

It seems that the only way of resolving this question is by recourse to the theory of "truly international public policy". First of all, it goes without saying that if the mandatory law excluded was considered to be contrary to truly international public policy by virtue of its content, an arbitrator would have to give effect to the parties' intention of excluding its application (e.g., a law establishing a racial discrimination). Likewise, if the object of that law is to guarantee the respect of principles considered by the arbitrator as forming part of truly international public policy, the arbitrator would have to make that law, or at least its principles, prevail over the will of the parties. But situations as clear cut as this are seldom met with in practice.

In fact, once it is admitted that in exceptional cases an arbitrator can in the name of a concept of truly international public policy refuse to give effect to certain agreements by parties – such as cases of corruption – one is led to the conclusion that in the same way an arbitrator should not agree to be an accomplice in a deliberate fraud on a mandatory rule that the arbitrator considers has an undisputed right to be applied.

Like every case of overriding international public policy, it is all a question of sensitivity. It seems, however, that if he wishes to avoid abuse of office, the international arbitrator has to guarantee as a minimum the respect of the mandatory rules of the place of performance of the contract, which the arbitrators consider to apply as a matter of course when the parties have not chosen a *lex contractus* (*cf.* No. 53).

b. *The* lex contractus *is determined by the arbitrator.*

52. As we mentioned above, (*cf.* No. 44) in the absence of the concept of competent law, all national or a-national laws have the same weight so long as the arbitrator has not decided that one or more of them are to be applied. Consequently, there is nothing to prevent the application of a mandatory law foreign to the law designated by the arbitrator as the *lex contractus*. In fact, in such a case the arbitrator will decide to restrict the field of application of the *lex contractus* by excluding from its operation those questions he considers should be subject to one or other mandatory law which in his view has a serious right to be applied.

53. Basically this will be a matter of mandatory laws of the state where the contract is performed. The 1983 ICC award in Case No. 4132 (*cf.* No. 44 above) is a good example of this since it applied not only the Korean competition law rules – the *lex contractus* determined by the arbitrator – but also the provisions of the Treaty of Rome because the contract was performed in Italy. The arbitrator even took the view that he had to apply these policy laws automatically.

54. Another ICC award rendered in 1973 in Case No. 1859[48] makes the point even more clearly. Here the arbitrators combined the application of a-national rules – the general principles and customs of international trade – and the policy laws of the states where the contract was carried out.

> "No provision was made in the contract and the parties did not agree on a law that they claimed was to apply to govern the problems of performance resulting from the contract . . . but to the contrary, they asked for their national law to be applied.
> Since the contract must be performed in Lebanon, Syria and Jordan, it is a sure fact that the Lebanese importer was obliged to comply with the mandatory rules of the countries of importation and that the Japanese party cannot now claim that those rules cannot be raised against him.
> Any merchant of a country who attempts to sell his products in another country is bound to respect the mandatory rules of the country of reception and cannot claim to be unaware of or not to respect mandatory laws on the regulation governing the importation of his goods, particularly when this law or regulation existed at the time of the performance of the contract.
> The contract had to be performed in three different countries. The selection of one particular law to apply to the contract would present a number of difficulties. The parties, however, intended to refer to the general principles and customs of international trade in this case."

48. *Cf.* the extracts from this award in Y. Derains, "Le statut des usages du commerce international devant les juridictions arbitrales", Rev. Arb. (1973) p. 122.

This recognition of the natural vocation of the mandatory rules of the place of performance of the contract, whatever the *lex contractus*, is also illustrated by an award in 1974 in ICC Case No. 2136.[49] This was a dispute involving problems of performance of a licence granted by a German firm to a Spanish firm.

> "... it is certain that the condemnation of the plaintiff to the payment of the duties of licence minima depends in large measure on the question of determining whether the riders no. 1, 2 and 3 to the licence contract have been officially approved and have thus acquired legal status. Even though the licence contract would have been subject to German law, the consequences of a failure to obtain authorization must be examined according to Spanish law."

There is no doubt in the mind of the arbitrators that the legal status of additional clauses to a contract subject to German law have to be evaluated under Spanish law, this because of the lack of authorization required by a mandatory rule of the place of performance.

55. Some arbitrators, although not as many, also consider that there are grounds for applying the mandatory rules of the parties' respective laws. For example, an award rendered in 1973 in ICC Case No. 2178[50] contained the statement:

> "One can also question in arbitral practice the reference to a *lex fori* to determine the applicable substantive law. The narrow links between State Courts and their national law which compel the application of the *lex fori* to the solution of problems of conflict of laws that present themselves to national jurisdictions are absent in an arbitration proceedings which is based on the will of the parties. As long as it does not relate to a law of public policy which applies to the parties within the realm of their respective rights and which the arbitrators must take into consideration, it is therefore up to the arbitrators to decide, considering the facts and circumstances of each case, the law to which the litigious matters are most clearly related as far as substance is concerned".

However, another ICC award rendered in 1978 in Case Nos. 2477/2978/3033,[51] like the award in Case No. 1512 mentioned above (*cf.* No. 49), seems to preclude the operation of the mandatory laws of the parties' respective countries when these are foreign to the *lex contractus*. The case involved a dispute between Swedish shipyards and a Libyan buyer. The arbitral tribunal refused to apply Libyan laws and regulations relating to the boycott of Israel since the contract was subject to Swedish law:

> "The application of the Swedish law leads to the obvious consequences that the Libyan boycott law and regulations cannot apply to these contracts – except if a special reference is made in the contracts to this boycott law."

56. It would, therefore, appear that there is no unanimous viewpoint among arbitrators as to the applicability of mandatory rules foreign to the *lex contractus*

49. *Cf.* Y. Derains, "Possible Conflict of Laws", *supra* n. 4, p. 182.
50. *Ibid*, p. 184.
51. *Cf.* Yearbook, Vol. VI (1981) p. 133.

when this law has not been chosen by the parties. The majority seem to tend towards favoring the application of mandatory rules of the place of performance of the contract. It is clear that opinions are much more divided on the question of mandatory rules of the parties' respective countries.

As a matter of fact, I have taken the view[52] that here too it was the concern to respond to the legitimate expectations of the parties that guided the arbitrators when they had to make a ruling on the applicability of mandatory rules foreign to the *lex contractus*. This is why in the vast majority of cases the arbitrator will apply mandatory rules of the place of performance of the contract, or more precisely, of the contractual obligation whose performance is in question. International practice is in fact to respect the mandatory rules of the states in which a contract is being performed. These laws come within the domain of the contract.

If there is no stipulation to the contrary in the contract, the parties are entitled to legitimately expect the arbitrator to presume that their agreement did indeed accord with that practice.

Thus, it is only if a mandatory rule of the place of performance is incompatible with truly international public policy that an arbitrator can exclude its application.

The same rule apparently does not apply in cases where mandatory rules of the country of one or other of the parties are concerned and the contract is not performed in that country.

GENERAL CONCLUSIONS

57. At the end of this study, which is of necessity incomplete, several conclusions as to public policy and the law applicable to the merits of the case in international arbitration can be drawn.

Firstly, it has been noted that the arbitrator is basically faced with two forms of public policy – if truly international public policy is excluded: the domestic public policy rules of the *lex contractus* and mandatory rules from elsewhere. Next, it can be observed that the arbitrator's position is different depending whether the parties have chosen the *lex contractus* or whether the arbitrator has determined it himself.

Indeed, the arbitrator has to respect the will of the parties. Without going along with the view of Pierre Mayer entirely when he states that: "the arbitrator falls within a system created by the contract and therefore has no heteronomous power in relation to the parties",[53] one can take the view that the arbitrator is bound to give effect (except if there is an infringement of truly international public policy) to the will of the parties, whether this is expressed directly by the adoption of contractual stipulations or indirectly by the choice of rules that are to be applied to the contract.

---

52. *Cf.* Y. Derains, "Les normes d'application immédiate dans la jurisprudence arbitrale internationale", in Études offertes à B. Goldman, p. 45.
53. P. Mayer, "Le mythe de l'ordre juridique de base", in Études offertes à B. Goldman, p. 215.

58. Consequently, when the parties have chosen the *lex contractus*, it must be applied by the arbitrator as it stands and with its public policy provisions even if they run contrary to the contractual stipulations, unless the arbitrator considers that the parties intended to exclude these public policy provisions. In such a case, the arbitrator ought to respect the will of the parties who could just as well have chosen a law that did not contain the public policy provisions in question to be the *lex contractus*.

59. With regard to the mandatory rules of the *lex contractus* the problem is different. These laws are likely to be entitled to be applied whatever the proper law of the contract. Thus, if the arbitrator were to consider that the parties had wished to avoid them, he should only give effect to their intention if he was of the opinion that this was not contrary to truly international public policy.

60. Where parties have not chosen the *lex contractus*, in the absence of concepts of competent law and foreign law, all laws have the same weight so long as the arbitrator has not decided to apply one or more of them. Because of his concern to respect the legitimate expectation of the parties who could have chosen any law, national or a-national, or even a combination of several laws, as the *lex contractus*, an arbitrator must never designate as the *lex contractus* a law whose public policy provisions run contrary to the contractual stipulations.

61. So far as mandatory rules are concerned, when the parties have failed to stipulate the *lex contractus*, the arbitrator does not have to determine that law prior to deciding on the applicability of a mandatory rule. The arbitrator must apply that rule directly if he considers that its operation falls within the legitimate expectation of the parties.

It follows from arbitration practice that the application of the mandatory rules of the place of performance should be deemed to correspond to the parties' legitimate expectations.

62. In the course of this study, I have not dealt with the problems of enforcement of awards in relation to the application or infringement of a rule of domestic policy or a mandatory rule. It would be incorrect to state that the arbitrator ought not to take this into consideration, because he is always concerned about the effectiveness of his decision.

However, this consideration ought not to appear in his written argument on the applicable law since he has no possibility of envisaging where his decision will be enforced.

Very often which of the parties wins the case depends on the application or non-application of a mandatory rule. Moreover, because assets are often distributed between different countries the arbitrator has no means of knowing that an award will be enforced in one particular country. Having said this, in view of his practical knowledge of the case, the arbitrator does in fact envisage the probable place or places where the award might be enforced and generally bears this in mind even though he does not state the fact.

Cases where the public policy or mandatory rules in question belong to the place of arbitration pose a special problem.

In fact, the arbitrator must always take into account the risk that these mandatory rules are considered to be international public policy rules in the country where the arbitration takes place and, if this is the case, respect them so as to avoid the ever-possible action for setting aside of the award.

When the international public policy of the place of arbitration or of the probable place of enforcement is involved, the arbitrator must therefore – in accordance with a process characteristic of international arbitration – temper the results of a purely legal analysis of the problems linked to the intervention of public policy in the determination of the law applicable to the merits of the case by taking into consideration the effectiveness of his decision.

Transnational (or Truly International) Public Policy and International Arbitration*

*Pierre Lalive***

TABLE OF CONTENTS

---

* With the cooperation of Mr. P. M. Patocchi, Docteur en droit; Attorney-at-law; Maître-Assistant at the Faculty of Law of Geneva.

** Professor at the University of Geneva; Counsel, Lalive, Budin & Partners, Geneva, Member of the Institute of International Law; Member of ICCA; President of the Swiss Arbitration Association, President of the ICC Institute of International Business Law and Practice.

N.B. The reader in a hurry is advised to read the *Fourth part* only. The reader in a great hurry need only read the Conclusion (Nos. 180–186).
The text is an English translation from the French original.

"The moral order of the world has its rights just as the material order"

Louis Kossuth (Memories and Writings from the Time of Exile)

I. INTRODUCTION

1. In the whole field, in full expansion, of commercial international arbitration, few subjects are more vague, more difficult to seize and more controversial than that of the existence, contents and function of a public policy which would be "really" or "truly" international, and which it is better, if only for the sake of convenience, to call "transnational".

2. The limits of the present Report do not of course allow a thorough examination of the subject and no "final" conclusion will be suggested (if there is such a thing as a "final" conclusion in scientific and in particular legal matters!). An attempt will however be made to clarify the terms of the problem with a view to the discussion which shall take place in New York.

3. A first task will be to attempt to clarify *terminology*. There is indeed little doubt that the subject, already difficult in itself, is made more obscure by the imprecisions, the diversity and sometimes the confusion in the vocabulary used, as shown for instance by the well-known ambiguity of the word "international".

4. With regard to its structure, the present Report does not begin, on purpose, with a discussion of the substance of the subject, i.e., the analysis of the decisions (comparatively rare, for obvious reasons, for instance in cases of bribery) when the international arbitrator has resorted to the concept of a "really international" public policy. For a good understanding of the subject, it appeared indispensable to begin with an outline of certain basic elements or facts of private international law with regard to public policy, on the one hand and, on the other hand, to recall the particular position of the international arbitrator in private international law, a position which is totally different from that of a national judge.

5. The present Report will then discuss the possible contents of transnational public policy in judicial practice. Such a study appears interesting for three reasons: the judicial practice of States is quantitatively important (much more so than published arbitral awards), notwithstanding a clear and understandable reluctance of judges with regard to the concept under discussion. Second, a comparison between the practice of judges and the practice of arbitrators is in itself significant, whatever the subject concerned. Third, it is interesting to

observe how judicial practice, in its recent evolution, has gradually broadened its horizons, from the sole taking into consideration of the public policy of the forum to that of the public policy of a foreign State, then of the public policy common to several States, and finally of a public policy more and more international.

II. FIRST PART: PUBLIC POLICY IN PRIVATE INTERNATIONAL LAW

6. From an examination of arbitral practice, of judicial practice in international arbitration matters or of doctrinal writings on the subject, one can often perceive, not only a great diversity in the vocabulary and ambiguities, but also a definite ignorance of the fundamental principles and mechanisms of private international law. Such ambiguities and confusions are harmful in practice to the development of international arbitration, much more so than is commonly realized in arbitration circles. As an example, it should be sufficient to mention the "automatic" assimilation – which is often made, without much thought, by judges – between local "mandatory" rules and the international public policy of the forum, from which follows on occasions the annulment or refusal of recognition of arbitral awards, without any substantive reason.

1. The Concept of Public Policy in General

7. In municipal law, the concept of public policy is often used to designate "imperative" or mandatory rules, from which the parties cannot derogate.[1] The concept of public policy in private international law is, of necessity, a *different* one – the functions and the purpose of these two parts (domestic law and private international law) of a given legal order not being the same. It follows that, in the case law of many countries, a mandatory rule of domestic law does not necessarily prevail in *international matters*; in other words the judge need not necessarily resort to its "international public policy" in case such a rule has been violated.[2] Such distinction reflects the nature of things and in particular the very nature of private international law, a branch of the law which is *based on a fundamental distinction between "domestic" situations and "international" situations* (i.e., those which include one or more foreign elements sufficiently relevant to call for a particular treatment and the intervention of the private international law of the State). To take another example, in domestic private law, the so-called principle of "autonomy of the will" or contractual freedom is limited by the obligation to respect mandatory rules whereas, in private international law, it is well-known to have a totally different meaning (allowing the parties by their choice of law to

1. See Report by Y. Derains in this Volume, no. 1.
2. See, for example, Swiss Supreme Court in *Rothenberger* v. GEFA, ATF 93 II 379, 382: "The provisions of Article 493 Code of Obligations according to which a warranty must be in notarial form, are of mandatory nature. But this does not mean that they should also be considered as belonging to public policy". This is a permanent principle in Swiss case-law (see the case *Société des grands travaux de Marseille* v. *People's Republic of Bangladesh, Bangladesh Industrial Development Corporation*, ATF 102 Ia 574, *581*).

dismiss the rules, mandatory or not, of the law which, in the absence of choice, would have been applicable).

8. To mention such truisms might seem to warrant an apology but, in practice, they are often neglected, in particular in arbitration. One of the reasons is likely to be the very ambiguity of such terms as "domestic law", "public policy" or "*ordre public*", and "international". Private international law is (unless it is based on international conventions) a part of "domestic" law (although it must be distinguished from the substantive or "material" part of such domestic law). And the "domestic law" (in the broad sense) of a State, i.e., its legal order, includes *both* its domestic private law (with its "domestic public policy" and its mandatory rules) *and its private international law* with its "international public policy" (which is also, but in a broad sense, "domestic" or "municipal").

9. It is worth noting in passing that when Article V of the New York Convention of 10 June 1958 allows the non-recognition of an arbitral award if it is against the "public policy" of the country where the award has been rendered or of the country in which recognition is requested, one should carefully avoid the automatic assimilation or the *confusion* between those two kinds of "public policy". The confusion is particularly dangerous, and frequent, with regard to the *procedural public policy* of the State where the award has been rendered if such a State, or rather its legislation or case law, has not become fully conscious yet of the *specificity of international arbitration* by contrast to domestic arbitration and therefore applies to international arbitration, without adaptation nor exception, mandatory rules enacted and conceived for *domestic* arbitration.

10. Unless there are specific indications to the contrary, reference will hereinafter be made to public policy in the traditional sense of private international law, i.e., to the "international public policy" of a given State, such terms being taken as equivalent to those of *ordre public* (notwithstanding the difference drawn, at least until recent times, in English practice for example, between "public policy" and *ordre public* as observed in the Böckstiegel Report, note 2).

11. This traditional expression is used, first of all, in its "negative" sense, as a "reserve" or exception (*ordre public d'éviction* or *Vorbehaltsklausel*), i.e., as a general clause enabling the judge to reject the application of the foreign law normally applicable according to the conflict rule of the forum, as well as to refuse the recognition of foreign acts whenever such application of foreign law or such recognition acts would be incompatible with fundamental principles of the forum.[3] Public policy exercises therefore a *negative function* (depriving the foreign

---

3. While in continental systems, public policy is generally an obstacle to (a) the application of the normally applicable foreign law and (b) the recognition of a decision, arbitral award or other admissive act of a foreign country, in Anglo-American law a number of more particular situations are distinguished: see Rule 2 of Dicey & Morris, *The Conflict of Laws*, I, *83*:

"English courts will not enforce or recognise a right, power, capacity, disability or legal relationship arising under

law of its normal title of application or the foreign act of its faculty to be recognized). And it constitutes a *limit* to the functioning of the rules of private international law when the latter command either the application of foreign law or the recognition of a foreign act.

12. Thus defined, public policy constitutes a general principle of private international law[4] which exists in all legal systems, even in the absence of specific rules or judicial precedents to that effect and a principle which may be opposed to the application of foreign law even though the latter would be applicable by virtue of a conflict rule contained in an international convention, whether or not such convention has expressly formulated this reserve of public policy.[5]

a. *Conditions and functioning of the exception of public policy*

13. It is generally admitted that such exception only comes into play when certain conditions are fulfilled, which (in spite of a variety of formulations or technical expressions) express a very simple idea: the community concerned (here a national community, a State) must feel sufficiently concerned to impose the respect of its fundamental rules.

14. An observation is not devoid of interest for an understanding of our subject: such conditions of application of public policy can be summed up by the formula of the *"relativity" of public policy*, from three points of view: it must be appreciated *in concreto*, in relation to the circumstances of the concrete case and not (unless in extreme and particularly shocking cases) in relation to the abstract contents of a foreign rule;[6] public policy is also relative *in space* (in the absence of a sufficient

---

the law of a foreign country, if the enforcement or recognition of such right, power, capacity, disability or legal relationship would be inconsistent with the fundamental public policy of English law".

But the formulation of such particular cases of application of public policy has no influence on the definition of public policy as such, *cf.* CHESHIRE/NORTH, *Private International Law*, 131.

4. See W. WENGLER, "Die allgemeinen Rechtsgrundsätze des internationalen Privatrechts und ihre Kollisionen", Zeitschrift für offentliches Recht (Vienna), 23 (1943), 473–509 No. 2, *476–477*. The following rules are well-known examples of expressions of the concept of public policy: Article 26 of the Albanian Law of 21.11.1964; Article 14 of the Argentinian Civil Code of 1861; Article 17 of the Introductory Law to the Brazilian Civil Code of 4.9.1942; para. 36 of the Law of Czechoslovakia of 4.12.1963; Article 28 of the Egyptian Civil Code 1948; para. 4 of the Act of 5.12.1975 of the German Democratic Republic; Article 30 of the Introductory Law to the German Civil Code of 18.6.1896; Article 30 of the Law of Gabon of 29.7.1972; Article 33 of the Greek Civil Code 1940–1946; Article 23 of the Law of Guatemala of 25.1.1936; Article 31 of the Italian Civil Code of 1942; para. 30 of the Japanese Hôreî of 21.6.1896; para. 5 of the South Korean Law of 15.1.1962; Article 73 of Law No. 5 of 14.2.1961 of Kuwait; Article VIII of the Civil Code of Nicaragua of 1904; Article X of the Peruvian Civil Code of 1936; Article 6 of the Polish Law of 12.11.1965 on private international law; Article 22 of the Portuguese Civil Code of 1966; Article 851 of the Law of Senegal on family of 12.6.1972; Article 128 of the Soviet Law of 8.12.1961; Article 12.3 of the Spanish Civil Code of 1881 version of 31.5.1974; para. 25 of the Law of Taiwan of 6.6.1953; Article 2404 of the Civil Code of Uruguay of 1868.

5. W. WENGLER, *Internationales Privatrecht*, 77, and Note 57; H. BATIFFOL/P. LAGARDE, *Droit international privé*, I, 420, No. 263.

6. W. WENGLER, *Internationales Privatrecht*, 79; see, for example, the decision of the Swiss Federal Tribunal *Compagnie commerciale tangeroise* v. *Compagnie grainière S.A.*, ATF 72 II 405, *416*.

connection with the legal order of the forum, it will not come into play or will only have an indirect effect (*effet atténué*[7])). Finally, public policy is relative *in time* (the exception will only intervene against a present attack against the fundamental rules of the forum[8]).

15. This analysis, which is traditional at least in Continental Europe, is not unknown in English private international law (although the concept appears to have a more limited role, since English conflict rules seem to designate a foreign law less often). In the United States, the concept of relativity of public policy appears to be recognized notwithstanding terminological differences and the fact that, according to the so-called "new methods" based on "interest analysis", considerations of public policy appear to be integrated as a principal element of the conflictual reasoning.[9]

b. *"Positive" public policy*

16. Apart from the cases of its exceptional "derogation" to the normal functioning of the conflict rule, the same idea (of protection of fundamental principles of the legal order) intervenes in a different manner, in order to ensure the application of certain rules, having priority, of the *lex fori*. This is the "*positive function*" of public policy, a function which aims at imposing the application of the law of the forum, by means of unilateral conflict rules, or of "special reservations

---

7. This aspect of the relativity of public policy in space was first brought to light in the nineteenth century by F. KAHN, who deeply influenced German private international law (see P. BENVENUTI, *Comunità statale, comunità internazionale e ordine pubblico internazionale*, Milan, 1977, *56* and Note 4).

The *Swiss* Federal Tribunal clarified, in 1952, the hesitations of its prior case law and accepted that the so-called reservation of public policy can only intervene if the concrete situation has a sufficient connection (*Binnenbeziehung*; in later case law *eine schwer ins Gewicht fallende Binnenbeziehung*) with Switzerland (see *Loudon* v. *Schweiz. Bankverein*, ATF 78 II 243, *249*). In *German* case law the same condition is expressed by the term *Inlandsberührung*; *Italian* private international law is influenced by the same idea (P. BENVENUTI, *op. cit.*, 108ff. and references; VITTA, *Diritto internazionale privato*, I, *402–403*); the same is true in *French* private international law (H. BATIFFOL/P. LAGARDE, *Droit international privé*, I 413ff., N 357–1), where the concept is illustrated by the distinction between the full effect of public policy and the so-called limited effect (*effet atténué*).

In *English* law, public policy has a traditionally limited role, owing to the fact that English conflict rules confer competence less frequently than continental conflict rules to a foreign law; the idea of relativity of public policy is nevertheless well-known (DICEY & MORRIS, *The Conflict of Laws*, I, 83–84).

In the private international law of the *United States*, the so-called "new" methods have based the designation of the applicable law on the "interest analysis"; public policy is considered as one of the "pervasive problems" of conflict of laws (SCOLES/HAY, *Conflict of Laws*, 72ff.). Notwithstanding terminological differences, the idea of relativity of public policy in space is nevertheless known (SCOLES/HAY, *Conflict of Laws*, para. 3.16, *74–75*).

8. H. BATIFFOL/P. LAGARDE, *Droit international privé*, I, 412, No. 356. KEGEL, *Internationales Privatrecht*, 682, 307; *De Keller* v. *Maison de la Pensée française*, Clunet 1955, 122, obs. SIALELLI.

9. Such is the case for the so-called positive function of public policy in the doctrines based on "interest analysis".

of public policy" or, according to a terminology which has become somewhat fashionable in Europe, of laws of "necessary" or immediate" application.[10]

17. To sum up, the concept of international public policy of a given community, here of a State, is made up of a series of rules or principles concerning a variety of domains, having a varying strength of intensity, which form or express a kind of "hard core" of legal or moral values, whether in its negative or in its positive function.

2. *Concepts Akin to Public Policy*

18. A brief mention of other techniques is also called for, techniques which are revealed by an examination of comparative private international law and which also result in imposing (indirectly or directly) the respect of certain fundamental principles or essential values, as an exception to the normal functioning of rules of conflict of laws. Such a mention will prove useful, if only by way of comparison and contrast, in our later examination of transnational public policy in arbitration.

a. *Inapplication of foreign public law, in particular of penal or fiscal laws*

19. According to a theory still existing, although of declining popularity, the domain of private international law is supposed to be limited to conflicts between State rules of *private law*; the application of foreign law would therefore be possible only in domains belonging to "private law". Such a restrictive conception may well have important practical consequences (varying from one country to the other). A number of decisions have thus decided that foreign *public law* would be inapplicable *per se*,[11] or that it is not applicable in the same way as private law, but

---

10. See the important writings of Ph. FRANCESCAKIS on the subject and in particular
- "Quelques précisions sur les 'lois d'application immédiate' et leurs rapports avec les règles de conflits de lois", R 55 (1966) 1–18.
- "Lois d'application immédiate et règles de conflit" RDIPP 3 (1967), 691–697.
- "Est-ce qu'il y a du nouveau en matière d'ordre public?" Travaux 27–30 (1966–1969), 149–169, discussion: 169–178;
- "Ordre public", in: Répertoire I, 498–506;
- "Lois d'application immédiate et droit du travail – L'affaire du comité d'entreprise de la 'Compagnie des Wagons- Lits'", R. 63 (1974) 273–296.

For German doctrinal writings on the *Sonderanknüpfung* (on the application of the internationally mandatory rules of a foreign State), see *infra*, Note 60.

For a criticism, see, in particular, P. LALIVE, "Tendances et méthodes", RCADI 1955 (1977 II), *120–153*.

11. This principle was first outlined in an absolute manner by the Swiss Federal Tribunal which later attempted to qualify it in various ways, admitting, for instance, that foreign public law can be applied whenever Switzerland is bound to do so by an international treaty or whenever foreign public law "supports" the application in Switzerland of private law and helps in a prevailing or exclusive manner the protection of private interests (see *Schw. Bankgesellschaft* v. *Poljak*, ATF 95 II 109, *114–115*; and recently *Ungrad* v. *Ungrad*, Sem. jud. 102 (1981), 216 (résumé); ASDI XXXVII (1981), 254, 419, note P. LALIVE/A. BUCHER).

can exceptionally, or may sometimes, be "taken into consideration" by the forum,[12] or that it cannot be enforced (coercive application) to the benefit of a foreign State;[13] such affirmations have also been expressed as particular sub-rules in the field of criminal law or tax law, in English or American private international law.[14]

20. In 1975, the *Institute of International Law* adopted, after a thorough study of the problem, a Resolution which categorically condemns the so-called "principle of inapplicability of foreign public law".[15] The main grounds of such a position can be summed up as follows: the concept of international public policy is sufficient to guarantee the respect of the fundamental principles of the forum, and the alleged principle of inapplicability of foreign public law does not add anything to this traditional concept, and is not based on any valid reason. The Resolution further recalls the requirements of international collaboration or solidarity, which impose a more cooperative attitude towards foreign States and therefore also towards their public law. This idea should be kept in mind when examining the position of the international arbitrator.

b. *Fraus legis*

21. In the sense of the private international law of some countries (a sense which is quite precise and distinct from that of domestic law), there is *fraus legis* when parties manage to change or displace, in an artificial although formally legal manner, the localization from the connecting factor used in the conflict rule (of conflict of laws or conflict of jurisdictions), e.g., through a change of domicile or nationality: this in order to bring about the application of a definite law, or to create the jurisdiction of a particular tribunal, thereby obtaining a practical result which the normal functioning of the conflict rule would not have made possible.

22. The so-called exception of *fraus legis* is therefore distinct, according to prevailing doctrine, from that of international public policy, by its subjective or psychological element, i.e., the "fradulent" intention. In those legal systems

---

12. In this sense the exception introduced by Swiss cases as cited in the preceding note. See also H. BATIFFOL/P. LAGARDE, *Droit international privé*, I, *296*, No. 248.

13. KEGEL, *Internationales Privatrecht*, 673.

14. See Rule 3 DICEY & MORRIS:
"English courts have no jurisdiction to entertain an action:
(1) for the enforcement, either directly or indirectly, of a penal revenue, or other public law of a foreign State; or
(2) founded upon an act of State".
See DICEY & MORRIS, *The Conflict of Laws*, I, 89–99; CHESHIRE/NORTH, *Private International Law*, 131–145; SCOLES/HAY, *Conflict of Laws*, 75–78.

15. Ann. Inst. dr. int. Vol. 56, Session de Wiesbaden 1975, P. LALIVE, "Rapport préliminaire", *157—183*; "Questionnaire", *184–186*; "Observations des membres de la Vingtième Commission", *187–218*; P. LALIVE, "Rapport définitif", *219–259*; "Projet de résolution", *260–263*; "Observation des membres de la Vingtième Commission", *264–273*; "Projet de résolution", *274–278*; "Résolution", *250–253*.

which only sanction a fraud upon the *lex fori*,[16] it is, nevertheless, very near the notion of public policy, whereas in those countries where the concept is used also to sanction a fraud upon *foreign* law, it appears rather as an independent correction to the ordinary functioning of the conflict rules.

23. Be that as it may, the concept appears to have a particular position in the field of contracts, by reason of the existence of the so-called principle of "autonomy of the will", a universally-recognized principle although with different modalities or interpretations. If the rule itself (which allows the parties to choose the applicable law) has as one of its underlying motives the idea of restricting the possibilities of fraud, then the choice of the *lex contractus* is restricted in its scope by the requirement of a territorial connection or that of a legitimate interest in the choice. If, on the other hand, the rule allows, as is frequently the case, a totally free choice of law, then the relevant system of private international law may well recognize other corrective elements (such as the taking into consideration of foreign "public" or "police" laws), so that it is permitted to consider that the exception of *fraus legis* has lost its purpose.[17]

24. It is in French private international law, in particular, that this theory appears to have been favourably received,[18] while its importance seems to be rather small in comparative private international law.[19] Here, too, we are faced with a concept which appears *prima facie* able to play some role in international commercial arbitration. Let us think, for example, of the possible use by the parties both of the choice of arbitration and of a choice of applicable law in order to avoid the effect of a foreign mandatory law, of "international public policy" or "necessary application".

c. *Conformity of the normally applicable rule with the Constitution of the forum*

25. In some cases, the forum may take into account its Constitution in the conflictual reasoning, either through the formulation of special unilateral conflict rules for the Constitution,[20] or through the requirement that the application of the normally applicable foreign law be in conformity with the Constitution of the forum. There is no need to elaborate on such a hypothesis, which appears to be easily absorbed within the general theory of public policy,[21] a concept which, as

16. On these questions, see Ph. FRANCESCAKIS, *Verbo* "Fraude à la loi", *Encyclopédie Dalloz*, Nos. 13–15; note on this point the difference between Article 21, Portuguese Civil Code and Article 12, n. 4 of the Spanish Civil Code.
17. On the present state of the problem, see Ph. FRANCESCAKIS, "Fraude à la loi", Nos. 57–78.
18. See B. AUDIT, *La fraude à la loi en droit international privé*, Paris, 1974, and quotations.
19. E. VITTA, *Diritto internazionale privato*, 3 vol., Turin, I, 1972, 441–445.
20. On this subject, see the Swiss decision of the Federal Tribunal *D. and O.* v. *DJP*, ATF 106 II 180, on Article 58 of the Swiss Federal Constitution.
21. G. KEGEL, *Internationales privatrecht*, 308–311.

we have seen, is sufficiently general and flexible to allow judicial practice to solve as they arise the various questions which may be involved in a concrete case.

d. *Conformity of the normally applicable law with public international law*

26. Some general observations appear to be called for here, which will help later to situate better the problem of a "transnational public policy" in arbitration. They refer mainly to the relations between the traditional notion of "international public policy" (in a national system of private international law) on the one hand and, on the other hand, general or conventional public international law.

27. According to the "Act of State" doctrine, known in particular to American law, the courts of the forum have no jurisdiction or, rather, no power to scrutinize the validity of acts which a foreign State has carried out within its own territory or, more precisely, within its sphere of territorial competence. This rule thus creates a kind of immunity *ratione materiae* for certain foreign acts. It constitutes, therefore, rather than a concept neighbouring that of international public policy, a limit imposed on the domain of the public policy of the forum: since the forum refuses to examine the validity of a foreign act of government, its international public policy should, so to speak by definition, have no possibility to intervene. The Act of State doctrine and the principle of international public policy thus appear to be opposed rather than close to each other.[22]

28. What are the relationships between the "exception" of public policy of the State and public international law? Doctrinal writings on this subject seem inclined to include such question within the general theory of public policy and to consider that the *only* pertinent question is whether, how and to what extent the rules of the law of nations do contribute to the formation of the concept (shown above to be relative in space and in time) of the international public policy of a given State.[23] According to various writers, the role of the international public policy of a State depends neither on the question whether the State in question has accepted the "monist" or "dualist" doctrine, nor on the recognition by the State of the supremacy of public international law over the domestic legal order. The precise subject here under examination is said to bear only on the relations between the domestic law of the State (*lex fori*, including its private international law) with the law of nations; it does not relate to the relations between the normally applicable *foreign* law (according to the private international law of the forum), on the one hand, and the law of nations, on the other.[24]

29. For the purpose of the present Report, there is no need to discuss such

---

22. See I. SCHWANDER, *"Lois d'application immédiate". Sonderanknüpfung, IPR-Sachnormen und andere Ausnahmen von der gewöhnlichen Anknüpfung im internationalen Privatrecht.* Zurich, 1975, 82–83, and the quotations under Note 8.
23. G. BADIALI, *Ordine pubblico*, 129.
24. MENGOZZI, *Le disposizioni sulla legge in generale*, 362–363; see also D. SCHÜTZE, *Der internationale ordre public*, 42–45, and the quotations under Note 1, p. 51.

questions, for which it is, in any case, difficult to suggest general and absolute solutions. It should be enough to outline them briefly, on the basis of the traditional distinction between the *general* rules (custom and general principles) and the *particular* rules (conventional) of public international law.

30. What are the relations between the concept of the international public policy of the forum and *international treaties*?

31. If the forum *is* a party to a treaty, the international public policy of the forum would, of course, prevent the application of a foreign law which is contrary to the treaty.[25] It may also be said that the question does not arise in such a manner, inasmuch as the provisions of the treaty have a direct application in the State of the forum by reason of the priority of international law.[26]

32. When an international treaty has *not* been ratified by the State of the forum, can it be stated that the latter's "international public policy" is not concerned? Such an absolute answer would appear excessive, at least for multilateral treaties. The existence cannot be denied of treaties which either codify a pre-existing custom or express or imply principles having general application; in such cases the fact that the treaty concerned has not been ratified by the State of a forum would not suffice, *per se*, to justify a refusal to take such custom or general principles into consideration. In several countries, courts have not hesitated, and rightly, to take into consideration principles contained in international conventions which had *not* (or not yet) been ratified by the State.[27]

33. Such phenomenon is illustrated by two recent and significant examples, taken from European case law in the field of *protection of cultural property*, in connection with the UNESCO Convention of 1970 relating to measures aimed at prohibiting the illicit import, export and transfer of ownership of cultural goods. In both cases, one German, the other Italian, the UNESCO Convention was taken into consideration although it was not in force in the State of the forum:

In the case decided by the German Federal Court, on 22 June 1982, an insurance contract relating to artifacts illegally exported from Nigeria was considered as null and void as against *bonos mores* in the sense of the German Civil Code.[28]

---

25. In this sense W. WENGLER, *Internationales Privatrecht*, 75.

There is no need to examine here whether this is a case of "advanced application" of the treaty itself or, which is a different matter, a case of the recognition of a general principle contained in a treaty which the State of the forum has not ratified and does not intend to ratify.

26. In this sense B. GOLDMAN, Note after the decision of the Court of Appeal of Paris, Ière Ch. suppl., of 12 July 1984, *R.A.E.* v. *Southern Pacific Properties Limited and Southern Pacific Properties (Middle East)*, Clunet 1985, 129, 142, *154*.

Problems have arisen in connection with the application of foreign rules which were declared contrary to the European Convention on Human Rights; see on this the decision *Marckx* of the European Court of Human Rights of 13 June 1979 and the Note by M. STOCKER in StAZ 34 (1981), 16–22.

27. Such was the case for example in the decisions quoted below, Notes 28 and 29.

28. See the decision by the German Supreme Court of 22 June 1982 *Allg. Vers. G.H.* v. *E.K.*, BGHZ 59, 82, and the Note of A. BLECKMANN, ZaöRV 34 (1974), 112–132.

In the judgment of 25 March 1982 of the Tribunal of Torino, the Republic of Ecuador won the case although the Convention was *not* applicable as such, since it had come into force in Italy *after* the facts giving rise to litigation; but the judges underlined the fact that the Italian international public order was in any case based upon and inspired by essential values recognized by the Convention.[29]

34. There are, of course, other examples of international conventions which contain, expressly or implicitly, general principles capable of "nourishing" the international public order of States which had not ratified them (or had no intention of doing so). Several international conventions relating to the *traffic of armaments* and a decision of the Court of Paris of 9 February 1966 may be quoted in this respect.[30] Another example which comes to mind is that of the International Agreements on the High Sea relating to measures preventing *sea pollution* by all products or by radioactive waste, or measures aimed at preventing damage to international cables.[31]

35. Without discussing here the question, which attracted much attention in recent doctrinal writings, of *ius cogens*, one should also mention here, in passing, general public international law, i.e., international custom (as well as general principles[32]). By definition, international custom and the other general rules of the law of nations must be complied with by all members of the international community; and State organs, in particular courts, have many occasions to apply them (for instance, with regard to the international delimitation of jurisdictions for acts *iure imperii*, immunities, recognition of States, nationality, nationalizations, etc.). It may be said that the international public policy of the forum has no reason to intervene, properly speaking, whenever public international law applies by reason of its priority, and the legal situation for the State of the forum is here like that, mentioned above, where the rules of a ratified treaty are applicable. But it may also be thought that the international public policy of the forum does come into play, in its *positive* functions, in order to impose the respect, not of a "mandatory" rule (of the forum or of a foreign State) but of the rules of the law of nations.

---

29. See the decision of the Tribunal of Turin of 25 March 1982 *Repubblica dell' Ecuador – Casa della cultura ecuadoriana* v. *Danusso*, RDIPP 18 (1982), 625.

30. Court of Appeal of Paris, 9 II 1966, R. 1966, 264, note P. LOUIS-LUCAS.

This example is cited by L. MATRAY in a very interesting study "Arbitrage et ordre public international", typewritten p. 23; see by the same author his article in *The Art of Arbitration, Liber amicorum P. Sanders*, p. 242. The author refers here to the general act of the Brussels Conference of 2 July 1890, Art. 8, the Arrangement of 13 December 1906 between France, Great Britain and Italy, and lastly the International Convention of 17 June 1925 of the League of Nations on the repression of the traffic of armaments.

31. Articles 24 and 27 cited by L. MATRAY in his study quoted in the preceding note.

32. Reference is made here both to the general principles of the law of nations and to the principles mentioned in Article 38 para. 3 of the Statute of the International Court of Justice, which are recognized, according to the famous expression by Lord Phillimore, *in foro domestico, i.e.*, resulting from a comparative analysis of the main legal systems in the world.

III. SECOND PART: THE POSITION OF THE ARBITRATOR IN PRIVATE INTERNATIONAL LAW

36. The above-mentioned general considerations on the concept of public policy in private international law, useful as they may be, do not suffice to allow a complete understanding of the subject under discussion. They must be supplemented by a brief outline of the unique position of the arbitrator of international commerce, a position which is fundamentally different from that of a State judge.

37. A clear understanding of such particular position (which is one of the aspects of the *specificity of international arbitration*, the functions and main features of which are to a large extent different from those of *domestic* arbitration) is a pre-condition to any attempt at answering the question whether there does exist a "truly international" public policy or, rather, a "transnational public policy". Any observation of arbitration practice and any reading of doctrinal writings suffice to show, on this question as on many others in the domain of international arbitration, the danger of terminological confusions or of ambiguities on basic concepts and the premises of legal reasoning.

38. It would be futile to reopen the old theoretical or doctrinal discussions (such as those, inherited from certain municipal laws, on the "legal nature", jurisdictional or contractual, or mixed) of international arbitration. But it may be useful, in order to clarify the discussion, to state precisely the main parameters of the problem. In order to do so, it is necessary to recall what is the position of the arbitrator in private international law. The other Rapporteurs had also to deal with this problem, of course, although in different contexts, whether on the question of arbitrability of the dispute, of arbitral procedure or of the law applicable to the merits, and reference will have to be made to their reports on several occasions.

39. In particular, the reader should keep in mind the excellent analysis (with which we are to a large extent in agreement) of Mr. Yves Derains in his Report on "Public Policy and the Law Applicable to the Merits of the Dispute in International Arbitration".

40. At the beginning of the enquiry, two facts should be realized: (a) any judge is "sitting" at a "forum": he has a *lex fori*, *both* in the usual sense of a domestic legal system, of substantive rules, which his function is to "state" or apply, as well as a national system of private international law which he has to follow. Any international question put to the judge must be decided by him on the basis of this system of private international law (which includes rules of conflict of jurisdictions and rules of conflict of laws) and which necessarily includes also a concept of "international public policy", the meaning of which has been outlined above. Similarly, the national judge may be called upon, also on the basis of his national system of private international law, to "take into consideration" or even to "apply" *foreign* public policy (as he is authorized to do, for example, by Article

7 of the Rome Convention of the EEC on the law governing contractual obligations).

41. The position of the international arbitrator, as rightly observed by Mr. Yves Derains, "is fundamentally different from that of a national judge when called upon to solve a problem of conflict of laws" (no. 8). He has no "forum" properly speaking (nor has he any "seat", which is a common but dangerously ambiguous word to use).[33]

42. The international arbitrator, therefore, has no *lex fori* within the usual sense of the term in private international law, and there is hardly any advantage in the use of a terminology which is borrowed from the totally different context of judicial activities within a particular State. Such an absence of *lex fori* also means, as stated above, the absence of a (national) system of private international law.

43. It is, however, doubtful that such absence of *lex fori* within the meaning of private international law is, as submitted by Mr. Derains, a *consequence* of the freedom of the arbitrator (which regard to the designation of the law applicable to the merits), a freedom which is clearly recognized by many national laws, by recent international conventions as well as by the most important arbitration rules. It would seem to appear, on the contrary, that he enjoys such freedom because he has no *lex fori*! The international arbitrator is *not the organ of a State*; he is not bound by any national system of private international law, while being obliged to follow, or so it would seem, the *general principles* of private international law, which recognize both the autonomy of the will of the parties and the freedom, for the international arbitrator, to disregard on occasions the "conflictual method" in order to choose the "direct way" and apply, for example, general principles of law or the *lex mercatoria*.[34]

44. While he is clearly not an organ of the State, the international arbitrator is not acting in a legal vacuum and is not called upon to decide, so to speak, as if he did not belong to this world! The question may be raised here, in passing (and it appears to be connected with that of the existence of a transnational public policy) whether the arbitrator is not, perhaps, the organ of the international community, be it the community of States[35] or the "international community of

33. The expression or image of the "seat" together with that of the arbitral "tribunal" lead to many confusions, which are well-illustrated in the theory, now in decline, which tends to deduce from the so-called "seat" the law applicable to the arbitral procedure. As a matter of fact, it is not the "seat" of the arbitration which can or should determine the applicable law but much rather, to the contrary, the applicable law which can decide if the *place* of the arbitration is a "seat" or not!

34. See O. LANDO, "The Lex Mercatoria in International Commercial Arbitration", ICLQ 34 (1985), 747–768.

35. This community received for instance an expression in the Final Act of the Helsinki Conference on Security or in the unanimous vote of the General Assembly of the United Nations in 1985 which adopted the UNCITRAL Model Law on Arbitration. See on this point the observations made by many writers, such as René David, on the tolerance or general acceptance by States as to a kind of distribution of functions between State courts on the one hand and international arbitration mechanisms on the other.

businessmen" (in which more and more States and State organs appear to be active) or both international communities. It might be contended that, since States have refrained from creating, except in very rare cases, really international private law jurisdictions (such as the Iran–US Claims Tribunal in The Hague), the extraordinary expansion of commercial international arbitration is due to the need to fill in this "gap" in international organization. It stands to reason that any answer given to such questions is bound to have to some extent a "political-philosophical" character and is likely to have a bearing on the analysis of our subject.

45. It may also be observed in passing that such international jurisdictions (inter-States, like the International Court of Justice, or "private" like the Mixed Arbitral Tribunals after World War I[36] or certain international commissions after World War II) have no *lex fori* either, and, therefore, no particular systems of private international law; they have, thus, no conflict rules of their own nor any particular concept of "public policy". But they have on occasions resorted to general principles of private international law or to a national "international public policy".[37]

46. To sum up, since he has no *lex fori* and, therefore, no particular conflict rules (with the exception of general principles such as the universally-recognized principle of "autonomy of the will"), the international arbitrator has no (national) law which is a priori applicable and, as shown by Y. Derains following B. Goldman, is not confronted with any "foreign" law properly speaking. For him, "all State laws have the same value and none has a privileged position, a fact which has a variety of important consequences, for instance, with regard to public policy" (own translation).[38]

47. If one considers the concept of public policy as a necessary element of any (national) system of private international law and as a compulsory counterpart in the conflictual mechanism, one is tempted to conclude that, since he has no *lex fori* within the meaning previously indicated, the international arbitrator does not, likewise, have at his disposal a concept of "international public policy" or, perhaps (which is not the same thing) that for him this concept has no function.

48. Such a conclusion would obviously be erroneous, as clearly shown for

---

36. According to the Romanian-German Mixed Arbitral Tribunal, in its decision of 16 June 1925 (Recueil TAM, p. 200): "since they do not belong to any State and meet wherever they wish, mixed arbitral tribunals have no *lex fori*".

37. On this subject, regarding the ICJ, see the Elisabeth Boll case between The Netherlands and Sweden, decision of 28 November 1959, ICJ Reports 1958, p. 55 and the Serbian and Brazilian Loans cases, PCIJ, 1929, Series A. Nos. 20–21, p. 12ff., cited in the Report by S. SCHWEBEL/S. LAHNE in this volume, p. 206. On mixed arbitral tribunals, see the well-known study by K. LIPSTEIN, "Conflict of Laws before International Tribunals" I, II, Transactions of the Grotius Society 27 (1941), p. 142–175 and 29 (1943), p. 51–83.

38. Y. DERAINS' Report, this volume, p. 232; these consequences do not relate only to the so-called negative public policy; it is submitted that they relate also to the so-called "positive" public policy.

instance by the three Reports submitted by our colleagues Böckstiegel, Derains and Schwebel-Lahne respectively on arbitrability, the law applicable to the merits and procedure. There is indeed no doubt, as observed by Yves Derains in the Introduction to his Report that public policy, negative as well as positive, "can affect the solutions given by an international arbitrator", be it on the subject of arbitrability, procedure or the merits of the dispute. In those various domains, international public policy (of a State – but of which State or States?) cannot possibly be ignored by the international arbitrator on the ground, or under the pretext, that the arbitrator is not an organ of the State. One reason among others is that he must strive to render a valid award capable of being recognized and enforced;[39] the international arbitrator is legally and morally bound to take into consideration to an adequate extent the international public policy of one or of several States, in order to meet the expectations of the parties and, more precisely, their "legitimate" expectations: the parties cannot legitimately expect the arbitrator to establish or sanction a violation of public policy.[40]

49. Assuming there does exist a transnational public policy (a question to be examined later), the question arises whether the international arbitrator has the power and the duty to take it into consideration either together with, or as a priority or even against one or the other relevant State public policies (of the forum, or of a foreign law such as the *lex contractus*, the law of the place of performance or possibly the law of a "third" interested State). Before answering such questions, it is useful and indeed indispensable first to examine the judicial practice of States.

IV. THIRD PART: TRANSNATIONAL PUBLIC POLICY IN JUDICIAL PRACTICE

50. It has been shown that, in private international law, the classic notion of (State) international public policy is marked by its evolutive and relative character and the difficulty, not to say the impossibility, of any precise definition. The same is true, so to speak a fortiori, for the notion of *transnational* public policy.

51. Even a cursory analysis of case law shows three factors which help to grasp the contents of the notion under examination. First, traditional public policy in private international law may contribute to the formation of specific rules (of substantive private international law) adapted to international situations, thus taking into account the needs of international trade. Second, its intervention in a given case does not always result in imposing the application of a particular and mandatory rule of the *lex fori*. Third, the public policy of the forum may also intervene in order to protect the (foreign) public policy of one or several States and lastly, that of the international community.

---

39. See on this subject Article 26 of the ICC Arbitration Rules.
40. See on this subject Y. DERAINS' Report in this volume Nos. 13ff. and in particular No. 14 in fine.

52. Undoubtedly, these various kinds of public policies are not distinct or independent enough to fall into clear-cut categories; this should in fact be a matter for satisfaction since it shows that, notwithstanding the "particularism" of legal systems, national laws often reveal a common core. Any attempt at classification and at an orderly presentation of the subject is thereby made more difficult, all the more so since judicial decisions on the subject are often motivated, or capable of being motivated, by a plurality and variety of grounds and reasonings.

53. Keeping in mind these explanations and reservations, we now propose to review a number of situations and judicial decisions which may be considered or interpreted as revealing, to some extent, the recognition of a transnational public policy.

1. The Formation of Specific Rules for International Relations

54. A classical example is found in the case of "*Messageries maritimes*", decided by the Court of Cassation of France on 21 June 1950:[41]

The case concerned a loan in Canadian gold dollars by the French company of "Messageries maritimes", which attempted to repay its bond holders in paper dollars, in keeping with a Canadian statute enacted after the date of the loan; this statute had devalued the dollar and forbidden gold clauses without distinguishing between internal and international payments. The Court of Cassation disregarded the Canadian statute and declared, in a now famous pronouncement, that the parties to such a contract were entitled to agree, even against the mandatory rules of a municipal law governing their contract, a gold value clause valid under a French law of 25 June 1928 in keeping with the French concept of international public policy.

55. This case shows that the concept of public policy enabled the creation of a rule (of "substantive" private international law) specific to international payments and different from the rule of French law applicable to domestic payments. This new rule was that of the validity of gold clauses in international contracts. According to Dean Lerebours-Pigeonnière, the case is based upon a public policy

> "which does not underlie the particularism of French domestic life and, quite to the contrary, is based on the desire that private transfrontier relations be governed by an international legal order . . . the exception of public policy leads here to the creation within French domestic law of a kind of *ius gentium* parallel to the domestic common law".[42]

---

41. R. 1950. 609, note by H. BATIFFOL; JCP 1950. II. 5812, note by J. Ph. LEVY; Gaz. Pal. 1950, II. 141; S. 1951 I. 1, note by J.-P. NIBOYET; D. 1951, 749, note by HAMEL.
See also P. LEREBOURS-PIGEONNIERE, "A propos du contrat international", Clunet 1951, 4–28.

42. Clunet 1951, *6, 14*.

56. Analogous examples of such a method may be found in several countries. One thinks here of some recent American cases, which seem to have received a widespread and well-deserved applause in the international community, in which the courts decided that certain mandatory or prohibitive rules were *only* "of *domestic* public policy" and should be disregarded in international relations in order to make way for more appropriate and less prohibitive rules.

57. Cases in point are the three well-known decisions in the cases *Zapata*,[43] *Scherk*[44] and *Mitsubishi*.[45] Suffice it to recall that, in the first case, of 1972, the Supreme Court of the United States decided, with regard to the validity of choice of forum clauses, that the restrictive tendency of American domestic law should not prevail over the requirements of international trade. In the second case, of 1974, the Supreme Court accepted the validity of an arbitration clause, having regard to the international character of the contract, thereby excluding the restrictions imposed by the Security Exchange Act on arbitrability. Lastly, the famous *Mitsubishi* decision accepts the argument, developed, *inter alia*, in the *amicus curiae* brief of the American Arbitration Association and decides that, in antitrust matters, the principle of non-arbitrability does not extend to international contracts. We can limit ourselves to these very brief indications and refer to the analysis and comments of our colleague and friend Professor Böckstiegel in his Report.[46]

58. It is worth noting that, in those cases, a rule of domestic law, of an imperative or "domestic public policy" character, is set aside, in international relations, in a manner which, *prima facie*, resembles that of the rejection of a normally applicable foreign law by the international public policy of the forum. But in fact, there is a greater analogy with the intervention of "positive" public policy which (instead of imposing as in the classical case the extension of a mandatory rule of domestic law to international situations) allows and indeed requires the application (and creation) of specific substantial rules adapted to the needs and context of international commerce.[47]

59. It seems possible to conclude that the function of international public policy may also be to enable the State of the forum to impose its views and requirements as to the proper and specific regulation needed by international situations, for "the national interest may precisely consist sometimes of taking into account and satisfying the interests and need of international trade, in the broadest sense of

43. 407 US 1, 92 S. Ct. 1907, 32 L. Ed. 2d 513 (1972). See also AJIL 66 (1972), 864 and the observations by G. R. DELAUME, "What is an International Contract? An American and a Gallic Dilemma", ICLQ 28 (1979), 258–279.
44. 417 US 506, 94 S. Ct. 2449, 41 L. Ed. 2d 270 (1974).
45. US Law Week, 25 June 1985, Vol. 53 No. 50, p. 5069 = 105 S. Ct. 3346 (1985). See also D. G. LANGE/S. WIESSNER, "Die Schiedsfähigkeit internationaler Antitrust-Streitigkeiten", RIW/AWD 31 (1985), 757–765; S. JARVIN, "Arbitrability of Antitrust Disputes", Swiss Review of International Competition Law, 1985, 53–65; D. G. GILL, "Note on the *Mitsubishi* v. *Soler* Decision", *ibidem*, 67–68.
46. K.-H. BÖCKSTIEGEL's Report in this Volume, p. 177ff.
47. Clunet 1951, *6, 14*.

this term, notwithstanding the rules of domestic law [rules which have been elaborated and imposed for domestic situations]."[48]

2. The Application of Rules Common to Several Systems

60. Notwithstanding the preceding observations, the prevailing doctrine appears today to restrict the intervention of the international public policy of the State to safeguarding mandatory rules and fundamental principles which are particular to the *lex fori*.[49] In certain countries, however, doctrinal writings or judicial decisions are found which recognize a broader concept of public policy and give it a more or less marked "supranational" meaning or contents.[50]

61. Examples are first found in the field of contracts, a field in which "mandatory" general principles appear to benefit from a very widespread international consensus whenever they express rules of "contractual morality", a morality which has in itself nothing local or national even though it is translated into mandatory rules of domestic law.

For instance, a French court decided that the sale of a foreign decoration – in the particular case the title of Commander of the Order of Queen Isabel the Catholic – was against public morality.[51]

The same result was reached by the Supreme Court of the United States with regard to a contract in which the seller was paying to the other party the exercise of illicit influence upon a third party with a view to obtaining the conclusion of a contract.[52]

Similarly, the Swiss Federal Tribunal decided that the contract aimed at the purchase of the illegal influence of a party upon a third person was against "good morals" and therefore totally null and void.[53]

62. It is indeed in cases of *bribery* that – as will be shown in the following part, on arbitral practice – many illustrations can be found of the efforts made at the international level, to "moralize" the practices of trade. International interests and the general interest in a normal functioning of international trade appear to coincide and to justify the conclusion that there does exist a principle of truly international or transnational public policy which sanctions corruption and

48. Ph. FRANCESCAKIS, "Ordre public", Encyclopédie Dalloz, No. 9.
49. In recent Italian doctrinal writings, see the book by M. PALAIA *L'ordone pubblico "internazionale"* which is mainly devoted to a demonstration of the alleged "domestic" nature of the principles of international public policy.
50. In his book *Comunità statale, comunità internazionale e ordine pubblico internazionale*, P. BENVENUTI contends that the Italian case law has adopted the wide concept, as it has referred since the nineteenth century to the "principles common to civilized nations". According to the author, some general principles having a supranational effect can be imposed by the international public policy of the forum.
51. Trib. comm., Seine, 15 November 1887, *Estibal* v. *Webb*, Clunet 1888, 389.
52. See *Oscaryan* v. *Wilchester Repeating Arm Co.* US Sup. Ct., 26 April 1881, Alb. L.J. vol. XXIV, 49; J. 1882, 445.
53. Swiss Federal Court in the case *G.* v. *L.*, lère Cour civ., 22 July 1980, résumé, Semé jud. 103 (1981), 192; SAS 53 (1981) 69.

"bribery contracts". But the delicate problem remains to determine precisely where the line should be drawn between legal and illegal contracts, between illegal bribery and legal "commissions".

63. In a decision given on 25 May 1948, the Civil Section of the French Court of Cassation considered that public policy was "the reservation of such principles of universal justice which are considered by French opinion as having an absolute international value."[54]

64. Similarly, Italian courts have often expressed the idea that international public policy aimed at safeguarding principles common to all civilized nations. According to the Italian Court of Cassation,

> "the respect of international public policy is based first and foremost on the need to safeguard a legal and moral minimum which is common to the feeling of several nations".[55]

65. The idea of an international public policy which is *common* (although part of State law) to various nations reappeared in French judicial practice with the famous case of the *Banque Ottomane*. In a decision of 19 March 1968, the Court of Appeal of Paris had clearly rejected the application of "principles of an alleged international public policy the existence of which is not recognized by any system of positive law and, in particular, not by French law".[56]

66. Facts and ideas have evolved since then. A decision by the Tribunal of Commerce of Paris, of 11 October 1982,[57] already shows a different perception:

> The plaintiffs contended that, in company law, the information of shareholders is so essential that the right to information, recognized by many legal systems, is promoted to "the rank of a general principle of international law" and recognized by a "specifically international public policy", superior to the international public policy to be found in the private international law of any given State.
>
> The Tribunal declared that "it would not be hostile to the application of the general rules of a common international law of companies, on the condition that such public policy be recognized in French law or in French judicial decisions. . . . The plaintiffs have not proved the existence of such an international public policy".

67. Lastly, in a third decision given in the same case of the Banque Ottomane, on

54. Cass. civ. 25 May 1948, D. 1948, 357, note P.L.P.; S. 1949. I. 21, note J.-P. NIBOYET; J. C. P. 1948. II. 4532, note VASSEUR; R. 89, note H. BATIFFOL.

55. *Alarcia Castells* v. *Hengstenberge e Procuratore generale presso la Corte di appello di Milano*, RDIPP XIX (1983), 364.

56. *Bakaljan et Hadjthomas* v. *Banque ottomane*, Clunet 1966, 137, note B. GOLDMAN; R. 1967, 85, note P. LAGARDE.

57. *Comité de défense des actionnaires de la Banque ottomane et autres* v. *Banque ottomane et autres*, R. 1984, 93, note SYNVET.

3 October 1984,[58] the Court of Appeal of Paris appears now to recognize the concept of a "common" international public policy, when holding that:

> "The security of international commercial and financial relations requires the recognition of a public policy which is, if not universal, at least common to the various legal systems which protect the interests of the shareholders of joint stock companies; that, in such circumstances, one cannot consider as against international public policy practices which offer the plaintiffs the minimum of safeguards which are recognized to the shareholders of banks established in England".

68. It follows from such cases that, "international" public policy remains always national by its source for the judges, but that it may well, however, on occasions, be inspired by supranational legislative purposes and therefore that it may have, *by its object*, a truly international purpose.

69. It is erroneous or far too narrow to state, as is often done in doctrinal writings, that the international public policy of the forum can have no other purpose or result but to impose the application of a mandatory rule or fundamental principle *of the domestic law* of the forum. Such a statement misses the point, since the real question is not to ascertain the source of international public policy, but it is to determine its precise normative contents.[59]

3. The Protection of Foreign Mandatory Rules or of Foreign Public Policy

70. Such a sub-title would have doubtless seemed a heresy some thirty or forty years ago. According to a classical doctrine, the essential validity of a contract depends on one law only which governs the whole contract (proper law or *lex contractus*). The quasi-universal recognition of the principle of autonomy of the will, on the one hand, and the traditional conception of international public policy of the forum (asssumed to aim solely at the protection of the fundamental principles of the *lex fori*) on the other hand, lead to a logical consequence: the violation of *foreign* rules (foreign to the *lex contractus* and to the *lex fori*) will in general not be sanctioned at all.

---

58. *Comité de défense des actionnaires de la Banque ottomane et autres* v. *Banque ottomane*, R. 1985, 526 note SYNVET.

59. See on this, the book already mentioned by P. BENVENUTI, who criticizes in a convincing manner the statements by a majority of legal writings and cases which often amount to *petitiones principii*:

> "Quei giudici che si limitano ad affermare che i principî di ordine pubblico internazionale non possono non essere "sempre" valori proprî dell 'ordinamento giuridico nazionale, non pervengono, allora, a dire niente di diverso e niente di più di quanto già sia ricavabile dalle sentenze che essi criticano. *In tal modo, essi si limitano a negare o, più semplicemente, a non tener conto di una esigenza di ulteriore specificazione circa il contenuto e la natura di alcuni principî di ordine pubblico internazionale* che quelle sentenze cercano di esprimere, e che consiste nel fatto che tali principî, pur essendo indiscutibilmente proprî all 'ordinamento particolare, riflettono una realtà che è propria anche ad un ambiente più ampio di quello circoscritto nei confini del singolo Stato e che viene genericamente definito come l'ambito di convivenza dei popoli civili". (*op. cit.*, p. 16. our italics).

71. Such a result is hardly satisfactory and may indeed be shocking from the point of view of ethics or of equity. Attempts have, therefore, been made to restrict the traditional principle. Some German writers, for instance, have suggested as early as the 1940's a theory allowing the application, in certain cases, of some foreign provisions which are internationally mandatory.[60] A well-known recent example is to be found, in European private international law, in Article VII of the Rome Convention on the law governing contractual obligations.[61]

72. Generally speaking, judicial practice has been cautious in this respect, and has hesitated to depart from the principle of the application of the proper law to the legality and morality of the contract. Some decisions, however, have shown a greater spirit of international cooperation and solidarity leading them to apply or at least to take into consideration some foreign provisions designed to be internationally mandatory; this amounts to an application of a foreign "international public policy" or, better, to an extension of the international public policy of the forum to cover and include the protection of essential interests of a foreign State.[62]

73. One of the leading cases in this respect in the well-known decision *Regazonni* v. *KC Sethia Ltd.*, decided in 1958 by the House of Lords.[63]

The facts are well-known: an international contract, concluded between a businessman domiciled in England and a businessman domiciled in Switzerland – a contract perfectly legal with regard to the English "proper law", was considered null and void according to Indian law which prohibited the trade of jute with South Africa, following the apartheid measures imposed on Indians.

74. The question which arose was whether the violation of a foreign law, which was neither the proper law nor the *lex fori*, nor (or so it seems) the law of the place of performance, could lead to an intervention of the international public policy of the forum (which was also that of the *lex contractus*). At least a short passage of this famous case warrants a citation, from the opinion of Viscount Simons:

> "It is, on the other hand, nothing else than *comity* which has influenced our courts to refuse as a matter of public policy to enforce, or to award damages for the breach of, a

60. See W. WENGLER, "Die Anknüpfung des zwingenden Schuldrechts im internationalen Privatrecht", Zeitschrift für rechtsvergleichende Rechtswissenschaft 54 (1940/41), 168–212; K. ZWEIGERT, "Nichterfüllung auf Grund ausländischer Leistungsverbote", RabelsZ. 14 (1942), 283–307; *idem*, Droit international privé et droit public, R. 1965, 645–666; K. H. NEUMAYER, "Autonomie de la volonté et dispositions impératives en droit international privé des obligations", R. 1957, 579–604 et R. 1958, 53–79.

For recent developments, see also I. SCHWANDER, "Lois d'application immédiate, Sonderanknüpfung, IPR-Sachnormen und andere Ausnahmen von der gewöhnlichen Anknüpfung im internationalen Privatrecht," Etudes suisses de droit international, No. 1, Zurich 1975; M. ERNE, "Vertragsgültigkeit und drittstaatliche Eingriffsnormen", Etudes suisses de droit international, No. 41, Zurich 1985.

61. See also, for Switzerland, Article 18 of the Draft Federal Code on private international law.

62. In this sense L. MATRAY, "Arbitrage et ordre public transnational", 14, and citations.

63. 1958 A.C. 301; [1957] 3 All E.R. 286; J. 1961. 1140.

contract which involves a violation of foreign law on foreign soil, and it is the limits of this principle that we have to examine . . .".

75. Conflicting interpretations of this case have been suggested. Is the decision a mere derogation (from the basic competence of the "proper law" of the contract) in favour of a foreign law closely connected with the contractual operation and which intended to impose the respect of its mandatory provisions? If this were so, the Regazzoni case would be a kind of *ante litteram* illustration of the modern theory of "special connection", of the "mandatory rules" (*lois de police*) of third States. According to another possible interpretation,[64] the House of Lords did not merely apply Indian law, instead of English law, to the legality of the contract; it extended the protection of the international public policy of the forum to the public policy of a foreign State (thereby intentionally neglecting, or so it may be assumed, the public policy of South Africa) and the decision would thus be a manifestation of a transnational public policy.

76. True it is that the decision appears to be based on the desire to recognize a certain solidarity with a friendly State (a member of the Commonwealth, but the same could be said of South Africa). It is an application of "comity", in the traditional sense of the great Dutch Statutists or of Joseph Story, or an example of what Savigny called the *freundliche Zulassung*, i.e., of a factor aimed at correcting the rigidity of the territoriality of private international law.[65] The Indian statute which was taken into consideration in that case was indeed a retaliation, but it was not aimed at safeguarding particular or "selfish" interests of the Indian State but rather, in the last analysis, to counter a racist legislation contrary to the elementary requirements of the protection of human rights. It stands to reason that the protection of human rights does belong to a common, and therefore transnational, public policy.[66] The interpretation of the Regazzoni case, therefore, can hardly be limited to one single ground or to one single legal interest: while showing solidarity towards a given State and offering its help by deciding the absolute nullity of a contract which would similarly have been annulled in India, the English courts were simultaneously upholding, and recognizing, the public policy of the international community.

77. Two other decisions, already quoted, one German, the other Italian, must be

---

64. See in particular J. DOLINGER, World Public Policy, 186–188; L. MATRAY, "Arbitrage et ordre public transnational", 243.
65. See M. GUTZWILLER, *Geschichte des International-privatrechts*, Bâle/Stuttgart, 1977, 136 ss.; *idem*, "Le développement historique du droit international privé", RCADI 29 (1929 IV), 291–398, *358*.
66. See, for example, B. GOLDMAN, "La protection internationale des droits de l'homme et l'ordre public international dans le fonctionnement de la règle de conflit de lois", in *René Cassin Amicorum Discipulorumque Liber*, Paris, 1969, I, 449–466; *idem*, "Les conflits de lois dans l'arbitrage international de droit privé", RCADI 109 (1963 II), 350–484, *430–443*, whose ideas have been developed by M. CHAPELLE in his doctor's dissertation; H. ROLIN, "Vers un ordre public réellement international", in *Hommage d'une génération de juristes au Président Basdevant*, Paris, 1960, 441–462; STÖCKER, "Internationaler ordre public zum Schutz der Menschenrechte", StAZ 34 (1981), 16–22.

mentioned here concerning *artifacts illegally exported* from Nigeria or Ecuador.[67] Without really "applying" the Nigerian or Ecuadorian statute prohibiting export, and without applying the UNESCO Convention which was not yet in force, the Court considered as against *bonos mores* the illegal traffic of cultural goods.

78. These cases, and in particular the decision of the German Bundesgerichtshof, appear to call for remarks analogous to those made about the Regazzoni case, in particular, upon the contrast existing between the formal reasoning of private international law and the actual facts of the case. The German Court applied the *lex fori*, which under its own conflict rules governed the contract, but, in reality, it was respecting a foreign law (of Nigeria) which was not applicable under the relevant conflict rule; this was done by means of the concept of "good morals". It should be observed here that this concept does not totally coincide, or so it would seem, with the purely domestic concept applied to those domestic contracts governed by German law. The notion belongs in fact to a morality specific to international trade, which includes the respect of foreign laws at least to the extent to which they protect the cultural heritage of a State. In other words, the court used a concept borrowed from the system of values of the international community rather than from that of a particular State, be it the forum or not.

79. In the same context, a number of decisions may be recalled which, sometimes in a contradictory manner, concerned *foreign export prohibitions*.

80. A first illustration may be found in the famous "*Borax cases*" decided by the German Federal Tribunal in the 1960's.

In the first case,[68] the plaintiff, who had bought in order to resell, had been unable to obtain from its own Danish buyer a declaration of non-export and, for that reason, the German defendant had been unable to obtain delivery in the United States and had been sued for damages as a result of the breach of contract. In the second, analogous[69] case, the buyer had purchased Borax from the United States in order to re-export it to Poland, and the dispute related to the validity of the insurance contract for maritime transport.

In both cases the Bundesgerichtshof held that the contract (of sale or of insurance) was null and void, since the violation of the American embargo was against good morals. The decisions observed that the parties had acted fraudulently in order to deceive the competent American authorities. Both cases are based largely on an analysis of the interests protected by the American embargo.

81. It is noteworthy that these German decisions take into consideration a *foreign* public policy or, in other words, a foreign *loi de police* or mandatory law (whereas the German Federal Republic had, on its part, enacted no similar statute); the decisions are based not only on the protection of *American* legitimate interests, but

67. See *supra*, Notes 28 and 29.
68. BGH, 27 XII 1960, BGHZ 34, 169 = NJW 1961, 822 = AWD 1961, 102 = MDR 1961, 406.
69. BGH, 24 V 1962, NJW 1962, 1436, 1962 note WARN = AWD 1962, 208 = MDR 1962, 719, 888 note SIEG.

also on the absence of damage to German economy and, first and foremost, on the *general interest* of "the whole of the Western free world" and, therefore, on the very interests of the Federal Republic. The question may be asked whether the decision would have been the same if the American embargo, for example, had been enacted *after* the execution of the contract and if, therefore, no intention to defraud had existed. Be that as it may, the method followed by the Court is significant: starting from an analysis of the interest protected by the foreign embargo, it notes the existence of a *common* interest (the protection of peace, *i.e.*, the underlying ground for the embargo on the export of sensitive material capable of reinforcing "the military strength of the East") and finally concludes therefrom that the foreign interest coincides with the national interest of the forum.

82. The decisions in the two "Borax cases", as is often the case with regard to international public policy, may well reflect the particular, and indeed political, circumstances of the period or the particular position of a given State, but this fact does not detract from their legal interest.

83. Analogous remarks may well be made, *mutatis mutandis*, with respect to those European decisions which *refused* to take into consideration other American measures. Two well-known cases need only be recalled here, in passing: one is the French decision in *Fruehauf* v. *Massardi*[70] – which is specific in the sense that an attempt had been made, not directly but indirectly, through instructions given by the American mother-company through its French subsidiary, to apply the foreign embargo – and the more recent, Dutch, decision in the *Sensor* case, concerning President Reagan's embargo of 1982 on deliveries of material for the construction of the Siberian pipeline.[71]

84. Contracts concerning *smuggling* have given rise for a fairly long time to judicial decisions in several countries, which considered them as null and void either on the basis of respect for foreign law, or because of solidarity with foreign States or by a sort of general and diffuse concern for contractual morality. Such a tendency appears to have prevailed in particular in German decisions[72] and in

70. JCP 1965, II, 14274 bis, with the conclusions of the Advocate General NEPVEU, see also W. L. CRAIG, "Application of the Trading with the Enemy Act to Foreign Corporations Owned by Americans: Reflections on FRUEHAUF v. MASSARDY", Harvard L.R. 83 (1970), 579–601.

It should be noted that recent French doctrinal writings invoked in that case a "truly international" public policy in order to justify a decision disregarding the foreign embargo, whereas the German Federal Tribunal relied on that same concept in order to reach the opposite result, *i.e.*, respect for the foreign embargo (see A. CHAPELLE, *Les fonctions de l'ordre public en droit international privé*, No. 450, p. 487).

71. See ILM 22 (1983), 66–73; Th.M. De BOER/R. KOTTING, "Der niederländische Richter und das US-Gasröhren-Embargo", IPRax 2 (1984), 108–112; J. BASEDOW, "Das amerikanische Pipeline-Embargo vor Gericht", RabelsZ. 47 (1983), 141–172; B. AUDIT, "Extra-territorialité et commerce international – L'affaire du gazoduc sibérien", R. 1983, 401–434.

72. For German decisions (including the old case law of the Reichsgericht), see M. ERNE, *Vertragsgültigkeit und drittstaatliche Eingriffsnormen*, 28–29, 31, and G. KEGEL in SOERGEL/G. KEGEL, *Einführungsgesetz*, 1983, vor Art. 7 EGBGB, No. 398.

the French case law of the first half of the twentieth century.[73] As an example one may quote a French judgment of about thirty years ago in which it was stated that

> "If French judges are not called upon to sanction in French courts the violations committed abroad against the public policy of a given State, nevertheless, they must consider as illegal and therefore devoid of validity smuggling operations which, as they violate foreign laws, do infringe as in the present case international public policy . . .".

85. Similar ideas have on occasion been expressed in Swiss judicial practice[74] although, at least in comparatively old decisions, it was often quite reluctant – like the case law of other countries according to a traditional attitude – to accept (or solely with very restrictive conditions) that the violation of a mandatory foreign rule could be a violation of "good morals", a reluctance which led to some harsh but not undeserved comments by F. A. Mann.[75] It may be noted, in passing, that some arbitrators have relied upon this restrictive judicial attitude and held that the applicable law did not permit them to take into consideration, for instance, foreign exchange regulations.[76]

86. It would be difficult and indeed rash to suggest a general conclusion on the basis of those few indications. One may, however, say that there is a definite evolution of judicial practice; it is less reluctant than earlier and it does show, rather cautiously and according to the whole circumstances of each concrete case, an increasing tendency to "sanction" violations of foreign law, be it that of a "third" State. This tendency is noticeable when several conditions are simultaneously realized: (a) that the contract has a sufficient connection with the foreign State the law of which has been violated; (b) that such foreign law has a mandatory or imperative character and insists on being applied, according to its own criteria; (c) that such foreign law aims at protecting interests which are not purely selfish but appear worthy of protection in a supranational perspective. When such conditions are fulfilled, it is no longer rare today that the courts of the forum take into consideration, in international economic relations, basic requirements of solidarity and of "comity". When performing this often delicate, not to say political, function, the judge of the forum, of course within the well-understood limits of its international public policy, accepts the task of protecting a *common* international public policy.

---

73. R. 1956, 580, note H. BATIFFOL. For citations, see M. ERNE, *Vertragsgültigkeit und drittstaatliche Eingriffsnormen*, 38–40.
74. See an isolated decision by the Tribunal of Commerce of Zurich, RSJ 64 (1968) 354.
75. *Suleyman* v. *Tungsram, Elektrizitäts AG*, ATF 76 II 33, *41*. F. A. MANN has also criticized the decision in *Atlas Trading Co.*, ATF 80 II 49; see "Eingriffsgesetze und Internationales Privatrecht", *in Beiträge zum internationalen Privatrecht*, Berlin, 1976, *189–190*; *idem*, "Conflict of Laws and Public Law", RCADI 132 (1971 I), *195–196*.
76. On this point, see the interesting ICC Award No. 1399, of 14 April 1966, quoted by J. LEW, *op. cit.* No. 422: ". . . French law is not concerned with foreign customs laws, and the fact of avoiding this foreign [Mexican] law is not in itself an illegal matter *because there is no collaboration between national legislation on these matters*".

87. This is not to say that the judge should or can blindly respect foreign and purely national political aims or bow before what some German writers called a "heterogeneous regulation". But, for the same writers, the judge could and should take into consideration mandatory foreign laws whenever they tend to safeguard a "typically international interest".

88. When certain recent provisions, such as Article VII of the Rome Convention, are kept in mind, it should be recognized that such theories have a great deal of truth: a State judge cannot of course, within the context of his own (national) private international law, go beyond the classical (national) concept of international public policy unless he is called upon to respect rules or principles which are based on an international consensus which is, if not universal, at least sufficiently widespread.

4. Transnational Public Policy and Public International Law

89. In the first part of the present Report, certain general considerations were submitted on the relationship between the concept of public policy and public international law. Another reference to the same subject is called for here in order to briefly conclude this survey of judicial practice.

90. It has been shown above that public international law may contribute to "nourish" or to define the contents of the international public policy of the forum, and that, on the other hand, the distinction between the two becomes blurred when public international law is applicable, as such, within the legal system of the forum.

91. Independently of such a case, there is little doubt that fundamental principles of the law of nations have been applied, more or less directly and through a variety of formulas, by national judges. A good example, already mentioned, is that of the protection of cultural goods, which belongs to a transnational public policy as shown by the decisions of the German Federal Tribunal and the Tribunal of Torino.[77] The *protection of cultural goods and of environment* would have played a more important role (as a criterion of the compatibility of the contract with transnational public policy) in the so-called Pyramids case,[78] decided by the Court of Appeal of Paris and now pending, at the time of writing, before the French Court of Cassation. If this had been the case, it might have been difficult to discern, in the reasons for the decision, what belonged to transnational public policy, on the one hand, and on the other hand, considerations of traditional international public policy, inasmuch as the UNESCO Convention of 16 November 1972 on the protection of the cultural and natural heritage is in force in France.[79]

77. See *supra*, Notes 28 and 29.
78. See *supra*, Note 26.
79. In this sense a note by B. GOLDMAN, Clunet 1985, 142, *154*.

92. Another field where vital interests of the international community are clearly at stake and where the intervention of international public policy is called for is the sale and *traffic of drugs*. On 14 June 1927,[80] the German Reichsgericht held that a contract for the import of heroin in India, in violation of the Treaty on Opium of 1912 and of Indian public law provisions was contrary to good morals and therefore totally null and void (the decision failed to specify clearly which States were actually bound by the said Treaty of 1912).

93. The Court of Paris held on 9 February 1966[81] that a contract organizing the traffic abroad of weapons, by private persons of foreign nationality, was contrary to the international public policy of France. The court said,

> "that the claim related to the performance of a contract of sale of arms, that such traffic was contrary to international public policy as expressed in particular by the General Act of the Brussels Conference of 2 July 1890, Article 8, by the Agreement of 13 December 1906 between France, Great Britain and Italy and lastly by the International Convention of 17 June 1925 concluded under the aegis of the League of Nations on the repression of arms traffic; that it follows also from French legislation as a whole on this subject and in particular of the Decree of 18 April 1939 that everything which relates to the trade of combat weapons is against French public policy."

94. The reference to French public policy in the present case appears to go beyond the traditional concept in private international law but it is ambiguous, inasmuch as the various international conventions referred to were in force in France.[82]

95. Finally, a very recent decision of the Swiss Federal Tribunal should be mentioned which relates to another of the evils which threaten vital interests of the international community, i.e., *terrorism*.[83] The legal point in dispute was the admissibility of a request by the United Kingdom for judicial assistance in criminal matters, a request to which a Swiss bank had expressed its opposition.

An English firm had been enjoined by the IRA to pay a ransom of £2 million and serious threats had been proferred by the Irish organization against the firm and one of its managers. The same amount appeared to have been transferred by the Swiss bank to the account of its subsidiary in New York, from which it had been re-transferred to an Irish bank in New York and later to the same bank in Ireland. The Swiss bank relied in particular on (a) the danger that the IRA would later similarly threaten some of the bank's customers and (b) the risk that the victim, having yielded to blackmail, be prosecuted under English law.

96. The Federal Tribunal rejected the opposition of the bank, since all the prescribed conditions for granting judicial assistance were fulfilled and it pointed

80. JW 1927, 2288 = IPRspr 1926/1927, No. 15.
81. Paris Court of Appeal, 9 II 1966, R. 1966. 264, note P. LOUIS-LUCAS.
82. In this sense P. LOUIS-LUCAS in his note, R. 1966, *272*.
83. Unpublished decision of 20 November 1985, reported in the newspaper "Neue Zürcher Zeitung" of 21 November 1985 No. 271, p. 34.

out that, in *all* States, there exists a major public interest in the prosecution of terrorists, an interest which must prevail over the private interests of the businessmen and agents concerned. No bank and no State member of the legal community of Western Europe, including Switzerland – stated the Swiss Supreme Court – can accept to become, through negligence, a turning-point or basis for the financial operations of terrorist movements.

97. From the preceding presentation, which did not attempt to be exhaustive, one thing at least seems clear: in an increasing number of cases, a national judge, although a State organ having the function to state and apply the law of a particular State and to ensure the respect of its fundamental principles (in particular by means of the traditional concept of external public policy) has not hesitated to recognize and give effect to a wider notion, more international or perhaps supranational, of public policy, based on the vital interests not only of the national community to which the judge belongs but also of a broader, regional or universal, international community.

98. The question then naturally arises: if such is the situation for the judge of a State, should not the international arbitrator also, and so to speak *a fortiori*, take into account *transnational* public policy and enforce it? This is the question which the last part of the present Report will attempt to answer.

V. FOURTH PART: CONTENTS AND REALITY OF TRANSNATIONAL PUBLIC POLICY IN ARBITRAL PRACTICE

1. *Introduction*

99. It is hardly necessary to emphasize the exceptional difficulty of the subject, for a variety of reasons which relate both to the sources and to the object of the present Report.

100. As to *sources*, every reader should know how difficult it is to get access to them and to obtain a global vision of arbitral practice. And what is known of such practice appears particularly scarce, for a plurality of reasons which it is useful to recall:

a. In the nature of things, there are and should be comparatively few opportunities for the international arbitrator to resort to the concept of transnational public policy; since the arbitrator can only be called upon to act on the basis of an agreement by the parties, it is up to one of them to invoke a contract whose execution or performance would be contrary to transnational public policy! A significant illustration in this respect is the classical example of bribery.
b. Even if the opportunity was offered to him, it is far from certain that the international arbitrator would have the courage, or as some would rather say the

foolishness, to express his decision in innovative formulas (such as a reference to transnational public policy) whenever he is able to motivate his decision in more traditional terms, which seem more likely to ensure the judicial recognition and enforcement of the award in the States concerned.

In contradistinction to a *judge*, who has all the necessary authority to render a judgment, if need be, on the basis of the public policy (national – international or even transnational) inspired by the international policy of his State, the *arbitrator* is likely to prefer, as grounds for his decision, such rules or notions (perhaps not necessarily of national origin) as are supported by a well-established *opinio juris*; this could of course be the case whenever transnational public policy is based on considerations of social *ethics*, but less frequently when transnational public policy would be largely inspired by *political* considerations.

c. It is understandable that, in general, the international arbitrator would show great caution when using his "creative powers" and would refrain from resorting unduly to concepts or standards as relative and difficult to define with certainty as that of public policy. It is of course much easier for the international arbitrator to refer in a given case to the international public policy *of a State*, since judicial precedents make it comparatively easy to establish its existence and its limits.

101. From this apparent scarcity of arbitral decisions on the subject, it would be erroneous to conclude that the concept of transnational public policy is either inexistent or useless. A first reason is the fact, previously mentioned, that several judicial decisions *did* refer to and even did recognize the concept of a common policy, truly international or universal, in appropriate cases; and this fact is all the more significant since, in most cases, the judge would have been able to arrive at the same practical result by resorting to the traditional concept of public policy within his own private international law.

102. There is reason to believe that, if judges have not hesitated to accept the idea of transnational public policy, international arbitrators by their very function and, let it be repeated, so to speak a fortiori, (a) *could* do the same and (b) *should* be naturally inclined to do the same, in order to reach practical conclusions, either negative (setting aside the normally applicable law or rules), or positive (imperative application, by priority, of certain superior and fundamental norms or principles essential in the law of international trade). In both cases this resort to transnational public policy should aim at protecting certain of the essential values and interests of the international community (of businessmen and States). Since he has no allegiance to a particular State, by the nature of his function, the international arbitrator could have greater difficulty than a judge when defining (at least in a case *primae impressionis*) the content of the international public policy *of a State*. But he would seem to be in a *better position* than a State judge when called upon to ascertain and understand the specific needs of the *international* community (at least that of businessmen), and it is precisely one of the reasons why the parties, *ex hypothesi*, have resorted to international arbitration.

103. Admittedly the task of determining, in a concrete case, the existence of a principle of transnational public policy may not be an easy one. But why should it be considered a priori as much more difficult than, in many cases, the task of the international arbitrator called upon to elicit and define, and then to apply, the usages of international trade or other "a-national" rules whenever applicable?

104. As a matter of fact, the two tasks appear closely connected or even identical, subject to some reservations to be mentioned later: and it is in any case of interest to compare to the question presently under examination the problem posed to the arbitrator by the application (and therefore by the prior determination) of the *lex mercatoria*. Such a comparison may be illustrated by reference to an excellent and recent study by Professor Ole Lando:[84]

> "An arbitrator applying the *lex mercatoria* will act as an inventor more often than one who applies national law. Faced with the restrictive legal material which the law merchant offers, he must often seek guidance elsewhere. His main source is the various legal systems. When they conflict he must make a choice or find a new solution. The *lex mercatoria* often becomes a creative process by this means.
>
> Arbitrators of different nationalities who have applied the *lex mercatoria* in collegiate arbitral tribunals have not experienced great difficulties in reaching consensus. . . .
>
> Most arbitrators have common ethics and common notions of how business should be conducted. That leads them in the same direction. . . . In their attempt to give reasons they sometimes realize that the issue is governed by a rule which has still to be framed. Even courts sometimes face such situation."

105. According to most recent studies on the subject, arbitral practice, at least in Europe, appears to accept more and more the application, unless of course the contract would preclude that, of the *lex mercatoria* to international disputes. As to the content of such "law merchant", it is worth noting in passing that it includes (according to Lando's article just mentioned) elements borrowed from a variety of sources, such as public international law.[85]

---

84. O. LANDO "The Lex Mercatoria in International Commercial Arbitration", 34 ICLQ (1985), *752*. It should be noted that the author rightly draws a distinction between "amiable composition" and an application of the "lex mercatoria". He writes in particular:

> "some of the authors who oppose the parties' right to choose the *lex mercatoria* will permit them to agree on amiable composition or decisions based on equity. This is, however, a yet more uncertain basis than the *lex mercatoria*. In spite of common traits, there is a difference between the *lex mercatoria* and equity. The *lex mercatoria* obliges the arbitrator to base his decision on the law merchant even when equity might lead him to another result" (p. 754–755).

And the author adds that

> "the choice of the *lex mercatoria* need not give the parties any opportunity to evade mandatory rules of law".

85. The author cites here the *Vienna Convention of 13 May 1969 on the Law of Treaties*; Article 42 of the *Washington Convention of the World Bank*; some uniform laws (such as those introduced by the *Vienna Convention on the International Sale of Goods*); general principles of law (*i.e.*, ICC Award No. 3327–81, cited in Clunet 1982, p. 973); certain rules, recommendations or codes of conduct enacted by international organizations; the usages of international trade, the general conditions for certain types of contracts and some arbitral "precedents".

106. Another fact is worthy of note: this tendency of arbitrators appears to have been supported, in recent times, in a significant manner, by doctrinal writings and some international conventions,[86] and also – which is perhaps even more striking – by some national *laws* (such as the French Decree on international arbitration), or certain *"judgments"*, in France, Austria and Italy in particular.[87]

107. Added to the judicial recognition, noted above, of the existence of a transnational public policy, these indications appear most significant: they seem to justify the conclusion that there does exist a general tendency of States (notwithstanding their legal "particularism" or even their narrow interests and selfishness as expressed by traditional "international public policy") to become more conscious of their increased *international solidarity*. Another factor did bear witness to that same tendency: the modern rejection of the alleged principle of "inapplicability of foreign public law" and the trend to apply, in certain circumstances, a foreign public policy or foreign mandatory rules (*lois de police étrangères*).

108. After these general observations, of a somewhat tentative character, we shall now review some examples (either real, likely or possible) of resort to transnational public policy by the international arbitrator.

109. Two preliminary remarks appear called for:

First, having regard to the scarcity of known arbitral decisions on the subject, it is justified to reason, by analogy, from the starting point of examples taken from court judgments, at least in those cases which could easily have arisen, or are likely to arise, also before international arbitrators.

Second, one should bear in mind the variety of the terminology used in arbitral awards, where it is not always easy to distinguish what really belongs to the concept of transnational public policy and what "merely" relates to general principles, common or fundamental principles of the law of international trade, of the *lex mercatoria*, of an emerging "transnational law" or also of an "international law of contracts". Among all these principles, it would appear that only which are really essential and are supported by a widespread, if not universal consensus, or as possessing, owing to their importance, a particular force and a particular imperative nature, will deserve to be considered as included in the concept of transnational public policy.

110. In traditional private international law, a characteristic feature of the notion of the international public policy of the State could be called its "polyvalent" or versatile character, i.e., the possibility to apply it in a great variety of fields. The same holds true in transnational relations, to the extent, of

86. See the *Geneva Convention of 21 April 1961*, Article VII para. 1 and 2, the already quoted Article 42 of the Washington Convention of 1965, Article 28 para. 4 of the *UNCITRAL Model Law on Arbitration.*

87. See the decision by the Italian Court of Cassation of 8 February 1932 (although it appears erroneous on other points as well-demonstrated by A. GIARDINA in Rivista di diritto internazionale privato e processuale, N. 4, 1982, p. 754–765) and the decision by the Supreme Court of Austria of 18 November 1982 (cited by L. MATRAY, Report, p. 16, note 1).

course, that they relate to trade. For the purpose of the present Report, the following examples will be divided into five categories, while bearing in mind the possibility of overlapping and the somewhat arbitrary character of any attempt at classification.

2. The Validity of the Contract

111. As any international arbitration is based on the contract and relates, nearly always, to a contractual dispute, it is, of course, in the field of contracts that most examples are likely to be found of arbitral recognition of fundamental principles capable of forming or "nourishing" the concept of transnational public policy. Various references have already been made above to interventions of judges or arbitrators aimed at protecting "bona fides", "good morals", fundamental principles of contractual morality or of natural law.

112. It would be wrong to assume, as seems to be done in certain studies on the subject, that the recognition by the international arbitrator of the moral character of certain transactions dates from 1963, with the justly famous award by Judge Lagergren, which will be commented upon later. Already in awards given in the last century, public policy was resorted to in order to safeguard morality in international trade relations.

113. Two cases in point are that of the ships "Créole" and "Maria Luz" respectively decided by the Mixed Commission of London on 15 January 1855, and by the Tsar of Russia, on 17–29 May 1875.[88] While they came to opposite results in fact, they were based on similar legal considerations, and they constitute a significant illustration of the role of transnational public policy (or rather, to use the terminology of the period, of the public policy of the "law of nations") in respect of human rights and, more precisely, of *slavery*.

The facts of the two cases were different but raised the same basic question: should the rights of ownership on slaves be recognized, when such slaves were transported by the "owner" in a ship which failed to reach its original destination following (in the case of the "Créole") a revolt of the slaves and (in the case of the "Maria Luz") their liberation by the Japanese authorities?

114. The first award, of 1855, does recognize the right of the owner on his slaves, but in terms which are worthy of note and clearly allow the conclusion that arbitrators deciding *today* would come to the opposite conclusion on the basis of transnational public policy:

> "We do not think that it is necessary to refer to authorities to demonstrate that slavery, however odious and contrary to the principles of justice and humanity, may be recognized by the law of a given country, and that, since it has in fact been established in several States, it cannot be contrary to the law of nations."

88. J.-P. NIBOYET, *Le rôle de la justice internationale*, 180–187.

115. The second award, of 1875, holds that the Japanese government, having freed the slaves in keeping with "its own laws and customs", has not violated "the general rules of the law of nations nor the provisions of particular treaties". The decision appears to have merely a historical interest and it would have been more significant if Japan had been bound by a bilateral treaty *prohibiting* the intervention of its maritime authorities in such a case, but had relied, nevertheless, on a superior principle of humanity or of the law of nations.

116. As to *bribery*, the award given by Mr. Lagergren in an ICC arbitration[89] has been so often quoted, and recently in the important Report of Professor Böckstiegel on public policy and arbitrability (see III.2.d.) that it is hardly necessary to comment it further. It would indeed be hard to dispute the validity, on the merits, of the arbitrators' observations, to the effect that "contracts which seriously violated bonos mores or international public policy are invalid . . .".

117. While he referred to *French law* as the proper law of the contract and added, probably *ex abundanti cautela*, that *Argentinian law* contained similar provisions, the arbitrator did refer to a general principle of law, of a fundamental nature (the prohibition of "bribery") and to the destructive effect of such violation on international trade: "such corruption is an international evil; it is contrary to good morals and to *an international public policy common to the community of nations* . . .".

118. It is irrelevant for the purpose of the present discussion that Judge Lagergren, perhaps influenced by a traditional British conception (which does not seem to have accepted yet the prevailing doctrine of the autonomy or "separability" of the arbitration clause) should have thought it necessary to decline his own jurisdiction, a solution which has generally been criticized by recent writers, such as Goldman, El-Kosheri and Leboulanger, and Böckstiegel.[90]

119. From this point of view, one should, therefore, approve the different approach adopted by an Austrian arbitrator in a recent case. It is worth noting that the arbitrator, with typical caution, based his condemnation of corruption *on a national law*, *i.e.*, French law which was the law of the contract, but added:

> "Lastly, one may also judge the case, apart from any national law, from the point of view of what is considered as morality in international relations".

120. Arbitral condemnation of corruption may thus be characterized as either the application of a general principle of law "recognized by civilized nations", or as the recognition of a "substantive law of necessary application", or as the resort

---

89. Award No. 1110 of 1963, cited and partly published by J. LEW, *Applicable Law in International Commercial Arbitration*, New York 1978, p. 553 ss.

90. See B. GOLDMAN, "The Complementary Roles of Judges and Arbitrators in Ensuring that International Commercial Arbitration is Effective", *ICC Court of Arbitration 60th Anniversary*, Paris 1984, p. 272, and A. S. EL-KOSHERI/Ph. LEBOULANGER "L'arbitrage face à la corruption et aux trafics d'influences", Revue de l'arbitrage 1984, p. 18, cited by K.-H.BÖCKSTIEGEL, Report p. 202.

to a "transnational public policy"; notwithstanding the variety of the labels or expressions used, the same concept is in fact involved.

121. From this point of view, arbitral practice appears to be in full harmony with judicial practice, as shown by a recent decision of the German "Bundesgerichtshof"[91] or by an old decision of the Supreme Court of the United States which, on 24 April 1881, refused to order the payment of a commission for the illicit use of influence, notwithstanding the fact, aptly emphasized by L. Matray, that the State whose citizen was involved in the transaction did *accept* such a bargain![92]

122. In an ICC award of 1982,[93] the question in dispute was the validity of a nexus of contracts between two Yugoslav firms and foreign firms. This was supposed to be an export–import transaction, but the export part of it was fictitious and solely designed to enable the Yugoslav firms to obtain – in violation of Yugoslav rules on foreign exchange and export credit – a credit in foreign currency for the purchase of consumer goods. The arbitrators first determined the true nature of the contractual operation and established the violation of Yugoslav law; they then concluded that such operations were "contrary not only to Yugoslav law but also to morality and bonos mores". According to the award, since the object of the contract was contrary to mandatory or public law rules, as well as contrary to morality, it was "absolutely null and void":

> "This principle is recognized in all countries and all systems of law. It does constitute an international rule, an element of the common law of contracts in the international field. In the present case, the parties deliberately concluded a fictitious contract, in violation of the governing Yugoslav legislation, in order to procure to the fictitious exporter a credit equally fictitious which he would not have been able to obtain otherwise. There is therefore a violation of law, morality and good morals".

123. In another ICC case,[94] the arbitrators were not deceived by the lawful appearance of a contract of commission and decided that the payment of bribes by a British firm was the cause of the obligation undertaken by a French firm. Deciding the nullity of the contract, the arbitrators made it clear that

> "This solution is not only in keeping with internal French public policy, it is also dictated by the concept of international public policy as is recognized by the majority of States".

124. In another case, between French and Iranian parties, the defendant contended that the "commissions" claimed were not payable because the contract was null and void.[95]

---

91. RIW/AWD 1985, 653, cited by K.-H. BÖCKSTIEGEL in his Report in this volume p. 202.
92. See *supra*, Notes 30 and 52.
93. ICC No. 2730, Clunet 1984, 914, Observations Y. DERAINS.
94. ICC No. 3913 of 1981, unpublished – extracts are published in a note by Y. DERAINS published with the award mentioned in the preceding note, in Clunet 1984, 920–921.
95. ICC Award No. 3916 of 1982, Clunet 1984, 930.

The award decides accordingly the nullity of the contract, but it is interesting to note that this conclusion is based on a detailed analysis of both Iranian and French laws. In particular, the award observes that in fact, during the years when the performance of the contract was taking place in Iran, "corruption or at least the sale of influence was in constant practice" so that it "was extremely difficult if not impossible to obtain any contract for public works without resorting to such methods", while the Iranian government had attempted, but in vain, to remedy this situation through various statutes.

125. In its formulation, this award is less explicit than the former ones as to the existence of a truly international public policy but it does reflect a similar approach and philosophy.

126. Again, an ICC case of 1982, already cited (No. 2730) clearly states that the immorality of such practices of bribery and sale of influence is based on a rule truly international in character, so that there is no doubt that such a rule must be considered as belonging to transnational public policy.

127. True it is that the concept of "good morals" in international trade relations has flexible and evolutive contents and limits (just as, by the way, *mutatis mutandis*, the domestic law concept of "good morals", although to a lesser degree since the national community involved is more homogeneous than the international community). While the difficulty to draw a clear-cut distinction between bribery and the "normal" payment of commissions according to trade usages should be kept in mind, it must be recognized that transnational public policy is directly involved by a type of behaviour contrary to principles whose ethical and legal bases are supported by a general consensus. The prohibition of such behaviour is not only provided for (if not always effectively enforced) by the domestic laws of most States; the reprehensible character of such practices also appears from a series of international instruments.[96–98]

128. International arbitration is now known to be "*the*" ordinary and normal method of settling disputes of international trade. It follows that the arbitrators'

96. Bribery in contracts has been studied by the United Nations either as a subject in itself or in the context of other subjects such as the activity of transnational corporations. See in particular "Resolution 3514 of the General Assembly, Resolution 2014 (LXI) of the Economic and Social Council (Corrupt Practices, Particularly Illicit Payments in International Commercial Transactions)", ILM XV (1976), 1222; "UN Commission on Transnational Corporations: Report of the Working Group on the Formulation of a Code of Conduct", ILM XVI (1977), 709; "Economic and Social Council: Report of the *Ad Hoc* Working Group on Corrupt Practices in International Commercial Transactions", ILM XVI (1977), 1236; "Report of the Committee of the Economic and Social Council on an International Agreement on Illicit Payments", ILM XVIII (1979), 1025; "Draft Code of Conduct of the UN on Transnational Corporations", ILM XXII (1983), 177 and XIII (1984), 626.

97. ICC, *L'exaction et la corruption dans les transactions commerciales*. Publication No. 315. See on these drafts ILM XVI (1977), 686 and ILM XVII (1978), 417.

On the ICC efforts towards a "moralization" in the field of bank guarantees, see J. DOHM, *Les garanties bancaires dans le commerce international*, Genève, 1986, No. 42.

98. "Council Regulation No. 2641/84 of 17 September 1984 on the strengthening of the common commercial policy with regard in particular to protection against illicit commercial practices", ILM XXIII (1984), 1419.

function is no longer (as would seem to appear from Judge Lagergren's approach in 1963) to declare admissible or inadmissible the request for arbitration of a person claiming the payment of commissions, according to the degree of contractual morality of the claimant (to some extent as a doctrine of "clean hands" might do). The protection of the superior interests of the international community, rather, requires the arbitrator, not to decline his jurisdiction, but to examine the merits and the conformity of the contract with the requirements of transnational public policy.

129. What other types of conduct (apart from bribery) will be considered as contrary to *bonos mores* (a notion which appears to be an essential part of that of transnational public policy)? Other examples are contractual practices aimed at facilitating drug traffic,[99] the traffic of arms between private persons (generally considered as against the international public policy of those very States which claim the monopoly of this disreputable activity!), contracts aimed at favoring kidnapping, murder, or generally the subversions or evasion of the imperative laws of a sovereign State (such as through the employment of mercenaries) or violations of human rights,[100] etc.

130. Analogous considerations could be made about contracts and the illicit transfer of cultural goods (but it should be noted, in passing, that the international consensus existing in this domain appears somewhat more limited than what a reader of UNESCO Conventions might believe, since there are some conflicts of interests between importing and exporting countries of cultural goods, in particular of artifacts and works of art.[101]

131. In all those fields, arbitral practice could usefully rely upon those court judgments which, as we have seen, show an increasing consciousness of the need

99. UN General Assembly, "Resolution 393/141 (International Campaign Against Traffic in Narcotic Drugs)"; "Resolution 39/142 (Declaration on the Control of Drug Trafficking and Drug Abuse)" and "Resolution 39/143 (International Campaign Against Traffic in Drugs)", ILM XXIV (1985), 1157.

100. On terrorism, see, for example, Conseil de l'Europe, "Recommendation Concerning International Cooperation in the Prosecution and Punishment of Acts of Terrorism", ILM XXI (1982), 199; Communautés Européennes, "Agreement Concerning the Application of the European Convention on the Suppression of Terrorism Among the Member States", ILM XIX (1980), 325; General Assembly of the UN, "Resolution 34/145 (Measures to prevent international terrorism which endangers or takes innocent human lives or jeopardizes fundamental freedoms, . . .)", ILM XIX (1980), 533; General Assembly of the UN, "Drafting of an International Convention Against the Taking of Hostages", ILM XVIII (1979), 1456.

On human rights, see, for example, Commission on Human Rights, UN, "Draft Convention Against Torture and Other Cruel, Inhuman or Degrading Treatment or Punishment", ILM XIX (1980), 647; Organization of American States, Inter-American Juridical Committee; "Draft Convention 1/11 Defining Torture as an International Crime", ILM XIX (1980), 618. – See also the excellent book written by J. LEW, *op. cit.*, No. 407.

101. See the recent doctoral dissertation by Q. BYRNE-SUTTON, *Le trafic international des biens culturels sous l'angle de leur revendication par l'Etat d'origine* (*Aspects de droit international privé*), Geneva – to be published.

for greater international solidarity and the recognition of an emerging transnational public policy.[102]

132. The *validity of the contract* may also be questioned, before the arbitrator, in other fields, e.g., in the case of contracts violating embargos of economic sanctions recommended by international organizations (such as the well-known case of the sanctions against Rhodesia). Here also, arbitral practice could gradually develop and render more precise the experience made by judicial practice, through concepts such as those of "good morals" or of *comitas gentium*. Let us imagine for example that a dispute like that in *Regazzoni* v. *Sethia*[103] is brought before an international arbitrator. It cannot be excluded that the arbitrator, notwithstanding a natural reluctance to adopt political positions, could react in a manner very similar to that of the English courts.

3. *The Common Law of International Arbitration*

133. There is little doubt that a number of essential principles of the international law of arbitration have acquired the character, or the "dignity", of general principles of the law of international trade; arbitrators no longer hesitate to apply them as a common law (and the terminology they use appears of little relevance, e.g., a substantive private international law common to several States or common to both international law and the private international law of the State, or *lex mercatoria*, etc.). There is no denying that such principles enjoy a general acceptance or "consensus" in international practice (while other principles appear to be in the process of acquiring such consensus). But the question remains whether these principles must *necessarily* prevail, *as a part of a transnational public policy*, over the normally applicable rules designated either "directly" by the parties or by the traditional method of a choice of domestic law.

134. The question also arises – although this may be rare in practice – whether the transnational public policy of the arbitrator should lead him, in a given case, to ignore the international public policy of a certain State, be it that of the place of arbitration or one of the States concerned in the dispute.[104]

135. A general and abstract answer does not appear to have much sense, especially since the concept of public policy, as we have seen, has a dynamic and evolutive character and must be considered *in concreto*, in the light of all the circumstances of the case. However, it can probably be asserted that certain principles of the law of international arbitration, because they receive general acceptance and because of this fundamental character, should be recognized as particularly imperative and having acceded to the "rank" of transnational public policy.

---

102. See *supra*, No. 50ff.
103. See *supra*, Note 63.
104. For examples of such rules of truly international public policy, see above No. 111ff.

136. Such appears to be the case for several and perhaps all of the principles which, for instance, recognize the impossibility for a contracting State, or a State company or public organization (a) after the execution of the contract containing an arbitration clause to invoke its incapacity to arbitrate; (b) to challenge the validity of the arbitration clause on the basis of absence of special powers to sign the contract; (c) unilaterally to rescind an international arbitration clause, either directly, or through retroactive legislation; (d) to contend that its immunity of jurisdiction entails the invalidity of the arbitration clause and thus the arbitrators' lack of jurisdiction; (e) to rely on the sovereignty of the State as a ground for the *restrictive* interpretation of the arbitration undertaking contained in an international contract.

a. *Subjective non-arbitrability or incapacity of the State to arbitrate*

137. There is no need to repeat here the analysis and distinctions put forward by Professor Böckstiegel, in his Report (see III.2.e) and his other works on the subject, and the major role played in international commercial arbitration by this problem is well-known. Particularly enlightened court decisions in certain States, *e.g.*, in France, have found an appropriate answer to the objection which the State or a public entity attempted to base on its municipal law. Depending on the interpretation given to such court decisions, the answer was the creation of a domestic rule of substantive private international law or an intervention of the "positive" international public policy of the State. When the question of the power to arbitrate is characterized as one of capacity, there is much strength, in classical private international law, in a conflict rule favouring the application of the "personal law", *i.e.*, the law of the State or public entity involved. If such is the normally applicable law, then it is up to the concept of public policy to intervene in order to avoid a result which would be morally unacceptable and harmful to the very interests of the State as an actor in international trade.

138. In the countries where the courts were incapable or unwilling to find the adequate answer (such as a restriction of the alleged incapacity to purely domestic situations), the international arbitrator may have to deal with it in the guise of an objection to his jurisdiction. There is no doubt that the general trend of arbitral practice today tends to reject this kind of objection (a rejection which can be expressed according to a variety of formulas, as aptly observed by Böckstiegel, p.187 and 203): application of the principle of good faith, of the notion of *venire contra factum proprium*, of abuse of right, of estoppel or of international public policy. Such rejection appears to be based on two lines of reasoning, one ethical, the other practical: on the one hand, there is an obvious moral reason for not allowing a State or public entity to invoke, after having signed an arbitration undertaking, its own domestic incapacity; on the other, such type of behaviour would gravely undermine the trust and security which are indispensable to the normal functioning of international trade, in particular with States, and it would be clearly against the general interests of States (an argument which is in full harmony, by the way, with the very conduct of States, the vast majority of which respect international arbitration undertakings). By the nature of his function, the

international arbitrator has to protect a certain basic "contractual morality" and the superior interests of international trade, and he is therefore called upon, in the nature of things, to resort to the concept of transnational public policy, if need be, against the international public policy of a particular State. A good example of such a situation is found in the recent award, of 18 November 1983, in an *ad hoc* arbitration *Benteler* v. *the Belgian State.*[105] The same principle is expressly recognized by Article 178 of the Swiss Draft Code on Private International Law.

b. *Absence of special powers (of the signatory of an arbitration undertaking)*

139. Analogous observations may be made with regard to this second type of objection. The principle of *bona fides* as well as the security of international transactions do not permit that a State or public entity be allowed to invoke, after the execution of a contract, alleged irregularities such as the absence of those special powers which would for instance be required under domestic law for the signing of arbitration undertakings. But some distinctions have to be drawn in such a case, as shown by the recent ICC arbitration award (No. 3896) in the case *Framatome-Atomic Energy Organization of Iran:*[105bis] it stands to reason that the objection would prevail if the foreign contractual party knew, or should have known, the alleged irregularities, or had failed, in the circumstances, to exercise proper care.

140. Apart from the exceptional case when the foreign contracting party did know the absence of special powers or other irregularity or had seriously failed to show "due diligence", arbitral practice clearly tends to reject – as against fundamental principles of arbitration law (principles which include perhaps the idea of *favor validitatis*) the defence or objection to jurisdiction which is based either on the idea of incapacity to arbitrate or of the invalidity or formal irregularity of the undertaking. Lastly, it may be added that, for the defending State or State entity, such objections are difficult to reconcile with the higher principle of *bona fides*, all the more so since, in the nature of things, the objection is often raised at a time when the main contract (if not the arbitration clause itself) has already been performed to some degree by both parties, which does constitute ratification by conduct![106]

c. *Unilateral rescission of the arbitration undertaking*

141. A well-known precedent is the famous *Losinger* case,[107] where the Kingdom of Yugoslavia used retroactive legislation in order to annul a prior arbitration undertaking. Another case in point, and a more recent one, is the case *Topco Calasiatic* v. *Libyan Government*, where the latter government initially challenged the power of the President of the International Court of Justice to designate the sole arbitrator on the ground that the arbitration clause which conferred to the

105. Journal des tribunaux, Brussels, 1984, 230, cited by K.-H. BÖCKSTIEGEL, Report, note 84.
105.bis Clunet 1983, 914, note S. JARVIN, *Yearbook Commercial Arbitration*, Vol. X (1985) 47.
106. On this question, see again the Award *Framatome* v. *AEOI*, already cited.
107. PCIJ Series A–B, Fasc., No. 67 and 69; Series C, Fasc. No. 78.

President such authority had itself been annulled, together with the whole arbitration clause, by the Libyan Decree of Nationalization.[108]

142. The general rejection of such State attempts to renege on their promise to arbitrate may be interpreted as based on an application of the "separability" or "autonomy" of the arbitration clause, which is a generally recognized principle (although a country like England appears to be reluctant to accept it).[109] But it must be seen rather as a direct application of the concept of good faith or *bona fides*[110] and is a fundamental principle of common sense as well as of the law of international arbitration.

d. *Immunity from jurisdiction?*

143. A similar fundamental principle, closely related to the preceding one, does not allow a State which has signed an international arbitration clause to invoke later its immunity from jurisdiction in order to challenge the jurisdiction of the arbitrator. Such a claim would be in total contradiction with the practice and behaviour of most States, a practice from which it follows that the signing of an arbitration clause is, or is equivalent to, a waiver of immunity from jurisdiction, perhaps implied but certain.[111]

e. *Restrictive interpretation of State undertakings*

144. A different principle, based however on similar underlying considerations – and which has been recognized for example in one of the ICSID awards[112] – has led international arbitrators to reject the claim that the quality of sovereign State would suffice to justify the *restrictive* interpretation of arbitration undertakings in an international contract. This would seem to be a mere application of the principle of equality of the parties in arbitration rather than a principle of interpretation properly speaking (and it would seem difficult, a priori, to consider principles of interpretation as capable of constituting or "nourishing" the concepts of transnational public policy).[112bis]

108. On this point, see the Preliminary Award by Professor DUPUY – unpublished – on his jurisdiction, dated 27 November 1975, p. 7ff.

109. See for example, J. STEYN, "England", in *International Handbook on Commercial Arbitration*, p. 9.

110. On good faith as a general principle of law, see BIN CHENG *General Principles of Law*, London, 1953, 105ff.

111. See, for example, a recent study by M. BLESSING/Th. BURCKHARDT, "Sovereign Immunity – A Pitfall in State Arbitration?", in *Swiss Essays on International Arbitration*, Zurich, 1984, 107–123.

112. *Amco Asia Corporation et al.* and *Indonesia*, ILM XXIII (1984) 351 (jurisdiction); XXIV (1985) 1022 (merits).

112.bis All the more so since principles of interpretation should rather be considered, it is submitted, as recipes or methods which may guide the arbitrator in the art of interpretation, and not as rules of law.

4. Procedure

145. The very first fundamental principle of arbitration, and in particular of arbitral procedure, is undoubtedly that of the *impartiality* of the arbitrator, a principle which partly overlaps with the general principle of law *nemo iudex in causa sua.*[113] Reference should be made here to the Schwebel-Lahne Report, which contains many illustrations of national practice or, more precisely, of application of the international public policy of States. An example is the German decision of the Oberlandesgericht of Cologne, on 10 June 1976,[114] where the arbitrators' impartiality was considered as "a fundamental principle both of the German legal system and of the international legal order". According to another German decision, given by the Supreme Court of the Federal Republic,[115] the prohibition to decide in one's own cause is a guarantee of the impartiality of the judge and arbitrator and the respect of this principle belongs to those rules of procedure which are absolutely mandatory.[116]

146. The other fundamental principles of any arbitral procedure can be summed up by the concept of *equality of the parties* and in particular by the old Roman principle *audiatur et altera pars* (or "principle of contradiction"). This is the well-known concept of "due process" which is summed up in the Schwebel Report p. 216.

The fact that the public policy requirements of due process are so obvious in the conduct of arbitral proceedings has the result that cases in which such questions have arisen are neither many nor controversial.[117] The shared, general principles of international due process in this sphere are (a) equal treatment of the parties, (b) fair notice (both of the appointment of arbitrators and the conduct of proceedings), and (c) fair opportunity to present the case. These principles characterize model laws and rules and municipal legislation as shown by UNCITRAL's Model Law, Article 19(3), Article 24(3), etc.

147. Those principles are undoubtedly a part of transnational public policy, as is demonstrated, on the one hand, by the remarkable harmony between national decisions and internal practices (or, in other words, by the coincidence of the concepts of domestic international public policy) and, on the other hand, their recognition by international instruments such as UNCITRAL Model Law, as well as by the practice of international jurisdictions or commissions.[118]

113. See for example BIN CHENG, *op. cit.* in note 110, at p. 279ff.
114. See S. SCHWEBEL/S. LAHNE, Reports in this volume, p. 213; *Yearbook Commercial Arbitration*, Vol. IV, (1979) p. 258, 260.
115. Decision of 7 March 1985, NJW 1985 II, 1903–1905, cited by L. MATRAY in his Report, p. 10.
116. In this case, the arbitrator took a decision without calling for evidence or estimating the proof, after a party had refused to pay an advance on the arbitrator's fees.
117. This opinion or its expression is perhaps excessively optimistic, at least if attention is drawn not to the principles themselves but to their modalities and their application in practice.
118. On this subject, see the standard work, already quoted, by Professor BIN CHENG, above, Note 110.

148. Can a similar statement be made about certain general principles with regard to proof? An affirmative answer is called for without doubt, with regard, for instance, to the inadmissibility of "secret proof",[119] which would be a glaring breach of the equality of the parties. It is more difficult to suggest an answer with regard to the principle *Actori incumbit probatio* – which an ICC award of 1981 considered as belonging to transnational public policy.[120] Caution is required before accepting that a given principle or idea has already found its place within the concept of transnational public policy. Such hesitation or caution appears to be justified by two considerations: on the one hand, the diversity of national procedures, the often formalist and detailed character of laws in such matters render slower and more difficult the gradual birth of general principles of law based upon a comparative analysis (although the diversity of procedural systems appears to decrease, at least in arbitral practice). On the other hand, the nature of arbitration, and in particular the specificity of international arbitration, hardly permit a simple transposition to arbitration of those general principles which emerge from a comparison of national rules of *judicial* procedure. Account must be taken, in particular, of the exceptions or adaptations required by the higher principle of good faith, in particular, in the field of proof. As an example, an ICC award of 1975[121] may be quoted:

> ". . . Reference must be made here to the rules which relate to the burden of proof, although arbitrators are not bound to apply such rules in the same strict manner at some State courts. Moreover, both parties are in duty bound to cooperate, according to the principle of good faith, to the administration of proof, in particular in arbitration."

149. There is little doubt that arbitral practice reveals a definite reluctance (which may be sometimes exaggerated and even a source of injustice) to rely on a strict distribution of the burden of proof and, more generally, on a strict application of rules of procedure. The context and general spirit of international arbitration, its flexibility, its liberalism and its absence of formalism are characteristics of arbitration and they do not favour (apart from fundamental principles such as those already referred to) the gradual emergence or recognition of transnational public policy with regard to proof.

150. In the matter of arbitral jurisdiction, the question may arise whether the so-called principle of *compétence-compétence* of the arbitrator has not become (notwithstanding a certain reluctance of some national systems, influenced by

---

119. In this sense, German lawyers speak of *Parteiöffentlichkeit der Beweisaufnahme*. An extraordinary example is found in a recent ICC award, of 1985, between a French company and an Asian public corporation: after a breach of contract, the French company invoked "force majeure" relying on secret instructions by the French Government, and a majority of arbitrators accepted as a "proof" of the alleged governmental decision the reading aloud by a "witness" of a decision (on the last day of the proceedings), the text of which was never communicated or filed to the other party or to the arbitral tribunal!

120. ICC Award No. 3344 of 1981, Clunet 1982, 978, note Y. DERAINS; see also the award of President Cassin in the famous case of the "cargaisons déroutées", R. 1956, 278, *286*.

121. Award No. 1434 of 1975, Clunet 1976, 978, note Y. DERAINS.

the Anglo-American tradition) a fundamental principle of transnational public policy, especially now that it has been recognized by various international instruments. An analogous question could be asked in respect of the principle of *autonomy of the arbitration clause* already mentioned.

151. What about the *obligation to motivate* the award, in the absence of an agreement of the parties to the contrary? The Geneva Convention of 1961 (Article VIII) provides that "the parties shall be presumed to have agreed that reasons shall be given for the award" unless they expressly agreed to the contrary or "have assented to an arbitral procedure under which it is not customary to give reasons for awards" but this assent can always be nullified by one party before the end of the hearing or before the making of the award. In any case, the absence of reasons can never conceal a violation of due process.[122]

5. General Principles of Private International Law

152. As shown in the Second Part of the present Report, the international arbitrator, *ex natura rerum*, has no *lex fori* and therefore no national system of private international law. This does not and cannot mean that he enjoys *unlimited* freedom and has no guiding principles, not to speak in terms of a "system of private international law (which is a controversial term, for reasons of general theory of law, as shown by the discussions about the concept of *lex mercatoria*). It is submitted that the international arbitrator does have, and is bound by, a private international law, but that such private international law can only be a "transnational" one, constituted as it is by a number of general principles, either common to all the parties (including States) concerned by a given case, or universal.

153. As to the exact number and contents of such general principles of common private international law, doctrinal opinions do of course vary. It is however possible to cite those principles, already mentioned above in a different context, relating to the validity of the international contract, the law of arbitration or even international procedure (e.g., on the impossibility for a State or State party to rely on its own incapacity under domestic law or to rescind the arbitral clause unilaterally). Without repeating what has previously been said about those principles, we should like to discuss briefly three general principles clearly belonging to private international law (whether "conflictual" or "material"): (a) the principle of autonomy of the will, (b) the principle of the "closest connection" and (c) the principle of the legitimate expectations of the parties.

a. *The autonomy of the will*

154. This principle is so generally recognized in all national systems of private

122. See the Report by L. MATRAY, p. 8.

international law that it may be considered as an international *custom*[123] or as a "general principle of law recognized by civilized nations" (within the meaning of Article 38(3) of the Statute of the International Court of Justice) or as a central element of the *lex mercatoria*. The acceptance of the principle (although perhaps not of its exact limits or modalities of application) is indeed so universal that, according to some writers, whenever the parties have chosen the applicable "law" or "rules", the question of the private international law of the arbitrator has implicitly been solved so that it would be superfluous to attempt to ascertain it.[124]

155. On the practical level, this point of view is quite understandable, but it does not really explain the problem as a whole and, for instance, does not explain on what basis an international arbitrator could solve a dispute on the limits or modalities of such principle. Logically speaking, this could only be on the basis of a transnational and common private international law. Reference may be made here, as an example, to an ICC award of 1975,[125] where the arbitrator did analyze in detail the question of the applicable law notwithstanding the existence of a choice by the parties themselves.

156. Such indications may suffice for the purpose of the present Report; their interest is in general more theoretical than practical, inasmuch as the choice (by the parties or by the arbitrator) of the applicable law is not a reason for refusing to recognize the award, within the meaning of Article V of the New York Convention of 1958, so that the international arbitrator has a wide freedom of action, as aptly shown by Mr. Yves Derains in his Report (in particular, nos. 4–9).

157. In an ICC award of 1971, in the famous *Dalmia Cement* case, the defendant had insisted on the idea that "the power to choose the applicable law is necessarily based on law and therefore can have no effect until and unless it is connected with a given system of law".[126] While this well-known logical argument did contain a grain of truth, the present writer came, as single arbitrator, to the conclusion that it was irrelevant since the fundamental principle of autonomy of the will was universally accepted; and he ventured the following opinion, which he still holds, that:

"Few principles are more universally admitted in private international law than the one

123. In this sense E. HAMBRO, "The Relations Between International Law and Conflict Law", RCADI 105 (1962 I), 1–68, *55–63*, and the award *Topco/Calasiatic* v. *Libyan Government*, Clunet 1977, 350 ss., *353*, No. 25.

124. See, for example, Ph. FOUCHARD, *L'arbitrage commercial international*, Paris, 1965, 360; J. LEW, *Applicable Law in International Commercial Arbitration*, Dobbs Ferry (NY)/Alphen a/d Rijn, 1978, 67 N 82, 83–84 N 202.

125. ICC Award No. 1434 of 1975, Clunet 1976, 978, note Y. DERAINS.

126. ICC Award No. 1512 of 1971, Clunet 1974, 904, Note Y. DERAINS/R. THOMPSON, in the case *Dalmia Cement* v. *National Bank of Pakistan*, [1974] 3 All E.R. 189; [1974] 2 Lloyd's Rep. 98, a case which may be mentioned by name since it has become public following the defendant's (unsuccessful) attempts to have the award annulled by the English courts.

implied by the usual expression of "proper law of the contract", according to which the law governing the contract is that which has been chosen by the parties, either expressly, or (with some differences or shades of opinion in the various national systems) implicitly. . . . The parties having made an express choice in the present case, it is therefore unnecessary to examine precedents or doctrinal writings on the implied intention of the parties or the power of the arbitrator to interfere with the choice of law, or to examine which facts or elements of the case have to be taken into consideration in order to decide with which legal system the contract is most closely connected. The arbitrator has no power to substitute his own choice to that of the parties, as soon as there does exist an express, clear and unambiguous choice and no valid reason has been alleged which could lead to a refusal to give effect to the choice of the parties."

158. Similarly, the *Topco-Calasiatic* award, already cited, states that:

> "All legal systems . . . apply the principle of autonomy of the will to international contracts. As to the merits, all legal systems recognize this principle, which appears therefore as universally accepted, even if it is not always interpreted or applied exactly in the same sense or with the same effect . . .".[127]

159. It should also be recalled that the principle of autonomy of the will is recognized in a much more liberal way in the (transnational) private international law of arbitration – and in particular in the case of arbitration with a State or public entity – than in national systems of conflict of laws. As a result one may mention the recognition for example of the power of the parties to choose several laws to govern their contract, to insert so-called stabilization clauses, to set aside or discard any national law and to choose "rules" (as is shown by international instruments such as Article 42 of the Washington Convention of 1965 of the World Bank or Article 28, (i), of UNCITRAL Model Law, not forgetting provisions like Article 1496, of 1981, of the new French Code of Civil Procedure (as cited in Yves Derain's Report, no. 7).[128]

160. It seems to be more and more accepted, in the private international law of arbitration, that the principle of autonomy of the will permits the parties to "denationalize" their contract, through clauses referring to good faith, equity, the general principles of law, the *lex mercatoria*, or indeed by clauses of a mere "negative" choice which reject, in part or in total, any particular State law.[129]

161. To sum up, it is a fundamental principle of transnational private international law that the choice by the parties of the "law", principles or rules

---

127. See *supra*, Note 123.
128. On this question, see, for example, P. LALIVE, "L'État en tant que partie à des contrats de concession ou d'investissements conclus avec des sociétés privées étrangères", *in New Directions in International Trade Law*, Dobbs Ferry, New York, I, 317, 373, *330* No. 23; and the "Athens Resolution of the Institute of of International Law", 1979, following a report by G. VAN HECKE, Ann. Inst. Dr. Int. Vol. 58 II 192ff.
129. As an example of "partial" choice, half negative and half positive, one may perhaps quote the arbitral clause in the arbitration agreement between the Government of Kuwait and Aminoil; see also the arbitration clauses in the Libyan oil arbitrations referring to principles common to Libyan law and international law, etc.

governing the contract must be respected, as a general rule, by the arbitrators in international trade who have no power to substitute another choice to that of the parties.

162. In a case decided by the Arbitration Commission of the Chamber of Commerce of Romania, however, the arbitrators did not take into account the choice by the parties of the applicable law, as the law of Greece was in their opinion *more appropriate* to govern a contract of sale of books than the chosen Romanian law.[130]

163. Their approach may well appear much closer to that of a State *judge* than of that of an international arbitrator, at least in the "Western" sense of the term – a fact which may perhaps be explained by the particular nature of the permanent Arbitration Commissions in Socialist countries and by the great importance, in that particular context, of the system of conflict rules of the seat of arbitration. On the other hand, one may note that this award has the "virtue", if it is one, to prefer a "foreign" law to the domestic law of the "seat" of arbitration.

164. It is difficult to accept, in the private international law of commercial arbitration, in principle, such freedom of the arbitrators to reject the law or rules chosen by the parties and to substitute the arbitrators' own judgment on what is "most appropriate" to the judgment of the parties themselves. But what can be, and indeed should be admitted, it is submitted, is not only the *freedom* of the international arbitrator but also the *duty* to disregard the choice of the parties, if this is required by a really international or transnational public policy. This is both a logical, advisable and inevitable transposition, to the domain of international arbitration, of the relationship which, in domestic private international law, exists between the normally applicable law and international public policy (of the State). There is no need to repeat here what was said above about the cases (e.g., of bribery, drug traffic, etc.) where the international arbitrator can and indeed must disregard the rules of the applicable law.

b. *The criterion of the closest connection*

165. In the absence of a choice by the parties, all the existing conflict rules (in State systems of private international law) relating to contracts appear to be based on the idea of the "closest connection" (and there is no need to discuss here whether such connection must be territorial or can be merely a rational one). This fact may lead one to consider that this is also a general principle of private international law, a principle which is likewise somewhat vague and undetermined. However, account should be taken of the great liberty of the arbitrator (as underlined by Mr. Derains) with regard to the selection of the

130. See J. LEW, *op. cit.*, 134.

applicable "law", and one should also keep in mind that there is no clear-cut distinction nor any total opposition between the so-called "subjective connection" and the "objective connection" in matters of contracts. This being the case is it possible to assert that the international arbitrator is bound, by a general principle of transnational private international law, to determine in each case with which State law the contract has the "closest connection"? A negative answer appears to be called for, inasmuch as modern practice clearly allows the arbitrator, again failing a choice by the parties, to disregard any State law – an approach which appears to amount to saying that the contract has in fact its "closest connection" with the international community of merchants (hence a resort to the *lex mercatoria*, to the usages of international trade, general principles, and the like).

166. It is, however, doubtful that the freedom of the arbitrator should be here considered as totally unlimited or should be placed so to speak on the same level as the autonomy of the will *of the parties*. As this problem can hardly be explored fully within the limits of the present Report, it may suffice to submit the provisional conclusion that (again in the absence of a choice by the parties) the international arbitrator should take inspiration from the idea of "closest connection" (but that this connection need not always and necessarily be "territorial", i.e., limited to the connection with a given State law).

c. *The legitimate expectations of the parties*

167. It is submitted that, in the private international law of arbitration, there exists a general principle which obliges the arbitrator to respect the legitimate expectations of the parties as they emerge from the contract, in accordance with the mission conferred upon him. The function of the arbitrator, as defined by the parties in the exercise of their autonomy, is to give a solution to the dispute on the basis of the rules chosen or objectively applicable and, it may be added, a solution safeguarding the higher interests of international trade in accordance with the common "expectations" of the parties. It is perhaps not decisive whether this is an independent "general principle" or one of the composing elements of the mission of the arbitrator. But it must be recognized that the use of one or the other of these various expressions or formulas is not entirely neutral; by stressing one particular aspect rather than another of the arbitral mission, one may be led, consciously or not, to give priority, in a given case, either to individualism and the particular interest of the parties or, to the contrary, to a transnational public policy capable of countering the common will of the parties.

168. One fundamental value in this field is undoubtedly foreseeability, which constitutes one of the traditional justifications of the autonomy of the will in private international law. There is no doubt that the international arbitrator, when performing his function, must have what the Supreme Court of the United States, in the famous *Mitsubishi* v. *Soler* case, called a "sensitivity to the need of the international commercial system for predictability in the resolution of disputes".

And this calls, for example, for the use of such rules or principles of interpretation of contracts which are generally recognized.[131]

169. The parties trust that their common will and expectations will be respected by the arbitrator, but this can be assumed to mean only the "*legitimate* expectations" of the parties. And this is obviously where the concept of transnational public policy comes in. The international arbitrator is only bound to take into account those expectations of the parties which are "legitimate" and, by reason of this characterization, he may have to apply or take into consideration, in a given case, not only the (classical) "international public policy" of one of the State directly concerned, but also and first of all transnational public policy (two concepts which, let it be repeated, frequently overlap but which may also happen to play in opposite directions, in which case transnational public policy should prevail).

6. *Other General Principles*

170. A few other general principles should finally be briefly recalled – most of which have already been mentioned in different contexts – and a great deal of which stem more or less directly from public international law, be it general or conventional public international law or what is sometimes called "economic international law".

171. Both judicial and arbitral practice revealed, in fairly numerous cases, interventions of a transnational public policy based upon an observation of the present state of development of the law of nations. One need not examine again such very general principles as that of good faith, of the prohibition of abuse of right (estoppel, *venire contra factum proprium*) or other aspects of a universal notion of "good morals" or elementary contractual morality. But it is interesting to note that, in several cases, when the arbitrator applies (or one might rather say "creates and applies") transnational public policy, he does so with reference to certain multilateral treaties or other international texts (such as recommendations, resolutions of international organizations, codes of conduct, etc.).

172. At least a passing mention must be made of a particular form of international public policy which might be called "multinational" or "common" or *"community" public policy* (well-known examples are Articles 2 and 85–86 of the Treaty of Rome establishing the EEC or, according to certain writers, the imperative provisions flowing from the General Conditions of Sale and Delivery

---

131. ICC Award No. 1434 of 1975, Clunet 1976, 978. ICC Award No. 3380 of 1980, Clunet 1981, 927. Interim Award No. 2321 of 1974, Clunet 1975, 938. See also the famous award of President Cassin (in the "cargaisons déroutées" case): an example of universally-recognized rules of interpretation is that of effectiveness *ut res magis valeat quam pereat*.

of the CMEA countries.[132] Whether this common or community public policy is incorporated within the internal public policy of the member States is no particular phenomenon and does not prevent it being a matter of a transnational (non-universal) or "multinational" public policy.

173. The question, of course, arises – which cannot be discussed in the present Report – whether or to what extent such a common or regional public policy must be taken into account, for instance, in an international arbitration taking place in a third country, between parties one of which or both are foreign to the community of States concerned. One general remark may however be put forward here: although the law of international arbitration is characterized by liberalism and the autonomy of the parties, it can hardly be accepted as a legitimate means to evade or nullify either the strictly mandatory rules or rules of international public policy of a State directly concerned or the principles of transnational public policy.[133]

174. Let us return to transnational public policy strictly speaking, whose various applications, in judicial practice and in arbitration, have already been mentioned above. What is particularly worthy of note here is the influence of international treaties or other international instruments on the observation, determination and application of such transnational public policy.

175. A case in point is that of bribery, where the influence should not be underestimated of the studies, recommendations and resolutions of the United Nations,[134] the International Chamber of Commerce[135] or the European Communities.[136] The same observation may be made with respect to drug traffic and the important Resolutions of the United Nations on the subject[137] or with respect to terrorism, where recommendations of the Council of Europe, of the United Nations, or an Agreement of the European Communities regarding the application of the European Convention on the Suppression of Terrorism should be mentioned.[138]

176. The same is true with regard to the international protection of human rights, and the influence of the Universal Declaration on Human Rights, and the work of the UN Commission on Human Rights or of the Organization of American States.[139] Reference may also be made to the examples cited above, at the beginning of this Report, on the protection of the cultural heritage of States and the UNESCO Conventions, a subject where the most "advanced" position appears to have been that of the German courts.

132. In this sense, J. LEW, *op. cit.*, Nos. 406 and 412.
133. On the community law of competition, see BÖCKSTIEGEL's Report, p. 194.
134. See *supra*, Note 96.
135. See *supra*, Note 97.
136. See *supra*, Note 98.
137. See *supra*, Note 99.
138. See *supra*, Note 100.
139. See *supra*, Notes 100 and 66.

177. A distinction should of course be drawn in this context between general principles recognized or implicitly accepted by international treaties in force, on the one hand, and those principles recognized in treaties which are not in force or not yet in force. One should also distinguish, of course, the influence of treaties from that of other instruments of international origin, and among the latter a distinction should be made between the texts adopted by international governmental organizations (such as UN Organizations, the OECD, etc.) and, on the other hand, texts adopted by NGOs like the International Chamber of Commerce.

178. On several occasions and in particular in disputes arising from measures of *nationalization* or unilateral abrogation of international contracts, international arbitrators have had to examine the exact role and scope of certain "resolutions" or "recommendations" voted or adopted by consensus by some international organizations (for instance when the arbitrators had to apply "generally recognized principles" or "principles common to international law and to the law of the nationalizing State").[140] When confronted, for instance, with an argument based on the so-called "new international economic order", the arbitrators had to ascertain the exact degree of general approbation or consensus existing in the international community. Well-known examples are the arbitral awards given in the Libyan nationalization cases, in particular in the *Topco-Calasiatic* case, and, more recently, by the award of 24 March 1982 in the *Aminoil-Kuwait* case.[141]

179. Arbitral awards show, as could be expected, a great variety of formulations, from which many controversies, often more political than scientific, arise. Some common or permanent features, nevertheless, seem to characterize this arbitral practice: the arbitrators of international trade always attempt first to ascertain the rules governing the dispute, by an interpretation of the mission conferred upon them in the arbitration clause, arbitration agreement or "choice of law clause" and such contractual clauses can hardly be considered, in general, as masterpieces in clarity or precision, for obvious reasons. From a number of international texts and from the practice of States, the arbitrators may thus have to try to deduce the existence of generally (or universally) recognized principles – a difficult task indeed but not an impossible one, as shown by many arbitral awards. Once the existence of such principles has been observed, the problem remains whether they have such an imperative or mandatory character as to have to be applied, either because of a direct choice by the parties, or because they may be characterized as *ius cogens* or transnational public policy. Is this solution only or primarily a matter of personal and subjective choice of the arbitrators, or a "question of sensitiveness" if one may use the expression of Mr. Derains about

140. According to an opinion widely accepted in arbitral practice, only Resolution 1803 (XVII) expresses the present state of positive international law on the subject. Article 4 of this Resolution provides for the possibility of nationalization for reasons of public utility, security or national interest and foresees adequate compensation in accordance with the positive law of the State and in conformity with international law.

141. *Texaco/Calasiatic*, Clunet 1977, 350, *374 No. 79* and *379 Nos. 87–88*; *Liamco* ILM XX (1981), 1–87, *120—121*; *Aminoil*, Clunet 1982, 869, *900 No. 143.*

the negative international public policy? Will the arbitrator's decision be merely a subjective or even arbitrary one? Is the arbitrator's function here one of "creation of law", which goes beyond admissible limits, unless he is authorized to act *ex aequo et bono*, as *amiable compositeur*? Such are some of the questions or objections which should at least tentatively be answered, by way of conclusion.

VI. CONCLUSION

180. As was emphasized at the outset but this need perhaps be repeated, the topic of the present Report, by its object and its nature, was one of particular difficulty.

181. By its object, first, since the very concept and the existence of a transnational public policy, or truly international public policy, have been questioned or denied. The question may thus be asked whether, in contradistinction to the three other Reports on public policy, by Böckstiegel, Derains and Schwebel-Lahne, the present Report has tried to study a ghost or a myth?

182. By its *nature* then, and its character which is both "multidisciplinary" and protean, the theme of the present Report offers considerable resistance to scientific analysis. One reason, but not the main one, is that (like the concepts of domestic public policy or, in traditional private international law, that of "international" public policy) it touches a very great variety of subjects (contracts, procedure, competition law, administrative law, protection of human rights, exchange control, etc.). This is indeed a "transfrontier" topic in various senses of the term, since it overlaps both private international law and involves, in particular, the difficult and changing question of the relationship between the law of nations and municipal law in the sphere of international economic relations.

183. As an example, the present study has shown the influence – and one might say the partial osmosis – of the (really international) public policy of the *law of nations* upon, or in, the concept of transnational public policy. We are here in the field of international trade arbitration, a field in rapid quantitative but also qualitative expansion which concerns, it must be repeated, the settlement of disputes in the *international community of businessmen* (a community which seems to involve more and more States and public entities). It follows that any question on the role of the arbitrator and its specific functions (in contradistinction to those of a State court) is closely related to a series of fundamental questions and theoretical controversies, on international organization, on the definition of law, on the role of rules, principles, standards, etc., on the role of States, on the "creative" power of the judge and of the arbitrator, to quote only a few! One need only think here of the doctrinal debates on the *lex mercatoria*, on the notion of "transnational law", equity and the like!

184. It stands to reason that the present Report did not and could not attempt to reopen or to conclude such fundamental controversies, which are both theoretical and practical, legal and political. But the danger was great, and perhaps impossible to avoid entirely, to seem to decide or take sides in such doctrinal controversies, if only because of the use of a particular terminology.

185. Be that as it may, one should recall that, in private international law, the traditional concept of a State's "international public policy" was largely based on a *feeling* of law and justice in a given community. The same is probably inevitable with regard to transnational public policy and to the international community (of businessmen, or States, or both), so that it may be contended, without verbal precautions, that, in the final analysis, a great deal if not everything is a question of personal feeling or sensitiveness, or of *Weltanschauung*!

186. The results of the present study can, nevertheless, be summed up, at least for the purpose of discussion, in the following propositions:

1. There exists a notion of transnational, or really international, public policy. This has sometimes been denied or questioned, at least until recent times. One should recall here the evolution of French court practice. As for the Swiss Federal Tribunal, it expressed in a dictum of 1976[142] its lack of understanding and scepticism, when it stated that international public policy was "rather a formula propounded by some writers who do not seem to ascribe to it a precise or an unequivocal meaning". Somewhat similarly, President Jean Robert[143] observed

---

142. *Société des grands travaux de Marseille* v. *People's Republic of Bangladesh*, ATF 102 Ia 574, *583*:

> "The appellant invokes also, apart from Swiss public policy, an 'international public policy' which would prevent the application of the Bangladesh decree in the present instance. This concept seems never to have been used by the Federal Tribunal. . . . It seems to be a formula put forward by some writers who do not ascribe to it a very precise or unambiguous meaning (see for instance SCHNITZER, *Handbuch des internationalen Privatrechts, 4 ed.*, I. 229 ff.; SCHÖNENBERGER/JÄGGI, *op. cit.* p. 115; LALIVE, ASDI 1971, p. 137; GENTINETTA *Die lex fori internationaler Handelsschiedsgerichte*, 1973, 264 and 266).
>
> It is difficult to see in what way this so-called 'international public policy' would limit the application of foreign law more or in another manner than the classical 'reserve' of Swiss public policy. Since the appellant does not give indications to that effect, it is unnecessary to examine the question further" (translation).

For a criticism of this very controversial decision, see P. LALIVE, "Arbitrage international et ordre public suisse", in Revue de droit suisse 97 (1981 I), 529–551.

143. J. ROBERT (*L'arbitrage*, 358) expresses a negative opinion as follows:

> "Decisions, it must be stated, have not recognized to date the concept of a truly international public policy . . .".

But the writer adds that certain rules (such as those contained in the European Declaration on Human Rights, of 4 November 1950, could constitute such a concept and he concludes that

> "the possibility cannot be excluded, therefore, that, in a comparatively near future, a really international public policy would appear on such a basis, with the help of court decisions".

French court decisions appear as a matter of fact to have recognized such concept of a truly

a few years ago, but with appropriate caution, that "judicial decisions do not seem to have recognized to date the concept of a truly international public policy". But he conceded that, having regard, for example, to the principles of the European Declaration on Human Rights on 4 November 1950.

> "One cannot exclude the possibility that, in a comparatively near future, a really international public policy would appear on that basis, with the help of court decisions."

2. *Any observation of modern practice*, whether of State judges (Third Part) or of international arbitrators (Fourth Part) shows that it is impossible to deny the existence of the concept of transnational public policy, nor can the variety of its possible applications, nor its interest be questioned (an interest which, as will presently be shown, should not however be over-estimated). This being the case, it is submitted that there is no important reason to distinguish, as has sometimes been suggested, between a really international public policy by its contents (while national by its source), on the one hand, and a public policy which is really international both by its contents and by its source", on the other hand.[144]

3. *There is no valid theoretical reason to challenge the acceptance of a concept of transnational or really international public policy*, a concept which, in practice, whether in the law of nations or in the law of international trade, has been recognized as real for quite a long time.

a. It is sometimes objected that the concept is *vague* and undetermined, but the same objection holds true, or is equally erroneous, for the traditional concept of the private international law of States. The wise remarks of the late Henri Rolin[145] should be kept in mind:

> "Just as public policy, good morals escape any attempt at a precise definition or an exhaustive enumeration. The concept is hardly mentioned in most legislations . . . and is in general included in the concept of "public policy". In fact, however, a concern for respect of good morals plays an important role in the elaboration of positive law, not only as a source of inspiration for the legislator, but also as the starting point of an exceptionally abundant and solid case law".

b. As a "substitute for a true international commercial jurisdiction", according to Ion Nestor's formula,[146] the international arbitrator, when called upon to solve a dispute on the basis of law, uses *a variety of methods* (conflict rules or substantive

---

international public policy in the last decision in the Ottoman Bank case (see *supra* Note 47); but it would not seem necessary that judicial practice recognizes the concept as such or in so many words; what is decisive is that court decisions do recognize the existence of common principles of public policy, that they apply them and sanction their violation and on such basis, it is up to doctrinal writings to build up concepts and categories.

144. In this sense A. CHAPELLE, *op. cit.*, 512–527, *513*. The distinction appears to have mainly a scientific interest; what is more important is the proof that there does exist a general principle or a rule having a particularly mandatory character and based on a sufficiently widespread consensus in the international community of businessmen and States.

145. See H. ROLIN, *Vers un ordre public réellement international*, *442*, No. 2; see also on this point J. ROBERT, *op. cit.*, No. 423, *357*.

146. Report of 1 March 1972 to the 5th Session of UNCITRAL Document A/CN9/64.

private international law) and can resort to *a plurality of sources*. To the extent, in particular, to which he relies on general principles of law and the usages of international trade, it can hardly be denied that *he does contribute to the creation of the positive law of international trade*. And the notion of public policy is a necessary component, as a corrective or equitable superior element, of the whole body of rules applied by the international arbitrator and which make up the (composite) "legal system" which he is called upon both to apply and to produce.[147] It has been contended by some writers, mostly specialists of public international law, that the "usages of international trade", the general principles, "transnational law" or the *lex mercatoria*, do not constitute *per se* a "legal *system*".[148] This objection is hardly convincing: on the one hand, neither the parties, nor the arbitrators, nor State judges care very much in practice whether or not the rules of principles applied in arbitration do constitute "a system" or not. On the other hand, and more decisively, it is irrelevant – as has been aptly pointed out by Alf Ross and other writers, particularly in Scandinavia – whether the *lex mercatoria* does constitute or not a "system" or a *complete* whole, inasmuch as the domestic legal order itself cannot be considered as "complete" either. Some theoreticians clearly over-emphasize the difficulties there may be to determine or to apply such "general principles".[149]

4. In international arbitration, *the concept of transnational public policy would appear to have a dual function, both negative and positive* (in a somewhat analogous manner as, in national private international law, the concept of "international public policy"):
a. It has a *negative function, i.e.*, of exclusion, partly to be compared to that of the "exception" of public policy in traditional private international law,[150] but it is different insofar as it may lead, not only to exclude, in a given case, the laws or rules which are normally applicable by virtue of a choice of law or of a "objective" connection, but *also* to reject any intervention of the international public policy of a State. Thus, transnational public policy may give priority to the traditional international public policy of one State rather than to that of another State: let us suppose that an international arbitrator would have been asked to settle the dispute in *Regazzoni* v. *Sethia*: there is no doubt that he would have given priority to a transnational public policy hostile to any measures inspired by apartheid. The same is of course true of the international *judge*, as already noted in 1932 by Niboyet:[151]

"He (the international judge) shall not apply the foreign law – and one may add: neither

147. See P. LALIVE, "Sur la contribution de l'arbitrage au développement d'un droit du commerce international", in *Les relations internationales dans un monde en mutation*, Institut universitaire de hautes études internationales, Genève, 1977, 387–407. On the controversies relating to the "lex mercatoria", see the study by O. LANDO, mentioned above, Note 84, and the classical study by B. GOLDMAN, in *Archives de Philosophie du droit*, 1954, 177ff.
148. Sic J. VERHOEVEN, in "Le contrat économique international", *Journées Jean Dabin*, 1977, *28.*
149. In this sense O. LANDO, cited in Note 84, p. 748 and Note 8.
150. See *supra*, Nos. 11ff.
151. J. P. NIBOYET, "Le rôle de la justice internationale en droit international privé, cited by H. ROLIN, *op. cit. supra*, Note 145.

shall he apply the notion of national public policy invoked – if it violates *international public policy* in the strict sense of the term, that is to say that of civilized nations".

Two observations may be added on the question of the "negative" transnational public policy. On the one hand, it is unlikely to play a role whenever the rules chosen by the parties, or applicable to the merits on an objective basis, happen to be general principles or usages of the international trade. On the other hand, the negative function of public policy appears to be secondary, as judiciously remarked by Julian Lew[152] in relation to its "positive" function, in which it is often likely to be absorbed: the main function of transnational public policy is to directly and positively influence the decision of the arbitrators, whenever fundamental and universal notions of contractual morality or the fundamental interests of international trade are involved.

5. As to the *conditions for intervention of transnational public policy*, they appear analogous, although not identical, to those of the traditional "international public policy" of a State. One of these conditions, well-known in comparative private international law, was that, as shown above, the factual situation should have *a sufficient connection* with the State of the forum which, in other words, must be sufficiently "concerned". There is no ground for such a condition,[153] in principle, in international arbitration – as least in the normal cases, where the arbitration takes place in a *neutral* country, which has been chosen precisely because of its *absence* of connection with the matter in dispute. In other words, the condition of a sufficient "connection" is always fulfilled, so to speak by definition, in international arbitration, as soon as the interests of international trade are involved, and it is hardly necessary to recall here the risks of confusion and error which arise out of a strictly territorial conception of the so-called "seat" of the arbitration.

The problem arises mainly or only, it would seem, when a "*regional*" transnational public policy (such as EEC common public policy) is involved, in particular, if the arbitrator was chosen *outside* such community and when the parties do *not* belong to it.

6. *Transnational public policy governs the actions of both the parties and the arbitrator.* The former cannot attempt, for instance, to obtain through arbitration the recognition or enforcement, whether direct or indirect, of an international contract which would be against *bonos mores* by its object (traffic of drugs, assistance to subversion or terrorism, etc.) or by the circumstances of its execution (bribery). As to the arbitrator, he would be committing himself a violation of transnational public policy – which he must protect and guarantee, if he happened to condone its violations by the parties or types of behaviour which are against good faith (this would be the case, for example, if he approved or recognized, against principles mentioned above, the allegation by the State of its own incapacity to arbitrate or a

152. *Op. cit.*, 539, No. 413.
153. "Binnenbeziehung" or "Inlandsberührung".

unilateral rescission of the arbitration clause). Similar principles are valid, as previously stated, in the domain of arbitral procedure.

As an example, a recent ICC award may be mentioned when the arbitrator, in violation of his duty to impose the respect for transnational public policy, merely bowed before political expediency and accepted an event as "force majeure" on the basis of a *secret* act of government, the existence of which had never been proved but was only alleged *orally* and indirectly, many years after the breach of contract, at the very end of the arbitral procedure!

The question may be asked whether, when the conditions are fulfilled, the arbitrator should resort to the concept of transnational public policy only upon the request of one party or *ex officio*. It is difficult to give a general answer to this question, especially when one bears in mind the *relative and dynamic* character of the concept and the variety of its possible applications; but *ex officio* application appears preferable whenever fundamental ethical and social values are concerned and when it appears that a decision ignoring transnational public policy could, to use the terms of the Supreme Court of the United States in *Scherk*, "damage the fabric of international commerce and trade" or, to resort to another expression, be incompatible with universal principles of justice.

7. As clearly appears from an examination of arbitral or judicial practice, the respective domains of "classical" international public policy of States and of transnational public policy *largely coincide*, each of them "feeding" so to speak the other or others (and there is little need to determine here according to which exact process or in what direction this kind of osmosis takes place, since the modalities of such process are inevitably influenced, in each State, by national conceptions on the relationship between the international legal order and the national, domestic legal order). However this may be, there can be no total identity or assimilation between the two kinds of "public policies", inasmuch as the State international public policy inevitably retains a particular or even selfish character, at least in part. Similarly, the fundamental values and interests of a given State can hardly coincide fully with the values and fundamental interests of the international community, just as the national concept of "international public policy" cannot be identified with that of transnational public policy.

8. Since all national laws are "foreign" in a way, for the *international arbitrator*, and, therefore, all State "public policies" are foreign, although not necessarily to the same extent, *it may happen*, as shown above, *that the international arbitrator has to take into account*, like a State judge, *a State international public policy* (whether positive or negative). Positive, which may be the case, for example, of the public policy of the "proper law" or of the law of the place of performance, or also of the foreign "mandatory rules" according to the theory of "special connection" (or *Sonderanknüpfung*) – or "negative", in order to exclude the possibility of an award which would not be recognized or enforced in a given State. But, contrary to a State judge for whom resort to transnational public policy appears to remain exceptional, the international arbitrator should first take into account the public policy of the international community of merchants (including, let it be repeated once more, many States or public entities). Like any law, the concept of public policy postulates the existence of a certain community and of certain common fundamental values, and the position of the international arbitrator confronted with the concept of transnational public policy can hardly be understood if its specific functions and position, outlined above, are not kept in mind.[154]

9. True it is, of course, that *the main function of the arbitrator is to perform the task conferred upon him by the parties* (as the whole law of international arbitration is based upon autonomy of the will and liberalism, as stated above). From this point of view, the fear may be felt by some that a recourse to such concept, evolutive, dynamic and therefore imprecise as it necessarily is, may eventually lead to abuse. Such a fear is understandable, but two arguments at least should be advanced by way of answer:

a. It may well be that the intervention of transnational public policy does amount (like in traditional private international law before a court) to a restriction to the autonomy of the will (although it is hard to see how it could be an *additional* restriction, since most national legal orders and public policies already incorporate, as shown above, precisely those common values, ethical or social, which are expressed by transnational public policy, e.g., in the case of corruption). But transnational public policy may also be, quite to the contrary, a *support* for the autonomy of the will and a useful means of the liberalism characteristic of international trade and generally recognized by States today, whatever their own economic and political domestic system. The concept may well lead the arbitrator to disregard the particular and selfish interest of a given State in order to respect the superior values of the international community (as would seem to be illustrated by the examples of the incapacity of the State to arbitrate or its impossibility unilaterally to rescind its own arbitration undertaking).

b. On the other hand, autonomy of the will or "legal liberalism" can only exist within the general limits of the law of the international community, that is to say provided the superior requirements of ethics and of a minimum of solidarity are observed in the said community.

10. Such statements, general though they are, should presumably help to pacify the understandable, although exaggerated *fears of some opponents of a "law of international trade" or of "lex mercatoria"* who, a few years ago, claimed to be worried by what they described as "the abdication" of States before the so-called "multinational and private powers"![155]

---

154. See K.-H. BÖCKSTIEGEL's Report in this volume, p. 179 and 180.

155. A good example of this preoccupation, particularly widespread in leftist legal circles, deserves to be cited here:

."Today political authorites in traditional democracies discover with astonishment that they no longer dominate their own territory: delocalized private economic powers have taken over access to natural products and sources of energy, as well as of the techniques necessary to transport and commercialize them . . . The drama (sic!) of contemporary international Society is that it failed to build up an international power capable of resisting such private economic powers which arose under the protection of national laws all the more favourable to them since

Such line of argument is misconceived and forgets the essential features of the modern world as well as the reasons of the extraordinary expansion of commercial international arbitration: far from "abdicating" anything, States have chosen, in their own interests as they saw them, to participate in international trade, either directly, or through a "public" enterprise or organism, and to resort to contractual methods (private, public or "mixed") and they have adopted, in relation to the business practices of the international community of merchants, an attitude of both *tolerance and supervision* which was excellently analyzed by Professors T. Popescu and R. David, in their general Reports to the Rome Conference of the International Institute for the Unification of Private Law (UNIDROIT) in September 1976.[156] Since they were conscious of the totally inadequate adaptation of domestic laws to the needs of international commerce and of the difficulty to come to a general agreement on a uniform international law of trade, States preferred to leave to the international community of merchants a *vast power of self-regulation*. Such tolerance is of course limited through a supervision *a posteriori* of arbitration as well as through a number of important interventions of each State in economic life, while simultaneously there is a not inconsiderable effort towards the gradual development, through conventions or otherwise, of the law of international trade.

Transnational public policy constitutes in a way a limitation to this tolerance, but also a guarantee that this tolerance will be allowed to remain. Such limitation is clearly justified since it allows for the incorporation in the law of international arbitration, as soon as there is a sufficient consensus, of fundamental values and of interests which are superior to those "private economic powers" which appear so threatening to some.

Thanks to its evolutive and dynamic character, so often emphasized above, the concept of transnational public policy allows today, and will allow in the future, the incorporation in arbitration of the *new needs and ideas* of the international community, in particular of the interests of developing States as expressed, for instance, by or implied in the concept of "new international economic order". Also from this point of view, therefore, the concept of transnational public policy appears to be an indispensable and important *dynamic* factor in the development, through arbitration, of a law of international trade.

11. However, *it would be erroneous to over-estimate its importance today*, the frequency of its applications or its possibilities of intervention. We have seen that, in classical private international law (of individual States), the judge had to show great care and caution before deciding to resort to the "exception" of public policy or to accept the "positive" role of the concept. *Mutatis mutandis*, a similar caution

these powers helped the States' will of domination and exploitation which Lenin called imperialism, the manifestations of which are either aggressive (as in the case of colonial powers in the nineteenth century or in the case of the United States in the twentieth century) or discreet (in the case of Switzerland as described by the recent work of J. Ziegler)" (translation from the book of FRANÇOIS RIGAUX, *Droit public et droit privé dans les relations internationales*, 1977, p. 443, 444).

156. R. DAVID, "Le droit du commerce international: une nouvelle tâche pour les législateurs nationaux ou une nouvelle *lex mercatoria? in New Directions . . .*, cited above in Note 128, p. 5–20; T. R. POPESCU, same title, *ibidem*, p. 21–49.

appears to be called for with regard to transnational public policy. Keeping in mind the comparative scarcity of known arbitral awards on the subject, there is little reason to fear that international arbitrators will abuse the power implied by their function – a function which, by the nature of things and by the common will or the legitimate expectations of the parties, does include the application or taking into consideration of transnational public policy.

VII. SELECTED BIBLIOGRAPHY

BADIALI, G., *Ordine pubblico e diritto straniero*, Milan, 1963, 123–152.

BARILE, G., *I principi fondamentali della comunità statale e il coordinamento fra i sistemi* (*L'ordine pubblico internazionale*), Padua, 1969, 77–81.

BENVENUTI, P., *Comunità statale, comunità internazionale e ordine pubblico internazionale*, Milan, 1977.

BLECKMANN, A., "Sittenwidrigkeit wegen Verstosses gegen den ordre public international", ZaöRV 34 (1974), 112–132.

CHAPELLE, A., *Les fonctions de l'ordre public en droit international privé*, thèse de doctorat, dactyl., Université de Paris II, 1979, 653.

DOLINGER, J., "World Public Policy: Real International Public Policy in the Conflict of Laws", Texas International Law J. 17 (1982), 167–193.

DOMKE, M., "Towards an 'International' Public Policy in Commercial Arbitration", in *Festschrift für A. Bülow*, Cologne/Berlin/Bonn/Munich, 1981, 49–58.

GOLDMAN, B., "La protection internationale des droits de l'homme et l'ordre public international dans le fonctionnement de la règle de conflit de lois", in *René Cassin Amicorum Discipulorumque Liber*, Paris, 1969, I, 449–466.

GOLDMAN, B., "Les conflits de lois dans l'arbitrage international de droit privé", RCADI 109 (1963 II), 350–484, *430–443.*

GOLDMAN, B., Note sous Cour d'appel de Paris, (Ière Ch. suppl.), 12 VII 1984, *R.A.E. c/Southern Pacific Properties Ltd. et Southern Pacific Properties* (*Middle East*), J. 1985, 130, *142–158.*

EL KOSHERI, A. S./LEBOULANGER, Ph., "L'arbitrage face à la corruption et aux trafics d'influence", Rev. arb. 1984, 3–18.

LALIVE, P., "Arbitrage international et ordre public suisse," RDS 97 (1981 I), 529–551.

LEW, J. D. M., *Applicable Law in International Commercial Arbitration*, New York/Alphen a/d Rijn, 1978, 531–580.

LOUIS-LUCAS, P., Note sous Cour d'appel de Paris, (5è Ch.), 9 II 1966, *Favier c/ Soc. Anderssen*, R. 1966, 264, *266–272.*

MATRAY, L., "Arbitrage et ordre public transnational", in *The Art of Arbitration, Liber Amicorum P. Sanders*, Deventer, 1982, 241–251.

MAYER, P., "Le contrat illicite", Rev. arb. 1984, 205–223.

NIBOYET, J.-P., "Le rôle de la justice internationale en droit international privé: conflit de lois", RCADI 40 (1932 II), 157–233.

PALAIA, N., *L'ordine pubblico "internazionale"*, Padua, 1974, 14–23.

PENTZLIN, F., *Der universelle ordre public im Wirtschaftsrecht als ein Ordnungsprinzip des innerstaatlichen Rechts*, Munich, 1985.

RIGAUX, F., *Droit public et droit privé dans les relations internationales*, Paris, 1977.

ROBERT, J., (Avec la collaboration de B. MOREAU) *L'arbitrage – Droit interne. Droit international privé, Paris*, 1983, 5ème éd.

ROLIN, H., "Vers un ordre public réellement international", in *Hommage d'une génération de juristes au Président Basdevant*, Paris, 1960, 441–462.

SCHÜTZ, D., *Der internationale ordre public. Der Ausschluss völkerrechtswidrigen fremden Rechts im internationalen Privatrecht der Bundesrepublik Deutschland*, Frankfurt/Bern/New York, 1984.

SEIDL-HOHENVELDERN, I., "L'ordre public international et la fraude à la loi", in *Mélanges offerts à J. MAURY*, Paris, 1960, 2 vol., I, 473–483.

STÖCKER, H., "Internationaler ordre public zum Schutz der Menschenrechte", StAZ 34 (1981), 16–22.

WIETHÖLTER, R./JÄNICKE, G., *"Zur Frage des internationalen ordre public"*, *Berichte der deutschen Gesellschaft für Völkerrecht*, *Heft 7*, Karlsruhe, 1965, 77–185.

Commentaries
Working Group II
Public Policy in Arbitration

Public Policy under Egyptian Law

*Ahmed S. El-Kosheri**

1. In regard to arbitration, the Egyptian legal system adopts an attitude characterized by the co-existence of two conflicting considerations: on the one hand, formal recognition of arbitration as a legitimate means to settle disputes between all parties concerned; and on the other hand, the presence of certain outdated rules which permitted the emergence in practice of an increasing tendency towards the utilization of certain techniques conceived for the purpose of obstructing the arbitral process.

2. In fact, the basic legislative texts relevant to arbitration are essentially those contained in the 1968 Code of Civil and Commercial Procedures (Articles 501–513). The rules formulated in said Articles of the Code are exclusively adopted to govern internal (i.e., domestic) arbitration, and do not take into account any potential international dimensions. Reference to arbitration in the field of international relationships can only be found in two other Articles of the same Code of Civil and Commercial Procedures: Articles 299 and 301.

In Article 301, the Egyptian legislator confirmed the established rule according to which the provisions of the relevant international treaties already existing or to be concluded in the future between Egypt and other States should prevail (including the New York Convention ratified and duly promulgated since 1959).

3. Article 299, primarily, provides for a total assimilation between foreign judicial decisions and the arbitral awards rendered abroad with regard to the conditions required for their enforcement in Egypt. The significance of said assimilation resides essentially in the fact that it reveals a certain spirit which dominated the entire subject of international commercial arbitration from the standpoint of those who drafted the 1968 Code of Civil and Commercial Procedures. In reality, the rule in question reflected an adherence by the Egyptian legislator to those doctrinal theories which remained basically unfavorable to the recognition of international commercial arbitration as "autonomous" in nature.

4. In line with that general philosophy, the said Article 299 contained another rule according to which the arbitral award has to be rendered in respect to a subject matter which is arbitrable under Egyptian Law. In determining the scope of those subject matters which are not arbitrable under Egyptian Law, Article 501 of Civil and Commercial Code stipulates:

* Professor of Law, Ain Chams University; Lawyer; member of ICCA.

"Arbitration is prohibited in matters which could not be the subject of a compromise".

5. Reference has to be made in this respect to the rule of general applicability in the Civil Code which establishes in Article 551 that the parties cannot possibly compromise out of court with regard to matters of "personal status" or those considered of "public policy".

6. Leaving aside the domain which obviously falls outside the scope of commercial international arbitration (i.e., questions related to "personal status"), no legislative text exists which defines or enumerates the other relevant category; i.e., what are the matters to be considered excluded because they are of "public policy". Accordingly, the determination has to be undertaken by the domestic courts as guided by the doctrine. But, in practice, no reported court decisions had been rendered in the past; a situation which leaves the question open regarding all the classical examples of non-arbitrability encountered by the domestic courts, such as competition disputes, industrial property rights, etc.

7. In the absence of a case law upon which to rely fully, the non-arbitrability issue remains controversial under Egyptian Law. The doctrinal opinions are divided among two tendencies. A first tendency, which includes the internationally oriented commercialists as well as private international law scholars, favors a restrictive interpretation of the concept of "public policy" in a manner that would not justify excluding the arbitrability of a given dispute simply because the subject matter is regulated by certain mandatory public law rules or touches upon some aspects of general interest. The authors representing that first tendency – having the advantage of being open to the realities of the present world and aware of the relevant comparative law teachings – foresee no legal obstacle to arbitration of trademarks or other industrial property rights. Similarly, for them, a petition in bankruptcy can form the object of an arbitration. Equally, a dispute between a foreign company and its locally registered agent or distributor could be freely arbitrated, as well as any dispute related to a construction contract or public works, in spite of the fact that such contracts pertain to matters of urbanization or general utilities governed necessarily by the various domestic regulations.

8. On the other hand, other doctrinal writings opt for a different tendency which favors restricting as much as possible the recourse to international commercial arbitration through interpretation of the concept of "public policy" in a manner that introduces a new distinction between: (i) a first category of subject matters which are not arbitrable either in Egypt or out of Egypt; and (ii) a second innovated category of subject matters perfectly arbitrable according to the domestic law provisions in Egypt, but non-arbitrable out of Egypt under the procedural rules of a foreign law or of an international permanent arbitral institution, like the ICC or the AAA Rules. The main concern which motivates the authors advocating that distinction appears to be an inherently chauvinistic approach leading them to favor an over-extensive interpretation of the concept of "public policy" to include thereunder all matters falling normally under the

exclusive jurisdiction of Egyptian courts. Such exclusive jurisdiction explicitly constitutes an obstacle to the enforcement of a foreign judicial decision according to Article 298, para. 1; and by virtue of the assimilation provided for in Article 299 the same obstacle extends equally to all foreign arbitral awards.

9. This argument recently exercised a great influence on the conduct of some Egyptian defendants involved in ICC arbitration proceedings who found it attractive to try to evade the binding legal effects of the arbitration clauses previously agreed upon. At least on two occasions known to us, that doctrinal opinion was invoked by seizing the Egyptian courts, summoning the ICC, and requesting the issuance of an injunction to prohibit the ICC from proceeding. In one of those two cases, a provisional injunction rendered by a judge in the Southern Cairo Court (Order dated 31 December 1983 in Case No. 11477/1983) was automatically vacated when an amicable settlement took place subsequently and the Egyptian party abandoned his case. The other case is still pending in front of the Southern Cairo Court (Case No. 265/1984), in spite of the fact that the Egyptian party had previously raised that argument in front of the sole arbitrator conducting the case (ICC Arbitration Case No. 4589), and the arbitrator refuted it in an interim award rendered on 13 April 1984.

10. Hopefully, the two recent examples mentioned above will be isolated incidents, especially when taking into consideration that the first comprehensive Egyptian textbook on *Arbitration in Private International Relations* (published in 1984) clearly demonstrated the fragility of the arguments supporting the above-stated doctrinal opinion which considered as a matter of "public policy", and hence non-arbitrable out of Egypt or according to alien rules of procedure, all disputes falling initially under the exclusive jurisdiction of the Egyptian courts.

The severe criticism addressed against said chauvinistic opinion, completely detached from contemporary realities, has the solid backing of a judgment rendered by the Egyptian *Cour de Cassation* on 12 April 1956, which refused to consider as a matter touching public policy the submission to arbitration out of Egypt through foreign arbitrators operating under rules of procedure other than Egyptian domestic rules. The fact that the Supreme Court relied on Article 841 of the old Code of Civil and Commercial Procedures does not diminish the authority of its judgment, since no substantial legislative changes have been introduced thereafter in a manner that would justify disregarding the solution it adopted.

11. The same type of problems emerged with regard to the mandatory nature of certain procedural rules provided for in the Egyptian Code of Procedures. The issue has been raised recently in front of Egyptian courts concerning Article 502, para. 3, which stipulates:

> "Without prejudice to the provisions contained in special legislative acts, the arbitrators have to be nominated either in the arbitration agreement or in a separate agreement".

The rule in question – which made its appearance for the first time in the 1968 new Code of Procedures – was interpreted by the same authors as being unfavorable to the expansion of commercial international arbitration because it requires the direct involvement of the parties themselves in selecting the arbitrators by names. Accordingly, there can be no possible solution under the Egyptian legal system to remedy the failure by the two parties to agree on the name(s) of the arbitrator(s). In other terms, not only does the diligent party have no way whatsoever to force arbitration on the reluctant party through the intervention of a domestic court to substitute itself for the latter in appointing the arbitrator(s), but also such appointment cannot be obtained by recourse to the rules of procedure of the permanent international institution according to which the parties have agreed that the arbitration shall proceed.

12. Consequently, in recent years, some Egyptian parties – who thought they could be successful in frustrating the arbitration proceedings engaged against them under the rules of certain permanent arbitral institutions like the ICC – attacked the legality of the proceedings engaged in front of those arbitral tribunals formed without their explicit consent to the appointment of each arbitrator personally.

Claiming that the right to nominate arbitrators who enjoy the mutual confidence of both parties is a rule of public policy, the Egyptian defendants – hostile to all forms of institutional arbitration – proceeded through three different methods: (i) requesting the Egyptian courts to order the stopping of all proceedings in front of the arbitral tribunal constituted by the permanent institution concerned in conformity with its rules and regulations; (ii) invoking the nullity based upon the provision of Article 502, para. 3, in front of the arbitral tribunal itself; or (iii) waiting for a request to obtain the enforcement of an award already obtained against the Egyptian party, and raising the public policy defence in front of the Egyptian court in order to obtain the refusal of the enforcement of the award.

13. The first technique concerns those direct actions brought in front of Egyptian courts seeking to stop the arbitral proceedings already engaged either in Egypt or in cases where the site of arbitration is outside the country. Said technique has been frequently utilized in recent years, even by the body representing the governmental authorities in front of courts (*Contentieux d'Etat*). New first instance judges in both Cairo and Port Said manifested a certain willingness to follow that point of view without questioning the effectiveness of their orders or the basis on which they could extend their jurisdiction to issue injunctions to permanent arbitration institutions located abroad. The Government does not seem sufficiently concerned about the long-term damaging effects that will be caused by maintaining that attitude.

14. The second technique of pleading the nullity because of a violation of public policy in front of the arbitral tribunal itself had been equally tested, at least in one instance where the site of arbitration was in Cairo. But the sole arbitrator appointed by the ICC put an end to any controversy in a decisive manner by declaring that: "Article 502(3) of the Egyptian Code of Civil and Commercial

Procedure is not part of public policy" (Award rendered 5 April 1984 in ICC Case No. 4406).

15. The third technique of objecting to the enforcement of the arbitral award for being contrary to public policy is more significant, since it concerns the normal method of testing the applicability of an Egyptian rule deemed of mandatory nature to arbitration that took place outside of Egypt under procedural rules which contain no such requirement. In other words, it raises the problem of determining whether the concept of "international public policy" is narrower than the concept of "internal public policy".

The Egyptian *Cour de Cassation* was confronted with that issue on two occasions in recent years, when the Alexandria Court of Appeal refused to grant the *exequatur* on the basis that the arbitrators who rendered the award (in England, in one case, and in France, in the other case) had not been nominated by the parties themselves in conformity with Article 502, para. 3 of the Egyptian Code of Procedures. The highest judicial court rejected that argument by starting in its first decision of 26 April 1982 (Case No. 714 – judicial year 47) that:

> "It is unacceptable to claim the exclusion of the applicable English law under the pretext that it violates Article 502 (3) Procedures, even if we assume that this is true. The possibility of excluding the rules of the foreign applicable law is conditioned according to Article 28 of the Civil Code upon the proof that these rules are contrary to public policy in Egypt, i.e., in conflict with social, political, economic or moral bases which relate to the supreme interests of the community. Thus, it is not sufficient that they (the foreign rules) contradict a mandatory legal text.
>
> Consequently, since Article 502 (3) Procedures, when requiring the necessary mentioning of the arbitrators' name in the arbitration agreement or in an independent agreement, does not relate to public policy as previously stated, its violation could not be considered sufficient justification to exclude the application of the foreign governing law." (Our translation from the Arabic text as reported by Judge Ahmed Hosni in his book: *The Case-Law of the Cour de Cassation in Maritime Problems*, Alexandria, 2nd edition, 1982, pp. 75–76).

The second decision rendered on 13 June 1983 (Case No. 1259 – judicial year 49) confirmed that:

> "Article 502 (3) of the Code of Procedures . . . does not relate to the public policy as previously indicated". (Our translation from the Arabic text as reported by Professor Samia Rashed in her new book: *Arbitration under the Afro-Asian Regional Centre in Cairo, and its submission to the Egyptian Legal System*, Cairo, 1985, p. 82).

16. With regard to the other procedural aspects of arbitration, it has to be noted that the absence of reported judicial precedents has not prevented the domestic doctrine from conceiving the possible recourse to the concept of public policy in certain hypotheses.

A classical example in this respect is provided in relation to Article 502, para. 2 of the Egyptian Code of Procedures which absolutely prohibits that the number of the arbitrators could be other than uneven. Accordingly, all proceedings carried out in front of an arbitral panel composed of two persons only have to be considered contrary to the international public policy as conceived in Egypt, even if not in violation to the rules applicable at the place where the proceedings took place.

17. On the other hand, under the influence of the predominant legislative concept according to which arbitration accomplishes a function that is essentially of a "judicial" nature, the prevailing doctrine considers as public policy the explicit requirement stipulated in Article 507 of the Egyptian Code of Procedures concerning the necessity of expressing in the award the reasons on which the arbitrators have based their decision. Therefore, the absence of reasons prevents an award from being enforceable in Egypt, regardless of whether or not the law of the country where the award has been rendered requires the issuance of a reasoned award.

18. Equally, the Egyptian procedural law authors tend to consider as public policy the implicit requirement under the same Article 507 related to the need for all arbitrators to participate in the deliberations to be regularly held in order to secure arriving at a majority opinion after a true exchange of views among all of them. Consequently, in accordance with said doctrinal position, no award can be considered validly rendered if one of the arbitrators had refused to participate in the deliberations. Nevertheless, it would seem excessive to construe this particular rule regarding deliberation in a manner that renders it of international public policy, in the sense of becoming applicable to all arbitration proceedings taking place outside the country, and in the application of procedural rules which contain no similar requirement.

19. The same tendency towards overextending the concept of public policy can be attested equally with regard to the rules governing the substance of the dispute, particularly in the field of condemning the debtor to pay moratory interests exceeding certain limits.

A few years ago, the Cairo Court of Appeal was confronted with a case in which a British company sought enforcement of an award rendered in London condemning an Egyptian foreign trade company to pay as indemnity for the breach of a contractual obligation a given amount of dollars, plus interest thereupon from the date of the breach at the rate of 8% per annum. The Cairo Court of Appeal ordered the enforcement of the principal amount of indemnity, but refused to allow the enforcement of that part of the award related to the interest for being considered contrary to the Egyptian public policy which imposes a ceiling of 5% as the maximum permitted rate of interest (Judgment rendered on 21 January 1982 in Case No. 3755 for the 97th judicial year).

The recourse lodged against the refusal to enforce interest at the rate of 8% is still pending in front of the Egyptian *Cour de Cassation* (Case No. 815 for the 52nd judicial year, filed on 18 March 1982).

20. Said case provides a unique opportunity for the highest judicial court to indicate its attitude with regard to the concept of public policy, and whether the

Egyptian courts have to recognize the existence of an international public policy more limited than the internal law concept. In essence, the Egyptian *Cour de Cassation* has to determine whether the line traced in 1982–1983 regarding Article 502 (3) (see *Supra* 15) extends to cover the politically sensitive issue of interests deemed anti-Islamic by the religious fundamentalists who were dissatisfied with the recent ruling of the Constitutional Supreme Court which upheld the Civil Code provisions authorizing the principle of allocating moratory interest.

If the already established case law (which refused to apply the restriction imposed by Article 502 (3) of the Code of Procedures to arbitration proceedings conducted under English law in London) is maintained, the Egyptian *Cour de Cassation* can safely overrule the challenged decision in a manner that enforces the distinction between: (i) mandatory internal rules applicable only whenever the Egyptian law is the governing legal system; and (ii) a more restricted number of basic principles reflecting the supreme values deemed fundamental for the national community, forming what may be called an international public order, the violation of which justifies excluding the solutions initially envisaged by the law governing the substantive disputed issues.

Consequently, a British award condemning the losing party to pay a moratory interest at the rate of 8% should be considered perfectly enforceable in Egypt, since such condemnation does not damage the supreme national values deemed of international public policy, particularly when taking into consideration that the Government of Egypt – itself or through its agencies – authorizes and undertakes financial banking transactions based on interest rates exceeding by large 7% per annum.

21. The situation has to be considered as essentially different when the mandatory domestic rule reflects a fundamental legal value, the promotion of which is necessary in view of safeguarding certain community objectives of prime importance. This was precisely the case in an ICC arbitration where the Egyptian judge who acted as sole arbitrator had to decide upon the legality of certain payments promised as a counterpart for services aiming to facilitate obtaining a military procurement contract. The Egyptian sole arbitrator declared the claimed payments illegal because they were promised within the framework of an agreement having as its exclusive purpose the corruption of those vital institutions which must be kept immune from any possible traffic of influence. In said instance, Egyptian law was declared the governing law, and, accordingly, the sole arbitrator relied on the Egyptian domestic concept of nullity for illegal cause as a mandatory rule of national public policy (Award rendered in ICC Case No. 4409).

22. Obviously, the solution would have been the same if the governing law were a system other than the Egyptian law. But the only difference in such hypothesis, in comparison with the above-mentioned arbitration case, would be to uphold the illegality of payments related to corruption on the basis of a truly international public policy reflecting superior values pertaining to the maintenance and development of sound economic relationships throughout the world community, i.e., in conformity with some morality norms which have to dominate universally.

23. In conclusion, it seems safe to state that the Egyptian courts have had no opportunity yet to elaborate on the applicability of that concept of public policy which could be qualified as truly international in its nature and objectives.

Nevertheless, such negative assessment cannot be interpreted to exclude the potential adoption by the domestic courts of said concept whenever deemed appropriate. The case law to be elaborated in this respect will necessarily rely upon generally recognized principles of effectiveness, fairness and justice both procedurally and substantively; and these general principles constitute – together with the international obligations emerging under the relevant multilateral and bilateral treaties – the core of a truly international public policy under formation. In particular, sooner or later, the Egyptian *Cour de Cassation* will be requested to invoke the predominant character of said international public policy in order to condemn the various maneuvers undertaken by those Egyptian defendants who are trying to escape their obligation to arbitrate under the false cover of a pseudo domestic public policy.

Public Policy and International Commercial Arbitration: An Argentine View

*Horacio A. Grigera Naón**

This topic is to be analyzed with regard to four different aspects:

(i) public policy and arbitral proceedings or awards taking place or rendered in Argentina with regard to an international transaction;
(ii) public policy and the invocation of an arbitral agreement regarding an international transaction before Argentina courts for compelling arbitration or for obtaining a stay of court proceedings in Argentina;
(iii) public policy and recognition or enforcement of foreign arbitral awards in Argentina;
(iv) public policy, *lex mercatoria* and *ordre public vraiment international* from the Argentine perspective.

(i) Arbitral proceedings and awards in Argentina have to be compatible with the essential principles of fairness and justice which are a part of both Argentine internal and international public policy.[1] For instance, the due process guarantee embodied in Article 18 of the Argentine Constitution requires that every party to a controversy to be adjudicated have a fair opportunity to be heard and to state his or her case.

Arbitral proceedings – national or international – fall within the scope of this public policy provision. With regard to *de ure* arbitration – in the course of which arbitrators are expected to strictly abide by the applicable rules of law governing both the substance of the dispute and the arbitral proceedings themselves – failure to meet this standard, or the fact that the arbitrator has made an "essential procedural error" can lead to the setting aside of the award. The same will happen if the award has been made after the deadline established therefor in the terms of reference or if it decides on issues not submitted to arbitration (Art. 760(2) National Code of Civil and Commercial Procedure, hereinafter referred to as Cpr.).

* Professor of Private International Law at the University of Buenos Aires and the Museo Social Argentino University. Attorney and Doctor of Law and Social Sciences (University of Buenos Aires); LLM, SJD (Harvard University).

1. H. A. Grigera Naón, "Les Règles de Droit limitant leur propre domaine d'application: doctrine comparée et droit argentin", *Rechtsvergleichung, Europarecht und Rechtsintegration, Gedächtnisschrift für Leontin Constantinesco*, at 25 & fol. (1983).

Arbitral proceedings where arbitrators have *ex aequo et bono* adjudicating powers (*amigables componedores*) also have to comply with due process constitutional requirements. Their awards can be also set aside if rendered after the expiration of the agreed term or when they decide issues not submitted to arbitration (Art. 771 Cpr.).

There also are additional grounds pertaining to general public policy reasons for challenging both *de iure* and *ex aequo et bono* awards rendered in Argentina in international cases:

1. Matters which cannot be freely settled or compromised by agreement of the parties cannot be submitted to arbitration (Art. 737 Cpr.).

This provision basically refers to two hypotheses:

a. matters which on account of public policy reasons are deemed non-arbitrable (certain aspects of company law, foreign investment law, antitrust, trademark and patent legislation, legal capacity of persons and family law, *inter alia*);
b. matters where there is exclusive jurisdiction of Argentine courts (matters where the Argentine State is a party and where, in addition, federal laws or provisions of the Argentine Constitution are applicable (Art. 100); questions where the exercise of sovereign powers of the State, such as the exercise of its taxing powers or the attribution or denial of nationality to individuals, are directly implicated.[2])

In all such cases, no arbitration – local or international – will be allowed.

Nevertheless, it is conceivable that if an international arbitration takes place in Argentina, internal imperative or public policy norms will not necessarily apply even in the eyes of an Argentine judge called to decide on the setting aside of the award.[3] Thus, matters which cannot be arbitrated in entirely local settings might become arbitrable in international ones.

However, concerns of national protection in certain vital aspects of the Argentine economy related to international commercial and economic intercourse can also validly lead to exactly the opposite outcome. For instance, precisely because the controversy is an international one, matters which can normally be arbitrated in Argentina may be rendered non-arbitrable outside of Argentina.

2. International cases which are generally deemed arbitrable under Argentine law, but where the substance of the award goes against Argentine international public policy.

In general, it is unlikely that an Argentine judge will question the substance of the arbitral award or the results attained through the choice of law made by the arbitrators or the parties to the arbitrated dispute unless there is evidence (at

2. *Id.*, at 3; H. Grigera Naón & J. Samtleben, "Schiedsgerichtsbarkeit in Argentinien", 10 RIW 728 (1983).
3. H. A. Grigera Naón, "El arbitraje comercial en América Latina", 4 Revista del Derecho Industrial 17/18 (1980).

least when the dispute arises from an international contract) that the award leads to a.) a violation of general principles of morality and justice shared by Argentina and the international community or specific to Argentine society or concerning basic grounds of the Argentine legal system, society or economic structure and policies;[4] or b.) a violation of foreign mandatory laws which should be applied both on account of Argentine private international law ("place of contractual performance"[5] and of the interests and policies underlying such laws (*fraude à la loi étrangère*);[6] or c.) a violation of Argentine mandatory laws of the Argentine "place of contractual performance" imperatively requiring international application (*fraude à la loi propre*);[7] or d.) a violation of Argentine or foreign "direct"

4. Art. 14 (1) and (2), Argentine Civil Code, hereinafter referred to as CC.

5. Although the majority of the Argentine doctrine contends that the parties to an international contract are free to choose the applicable law, it is also a fact that no reference to private autonomy is made in Arts. 1205 and fol. of the Argentine Civil Code on the law applicable to international contracts. As a result, the place of conclusion of the contract only plays an occasional or at most subsidiary role (Art. 1205 CC); private autonomy of the parties in the choice of law is limited by the "mandatory" rules of the "place of the contractual performance" (Arts. 1209 and fol. CC).

In this regard, the expression "place of contractual performance" of the Argentine Civil Code can only be tantamount to the contractual localization determined *ad hoc* by the judge for each contractual relationship through the grouping of contacts process which enables the determination of the law applicable to the substance of the international contract. Only in the very unlikely hypotheses where it will be impossible to determine where the contacts predominantly group themselves will the judge resort to subsidiary "fixed" and "hard and fast" connecting factors individually bringing about the designation of the applicable law, (such as the domicile of the debtor and the place of contractual conclusion (Arts. 1205, 1212/14 CC)), though it is to be remarked that at this stage these must have already played a role as contacts in the preliminary (and most probably successful and final) step of the grouping process leading to the *ad hoc* determination of the "place of contractual performance" (See H. A. Grigera Naón: "International Contract Law, 'Lois de Police' and self-applicating rules: an Argentine outlook"; 19 Vorträge Reden und Berichte aus dem Europa Institut, Universität des Saarlandes; by the same author, "Les Contrats Internationaux en Argentine", 7 DPCI, 427 & fol. (1981). As to the meaning of "mandatory" rules of the "place of contractual performance" in the international sense, see footnotes 5. and 6. *infra*).

6. It is up to the judge to decide in the face of each controverted issue if the policies and interests of the otherwise strictly local substantive norms indicated by the contractual localization ("place of contractual performance") or the wider forum's interests and policies implicated by international transactions and international commerce make such norms require extraterritorial application despite their originally exclusive relevance for entirely local transactions. The initial presumption will be that the imperative substantive rules of the "place of contractual performance" apply to international cases and limit choice of law autonomy. But such presumption can be rebutted by showing that in face of the concrete dispute to be decided there are no interests and policies requiring the extraterritorial application of originally entirely locally-oriented substantive norms. The "place of contractual performance" as connecting factor then acquires a functional meaning according to which contacts, substantive legal rules of the concerned forum and underlying or relevant forum policies continuously interact much in the way they do under functional and interest analysis characteristic of US conflict of laws doctrines. (See D. T. Trautman, "Some Notes on the Theory of Choice of Law Clauses", 35 Mercer L. Rev., 535 (1984); Scoles & Hay, *Conflict of Laws*, 652 & fol. (1982)).

7. Argentine law (like the law of the Federal Republic of Germany: B. Dickson, "The Reform of Private International Law in Germany", 34 ICLQ, 242 (1985)) also encompasses within its broad notion of international public policy – clearly exceeding the "strict" notion which we have previously considered – the *fraude à la loi* doctrine. *Fraude à la loi* in the private international law sense refers to any maneuvers addressed at frustrating the application of the law which should normally apply if the private international law system of the forum operated without any artificially created distortions.

Arts. 1207 and 1208 CC respond to this notion providing that (i) any contract concluded abroad for

rules also requiring extraterritorial application[8] irrespective of the indications of

---

evading otherwise applicable Argentine mandatory law or (ii) any contract made in Argentina for evading the application of foreign mandatory law will be rendered null and void. Thus, by condemning both *fraude à la loi propre et fraude à la loi étrangère* the Argentine legislator underscores the imperative character of the Argentine private international law and the necessary application, even *ex officio*, of national or foreign mandatory laws designated by the Argentine private international law. Such imperative nature of Argentine private international law becomes then a part of Argentine principles of public policy in the international sense and leads to the *ex officio* application by an Argentine judge of foreign laws designated through Argentine private international law choice of law methodologies.

8. Although not identical with the notion of international public policy, but still close to it because of having a bearing on the amount of foreign law an Argentine court will be ready to apply when it is to decide an international dispute, the growing literature and court decisions in Argentina favor the unilateral application of originally local or municipal substantive norms to international cases (I. Winizky & H. Grigera Naón, "El art. 30 del Dto./Ley 19.550 y la acutación internacional de las sociedades comerciales en el ámbito de los Tratados de Montevideo de 1889 y 1940", 38 Revista del Derecho Comercial y de las Obligaciones, 133 & fol. (1974); H. Grigera Naón, *supra*, at note 1; A. Boggiano, I *Derecho Internacional Privado*, 313 & fol. (1983)). This will happen, according to our views, when interests and policies underlying a specific substantive rule or principle or evidenced through them, would be frustrated if any such rule did not receive international application. The latter will therefore not depend on the traditional conflict of laws "hard and fast" technique of determining the applicable law through the localization of the different connecting factors individually ascribed to the diverse abstract categories, where all legal relationships are to be necessarily and respectively inserted. On the contrary, the area of application of each substantive legal rule is to be determined by solely considering the strength of the interests and policies underlying it in light of the controverted issue and of the connections of the latter with the legal order to which such rule belongs. It is the interaction of all these elements: interests, policies, disputed issue and contacts "creating interests" which is to determine if a *loi de police* exists and is to be applied or not (*Allstate Ins. Co.* v. *Hague*, 449 US 302 313 S.Ct. 633 (1981)). The *loi de police* technique differs from the traditional international public policy notion because (i) the policies determining the extraterritorial application of otherwise municipal substantive rules do not respond to general principles abstracted from the whole of the legal system or societal organization or to broad conceptions of morality and justice, but reflect concrete and specific interests and policies which account for the existence of that norm in the legal order, or correspond to the field of law to which that norm belongs and (ii) *lois de police* do not seek exceptionally to avoid the otherwise normal application of foreign law, but once their conditions of application are given, they immediately apply to the issue at stake, thereby *ab initio* (a) excluding both the eventual application of foreign laws and of any "indirect" conflict of law rules of the legal order to which they belong and (b) simultaneously superseding any choice of law made by the parties which would deny application to the *loi de police* concerned.

Very close to *lois de police* are rules of immediate application. The latter are substantive rules whose *ab initio* principal purpose is to apply directly to international transactions pursuant to specific policies established by the legislator. Therefore, unlike *lois de police*, laws of immediate application are not originally local or municipal rules of law which on account of the specific issue at stake require extraterritorial application. Normally, laws of immediate application share the strict mandatory character of *lois de police* and their application cannot be prevented by a contrary choice of law of the parties. Moreover, like *lois de police*, they usually unilaterally and directly govern legal relationships falling within their scope without resorting to the "indirect" or "conflictual" choice of law technique. We shall jointly refer to *lois de police* and laws of immediate application as "direct rules".

The *lois de police* technique is generally contemplated in Art. 14(1) CC, giving priority to the application of Argentine public law norms over the application of foreign law, and Art. 1206 CC, determining the direct application of Argentine substantive laws to international contracts, when so required by the interests of the State or of its inhabitants. *Examples* of laws of immediate application are Arts. 14(4), CC giving priority to the application of Argentine law if more favorable to the validity of an international contract, and Art. 855(2) Argentine Commercial Code, imposing a 2-year statute of limitations for contracts of carriage of goods with a destination outside of Argentina.

traditional "indirect" conflict of law rules having the "place of contractual performance" as connecting factor.

All these hypotheses are really different examples of violations of Argentine international public policy in its broadest sense which might lead an Argentine judge to set aside arbitral awards rendered in Argentina when the controversy originated in an international contract.

It is also to be borne in mind that the above considerations on arbitrability of disputes and operation of international public policy in connection with international commercial arbitration do not necessarily imply an abusive interference of Argentine judges in arbitrations held in Argentina because, as already pointed out, the interests and policies to be evaluated within the framework of entirely local transactions do not wholly coincide with those considered when international transactions are at stake.

In this latter context, general concerns of predictability, fairness, fostering of international commercial and economic intercourse, reciprocity, harmony, lowering of costs, unification of international trade law, functional coordination of mandatory norms of national origin governing international trade and economic transactions and swiftness of international economic and international transactions are to be analyzed on the same footing as specific interests and policies underlying each national mandatory substantive norm.[9] Thus, the application of a norm preventing the arbitrability of certain disputes in local settings, or the application of mandatory prohibitive norms for totally local transactions is not necessarily warranted in international cases when, after weighing together the interests and policies underlying such provisions for entirely local cases and those pertaining to international ones, the conclusion is reached that the specificity of the international issue at stake constrains the applicability of the mandatory rule only to local transactions.[10]

(ii) What has been generally said in (i) is also true when the validity of an arbitral clause concerning an international transaction is invoked. Nevertheless, in such instances, the invalidity of the arbitral clause is rather more likely to ensue because there is a public policy reason, relevant for arbitration in an international settings, specifically forbidding arbitration in the instant case – probably expressed through *lois de police* concretely excluding international or *foreign* arbitrations – than because there is a possible violation of Argentine international public policy if an arbitration were carried out under such arbitral clause.

The reason for this is that it will be very difficult – and most often impossible – to determine before the arbitration has even started if it will lead to a solution incompatible with Argentine international public policy (either as a violation of general principles of morality, justice and social or economic organization or of the fundamental mechanisms for the designation of the applicable law on which the Argentine private international law system is grounded); or that future arbitral proceedings pursuant to the questioned arbitral agreement will be

9. A. T. von Mehren, "Choice of Law and the Problem of Justice", 41 Law & Contemp. Probs., 25 & fol. (1977).

10. Grigera Naón & Samtleben, *supra* note 2 at 726; H. A. Grigera Naón, "National Report Argentina", *International Handbook on Commercial Arbitration*, P. Sanders General Editor, Supplement III, 1 & fol. (1985).

carried out in a way incompatible with Argentine international public policy. Only if such incompatibility appears from the arbitral clause itself or from the instructions given to the arbitrators, or from other circumstances evidenced by the contract where the arbitral clause is inserted (such as the choice of law provisions to be applied by the arbitrator according to the will of the parties), can an Argentine judge deny validity and effects to an arbitral clause corresponding to an international transaction as contrary to Argentine international public policy.

It is also relevant to point out that the general opinion of the Argentine authors and court decisions does not seem to grant absolute independence to the arbitral clause from the contract where it has been inserted. Moreover, it appears that issues of inexistence of the contract containing the arbitral clause and of contractual invalidity necessarily reaching the arbitral clause cannot be settled through arbitration under such clause and are to be decided by national courts.[11] For this reason, there is no contrary evidence that an Argentine court will not consider the application of mandatory legal norms wishing to receive extraterritorial application belonging to the "place of performance" of the transaction submitted to arbitration for determining the validity and effects of the arbitral clause itself, as well as relevant "direct rules" of its own and foreign "interested" fora.

(iii) Arbitral awards rendered outside of Argentina will not be recognized or enforced in the country if they are contrary to Argentine "principles of public policy", if they decide issues which cannot be arbitrated or if the arbitral agreement covers an issue submitted to the exclusive jurisdiction of Argentine courts (Arts. 517 (4), 519 bis, 737 and 1 Cpr.).

In general terms, the requirements for recognition and enforcement of foreign arbitral awards rendered in international commercial disputes are based on the same public policy and arbitrability limitations already described with regard to the powers of judges to set aside arbitral awards rendered in Argentina or to the possibility of denying recognition or validity to arbitral clauses when international commercial or economic disputes have been submitted to arbitration.

Therefore, recognition and enforcement of foreign arbitral awards violating Argentine general principles of morality and justice or Argentine social, economic and political organization and policies, or Argentine or foreign relevant direct rules, or within the framework of international contracts, substantive mandatory norms of the "place of contractual performance" requiring international or extraterritorial application to the controverted issue (*fraude à la loi*), may be refused by Argentine courts.

Nevertheless, it is to be remarked that the recognition and enforcement of foreign arbitral awards bring to bear specific policies and interests which will certainly have a moderating impact on the evaluation of the weight to be given to the policies of the forum requiring the refusal of recognition or enforcement of a

11. H. A. Grigera Naón, "El Arbitraje Comercial en el Derecho Argentino Interno e Internacional Privado", 163 Revista de Derecho Mercantil, 115, 117/118 (Madrid 1982).

foreign award which has been issued in connection with a truly international case.

In this sense, there are general policies normally shared by the procedural law of the forum before which the foreign award is submitted and revealed by institutions such as *res iudicata* and the limitation of appeals or means of setting aside which can be raised against an already adjudicated matter, which must be weighed against other policies and interests of the forum's legal order or specific norms from which a denial of recognition or enforcement would ensue.

After such a weighing exercise is carried out, it should not be surprising if the conclusion is reached that awards in international commercial and economic matters which might have been set aside for public policy reasons if they had been rendered in Argentina, are likely to be fully recognized and enforced in that country because they already enjoy *res iudicata* effects abroad entitling the parties to the arbitrated dispute to expectations as to their reciprocal rights and obligations which would be radically and may be outrageously disturbed if the award were deprived of extraterritorial effects.[12] This is why Art. 517 (1) and (3) Cpr. (to which internal *renvoi* is made by Art. 519 bis Cpr. specifically referring to recognition and enforcement of foreign awards) requires that for recognition and enforcement in Argentina the foreign award must be endowed with *res iudicata* effects and be considered as such under the law of the country where it was made.

These principles of predictability and "repose"[13] concerning situations already adjudicated through final decisions will certainly induce the Argentine judge to prudently consider public policy principles under Argentine law so as not to unnecessarily disturb the expectations of the parties to an arbitral procedure and the fluidity of international commercial and economic exchanges unless there are superior national interests and policies underlying the Argentine relevant norms and principles clearly overpowering the concerns for the stability of international commercial arbitral adjudications.

(iv) It is to be pointed out that in light of the considerations heretofore made, no truly international or anational *lex mercatoria* or *ordre public vraiment international* underlying *lex mercatoria* will be admitted in the eyes of an Argentine court if contrary to the broad notion of Argentine international public policy as described.[14] In other words, such *lex mercatoria* or truly international public policy

12. A. T. von Mehren, "Adjudicatory Jurisdiction: General theories compared and evaluated", 63 Boston Univ. L. Rev., 279 & fol. (1983).

13. The principle of "repose" canvasses different policies involved in the recognition and enforcement of foreign adjudications, such as the avoidance of the duplication of efforts and the preservation of stability and unity in the decision-making process by diminishing the possibilities of attacking existing adjudications (foreign or local) regarding specific issues. Such policies lead within certain boundaries to sacrificing the principle of absolute correctness of the final decision, which might be better served, for instance, by authorizing a total review of the foreign award by the court where it is submitted for recognition and enforcement. As it has been said in this regard, the principle of repose: "... accepts the inherent imperfection of human knowledge and institutions and the need to put to rest quarrels and disputes so that the energies of individuals and resource of society can be devoted to more constructive tasks." On Mehren & Trautman: *The Law of Multistate Problems*, 835 (1965); 1983 mimeographed edition: V-4 & fol.

14. A critical appraisal of both *lex mercatoria* and *ordre public vraiment international* can be found in A. Kassis, *Théorie Gènérale des Usages du Commerce*, (1984).

will be acceptable if not incompatible a.) with Argentine "direct" rules; b.) with mandatory rules of the "place of contractual performance" requiring international application; or c.) with general principles of morality and justice or underlying the social and economic structure or social organization recognized or advanced by the Argentine community. Therefore, any arbitral award infringing any of these aspects or serving as an instrument for their evasion can be set aside by an Argentine court if rendered in Argentina or denied recognition or enforcement in Argentina if rendered abroad.

Problems of Public Policy – The Indian Perspective

*Fali S. Nariman**

I. THE BASIC OUTLOOK

In *Mitsubishi Motor Corporation* v. *Soler Chrysler-Plymouth, Inc.*[1], the Supreme Court of the United States stressed the need "to shake off the old judicial hostility to arbitration" and the necessity "for national courts to subordinate domestic notions of arbitrability to international policy favoring commercial arbitration". A year earlier, in *Renusagar Power Co. Ltd.* v. *General Electric Company*,[2] the Supreme Court of India, whilst permitting reference of disputes relating to money due under promissory notes and claims for compensatory damages in the nature of tort to the Court of Arbitration of the ICC in London, underlined the necessity of construing the provisions of the Foreign Awards (Recognition and Enforcement) Act, 1961 (giving effect to the New York Convention, 1958) in a liberal manner. The court said:

> "The Statement of Objects and Reasons shows that the Act seeks to achieve speedy settlement of disputes arising from international trade through Arbitration. The Act is a successor to the Arbitration (Protocol & Convention) Act, 1937 . . . The present Act was enacted, as its long title indicates, to give effect to the said New York International Convention on the Recognition and Enforcement of Foreign Awards to which India is a party. . . .
> It is obvious that since the Act is calculated and designed to subserve the cause of facilitating international trade and promotion thereof by providing for speedy settlement of disputes arising in such trade through arbitration, any expression or phrase occurring therein should receive, consistent with its literal and grammatical sense, a liberal construction."

However, in cases not covered by the laws implementing the Geneva Convention (and then the New York Convention) Indian courts have exhibited a

* Advocate at the Supreme Court of India, ICCA member.

1. A decision rendered on 2 July 1985 – by a sharply divided court – on whether a US court should enforce an agreement to resolve antitrust claims by arbitration, when the agreement arose from an international commercial transaction. Extracts cited in *Yearbook Commercial Arbitration*, Vol. XI (1986) pp. 555–566.
2. *Renusagar Power Co. Ltd.* v. *General Electric Company*: AIR 1985 SC 1156 at p. 1181 (decided on 16 August 1984) – Extracts from the judgment are also reported in *Yearbook Commercial Arbitration*, Vol. X (1985) pp. 431–449.

marked reluctance to concede jurisdiction of a claim arising under domestic law to a foreign or international tribunal.[3]

II. PUBLIC POLICY: ARBITRABILITY AND ARBITRAL PROCEDURE

Indian parties who have agreed to arbitration under rules and regulations of international controlling bodies (like the ICC) have often sought to extricate themselves from the contract by filing suits in India and resisting stay of proceedings under legislation enacted in India to give effect to the Geneva Convention (1923) and (later) to give effect to the New York Convention (1958).[4] According to the plain language of Article II (3) of the New York Convention, the court of the contracting State, when seized of an action in a matter in respect of which the parties have executed an arbitration agreement, is obliged at the request of one of the parties "to *refer* the parties to arbitration unless it finds that the said agreement is null and void, inoperative and incapable of being performed". In the implementing Acts in India, the expression "*refer* the parties to arbitration" is not reproduced; it is rephrased and expressed in its technical procedural sense ("shall make an order staying the proceedings").[5] The absence of the more positive language of the Convention (to "refer"), though of little consequence in law, has given rise (and some plausibility) to exculpatory pleas based on alleged public policy. Fortunately, in the main such pleas have been rejected by the courts in India:

(i) Some years ago, in *Societé de Traction d'Electricité Societé Anonyme* v. *Kamani Engineering*

---

3. In contracts providing for resolutions of disputes by arbitration outside India, Indian courts have frequently exercised their discretionary power under Section 34 of the Indian Arbitration Act, 1940 – a statute primarily enacted for purposes of domestic arbitration – to refuse a stay of a legal proceeding within their jurisdiction (to enable the foreign arbitration to proceed), in cases where the Indian parties would be put to inconvenience and hardship, especially in view of statutory foreign exchange restrictions; See *Michael Golodetz* v. *Sirajuddin & Co.* (AIR 1963 SC 1044) (where the contract was between an American company and an Indian firm, and which provided for resolution of disputes by arbitration in New York according to the Rules of the American Arbitration Association), and *Ramji Dayawala & Sons Pvt. Ltd.* v. *Invest Import* (AIR 1981 SC 2085) (where the contract between an Indian firm and a party in Yugoslavia provided for the settlement of the disputes by arbitration of the International Chamber of Commerce in Paris). In the first case, the Arbitration Protocol and Convention Act, 1937, giving effect in India to the provisions of the Geneva Convention (1923) was inapplicable, as the United States of America was not a party to the Geneva Convention. In the second case, Yugoslavia not being a party to the New York Convention, the provisions of the Foreign Awards (Recognition and Enforcement) Act, 1961, giving effect in India to the New York Convention (1958), was inapplicable. In both these cases, application by the foreign contractual party for a stay of proceedings (i.e., of a suit filed by the Indian party within the jurisdiction of Indian courts) was refused on the ground that in the totality of circumstances, including the fact that most of the evidence was in India, the interests of justice required the court's discretion being exercised in favour of the Indian contractual party.

4. The Arbitration Protocol and Convention Act, 1937 giving effect to the provisions of the Geneva Convention (1923) and the Foreign Awards (Recognition and Enforcement) Act, 1961 giving effect to the New York Convention (1958).

5. Section 3 of the Foreign Awards (Recognition and Enforcement) Act, 1961 – the same is the position in the UK. See Section I(1) of the Arbitration Act 1975.

Co. Ltd.[6] a bench of five judges of the Supreme Court of India overruled the decision of the Calcutta High Court which had taken the view that an Indian company could not submit disputes to arbitration according to a scheme different from the Indian Arbitration Act, 1940. This was in the context of an arbitration agreement entered into by the French company with the Indian company (Kamani) providing for arbitration in accordance with the rules of the International Chamber of Commerce (ICC). In the Companies Act, 1956 (s. 389) there was a provision that a company may by agreement refer to arbitration in accordance with the Indian Arbitration Act, 1940 existing or future differences between itself and any other company and that the provisions of the Arbitration Act, 1940 should apply to all arbitrations to which the company was a party. The court held that the provision was enabling and not exclusive; it did not prevent an Indian company from referring disputes to arbitration otherwise than under the Indian Arbitration Act. The Supreme Court held that an agreement to refer disputes in accordance with the rules of the ICC was not inconsistent with s. 389 of the Companies Act, 1956 – and that s. 47 of the Arbitration Act, 1940 itself contemplated reference to arbitration under any other law for the time being in force – such other law (it was held) included the Arbitration Protocol & Convention Act 6 of 1937 (enacted by the Indian Legislature to give effect to the Geneva Convention then in force).

(ii) More recently in *Union of India* v. *Owners of Vessel Hoegh Orchid and their Agents*,[7] (before the High Court of Gujarat) it was contended by the Central Government which was a contracting party in a charterparty contract with the owners of the Norwegian vessel Hoegh Orchid (which contract contained an arbitration clause) that enforcement of the arbitration clause and obligating the government to make a reference to foreign arbitration would amount to a denial of "the sovereign status of the State"; the Act implementing the New York Convention (it was said) is valid and binding only between citizens of different States; reliance was placed on Article 14 of the New York Convention.[8] The High Court (of Gujarat) refused to accept this specious plea. It held that a Contracting State was itself bound by the terms of the Convention, and that the only limitation in case of disputes between contracting parties was to be found in Article 1: that the dispute must arise out of a contract which is commercial in nature. The court held that since the New York Convention had been ratified both by India and by Norway (whose flag the ship in question was flying) enforcement of the arbitration clause would not amount to a denial of the "sovereignty of the Union of India".

Section 3 of the Foreign Awards (Recognition and Enforcement) Act, 1961, is couched in mandatory terms ("shall make an order staying the proceedings").[9]

6. AIR 1983 Guj. p. 34 – Extracts from the judgment in this case are also cited in *Yearbook Commercial Arbitration*, Vol. IX (1984) pp. 405–411.
7. Article 14: "A contracting State shall not be entitled to avail itself of the present Convention against other Contracting States except to the extent that it is itself bound to apply the Convention".
8. 1964(3) Supreme Court Reports 122.
9. "3. Stay of proceedings in respect of matters to be referred to arbitration. – Notwithstanding anything contained in the Arbitration Act, 1940, or in the Code of Civil Procedure, 1908, if any party to an agreement to which Article II of the Convention set forth in the Schedule applies, or any person claiming through or under him commences any legal proceedings in any court against any other party to the agreement or any person claiming through or under him in respect of any matter agreed to be referred to arbitration in such agreement, any party to such legal proceedings may, at any time after appearance and before filing a written statement or taking any other step in the proceedings, apply to the Court to stay the proceedings and the Court, unless satisfied that the agreement is null and void, inoperative or incapable of being performed or that there is not, in fact, any dispute between the parties with regard to the matter agreed to be referred, shall make an order staying the proceedings."

As a result, courts in India have now uniformly rejected the following pleas in support of the public policy defence, viz. difficulty of contesting arbitrations due to Foreign Exchange Regulations, inconvenience of tendering evidence available in India before foreign arbitral tribunals, and non-enforceability of non-speaking foreign awards. Whenever the Act implementing the New York Convention is applicable, such pleas have not been accepted. In 1975, a Division Bench of the Bombay High Court[10] held that it was the statutory obligation of the court of the Contracting State, at the request of one of the parties to the arbitration agreement, to ensure that the disputes are determined by arbitration, and that Section 3 of the Indian Act (Foreign Awards Recognition & Enforcement Act, 1961) obliged the court to stay proceedings in respect of matters referred to foreign arbitral tribunals.

More recently, in *Renusagar Power Co., Ltd.* v. *General Electric Co.*[11] it was again contended before a single judge (of the Bombay High Court) that the large amounts of deposit required under the Rules of the ICC and the costs of the foreign arbitration and the difficulty of obtaining foreign exchange for that purpose should be considered in not granting a stay of proceedings against the foreign company in the Indian court. The judge (Pendse J.) by his judgment dated 19/20 April 1985 rejected this contention. He said:

> "The Respondents also resisted the Petition on the ground that the evidence on which the Respondents desire to rely is in India and it would not be possible for them to secure foreign exchange for appearing and resisting the proceedings before the International Chamber of Commerce. The defence on this ground is totally misconceived. The mere fact that the evidence which the Respondents desire to lead is from this country is no answer to the claim of the Petitioners that the arbitration proceedings must continue and the suit instituted by the respondents should be stayed. As regards the difficulty in securing foreign exchange, the record indicates that the Respondents had made an application before the Reserve Bank of India for grant of foreign exchange for defending the proceedings before the arbitrators and have succeeded in securing the foreign exchange. The mere fact that the proceedings before the arbitrators to be conducted outside India might cause some hardship to the Respondents is no ground to by-pass the arbitration Clause contained in the contract. In case the party is permitted to resile from the arbitration clause on such ground, then International trade and commerce would come to a standstill. The Respondents have entered into the contract with open eyes and it is futile for them to claim that now they find it difficult to participate in the arbitration proceedings. The submission in this connection deserves to be repelled."

When the matter was taken in appeal this contention was not pressed – presumably because the statutory authority (the Reserve Bank of India) had in a letter addressed to Renusagar (the Indian party) stated that the Government was agreeable to release the estimated foreign exchange (350,000 US dollars) towards solicitors' costs of the arbitration.[12] In a further appeal carried by *Renusagar* to the

10. A decision rendered in February 1975 in Appeal No. 151 of 1970.

11. Cited above in note 2: the (unreported) judgment of Pendse J. was ultimately approved by the Supreme Court of India: *Renusagar Power Co. Ltd* v. *General Electric Co.* AIR 1985 SC 1156.

12. Under the Foreign Exchange Act 1973, no remittance from India is permitted without permission of the Reserve Bank of India. As a matter of practice the Reserve Bank grants such permission (for

Supreme Court of India, the highest court rejected each and every plea raised by the Indian company for not proceeding with the arbitration under the ICC Rules of Arbitration as agreed to. However, none of the pleas raised before the Supreme Court related to the public policy defence. However, the decision of the Supreme Court is of great importance to international commercial arbitration – in disallowing the contentions of *Renusagar Power Co. Ltd.*, the court has set a healthy trend, rejecting "parochial responses" to international commercial disputes. The entire decision proceeds on a strong presumption in favor of a freely negotiated contractual choice-of-forum provision, it has set the future pattern for courts in India: when required to interpret the provisions of the Foreign Awards (Recognition and Enforcement) Act, 1961, they must keep in mind its objective, namely, achieving speedy settlement of disputes arising from international trade through arbitration. Incidentally, in *Renusagar Power Co. Ltd.* v. *General Electric Co.* the Supreme Court also affirmed an earlier Bench decision of the High Court of Bombay (in *Fertilizer Corporation of India* v. *Chemical Construction Corporation*) which had upheld the validity of the Rules of Arbitration of the ICC as not violating Indian public policy. In *Fertilizer Corporation of India* v. *Chemical Construction Corporation*,[13] disputes and differences were to be settled by arbitration in conformity with the Rules of Arbitration of the International Chamber of Commerce, and the venue of the arbitration was to be in India. The proceedings before the arbitrators (it was conceded) were to be governed by the provisions of the Indian Arbitration Act, 1940. The contention was that some of the Rules of the ICC were inconsistent with the Indian Arbitration Act, 1940 and accordingly, the arbitration agreement itself was void being inconsistent with the provisions of law applicable in India and to enforce them would be contrary to public policy. The argument was rejected by a Division Bench of the Bombay High Court. The court examined the Rules of the ICC which were impugned and upheld their validity and applicability in India. It also held that "even if for the sake of argument any of these rules is void as being inconsistent with the law of a particular country, then *qua* the disputes which are governed by the law of that country such a rule has to be ignored and the provisions are clearly severable from the rest of the rules." Even the invalidity of any arbitral rule of procedure under the law of any particular country by which arbitration was to be governed did not affect the validity of the arbitration agreement and arbitration proceedings would have to be conducted in accordance with such of the rules framed by the ICC as were not inconsistent with the law of the country by which the arbitration proceedings were to be governed.

III. PUBLIC POLICY AND ENFORCEMENT OF AWARDS

A. Public sector companies in India have often benefited by the restrictive interpretation of the public policy defence in foreign courts – whilst enforcing

meeting costs of registration and making deposits of fees) in all cases where there are genuine disputes raised before foreign arbitral tribunals: i.e., where a foreign arbitration is not used as a device by parties to unlawfully remit monies abroad.

13. *Fertilizer Corporation of India* v. *Chemical Construction Corporation* (1973) 75 Bom LR 335.

international awards abroad. For instance, in 1981 the Fertilizer Corporation of India (FCI – a wholly-owned government company) petitioned the US District Court of Ohio for enforcement of an ICC award (in its favour) in the sum of US $300,000. The American company (IDI Management Inc.) against whom the award was enforceable asserted that the enforcement of the award would violate the public policy of the United States under Art. V(2)(*b*) inasmuch as the arbitrator nominated by the Indian company (FCI) had served as counsel for FCI in at least two other legal or arbitral proceedings which facts had not been disclosed to the American party. The District Court of Ohio rejected this defence holding:

> "The Court does not take lightly IDI's charge. In view of the unanimity of the Nitrophosphate Award, there is nothing to suggest actual bias or prejudice on Mr. Sen's part, yet we strongly believe that full disclosure of any possible interest or bias is the better rule whenever one is in a position to determine the rights of others. However, we do not find that nondisclosure of Mr. Sen's relationship with FCI has so tainted the proceedings as to nullify the award."[14]

The District Court also invoked the decision of the US Court of Appeals for the Second Circuit holding that the Convention's public policy defence should be construed narrowly (US Court of Appeals (2nd Cir.) 23 December 1974, *Parsons & Whittemore Overseas Co., Inc.*). The District Court quoted in particular the following passage:

> "Enforcement of foreign arbitral awards may be denied on this basis only where enforcement would violate the forum state's most basic notions of morality and justice."

They held that "the stronger public policy is that which favours arbitration both international and domestic."

B. The scope of Article V(2)(*b*) of the New York Convention – incorporated in Section 7(1)(*b*)(ii) of the Foreign Awards (Recognition and Enforcement) Act 1961 – has been specifically considered only in a few decisions. In *Mury Exportation* v. *Khaitan & Sons*,[15] the public policy defence was denied to an Indian party resisting enforcement of a foreign award in India. It was contended that if the foreign award was enforced in India it would defeat the Indian law of limitation. The High Court of Calcutta said that where parties chose by their contract that the arbitration would be in Paris (under the ICC Rules of Arbitration) they impliedly consented that the laws regulating the decision (including the law of limitation) would be the law of the forum and not Indian law. In *European Grain and Shipping Ltd.* v. *Seth Oil Mills Ltd.*,[16] a single judge of the High Court of Bombay (Pendse J.) granted the petition of the foreign party for the enforcement of an award in its favour under GAFTA Arbitration Rules. The petition for enforcement was filed under the Foreign Awards (Recognition and Enforcement)

---

14. *Yearbook Commercial Arbitration*, Vol. VII (1982) pp. 382–392.

15. AIR 1956 Cal. 644.

16. Unreported Decision dated 29 January 1983 (unrep.) of a single judge of the High Court of Bombay – extracts are reported in *Yearbook Commercial Arbitration*, Vol. IX (1984) pp. 411–415.

Act, 1961. The Indian Party had failed to supply to *European Grain* the agreed quantity of rice bran extractions under a sale contract of March 1976. *European Grain* informed *Seth Oil Mills* that the claim for damages would be referred to arbitration and proceeded to appoint its arbitrator under GAFTA. The Indian party (*Seth Oil Mills*) failed to appoint its arbitrator. The arbitration proceedings thereafter proceeded according to GAFTA Rules but *Seth Oil Mills* did not attend the arbitration proceedings in spite of being notified. By an award dated 17 May 1977 (an award without reasons) *Seth Oil Mills* was ordered to pay *European Grain*, £25,525 by way of damages. When they did not pay, *European Grain* filed a petition for enforcement of the award in the High Court of Bombay under the Foreign Awards (Recognition and Enforcement) Act, 1961. The High Court allowed the petition for enforcement overruling the plea of *Seth Oil Mills* that enforcement would be contrary to public policy. It was argued (by Seth Oil Mills) that before completion of the contract it had received from the Punjab State Government, a letter cancelling its export permit, thus making it impossible to complete the contract for export of rice bran, and this fact had been communicated to *European Grain*. Clause 18 of the contract expressly provided that in the case of prohibition of export, the contract had to be cancelled. It was submitted that taking these facts into consideration, it was obvious that the arbitrators had passed an award which was unsustainable in law and its enforcement would be contrary to public policy. The High Court rejected this contention, firstly on the ground that it was open to *Seth Oil Mills* to raise this contention before the arbitrator:

> "The contention of the respondent as to whether they were prevented from fulfilling the contract because of an executive act of the Government of Punjab was open for consideration before the arbitrator. The mere fact that the respondents did not choose to appear before the arbitrator and ascertain whether passing of the award was contrary to the law, and the failure of the respondents to fulfil the contract was for reasons mentioned in Clause 18 of the Contract."

And secondly, on the ground that the possibility of a party to the contract raising certain contentions before the arbitrator for the non-fulfilment of the contract was not sufficient to hold that the *enforcement* of the award was contrary to public policy:

> "Counsel for respondents made a valiant attempt to claim that though Sect. 7(1)(*b*)(ii) of the Act provides that the enforcement of the award should not be contrary to the public policy, still it is open for this court to consider whether passing of the award itself was contrary to public policy. It is not possible to accept this submission. It is possible that in a given case where the contract between the parties is totally illegal from its inception and in spite of it an award is passed, then the Court may very well refuse to enforce such an award as being contrary to public policy. But the mere fact that it was possible for the respondents to raise certain contentions before the arbitrator for non-fulfilment of the contract, is no ground to hold that enforcement of the award is contrary to public policy."

It was also contended that the failure to give reasons was sufficient to hold that the enforcement of the award would be contrary to public policy. This argument met the same fate:

> "There is no merit whatsoever in this contention. The Rules do not require the arbitrators to give any reasons and merely because the appeal is provided it does not require the arbitrators to set out the reasons. In any event, it is difficult to imagine how these grounds would suffice to claim that the enforcement of the Award could be contrary to the public policy."

A further consequential contention that the award did not reflect any material to support the basis of damages awarded in favour of *European Grain*, and that in the absence of there being such material pleaded before the court, the enforcement of the award would be contrary to public policy, was also rejected.

More recently, however, a single judge of another High Court[17] (the High Court of Delhi) refused to enforce an award made in London by the Court of Arbitration of the International Chamber of Commerce on the ground that its enforcement would violate Section 7(1)(*b*)(ii) of the Foreign Awards Act (implementing Articles V(2)(*b*) of the Convention). The contract was for supply of a specified quantity of steel coils by a government undertaking viz., the Steel Authority of India Ltd. (SAIL) to COSID (a New York corporation). The supplies were to be effected in two instalments. The plea of SAIL was that it was excused from performing the contract on the basis of the *force majeure* clause in the contract itself because of a ban imposed on exports of steel coils by the Government of India. The contention was disputed before the arbitrator by COSID which alleged breach of contract by SAIL and claimed damages. The arbitrator appointed by the International Chamber of Commerce upheld the claim of COSID. The judge (of the High Court of Delhi) held that although the question was raised before and decided by the arbitrator, it was not a specific question of law referred to the arbitrator and that the court could independently examine the aspect about the validity of the order of the Government of India banning exports in view of the provisions of Section 7(1)(*b*)(ii) of the Act (public policy). The arbitrator had held that the evidence produced in support of the ban did not have the force of law – and that (in his view) under Indian law, export could only be prohibited by a notification issued by the Central Government in the Official Gazette. The Attorney-General of India appearing for SAIL contended before the single judge that matters concerning import and export of goods were covered both by law and by the public policy of the country (governing imports and exports) as was current from time to time. When an order was made or a ban imposed by reason of priority for domestic needs on account of acute shortage of a commodity in the country such a matter would be a valid consideration of public good and therefore, of public policy. It was contended that a contract which was contrary to public policy was recognized as void under Section 23 of the Indian Contract Act 1872. The argument urged on behalf of COSID (before the High Court) that

17. COSID *Inc. & Anr.* v. *Steel Authority of India Ltd.* (unreported) – decision dated 12 July 1985 of a single judge of the High Court of Delhi in Suit 973A of 1982: now pending before an Appellate Bench of two judges of the same High Court. Extracts are reported in *Yearbook Commercial Arbitration*, Vol. XI (1986) pp. 502–507.

there was a distinction between domestic public policy and international public policy was not accepted. The judge whilst holding that the expression "public policy" under Section 7(1)(*b*)(ii) of the Act meant the public policy of India stated:

> "I also fail to understand what international public policy is involved in the present case which should have preference over the order of the Central Government banning export/shipment of HR Coils with immediate effect on the ground that there was acute shortage of this commodity in the country. If I have to accept the submission of Mr. Singhania on his concept of international public policy, as referred to above, then a foreign award like the present one has invariably to be enforced."

An appeal from the decision of the single judge has been taken and is admitted; it is now pending decision before a Division Bench of the same court – the High Court of Delhi. It is submitted that the single judge of the High Court has erroneously equated public policy with Indian national policy. The circumscribed public policy (*ordre public*) doctrine contemplated by the framers of the Convention has not been accepted. Obviously, Article V(2)(*b*) was not intended to offer the party who raised the plea of impossibility of performance before the arbitrators, a second chance before the court of enforcement. After all, the provision in the Article – and in the corresponding provision of the Indian Foreign Awards (Recognition and Enforcement) Act, 1961 – was solely designed to prevent enforcement of an award which, if it were a decree of the local court, would not and could not be enforced by the executing court as contrary to public policy. If a court in India were to hold finally that a specified event was not covered by a *force majeur* clause (in a particular contract) and passed a decree for the amount due, an executing court in India could not question the validity of that decree – as violating public policy. The real problem of course is that the decision of a foreign arbitral tribunal on points involved and raised before it is not regarded as having the same efficacy or validity as a decree or decision of an Indian court: this attitude is not peculiar to India. In *Mitsubishi Motor Corporation* v. *Soler* (cited above), the Supreme Court of the United States whilst permitting foreign arbitrators to proceed and adjudicate upon pleas regarding the effect of US antitrust laws on the contract has reserved the right of courts in the US to re-examine the award (when made) in the light of Article V(2)(*b*) of the New York Convention. Justice Blackmun speaking for the majority said:

> "Having permitted the arbitration to go forward, the national courts of the United States will have the opportunity at the award enforcement stage to ensure that the legitimate interest in the enforcement of the antitrust laws has been addressed. The Convention reserves to each signatory country the right to refuse enforcement of an award where the 'recognition or enforcement of the award would be contrary to the public policy of that country.' Art V(2)(*b*), 21 UST, at 2520. While the efficacy of the arbitral process requires that substantive review at the award-enforcement stage remain minimal, it would not require intrusive inquiry to ascertain that the tribunal took cognizance of the antitrust claims and actually decided them."

It does appear that even the Supreme Court of the United States is willing to cede jurisdiction of an antitrust claim or defence arising under domestic law to a foreign tribunal only if that Tribunal properly applies domestic law, and not otherwise!

C. The distinction between domestic public policy and international public policy has not been accepted in India – and is not likely to be accepted by Indian courts. The New York Convention itself leaves it to the discretion of the domestic court to refuse recognition of foreign arbitral awards where it finds that the recognition or enforcement of that award would be contrary "to the public policy *of that country*". In India contracts which the court regards as opposed to public policy are unenforceable and void.[18] Such contracts are generally those which involve: trading with the enemy, stifling criminal prosecutions, champerty and maintenance (i.e., financing litigation by a person who has no legal interest in it), contracts tending to interfere with the course of justice, agreements to procure marriages for reward, contracts in restraint of marriage and marriage agreements, agreements tending to create interest against duty, agreements transferring guardianship of infants and parental rights to third parties, trafficking by way of a sale of public offices, and agreements tending to create monopolies. Although the list of contracts opposed to public policy is not a closed one, courts in India are slow to invent new heads of public policy.[19]

In domestic arbitration in India certain matters are not referable to arbitration at all and awards adjudicating disputes under arbitral agreements relating to such matters would not be enforced: for instance, disputes regarding matrimonial matters, testamentary matters, matters relating to insolvency proceedings, or lunacy proceedings, questions relating to the guardianship of infants, questions relating to charities and charitable trusts, and agreements directed at stifling criminal proceedings.

All other matters of a civil nature can be validly referred to arbitration – these include *all* disputes of a commercial nature, and disputes regarding payment under promissory notes and other negotiable instruments and claims for compensatory damages in the nature of tort.[20] The fact that one of the parties to a commercial transaction contends that he has been discharged from the contract either by reason of *force majeure* or by subsequent illegality or the like would not make the dispute non-arbitrable.

---

18. Sect. 23 of the Indian Contract Act, 1872.

19. See *Gherulal Parakh* v. *Mahadeodas:* AIR 1959 SC 781. Subbarao. J. delivering the judgment of the Court said:
"Though the heads (of public policy) are not closed and though theoretically it may be permissible to evolve a new head under exceptional circumstances of a changing world, it is advisable in the interest of stability of society not to make any attempt to discover new heads in these days."

20. *Renusagar Power Co. Ltd.* v. *General Electric* cited above (AIR 1985 SC 1156). The ratio in the decision of the House of Lords in England – NOVA *Jersey Knit Ltd.* v. *Kammgarn Spinnerei* 1977 2 ALLER 463 HL (reversing a decision of the Court of Appeal) – to the effect that if bills of exchange were to contain an arbitration clause they would not be valid negotiable instruments has been doubted by the Supreme Court of India.

IV. CONCLUSION

In India, therefore, a foreign award would be enforceable and would be enforced under the law implementing the New York Convention, where it adjudicates on disputes arising out of contracts (commercial in nature) which contracts would not be regarded, under domestic law, as opposed to public policy under Section 23 of the Indian Contract Act, 1872.

In international commercial arbitration, a foreign award would not be regarded as contrary to public policy merely because the arbitral procedure was different from that prescribed in domestic arbitration, or because the Indian party has found it difficult to defend proceedings many thousands of miles away from its ordinary place of business. A foreign award would not be regarded as unenforceable merely because the Indian party could not conveniently assimilate and produce all its evidence before the foreign arbitral tribunal due to reluctance of witnesses in India to undertake the journey abroad (to depose to material facts), or because of non-availability or inadequacy of foreign exchange; nor because the foreign award contains no reasons, or awards the maximum amount stipulated in the contract by way of damages. It is submitted (notwithstanding the recent decision of a single judge of the High Court of Delhi) that under Indian law a foreign award would not be declared unenforceable merely because the foreign arbitral tribunal having power to interpret the contract has erroneously construed a *force majeure* clause contained in it, or after due consideration has held (albeit wrongly) that the proved circumstances of the case did not attract the provisions of that clause. Under the law in India, disputes as to whether performance of a commercial contract (containing an arbitration clause) has become impossible or by some subsequent event illegal or unlawful are arbitrable – consequently, an award determining such disputes is final and binding between the parties and enforceable in courts in India.

Public Policy as a Condition for Recognition and Enforcement of Foreign Court Judgments and Arbitral Awards in the USSR

*Konstantin L. Razumov**

Soviet law, as well as the law of most countries of the world, considers the compliance of foreign court judgments and arbitral awards with the public policy requirements of the respective country as a necessary condition for the recognition and enforcement of such judgments and awards. The competent authorities of the country where recognition or enforcement is sought (the country of recognition or enforcement) determine whether or not this condition has been followed on the basis of national rules, applicable international agreements and the practices adopted in that country for the application of the above rules.

The requirements to which foreign judgments and awards should correspond in order to be considered as complying with public policy, as a rule, are not identically formulated in the legislation of various countries.

In some countries, the law deals with the public policy in general.[1] In other countries, the legislation more or less specifies this notion.[2] However, even if the law does not provide at all for such a condition for enforcement (recognition), the compliance of foreign court judgments and arbitral awards with public policy is considered necessary by court practice and doctrine.[3]

In the Soviet Union, according to Article 63 of the Fundamentals of Civil Procedure, enforcement of foreign arbitral awards is provided for by respective agreements of the USSR with foreign states or by international conventions to which the USSR is a party. Since 1960, the Soviet Union has been a party to the New York Convention on the Recognition and Enforcement of Foreign Arbitral Awards of 10 June 1958, and has concluded a number of bilateral agreements on trade and shipping which contain a clause providing for the refusal of enforcement of arbitration awards which are found contrary to the public policy

* Professor of Law; Director, Arbitration Department at the USSR Chamber of Commerce and Industry, Moscow.

1. See, e.g., Sect. 797(7) of the Italian CCP, Sect. V(4)(1)(*a*) of the British Foreign Judgments (Reciprocal Enforcement) Act, 1933, Sect. 64 of the Czechoslovak Act No. 97/1963 on Private International Law and Procedure, etc.
2. See, e.g., Sect. 7 of the Indian Foreign Awards (Recognition and Enforcement) Act, 1961, Sect. 979 of the Iranian CC, Sect. 183(2)(3) of the CCP of the German Democratic Republic, etc.
3. Roth, G., *Vorbehalt des Orde Public gegenüber fremden gerichtlichen Entscheidungen.* Wurzburg, 1967, p. 3.

of the country where enforcement is sought (Austria, Cyprus, Federal Republic of Germany, Finland, Italy, Japan, Sweden, Switzerland).

An analogous rule may be found in Article V(2)(*b*) of the New York Convention of 1958, which provides for the possibility of refusing the recognition and enforcement of arbitral awards if the competent authority of the country where recognition and enforcement are sought finds that an award is contrary to the public policy of that country.

The above-mentioned Article 63 of the Fundamentals of Civil Procedure does not directly provide for the possibility of refusing recognition and enforcement of a foreign arbitral award if it is contrary to the public or social order of the country. It would be a mistake to conclude that the public policy rule may be applied in such a case by the Soviet Court. The public policy rule, however, may be applied by analogy with Article 128 of the Fundamentals of Civil Legislation stating that "Foreign Law is not applied if its application is contrary to the foundations of the Soviet systems".

It should be mentioned here that this problem will arise only in regard to arbitration awards made in a country which is not a party to the 1958 Convention.

When ratifying that Convention, the Presidium of the USSR Supreme Soviet declared that the Soviet Union "will apply the provisions of this Convention with regard to awards made in the territory of the States not party in the Convention on the basis of reciprocity only" (*Vedomosti* of the Supreme Soviet of the USSR, 1960, Nr. 46, Art. 421).

Lack of statutory definitions of public policy enables the competent authorities of the countries of enforcement to enjoy a wide discretion in determining the conformity of foreign arbitral awards with public policy. This conclusion is substantiated by the published court practice of a number of states.

It should be noted, also, that under the New York Convention, recognition and enforcement of awards may be refused not only because of public policy considerations of the country of enforcement (Art. V(2)(*b*)), but also due to the fact that the party against whom the award is invoked was not given proper notice of the arbitration proceedings (Art. V(1)(*b*)). Therefore, violation of the procedure for constituting the arbitral tribunal or for the notification of the defendant of the time and place of arbitration is not considered by the Convention as a violation of the public policy.

An analogous conclusion may be drawn from an analysis of many bilateral international agreements dealing with the procedure for the recognition and enforcement of foreign court judgments, where the requirement of timely notification of pending procedural actions is considered as a condition for the recognition or enforcement of judgments, but not as a condition of public policy. That can be seen clearly from a comparison of paragraphs 2 and 3 of Article 15 of the USSR – Iraq Agreement on Legal Assistance. Paragraph 2 of the above Agreement provides for the refusal of enforcement of judgments made in a foreign state due to a violation of the proper procedure for notification of the requirement to be present at the hearing. Paragraph 3 provides for the refusal of enforcement due to the judgment conflicting with the public policy of the country of enforcement.

The classification of untimely notification of the party as to time and place of court or arbitration proceedings as a public policy condition might give an opportunity to consider as such conditions other requirements in regard to recognition and enforcement of foreign judgments, e.g., the absence of another judgment concerning the same dispute, the compliance with jurisdiction rules, the legal force of the judgment sought to be recognized or enforced.

In this connection, it may be concluded that there is a tendency in international practice to consider the violation of procedural rights of the parties as an independent ground for the refusal of enforcement of foreign arbitral awards.

Thus, the violation of the procedural interests of a party against whom a judgment or an award was made is not a violation of public policy.

An analogous point of view was expressed in regard to the Moscow Convention on the Settlement by Arbitration of Civil Law Disputes Resulting from Relations of Economic and Scientific-Technical Cooperation of 26 May 1972.[4]

As described above, the process of determining whether a foreign award complies with the public policy requirements of the country of enforcement, is complicated and hardly predictable. Apparently, violations of public policy may include judgments concerning disputes out of relations which, in principle, can not be legally protected in the country of enforcement. This is precisely what is meant by Article 15(2) of the Code of Merchant Shipping prohibiting the application of foreign law if it is contrary to the foundations of the Soviet system.

In particular, it is a violation of public policy when a foreign jurisdiction binds the defendant to pay residents of a foreign state a certain amount of currency which cannot be transferred abroad under the law of the country of enforcement. It is evident that such a decision cannot be enforced, as it violates the laws and public policy of that country. In practice, a foreign judgment, delivered without regard to the prohibition by the competent state authority of the defendant's country to fulfil the defendant's and the plaintiff's obligation resulting in losses to the plaintiff, was also considered as violating the public policy of the enforcement country.

In this connection, an opinion advanced in foreign literature on the subject should be mentioned, an opinion according to which in those countries where there is a state monopoly of foreign trade, the refusal of the State to grant an export or import licence should not, as a rule, be considered as a circumstance relieving a state economic organization of that country from liability and in a foreign arbitration examining such a dispute, an award should be rendered in favor of the company suffering losses. We shall not deliberate here on the lack of a basis for such an approach from the point of view of the substantive law of various countries, including the USSR. If, however, in a foreign arbitration an award were to be rendered based on this erroneous approach, it will not be enforced in the Soviet Union since it will be considered as being contrary to Soviet public policy, namely, to the principle of separate civil property liability of Soviet foreign trade

4. See, Collection of the IV International Arbitration Congress Materials, Moscow, 1974, p. 419 (in Russian).

organizations for their own obligations for which the Soviet State carries no pecuniary (financial) responsibility.

In regard to the basic principles (Soviet public policy in the field of foreign trade) reference may also be made to the rules concerning the form and procedure for signing foreign trade transactions. The form of foreign trade transactions made by Soviet organizations and the procedure for their signing are determined by USSR legislation irrespective of the place of conclusion.[5]

Thus, if in a foreign arbitration an award is rendered in a case where a Soviet foreign trade organization has participated without taking into account the above provision and a foreign trade transaction concluded in violation of the established procedure is held to be valid, such an award can not be enforced in the USSR since it is contrary to the public policy.

One more aspect of the problem "arbitration – public policy" should be noted. In examining a particular case and rendering an award that will be enforced in a foreign state, the arbitral tribunal may not ignore the public policy of that state. It is necessary to be especially careful in motivating the award when the defendant pleads that the award will not be enforced because the arbitration tribunal is not competent to entertain the dispute between the parties. In this connection, a case considered by the Foreign Trade Arbitration Commission involving a Soviet foreign trade organization and an Italian firm may be of interest.

The Soviet foreign trade organization brought an action at the FTAC against an Italian firm. The latter, in its reply, asserted, *inter alia*, that the arbitration clause in the contract was invalid under the Italian law, the law of the place where the contract had been concluded: as a part of the general conditions of the contract unilaterally determined by the seller in his standard form, the clause was not confirmed by the defendant in writing as required by Articles 1341, 1342 of the Italian Civil Code. The firm also stated that the award of the arbitration tribunal based on such an arbitration clause would not be enforced in Italy since it would be contrary to the public policy of that country.

After examination of the documents the FTAC established that originals of the contract presented in the course of hearings showed that it had been concluded as an independent agreement, conditions mutually agreed upon by both parties.

The Commission took into account that the validity of the arbitration clause in the contract concluded between the parties in conflict should be fully and unconditionally recognized under Article 21 of the Soviet-Italian Agreement on Trade and Shipping of 1948, according to which the Contracting Parties agreed to recognize any clause on the arbitration of disputes relating to trade transactions concluded by their citizens, organizations and entities. Since the arbitration clause provided for the examination of disputes by the FTAC, the FTAC started the proceedings and considered the case on the merits.

Hence, the Commission acted on the basis of the priority of the provisions of the international agreement over the domestic Italian legislation that required special procedure for the confirmation of the validity of an arbitration clause.

5. See, the Decree of the USSR Council of Ministers "On the Procedure for Signing Foreign Trade Transactions" of 14 February 1978 (Collection of Decrees of the USSR Government, 1979, No. 19. Art. 121).

Stating that the form of the arbitration clause complies with the requirements of the Soviet-Italian Trade Agreement, the Commission, therefore, rejected the defendant's argument that recognition of the validity of the arbitration clause drawn up without regard to the requirements of the Italian legislation would be contrary to the public policy of Italy.

It should be noted, as a conclusion, that in the interest of stability and certainty in international trade relations and with the aim of further recognition and promotion of arbitration as the way of settling commercial disputes which is best suited to contemporary international trade, it is necessary to employ a very restrictive construction of international multilateral and bilateral conventions and agreements providing for the possibility of refusing enforcement of foreign arbitral awards because of public policy considerations.

The Application by the Arbitrator of Public Policy Rules to the Substance of the Dispute

*Ireneu Strenger**

I. INTRODUCTORY REMARKS

The subject is very important insofar as public policy strongly influences the actions of arbitrators, not only concerning the procedural development but also – and especially – concerning the application of the law that is to govern the dispute.

Public policy, not only in Brazil but also in other countries, being rather complex to be granted a comprehensive definition, results many times in awkward situations, hard to cope with.

The great plague which affects public policy as a legal institution is its strong social and political connotation. Often enough, the application of public policy results from expressions which are both equivocal and not precisely inserted in the law; such expressions admit a diversity of interpretations which may often be subjective.

If it would be possible to mention a utopian thought, we would say that it would be preferable not to have "public policy", since its presence is an obstacle to the application of foreign law, a circumstance which directly affects the scope of private international law and the dynamics of international relations.

Brazil is particularly sensitive to the effects of public policy in law, not being in any way grounded on concepts that might be useful for the creation of a general rule; there is not even a well-formed explicit legal expertise concerning the subject.

Legal dispositions are merely general concepts, leaving the judge a broad field in assessing the incidence of public policy as an exception to the application of foreign law.

A living example of such an assertion is Article 17 of the Introductory Law to the Brazilian Civil Code (*Lei de introducâo ao código civil*) which reads as follows:

> "Laws, acts and decisions of another country, as well as any statements of will, have no effect in Brazil when being contrary to national sovereignty, public policy or *bonos mores*."

This is a typical example of the extreme terminological broadness of legal concepts, leaving an open field for its effective application.

---

* Professor of International Private Law at the Law Faculty of the University of Sao Paulo.

The effect of all public policy exceptions is, basically, to offer firm soil for some territorialistic trends in the solution of conflicts of laws. In determining the character of public policy rules in private international law, three versions of it may be presented: firstly, public policy rules as *exceptions*, insofar as they acknowledge as a rule the *extraterritoriality*; secondly, public policy rules as *territorial rules*, because they are enforceable within the whole territory of the State, with exclusion of any other competent law; thirdly, public policy rules as *changeable and contemporary*, resulting from the fact that they may vary both in time and in space, owing to the diversity of criteria, both legal and judicial, prevailing in each country.

These characters are evidence of how difficult it is, if not altogether impossible, to conciliate national and transnational concerns, in order to establish a clear interpretative methodology, as well as to identify the essential point, in order to define public policy.

II. NATIONAL PUBLIC POLICY AND INTERNATIONAL PUBLIC POLICY

Contemporary legal systems specifically make distinctions between national public policy and international public policy, as is the case in France where such a bipartition is widely known and where there is a new law on arbitration.

In Brazil, on the other hand, not only is the legal *régime* of arbitration strictly linked to the territory, but it is also structured in accordance to strict formal provisions of mandatory rules, thus setting aside any possibility of absorption of foreign law, in spite of certain new tendencies resulting from judgments issued by the *Supremo Tribunal Federal* (Federal Supreme Court).

In any case, the Brazilian legal system is only acquainted with the so-called international public policy owing to the fact that it is mentioned in the *Código Bustamante*, the famous La Habana Treaty of 1928. This Treaty has not had any effect on judgments and is almost completely unknown in relation to international disputes.

Brazilian legal expertise is not especially extensive in the study of this subject. Personally, anyway, we have pleaded for a distinction between national and international public policy, mainly because legislators, when issuing a new rule, do so because it pertains to the interest of the society that a specific thing, person or obligation be regulated by the law in a precise way. But, in the great majority of cases, if it is necessary for the society to have a mandatory rule, it does not seem appropriate that such a rule be concretely formulated; such a rule adopts this or that content. It is this way because, in the great majority of cases, the commonwealth is concerned about the certainty of juridical obligations, but not in a specific appearance of such certainty.

In these circumstances, the understanding prevails that no contrary will of the parties and no contrary provision of a foreign law may gain the upper hand, within the limits of the territory of one State, to a correspondent provision of territorial law.

Although the distinction may – and should – be admitted in respect of this dichotomy between national and international public policy, Brazil withholds from accepting this distinction in its legal system.

This attitude has lead the Supreme Court of Brazil to a few contradictions, not knowing how to distinguish national public policy from international public policy, a few times extremely liberal, other times extremely strict in the acceptance or refusal of *exequatur* for foreign arbitral awards.

III. BRAZILIAN ARBITRAL TRADITION

Brazil has a poor tradition in the practice of arbitration, in spite of the fact that the *Código de processo civil* (Civil Procedure Code) has accepted arbitration as one of the ways for the solution of disputes.

This circumstance made possible the acknowledgement of foreign arbitral awards, which are related by nature to judicial decisions and which have similar power. This, in turn, makes possible the enforcement of such decisions in Brazil, in their full contents, but with strong and frequent hindrances resulting from national public policy, especially when the foreign arbitral award is not followed by a judicial *exequatur* or acknowledgement by the courts in the seat of the arbitration.

This lack of customary practice of arbitration brings, as a result, a certain instability in the decisions, sometimes leaning towards absolutism, other times leaning towards relativism, in respect to the matters which come from the foreign court, in the search of enforcement of such judgments.

In the development of this paper there is no room for checking procedural matters, but, foremost, we would like to concentrate on the problem of the substance of contracts, where a provision has been made for the settlement by arbitration of any eventual dispute between the parties.

In a first approach, we may, *a priori*, state that the principle of the autonomy of the will (*lex voluntatis*) has made great steps forward within the Brazilian legal system, in spite of the lack of express legal provisions, of mandatory rules or resulting from an option for the performance of the autonomy of the will. However, a strong tendency can be noticed to block the will of the parties, easily alleging a violation of public policy, such as was current practice until about ten years ago.

This practice has doubtlessly prevailed in international trade agreements, and the reason for this seems to be the acceptance or even the submission to current practices in international trade, embodied in a true *lex mercatoria* which is increasingly being applied in Brazil.

All these circumstances lead to a result which is already being clearly felt: the choice of the applicable law and the choice of the competent jurisdiction is largely adopted by specific clauses in international trade agreements.

Thus, if we admit the conception that *lex mercatoria* is a body of non-referring-to-a-State material-rules, which aim at the regulation of international economic relations, we will come to the conclusion that, inevitably, the countries will tend increasingly to adopt a notion of international public policy, not linked, progressively, to the so-called national public policy.

This does not mean that it will be necessary to have a uniform system, but that a natural *consensus* at an international level will coincide with the findings of the investigation made by Berthold Goldman (*Recueil des Cours*, 1963, page 430ff.) stressing the tendency which reflects a careful abeyance of the rule *pacta sunt servanda*, while asserting: "*on ne voit pas pourquoi ils n'auraient pas pour effet d'exclure les dispositions contraires d'un droit national, sous prétexte qu'il a été choisi par les parties; c'est, en effet, la fonction habituelle de l'ordre public qui s'exerce en droit international privé, quelle que soit la règle de rattachement ayant donné compétence à une loi déterminée et, en particulier, lorsqu'il s'agit de la loi d'autonomie applicable à un contrat*".

In this sense, when Professor Pieter Sanders states the question if arbitrators should apply public policy rules from a legal system different from the one primarily governing the contract, we answer, having in view the Brazilian practice, that, fundamentally, arbitrators should apply public policy rules governing the contract, although such a judicial attitude does not avoid the possibility that the award may be rendered unenforceable in regard to public policy rules at the place of enforcement.

Such an assertion also entails the impossibility of conceiving an agreement entirely alien to any national legal system.

It would be perfect if the arbitrator or the arbitrators knew the trends prevailing in the countries of the parties to the dispute, while ascertaining the character of the public policy rules, in order to avoid unsolvable situations at the enforcement of the decision. For instance, in Brazil, the prohibition of remittance or the agreement dealing with the remittance of royalties above 5% is a mandatory rule. Imagine that an arbitral award might adopt a higher level, because it is possible, in accordance with the national legal system of the country of the creditor; obviously such an arbitral award would be impossible to enforce in Brazil.

It seems, in this sense, that the performance of the arbitrator should not be restricted to the terms of the agreement. If the parties have chosen the applicable law, or if the applicable law results from the interpretation of the will of the parties, in any case, it will be necessary to check the validity of such a decision, in the light of the public policy of the national law which governs the legal obligation.

Another important aspect that should be considered is to what extent the autonomy of the will is acceptable. It seems reasonable that if parties choose as applicable law the law of a third country, in order to avoid their own national, excessively strict, rules, an invalid decision may result from the acknowledgement of fraud. Such is the case in the example suggested by Professor Sanders of a French company and German company making a contract under Swiss law, and fixing the place of arbitration in Switzerland, because, they admit, the arbitrator will not take into consideration the EEC Rules on competition as a French or German judge would do.

IV. CONCLUSION

Taking international trade as a point of view, we are bound to accept the statement that the arbitrator is not a guardian of public policy, but, on the other hand, nobody can deny that this power may be related to it, if we take into consideration that it is not the choice of a system of conflicts of law that matters, but the duty of taking public policy into consideration, keeping in mind that an international arbitrator does not have just one *lex arbitri*, but many.

With this purpose, I have summarized how the Brazilian tradition on arbitration stimulates such interpretations, which may not yet be understood in accordance with legal expertise regarding well-established prevailing jurisprudence, but reflect its main guidelines, within the realm of the poor Brazilian arbitral tradition.

International Arbitration and Public Policy. Comment on the Legal Practice in the German Democratic Republic

*Heinz Strohbach**

In the German Democratic Republic (GDR), disputes arising out of international commercial contracts and similar economic transactions are almost always settled by arbitration. Fortunately, at least for the arbitrators, there has been no need to make use of the procedure for setting aside an arbitral award by the court for many years. Moreover, there have been no cases reported where the recognition and enforcement of foreign awards gave rise to problems. Therefore, no judgments of higher courts and especially of the Supreme Court of the GDR are available on matters of public policy in arbitration. Thus, I only can comment on these questions from the point of view of an arbitrator without a body of relevant court judgments as back up.

A. PUBLIC POLICY AND ARBITRABILITY OF DISPUTES

The Court of Arbitration attached to the Chamber of Foreign Trade of the GDR has administered arbitration exclusively in non-domestic cases for more than 30 years. This has entailed a caseload of about 7,800 files. During this period there has been no case amongst these files with a State or Governmental body or similar authority as a party to the dispute.

The parties who appear in arbitrations held in this country are, on the one hand, foreign companies and, on the other hand, industrial enterprises or their specialized foreign-trade agencies, based on common (state) property and organized as legal persons according to the law of the GDR. Questions concerning public policy with regard to the legal status of these parties have never arisen in the last two decades. Nor have there been foreign exchange regulation disputes nor competition disputes. However, from time to time the question of arbitrability of industrial property rights arises.

According to Article 30(3) of the Act on the Constitution of the Courts of the German Democratic Republic (Judicature Act) of 27 September 1974, "*exclusive*

* President of the Court of Arbitration attached to the Chamber of Foreign Trade of the German Democratic Republic in Berlin; Deputy Director of the Institute for Foreign and Comparative Law (Academy of Political and Legal Science of the German Democratic Republic in Potsdam-Babelsberg); member of ICCA.

jurisdiction, in first instance in matters of *patent*, *design*, *trademark* and copyright law is vested in the Leipzig County Court . . ." (emphasis added). Consequently Article 37 of the same Act describes the competence of the Supreme Court as follows (*inter alia*):

> "The Supreme Court is competent . . . as court of second instance for hearing and deciding on the legal remedies of protest, appeal and complaint against decisions made by the county courts . . . as well as on the remedy of appeal against an award by the Board for nullity declarations of the Patent Office . . .".

The Act on Judicial Procedure in Civil, Family and Labor Matters (Civil Procedure Code) of 19 June 1975 also deals with questions of exclusive jurisdiction of the courts. In this connection, mention may be made of the two paragraphs of Article 22:

> "(1) Jurisdiction on claims arising from *rights to land or to a building* belongs exclusively to that district court in whose circuit the land or building is situated. . . .
> (2) Claims for compensation of damage or costs arising from pollution of territorial waters, inland lakes or rivers, are within the exclusive jurisdiction of that district court in whose circuit the pollution has taken place."

Finally, I may quote one of the basic rules of the international procedural law of the GDR contained in Article 185(2) of the Civil Procedure Code; it reads as follows:

> "Insofar as an action does not come within the exclusive jurisdiction of the courts of the German Democratic Republic, cognizance over and decision in a civil matter may, by written agreement between parties, whereof one has his domicile, abode or seat outside the German Democratic Republic be conferred to the jurisdiction of the courts of another State or . . . to an arbitration court."

From the legal provisions quoted above it follows, in my opinion, that, where no exclusive jurisdiction has been attributed to the courts of the GDR, if one of the parties has its domicile or seat outside the GDR, the parties may refer to arbitration. On the other hand, where exclusive jurisdiction is attributed to the courts, it would be against public policy to refer to arbitration.

Under the law of the GDR those disputes are not arbitrable the decision of which might lead directly to amendments of state registers or state records or to other means of state activities. Only the courts can ask the relevant state agency for entries in the register of patents, trademarks, etc. or in the land register, etc. Or to say it in the words of Professor Böckstiegel:

> "Since such rights are established by acts of state in a specific procedure established by each state . . . a dispute settlement procedure in which this state is not involved . . . cannot decide finally. The state who grants the right has also the authority to determine the procedure in which the validity of the right is decided in case of a dispute."

For the very same reason special kinds of water pollution disputes are not arbitrable, because they are, more or less, strongly connected with state activities in the field of environment protection.

And now the other side of the coin. Insofar as industrial property disputes do not influence entries in the register of patents, such disputes are arbitrable. Thus, the Court of Arbitration attached to the Chamber of Foreign Trade of the GDR has heard and decided disputes arising out of contracts of license.

Controversies on the use of a license, on breach of contract by revealing secret information obtained from the licensor, on damages and costs, etc. may be the subject of arbitral proceedings. Analogously the same principle applies to real estate disputes. It is worth mentioning that the Moscow Convention of 1972 on the settlement of civil law disputes by arbitration was unofficially supplemented by a list of non-arbitral subject matters. This list, established by the member-countries of CMEA, mentions in the first place disputes on the validity of patents, trademarks and similar rights.

B. PUBLIC POLICY AND ARBITRAL PROCEDURE

Arbitrators have to comply at least with the mandatory provisions of the law applicable to the procedure in force at the venue of arbitration.

The GDR law on (international) commercial arbitration (Ordinance on Arbitration Proceedings of 18 December 1975) follows the territorial approach, i.e., the Ordinance applies to all kinds of arbitration (permanent or administered arbitration, *ad hoc* arbitration) held within the boundaries of the GDR. Parties may not derogate from the mandatory provisions of this Ordinance.

But what are the mandatory provisions? The best way to discover them is to look at the grounds for setting aside an arbitral award or to deny its enforceability. According to these provisions (Article 24, Setting Aside of the Award; Article 28, Rejection of the Enforcement Declaration) all procedural rules which enable a party to make use of his right to present his case or to defend himself may be considered as mandatory. As an example, the due process rule of Article 15 of the Ordinance is quoted:

> "The arbitration court shall grant to the parties to the proceedings an opportunity to comment on mutual pleadings, on evidence given and on the settling of the dispute."

Another example is that under GDR law it is also mandatory that the award contain reasons.

Within the boundaries of these basic provisions of the GDR law on arbitration, parties are free to agree on arbitration rules, e.g., the Rules of the Court of Arbitration attached to the Chamber of Foreign Trade of the GDR if this arbitration body is approached, or the ECE or UNCITRAL Arbitration Rules in *ad hoc* arbitration.

Article 5 of the Ordinance provides:

> "(1) The procedure before a permanent arbitration court shall be determined by its arbitration rules.

(2) The procedure before a non-permanent arbitration court (*ad hoc* arbitration) shall be determined by an agreement between the parties to the proceedings. They may refer in their agreement to the model rules of arbitration which are customary in international commercial relations."

One may note here Section 12(2) of the Rules of the above-mentioned arbitration court which reads as follows:

"The Arbitration Court applies to the proceedings the Rules of the Arbitration Court. Beyond, it observes the legal provisions of the GDR concerning arbitration proceedings. *Otherwise the arbitration committee operates at its own discretion.*" (emphasis added)

Furthermore the grounds for setting aside an award or denying its enforceability established by the law of the GDR are more or less identical with the grounds listed in Article V of the New York Convention. Thus in practice there is no perceptible difference between the few mandatory rules in the arbitration law of the GDR, on the one hand, and public policy rules concerning the arbitral procedure, on the other hand. There is only one weak example showing a slight difference between international and internal public policy: violation of the requirement to give reasons for the award is a ground for setting aside an arbitral award rendered in the GDR. But this omission does not prevent recognition and enforcement of a foreign award, rendered in a country which does not require reasons to be given, if such recognition and enforcement is sought under Article V of the New York Convention 1958, the GDR being a party to this convention. In a case like this, the more restricted criterion of international public policy is applied.

For us, it is quite clear that arbitral proceedings held in the State X have, at least to some extent, to comply with the law on arbitration of State Y, if the winner of the case wishes to have the award recognized and enforced in the State Y. Not complying with mandatory procedural provisions of State Y does not *eo ipso* mean an infringement of this State's international public policy. The concept of international or real public policy is narrower than the concept of internal public policy, which is just another label for national arbitration and/or procedural rules.

The question is linked to the so-called problem of "delocalization" of arbitration. Up to now, arbitrators in the GDR saw no need for such a vehicle to promote commercial arbitration.

C. THE APPLICATION BY THE ARBITRATOR OF NATIONAL PUBLIC POLICY RULES

First of all it is to be emphasized that decisions of arbitrators of the Court of Arbitration attached to the Chamber of Foreign Trade of the GDR, as well as of similar arbitration courts in other member-countries of CMEA, are based on the relevant substantive law. Arbitrators fully recognize an unlimited party autonomy in choosing the applicable law. If no choice-of-law clause is agreed upon by the parties, the applicable substantive law is ascertained by using conflict of law rules. It is true that arbitrators of a permanent court of arbitration more or less stick to the private international law of the venue (choice of law rules of the *lex decisionis*).

Another question is the impact of public policy rules on the applicable substantive law. The term public policy rules is probably just as unclear as other terms like *loi de police*, immediately applicable law or absolutely mandatory law. Texts of The Hague Conference on Private International Law usually describe these rules as law of the forum which must be applied even to international situations irrespective of rules of conflict of laws. Sometimes this description includes also the possible application of such law of another State having a sufficiently close connection with a case.

Arbitrators of the Court of Arbitration attached to the Chamber of Foreign Trade of the GDR sometimes apply Foreign Trade Regulations of the GDR concerning the management of foreign trade when a GDR enterprise is a party to the dispute and the question of its competence to deal in foreign trade is involved. Comparable regulations of foreign States have not been applied in this arbitration practice. However, in dealing with breach of contract and hardship, arbitrators usually have taken into consideration the effects and results of such foreign regulations, e.g., denial of granting governmental licences for special kinds of contracts, provided that these regulations do not run counter to established rules and practices of international law.

In general, arbitrators are reluctant to go beyond contract clauses, trade usages and the civil, trade or commercial law applicable to the contrast in dispute when they have to decide on the case.

D. THE ARBITRATOR AND THE "REALLY" INTERNATIONAL PUBLIC POLICY

As to this question there are no experiences available in the practice of settling disputes by arbitration administered by the Chamber of Foreign Trade of the GDR. From our side there is no possibility to contribute to the arbitral case law on this issue.

Up to now the concept of "really" international public policy, i.e., the idea of having a kind of rules separated either from a given national legal system or from international conventions already in force, has met with doubts, scruples and hesitation. The realization of such a concept, in our view, makes it unforeseeable for the parties to know what norms, rules, criteria or standards the arbitrators are going to use in deciding the case. This means a disadvantage for the parties to the dispute.

Above all, this concept implies an evaluation of national legal systems or at least of their civil, trade or commercial law as to whether or not it is in contradiction with such artificial criteria composing "really" international public policy. In our world of today with its different and even contrary socio-economic and political systems and interests one of the main achievements is to proceed from the principle of equality of these "really" existing systems and their legal reflections in national laws. Arbitration should not question this achievement.

List of Written Communications

Working Group II
Alan Redfern
"International Public Policy: The New Standard"

General
V. S. Deshpande
"The Place of Arbitration"
Salah Al-Hejailan
"The Future of Euro-Arab Arbitration"
Satya R. Kar Roy
"Need to Economize Costs in International Commercial Arbitrations"

List of Oral Interventions to Working Group II

Wednesday, 7 May 1986

Dr. Th. Donner (Czechoslovakia)
Dr. Gyula Gál (Hungary)
Prof. Jürgen Lebuhn (FR Germany)
Arthur T. von Mehren (USA)
Heribert Golsong (USA)
Prof. Berthold Goldman (France)
Dul Chand Singhania (India)
Sarosh R. Zaiwalla (UK)
Dr. Herbert A. J. Nolst Baanders (Netherlands)
William L. Craig (France)
Carlos J. Bianchi (USA)
Hilmar Räschke-Kessler (FR Germany)
Dr. Julian D. M. Lew (UK)

Thursday, 8 May 1986

Pierre Bellet (France)
Charles N. Brower (Netherlands)
Prof. Fabio Bortolotti (Italy)
Prof. Berthold Goldman (France)
Dr. Gyula Gál (Hungary)
Arthur T. von Mehren (USA)
Prof. Dr. Udo Kornblum (FR Germany)
Jean-Claude Goldsmith (France)
William L. Craig (France)
Prof. Lars Hjerner (Sweden)
Dr. Julian D. M. Lew (UK)

Friday, 9 May 1986

Prof. Tudor R. Popescu (Romania)
Dr. Herbert A. J. Nolst Baanders (Netherlands)
Dr. Angelo Pesce (Italy)
Prof. Philippe Fouchard (France)
Robert B. von Mehren (USA)
Prof. Claude Reymond (Switzerland)
Michel Virally (Netherlands)
Dr. Jürgen Dohm (Switzerland)
Prof. Hans van Houtte (Belgium)

Arthur T. von Mehren (US)
Prof. Lars Hjerner (Sweden)
Thomas W. Hill (US)
Prof. Fabio Bortolotti (Italy)

List of Participants

Algeria

Djouadi, M. Ahmed
Attaché de Direction
SONATRACH, Dir.-Générale
10 Rue du Sahara
Alger

Haroun, Ali M.
Avocat, Haron & Bendimerad
Rue Ali Bomendjel 5
Alger

Kadi, Abdellatir
Avocat
21, Rue Ben M'Hidi
Alger

Argentina

Boggiano, Antonio
Lawyer, Professor
Marval & O'Farrell
Carlos Pellegrini 885
Buenos Aires 1338

Grigera Naón, Prof. Dr. Horacio A.
Professor of Private Int'l Law, Univ. of Buenos Aires; Attorney
José E. Uriburu 1318 PB
Buenos Aires 1114

Australia

De Fina, A.
Director, Australian Centre for International Commercial Arbitration
6th Floor, Building B, World Trade Centre
Melbourne 3005

Austria

Friedberg, Dr. Axel E.
Gonzagagasse 3
Vienna A-1010

Baier, Dr. Anton
Lawyer
Führichgasse 6
Vienna A-1010

Cihlar, Barbara
LLM
Kohlmarkt 4/19
Vienna A-1010

Fritsch, Dr. Friedrich
Rechtsanwalt
Dominikanerbastei 4
Vienna A – 1010

Herrmann, Dr. Gerold H.
Senior Legal Officer
UNCITRAL Secretariat
Vienna International Center, Rm E-0443
P.O. Box 500
Vienna A – 1400

Melis, Dr. Werner
ICCA member; Chairman, Arbitration Centre
Austrian Federal Economic Chamber
Wiedner Hauptstrasse 63
P.O. Box 190
Vienna A – 1045

Mosing, Dr. Friedrich
Attorney
Mölkerbastei 5
Vienna A – 1010

Neuteufel, Dr. Kurt
Secretary, Court of Arbitration
Vienna Commodity Exchange
(Wiener Warenbörse)
Wipplingerstrasse 34
Vienna A – 1011

Schwank, Dr. Friedrich J.
Law Offices of Dr. F. Schwank
Stock Exchange Building
Wipplingerstrasse 34
Vienna A– 1011

Weiss-Tessbach, Dr. iur. Oskar
Partner, Weiss-Tessbach Galle Benn-Ibler
Krilyszin & Gassauer
Rotenturmstrasse 13
Vienna A – 1010

Belgium

Brody, Laurence B.
Partner (ret.), Coudert Brothers
10 Rue du Magistrat
B-1050 Brussels

Dieryck, Christian
Partner, Kegels, Dieryck Van Looveren
Mechelsesteenweg 196
B-2018 Antwerp

Leroy, Philippe
Coupure 5
B-9000 Ghent

Schwartz, Eric A.
Partner, Law Offices of S. G. Archibald
30 Avenue Marnix, Boîte 7
B-1050 Brussels

Van Crombrugghe, Nicole
Lawyer, Lafili & Van Crombrugghe
6 Dreve des Renards, Boîte 11
B-1180 Brussels

Van Houtte, Prof. Hans K.
Professor of Law (Louvain)
Attorney, Coppens Horsmans & Malherbe
385 Avenue Louise, Boîte 1
B-1050 Brussels

Bulgaria

Popov, Lyubomir, K.
Professor, University of Sofia
Bd. Tolbuchin 61
Sofia 1000

Canada

Alary, Rene-C.
Lawyer, De grandpre Godin & Associés,
800 Victoria Square
P.O. Box 108
Montreal
QU H4Z 1C2

Alvarez, Henri C.
Lawyer, Russel & Dumoulin
1700–1075 West Georgia Street
Vancouver
BC V6E 3G2

Antaki, Prof. Nabil
President, Centre d'arbitrage commercial international au Canada (CACIC), Quebec
Professor, Law Fac. Université Laval
Cité universitaire
Quebec
QU G1K 7P4

Buchanan, John N.
Lawyer, Spiegel Sohmer
5 Place Ville Marie
Montreal
QU H3B 2G2

Chiasson, Edward C.
Partner, Ladner Downs
1708 Allison Road
Vancouver
BC V6T 1S9

Christmann, John H.
Arbitrator, Partner, Arbitration International-Mediation
50 Quebec Avenue, Apt. 2401
Toronto
Ont. M6P 4B4

Combs, John W.
President, John W. Combs Ltd.
82 Bloor Street
Toronto
Ont. M5S 1L9

Cosman, Robert W.
Lawyer, Arbitrators Institute of Canada
Fasken & Calvin, Barristers & Solicitors
P.O. Box 30
Toronto Dominion Centre
Toronto
Ont. M5K 1C1

Davidson, Prof. Paul J.
Secretary, Canadian Arbitration Conciliation and Amicable Composition Centre
Department of Law
Carleton University
Ottawa
Ont. K1S 5B6

Davies, Douglas C.
Consultant
11 Edgecombe Avenue
Toronto
Ont. M4N

Gait, Hilary M.,
John W. Combs Ltd.
82 Bloor Street West, Suite 200
Toronto
Ont. M5S-1L9

Keefe, John A.
Lawyer, Goodman & Goodman
20 Queen Street West
P.O. Box 30
Toronto
Ont. M5H 1V1

Kos-Rabcewicz Zubkowski, Prof. Dr. Ludwik J.
President, Canadian Arbitration Conciliation & Amicable Composition Centre
14 Henderson Ave s. 20
Ottawa
Ont. K1N 7P1

Lalonde, Marc
Lawyer, Stikeman Elliott
1155 Dorchester Blvd. West, 39th floor
Montreal,
QU H3B 3V2

McKelvey, E. Neil
Partner, McKelvey Macaulay Machum
44 Prince William Street
P.O. Box 7289, Sta. A
Saint John
NB E2L 4S6

McLaren, Prof. Richard H.
Faculty of Law,
University of Western Ontario
315 Regent Street
London
Ont. N6A 2H3

Mendes, Prof. Errol P.
Professor of Int'l Business Law
Faculty of Law
University of Western Ontario
London
Ont. N6A 3K7

Pomerleau, Manon
Lawyer, Molpecères Zikovsky Pomerleau
225, rue Nôtre-Dame
Quest Bureau 230
Montreal
QU H2Y 1T4

Prujener, Prof. Alain Y.
Vice President,
Centre d'arbitrage commercial international au Canada, CACIC, Quebec;
Professor, Law Fac. Université Laval
Cité universitaire
Quebec
QU G1K 7P4

Revay, Stephen G.
President, Revay & Associés Ltd.
4333 St. Catherine St. West
Montreal
QU H3Z 1P9

Smith, Hon. Brian R. D.
Attorney General, Province of British Colombia
232 Parliament Buildings
Victoria
BC V8V 1X4

Switzer, Ross G.
Partner, Ladner Downs
4227 West 15th
Vancouver
BC V6R 3A7

Thompson, Bonita
Senior Solicitor, Ministry of Attorney General
1301 865 Hornby Street
Vancouver
BC V6Z 1H4

Vandernoot, Henry J.
Chairman of the Board, Franki Canada Ltd.
4795 St. Catherine St. West
Westmount (Montreal)

Chile

Bierwirth, Emilio,
Vice President
Santiago Chamber of Commerce
Baztan 3153
Santiago

Eyzaguirre, Dr. Rafael E.
President, Inter-American Commercial Arbitration Commission; ICCA member
Moneda 1160,
11th Floor
Santiago de Chile

Oyarzun, José
Secretary, Inter-American Commercial Arbitration Commission
Casilla 1015,
Santiago

China, P.R.

Li, Xiaoming
Beijing

Tang, Houzhi
Deputy Secr. Gen., Foreign & Economic Trade Arbitration Commission,
China Council for the Promotion of Int'l Trade; ICCA member
1 Fuxingmen Wai Street
Beijing

Colombia

Bernal, Camilo
Legal Advisor, Empresa de Energía de Bogotá
Av. El Dorado No. 55–51
Bogotá

Czechoslovakia

Bubnik, Dr. iur. Gerhardt
Law Offices No. 1
Narodni tr. 32
Prague 1 116 66

Donner, Dr. iur Theodor
Attorney at Law
Law Offices No. 1
Narodni tr. 32
Prague 1 116 66

Hanák, Dr. Svetozar
Director, Czechoslovak Chamber of Commerce; ICCA member
Tr – SNB 35
Prague 10100

Klein, Dr. iur. Bohuslav
Director Legal Services, Czechoslovak Chamber of Commerce & Industry
Argentinska 38,
Prague 7 17005

Vojvodik, Dr. iur. Lubomir
Lawyer, Foreign Trade Corp.
Skodaexport
Vaclavske nam. 56
Prague 113 32

Denmark

Gulmann, Claus
Dean of Law School
Copenhagen University, Councellor to Denmark Provincial Chamber of Commerce
Emiliekildevej 7
Klampenborg DK-2960

Jacobi, Adam
Barrister & Solicitor
Montergade 1,
1116 Copenhagen Skovvej 61
Gentofte DK-2820

Magid, Per O.
Attorney at Law
Advokatfirmaet Jonas Bruun
38 Bredgade
Copenhagen K 1260

Meurs-Gerken, Paul R.
Advokat, T. Ingemann Hansen & P. R. Meurs-Gerken,
Amaliegade No. 22
DK-1256 Copenhagen K

Neergaard, Peter
Director, Denmark Prov. Chamber of Commerce
Folehavevej 155
Rungsted Kyst DK-2960

Philip, Prof. Dr. iur. Allan
Partner, Pontoppidan Philip & Partners
Frederiksgade 1
Copenhagen K DK-1265

Egypt

Aboul-Enein, Mohamed I. M.
Acting Director, Cairo Regional Centre for International Commercial Arbitration
3 Aboul Fida Str., 9th Floor
Cairo

El-Kosheri, Prof. Dr. Ahmed S.
Professor at the University of Cairo
Member, Arbitration Council Franco-Arab Chamber of Commerce; ICCA member;
Attorney, El-Kosheri & Rashed
16 Mamaal El-Sokar, Garden City
Cairo

F.R. Germany

Aden, Dr. Menno
Company Lawyer
Ruhrgas AG
Essen Am Gerichtshaus 1a
D-4300 Essen

Alberts, Dr. iur. Eduard E.
Lawyer
Kaiserwertherstr. 115
D-4000 Düsseldorf

Baumeister, RA Dr. iur. Helmuth
Attorney, Schlutius Espey & Partners
Kurze Mehren 2/Spitalerstrasse 4
D-2000 Hamburg 1

Beeg, RA Dr. Hans G.
Kurt Schumacher Strasse 30–32
D-6000 Frankfurt

Beusch, RA Dr. Karl
Attorney, Siemens AG
Wittelbacherplatz 2
D-8000 Munich 2

Böckstiegel, Prof. Dr. Karl-Heinz
President, Iran-United States Claims Tribunal
Professor at the University of Cologne
Parkstrasse 38
D–5060 Bergisch-Gladbach

Bopp, Thomas M.
University of Saarland
St. Ingberterstrasse 42
D-6600 Saarbrücken

Bredow, Dr. Jens
Director, German Arbitration Institute
German National Committee of the ICC
Postfach 100447
D-5000 Cologne

Caron, David
Attorney, Pillsbury Madison & Sutro

Eberth, Dr. Rolf
Legal Adviser, Commerzbank AG
Neue Mainzerstrasse 32–36
D-6000 Frankfurt/Main

Fischer-Zernin, Dr. G. Vincent
Lawyer, Hasche Albrecht Fischer
Valentinskamp 88
D-2000 Hamburg 36

Flad, Hubert H. F.
Senior Partner, Albert Flad & Schlosshahn
Constettenstrasse 66
D-6000 Frankfurt/Main

Glossner, Dr. Dr. Ottoarndt
ICCA member
Am Eichbühel 24
D-6242 Kronberg

Hobeck, RA Dr. Paul A.
Attorney, Siemens AG
Werner-von-Siemens Str. 50
D-8520 Erlangen

Hoffmann, Dr. Dietrich
Attorney-at-Law
Hoffmann, Liebs & Partner
Rotthäuser Weg 12
D-4000 Düsseldorf 12

Kornblum, Prof. Dr. Udo
Professor, Universität Stuttgart
Friedrichstr. 10
D-7000 Stuttgart 1

Landry, Dr. Klaus,
Lawyer, Modest Gündisch Landry
Poststrasse 9A
D-2000 Hamburg 36

Lebuhn, Prof. Dr. Jürgen H.
Attorney, Lebuhn & Puchta
Vorsetzen 35
D-2000 Hamburg 11

Lindemeyer, RA Dr. Bernd
Attorney
Kaiser-Friedrichstr. 13
D-5300 Bonn 1

Lionnet, RA Dr. Klaus W.
Attorney, Siemens AG
Werner-von-Siemens Str. 50
D-8520 Erlangen

Lörcher, Dr. Gino
Lawyer
Aleburger Str. 377
D-5000 Cologne 51

Nicklisch, Prof. Dr. Fritz F.
Professor, University of Heidelberg
Friedrich-Ebert-Anlage 6–10
D-6900 Heidelberg

Preyer, Dr. Hans-Dieter
Neuer Wall 42
D-2000 Hamburg 36

Räschke-Kessler, RA Hilmar
Bismarckstrasse 3
D-7505 Ettlingen

Sarkis, Dr. Sami
Attorney at Law
Stolzingstr. 21/7
D-8000 Munich

Schlosser, Prof. Pieter F.
University of Munich
Professor-Huber-Platz 2
D-8000 Munich

Seiffert, Prof. Dr. Wolfgang
University of Kiel
Am Schulgarten 26
D-2000 Hamburg 70

Swoboda, RA Michael
German Arbitration Institute
Adenauerallee 148
D-5300 Bonn 1

Teichert, Rolf A. H.
Director, International Council of Hides,
Skins & Leather Traders Association
Herrenhausallee 95
D-2000 Hamburg 65

Vollmer, Prof. Dr. Lothar E.
University Hohesheim
Ingwerweg 14
D-7000 Stuttgart 75

Von Ditfurth, Dr. Hoimar
Robert Bosch GmbH
Robert-Bosch-Platz 1
D-7016 Gerlinger-Schillerhöhe

Weber, RA Dolf
Partner, Pünder Volhard & Weber
Mainzer Landstrasse 46
D-6000 (FBC) Frankfurt/Main

Zimmer, RA Klaus Peter
Attorney
Citadellstrasse 21
D-4000 Düsseldorf

France

Ahdab, Abdul Hamid
Attorney at Law, Law Office Abdul
Hamid Ahdab
1, Rue Cognacq-Jay
Paris 75007

Armfelt, Andrew P.
Lawyer, Cameron Markby
4, Rue de la Planche
Paris 75007

Asthalter, Richard G.
Partner, Sullivan & Cromwell
8, Place Vendôme
Paris 75001

Augendre, Geneviève
Avocat, SCP G. Augendre et A. Fourment
134 Rue de Courcelles
Paris 75017

Baum, Axel H.
Partner, Hughes Hubbard & Reed
47 Avenue Georges Mandel
Paris 75116

Bellet, Pierre
Avocat
15, Avenue du Prés. Wilson
Paris 75016

Berlioz, Georges
Avocat, Berlioz Ferry David Lutz & Rochefort
68, Boulevard de Courcelles
Paris 75017

Bernard, Patrick
Partner, Bernard, Gillot, Tessler et Carton
127, Bld. Haussmann
Paris 75008

Bernard, Thierry
Avocat, SCP Robert Moreau & Associés
5, Rue de Stockholm
Paris 75008

Bond, Stephen R.
Secretary General, Court of Arbitration of the International Chamber of Commerce
38, Cours Albert Ier
Paris 75008

Bouckaert, Christian H.
Avocat, Cabinet Bouckaert
9, Avenue Hoche
Paris 75008

Briat, Martine
International Chamber of Commerce
38, Cours Albert Ier
Paris 75008

Carrez, Bernard M.
Lawyer, Giroux-Buhagiar & Partners
32, Ave. Georges Mandel
Paris 75116

Caslot-Serra, Jean P.
Directeur Adjoint
Banque Française du Commerce Extérieur

Chartier, Frederic
Lawyer, Cabinet Chartier Hourcade Jobard Connor
83, Avenue Foch
Paris 75116

Courbot, Jacques J.
Technical Expert, International Chamber of Commerce
5, Rue Denis Poisson
Paris 75017

Craig, William L.
Partner, Coudert Frères
52, Avenue des Champs Elysées
Paris 75008

Cuisinier, Jean H.
Executive Vice President, Spie-Batignolles
Tour Anjou
33, Quai de Dion-Bouton
Puteaux-Cedex 92814

Danet, Guy M.
Batonnier
1, rue Georges Berger
Paris 75017

David, Nicholas
Lawyer, Société Nationale Elf Aquitaine
Tour Elf
2, Place de la Coupole
Paris 92078

De Boisseson, Mathieu
Avocat
26, Cours Albert Ier
Paris 75008

De Grandcourt, Prof. Jean L.
Avocat
32, Avenue Georges Mandel
Paris 75116

Dellecker, Terence R.
Partner, Orlando Dellecker Ghriqui Mercey
98, Blvd. de Courcelles
Paris 75011

Den Hertog, Mr. Dick
Attorney, Stibbe Blaisse & De Jong
22, Place du Général Catroux
Paris 75017

Derains, Yves
Conseil Juridique, Derains-Gelinas
ICCA member
66, Avenue des Champs Elysées
Paris 75008

Delvolvé, Jean Louis
Avocat
38, Avenue Hoche
Paris 75008

Dompgnac Latour, Xavier
Total CFP
24, Rue Erlanger
Paris

Doumith, Roger
Ordre des Avocats
El Palacio de Justicia
Paris

Du Grandrut, Bernard
Avocat au Barreau de Paris: Ancien Batonnier
18, Avenue Bugeaud
Paris

El Houeiss, Rodrigue
Avocat
18, Avenue Mozart
Paris 75016

Emo, Pierre
Avocat
SCP Emo Hebert Le Bousse Labrunye
4, Avenue Gallieni
Mont St. Aignan 76013

Falque, Dominique A.
Partner, Debost Falque Carpentier & Barbe
48, Avenue Victor Hugo
Paris 75116

Flecheux, Georges
Avocat à la cour
17, Avenue de Lamballe
Paris 75016

Fouchard, Prof. Philippe
Professor University of Paris II
51 bis, Boulevard de Troyes
Talant 21240

Fouche, Gilbert J.
Corporate Lawyer, Thomson SA, Paris
83, Ave. Pierre Brossolette
Montrouge 92120

Fourest, Michel
Arbitrator, ICC and AAA
59, Quai Branly
Paris 75007

Funck-Brentano, Lise
198, Avenue Victor Hugo
Paris 75116

Funck-Brentano, Roland
198, Avenue Victor Hugo
Paris 75116

Gaillard, Prof. Emmanuel
Professor de Droit International à l'Univ. de Lille II; Avocat, Bredin Prat Saint-Esteben & Gaillard
130, Rue du Faubourg Saint-Honoré
Paris 75008

Gaudet, Michel
Chairman of the Court of Arbitration
International Chamber of Commerce,
ICCA member
38, Cours Albert Ier
Paris 75008

Gelinas, Paul A.
Lawyer, Derains-Gelinas
6, Avenue des Champs Elysées
Paris 75008

Ghozland, Patricia
Avocat
4, Rue de la Planche
Paris 75007

Goldman, Prof. Berthold
Prof. Emeritus, University of Paris
15, Rue Clement Marot
Paris 75008

Goldsmith, Jean-Claude
Member of the Paris Bar
J. C. Goldsmith & Associés
4, Avenue van Dyck
Paris 75008

Hagelsteen, Marie-Dominique
Dir. Juridique Elf Aquitaine
6, Quai du 4 Septembre
Boulogne 92100

Hanson, Maren
Attorney
139, Ave Victor Hugo
Paris 75116

Jarvin, Sigvard
General Counsel, Court of Arbitration of the International Chamber of Commerce
38, Cours Albert Ier
Paris 75008

Kemicha, Fathi
Secretary/Registrar
Euro-Arab Arbitration Center
91, Rue Lauriston
Paris 75116

Kudlick, Susan B.
Counsel, Schlumberger Ltd
42, rue Saint-Dominique
Paris 75007

Lazarski, Henry
Solicitor, Clifford Turner
36, Rue Brunel
Paris 75008

Leboulanger, Philippe
Avocat
Avenue Dù President Wilson
Paris 75116

Lee, William L.
Partner, Shearman & Sterling
21, Avenue Georges V
Paris 75008

Lesguillons, Prof. Henry
University of Paris X
26, Villa de la Réunion
Paris 75016

Meade, Richard C.
Attorney, Law Office of Richard C. Meade
15, Rue Theodule Ribot
Paris 75017

Moreau, Bertrand
Avocat, SCP Robert Moreau & Associés
5, Rue de Stockholm
Paris 75008

Petit, Bernard R.
Juge au Tribunal de Commerce de Paris;
Directeur Central CHISOVAC
6, Boulevard Suchet
Paris 75016

Pinchon, Prof. François F. J. L.
Ingénieur-Expert; Professeur, l'École Supérieure des Beaux Arts de Paris; Vice President la Compagnie des Experts (CCI – Comité Français)
12, Avenue Franklin D. Roosevelt
Paris 75008

Portier, Jean-Marc M. G.
Deputy General Counsel, SANOFI
99, Rue des Moines
Paris 75017

Prat, Jean-François
Avocat au Barreau de Paris, Bredin Prat Saint Esteben & Gaillard
130, Rue du Faubourg Saint-Honoré
Paris 75008

Ravaud, Didier P.
Avocat, Martinet Bataillon Barberon Ravaud
167 bis, Avenue Victor Hugo
Paris 75116

Robert, Jean
Avocat Honoraire;
ICCA Honorary President
5, Rue de Stockholm
Paris 75008

Ryziger, Paul-François
Avocat
125, Boulevard Malesherbes
Paris 75017

Saint Cene, Philippe
Chief Legal Department SNEA
Tour Elf, La Défense 6
Courbevoie 92400

Salans, Carl F.
Partner, Salans Hertzfeld Heilbronn et al.
1, Ave. Franklin D. Roosevelt
Paris 75008

Sarah, Alexandre T.
Chairman, Sarlex Consultants
182, Rue de l'Université
Paris 75007

Sefrioui, Abdelhay
Avocat à la Cour;
Vice President, Arbitration Centre at the Franco-Arab Chamber of Commerce
Abdelhay & Anne Sefrioui
6, Avenue Raymond Poincaré
Paris 75116

Sefrioui, Anne
Avocat à la Cour, Abdelhay & Anne Sefrioui
6, Avenue Raymond Poincaré
Paris 75116

Seppala, Christopher R.
Partner, Law Offices of S. G. Archibald
10, Avenue de Messine
Paris 75008

Sohier, Walter D.
Consultant, Frère Cholmeley
42, Avenue de President Wilson
Paris 75116

Stasi, Mario
16, Ave. Bd. Aquet
Paris

Thevenard, Jean Pierre
Conseiller, Spie Battignolles Tour d'Anjou
33, Quai de Dion Bouton
Puteaux 92814

Thieffry, Jean
Managing Partner, Thieffry & Associés
2, rue Dufrenoy
Paris 75116

Torem, Charles
Senior Partner, Coudert Frères
52, Avenue des Champs Elysées
Paris 75008

Touzani, Baccar
General Secretary, Franco-Arab Chamber of Commerce
93, Rue Lariston
Paris 75116

Tschanz, Pierre-Yves
Associate, White & Case
20, Place Vendôme
Paris 75001

Vuillard, Emmanuel
Lawyer, Framatome
International Legal Department
34ter, Rue de la Muette,
Maison Lafitte 78600

German D.R.

Strohbach, Prof. Dr. Heinz
President Court of Arbitration at the GDR Chamber of Foreign Trade;
Professor University of Potsdam-Babelsberg;
ICCA member
Am Kupfergraben 7
DDR-1020 Berlin

Greece

Dimolitsa, Antonias
Lawyer
12 Milioni Street
Athens 10673

Foustoucos, Dr. Anghelos C.
Attorney; Secretary-General, Greek Arbitration Association
Solonos 102
Athens 10680

Malouf, Khalil M.
Special Adviser, CCC International
32 Kifissias Ave.
Amaroussion
Athens

Hong Kong

Tisdall, Brian
Secretary General, Hong Kong
International Arbitration Centre
1 Arbuthnot Road
Hong Kong

Hungary

Balint, Eva
Legal Adviser, Medimpex Hungarian
Trading Co.
Vorosmarty ter 4
Budapest

Balog, Dr. Judit
Chief Legal Adviser, Tannimpex Foreign
Trading Company
Deak F. Str. 17
H-1052 Budapest

Gál, Dr. Gyula
Legal Adviser, Terimpex
Varga J.U. 8
Budapest VII

Hontvari, Dr. Matyas
Chief Legal Adviser, Metalimpex
Ora ut. 18/c.
H-1125 Budapest

Komaromi, Peter
Director, Legal Department, Hungarian
Chamber of Commerce
Kossuth Lajos ter 6–8
H-1055 Budapest

Korosi, Janos
Lignimpex
U. Honved n. 20
H-1393 Budapest

Lehoczky, Dr. Miklos
Lawyer, Artex Kulker Vall.
Munnich Ferenc u. 31
H-1390 Budapest

Szász, Prof. Dr. Iván
Member, Presidium Court of Arbitration at
the Hungarian Chamber of Commerce;
ICCA member
Voros Hadsereg utja 104–106
H-1021 Budapest

Vigh, Dr. Jozsef
Legal Adviser, Licensia Bajcsy
Zsilinszky ut. 16
H-1051 Budapest

India

Bhandari, Sarvjit
Singhania & Co.
B-92 Himalaya House
K.G. Marg New Delhi 1

Deshpande, Chief Justice Vasant S.
Singhania & Co.
A-19 Geetanjali Enclave
New Delhi – 110 017

Kar Roy, Satya R.
Technical Director, S. R. Kar Roy &
Associates
South Office Para
Ranohi 834 002

Leybourne Callaghan, Robert W.
Négociations Internationales, SA Ltd.
Dublin, London, Zurich, Singapore
Sidney Royal Yacht Club Chambers,
Apollo Bunder
Bombay 400 049

Nariman, Fali S.
Advocate at the Supreme Court,
President LAWASIA,
ICCA member
F-21/22 Hauz Khaz Enclave
New Delhi 110016

Nirwani, S. C.
Secretary, The Indian Council of Arbitration
Federation House
Tansen Marg
New Delhi 1

Seth, J. C.
Secretary & Chief Law Officer NTPC

Singhania, Dul Chand
Advocate, Singhania & Co. Advocates
B-92 Himalaya Street
K.G. Marg New Delhi-1

Italy

Bernardini, Piero
General Counsel ENI
Ente Nazionale Idrocarburi ENI
Piazzale E. Mattei n. 1
Rome 00144

Bernini, Prof. Avv. Giorgio
ICCA President-Elect
Studio Bernini
Via Mascarella 94
Bologna 40126

Bortolotti, Prof. Avv. Fabio
Lawyer, Studio Legal Bortolotti Mathis & Associés
Via S. Dalmazzo 24
Torino 10122

De Palma, Vincenzo
Deputy Director, Legal Dept.
Banca Nazionale del Lavoro
Direzione Generale
Via Aureliana 2
Rome 00187

Draetta, Ugo
Counsel Sadelmi SpA
Via San Gregorio 34
Milan

Ferrante, Mauro
Secretary General ICCA
Secretary General, Associazione Italiana per l'Arbitrato
Via XX Settembre 5
Rome 00187

Gentile, Giovanni G.
Lawyer ENEL
Via G. B. Martini, 3
Rome 00198

Giardina, Prof. Andrea
Largo deo Teatro
Valle 6
Rome 00186

Leone, Avv. Gregorio
Lawyer, Camera Arbitrale Associazione Granaria
Via Canova 19A
Milan 20145

Maccomi, G. Franco
Lawyer, Baker & McKenzie
Via XX Settembre 1
Rome

Marano, Guido
Legal Counsel, Filippo Fochi SpA
Via S. Valentino N.2
Bologna 40122

Marin, Marco
First Vice President & Legal Counsel
Banco di Napoli, Serv. Legale
Via Aniello Falcone
Naples 80127

Minoli, Marco
Lawyer, Studio Legale Minoli EC
Via Po 11,
Turin

Mirabelli, Prof. Giuseppe
Professor, Associazione Italiana per l'Arbitrato
Via Polibio 15
Rome 00136

Morera, Renzo M. R.
Avvocato
Via Pollaiolo 3
Roma 00197

Pesce, Dr. Avv. Angelo
Senior Partner, Studio Avv.
Dr. Angelo Pesce & Associati
Via del Giardini, 4
Milan 20121

Recchia, Prof. Avv. Giorgio
Professor of Law, Attorney
Via Arbia No. 23
Rome 00199

Rosauer, Giulio
Lawyer
Via Umbria, 7
Rome 00187

Rubino-Sammartano, Mauro
Partner, Studio Rubino-Sammartano e Associati
Via del Giardini 4
Milan 20121

Savarese, Michele
Lawyer IRI
Via Vittorio Veneto 89
Rome 00187

Schiavoni, Giorgio
Legal Counsel, Foster Wheeler Italiana
Via Porta Tenaglia 3
Milan 20123

Speranza, Sergio
Lawyer, Fubini Jorio Speranza Cavalli
Corso Vittorio Emmanuele 71
Turin 10128

Spolidoro, Sergio R.
Partner, Law Offices of Avv. Spolidoro
Via Mozart, 2
Milan 20122

Tedone, Dr. Roberto
Vice Dirett. di Succursale Banca Nazionale dell' Agricoltura
Via Salaria, 231
Rome 00199

Tesauro, Paolo
Attorney, Professor
Via Toledo, 156
Napoli 80134

Tubere, Rosalba
Lawyer, Studio Legale Minoli EC
Via Montebello 15
Turin

Ughi, Avv. Giovanni
Lawyer
Via Sant Andrea 19
Milan 20121

Visconti, Avv. Giuseppe Broggini Benatti
Portale Visconti
Milan

Japan

Arakwa, Taro
The Japan Shipping Exchange, Inc.
Mitsui Rokugokan, No. 8
Muromachi 2-chome
Nihonbashi, Chuo-Ku
Tokyo 103

Dogauchi, Masato
Associate Professor, University of Tokyo
Komaba 3-8-1 Meguro-ku
Tokyo 153

Doi, Prof. Teruo
Professor of Law
Waseda University 1545-40
Irumagawa Sayama-shi
Saitama-Ken 350-13

Hattori, Hiroshi
Director, The Japan Commercial Arbitration Association
3-2-2 Marunouchi, Chiyoda-ku
Tokyo 100

Shimoyama, Tomoo
The Japan Commercial Arbitration Association
3-2-2, Marunouchi, Chiyoda-ku
Tokyo 100

Taniguchi, Prof. Yasuhei
Faculty of Law
Kyoto University
Sakyo-ku
Kyoto 606

Tanimoto, Hironori
Executive Director
The Japan Shipping Exchange, Inc.
Mitsui Rokugokan, No. 8
Muromachi 2-chome
Nihonbashi, Chuo-ku
Tokyo 103

Korea (Rep.)

Kim, Kwang-Young
Secretary General,
The Korean Commercial Arbitration Board
10-1, 2-Ka, Hoehyun-Dong, Chung-ku
Seoul

Lebanon

Moussali, Antoine
Attorney
Furn Hayek Street
Beirut

Malaysia

Kitingan, Jeffrey G.
Director, Sabah Foundation
P.O. Box 11623
88817 Kota Kinabalu,
Sabah

Lalung, Semion
Legal Adviser, Sabah Foundation,
P.O. Box 11623
88817 Kota Kinabulu,
Sabah

Lim, Phaik Gan
Director AALCC Regional Centre for Arbitration, Kuala Lumpur
576 Jalan Sultan Salahuddin
Kuala Lumpur 50480

Mexico

Siqueiros, José L.
ICCA member
Attorney, Barrera Siqueiros y Torres Landa
Sinaloa 153
Mexico City DF 06700

Netherlands

Ameli, Koorosh H.
Ad hoc member, Iran-United States Claims Tribunal
Parkweg 13
2585 JH The Hague

Baanders, Dr. Herbert A. J.
Nolst Trenité Hoogenraad & Van Velzen
Korte Hoogstraat 30
3011 GL Rotterdam

Bos, Dr. Daniel
Publisher, Kluwer Law & Taxation Publishers
Staverenstraat 32015
Postbus 23
7400 GA Deventer

Brower, Charles N.
Judge, Iran-United States Claims Tribunal
Nassau Odijckstraat 55
2596 AG The Hague

Bulterman, Mr. Willem
Attorney-at-Law
P.O. Box 340
Melkpad 41
1250 AH Hilversum/Laren

Davids, Ester J.
Secretary, Royal Dutch Grain & Feed Trade Association
P.O. Box 202
3000 AE Rotterdam

Eshragh, Mohammad K.
Agent, Islamic Republic of Iran
Iran-United States Claims Tribunal
Klaverweide 200
2272 BX Voorburg

Freedberg, Judith A.
Department of International Commercial Arbitration
T.M.C. Asser Institute for International Law
Alexanderstraat 20–22
P.O. Box 30461
2500 GL The Hague

Hamel, Willem A.
Assistant Secretary-General
Iran-United States Claims Tribunal
Oranjelaan 33
3062 BP Rotterdam

Höcker, Anton
Partner, Höcker & Kamper
Roemer Visscherstraat 47
1054 EW Amsterdam

Holtzmann, Howard M.
Judge, Iran-United States Claims Tribunal;
ICCA Vice President
Parkweg 13
2585 JH The Hague

Meadows, G. Frances
Legal Assistant to the President
Iran-United States Claims Tribunal
Parkweg 13
2585 JH The Hague

Nieuwenhuis, Marcel
Publisher, Kluwer Law & Taxation Publishers
Staverenstraat 32015
P.O. Box 23
7400 GA Deventer

Sanders, Pieter
Lawyer, Hoogovens Groep B.V.
Zwarteweg 1
2111 AJ Aerdenhout

Sanders, Prof. Dr. Pieter
Emeritus Professor,
Erasmus University Rotterdam;
Outgoing ICCA President
Burg. Knappertlaan 134
3117 BD Schiedam

Schultsz, Prof, Jan. C.
Attorney, Blackstone Rueb & Van Boeschoten
Oranje Nassaulaan 47
1075 AK Amsterdam

Schwebel, Stephen M.
Judge, International Court of Justice
Carnegieplein 2
2517 KJ The Hague

Sillevis Smitt, J. Lodewijk W.
President, Netherlands Arbitration Institute;
Partner, De Brauw & Westbroek
Scheveningseweg 58
2517 KW The Hague

Van den Berg, Dr. Albert Jan
Partner, Van Doorne & Sjollema Advocaten
P.O. Box 22105
3003 DC Rotterdam

Van den Hoek, Paulus C.
Attorney, Stibbe Blaisse & De Jong
Rokin 92–96
1012 KZ Amsterdam

Van Sandick, Leonard H. W.
Partner, Loeff & Van der Ploeg
P.O. Box 21022, Blaak 333
3001 AA Rotterdam

Virally, Michel
Arbitrator, Iran-United States Claims Tribunal
Parkweg 13
2585 JH The Hague

Willems, Pieter J.
Partner, P. J. Willems & P. J. de Booij
Willemsparkweg 196
1071 HW Amsterdam

Wühler, Dr. Norbert
Iran-United States Claims Tribunal
Parkweg 13
2585 JH The Hague

New Zealand

O'Connor, Michael R.
Principal, Sanders O'Connor & Partners
P.O. Box 748
New Plymouth

Nigeria

Adebayo, Ariyo
Attorney
2 Benjamin Lane, P.O. Box 7509
Lagos

Adegbite, Dr. Lateef O.
Partner, Lateef Adegbite & Co.
Investment House, 2nd Floor
Flat 2 21/25 Broad Str.
Odunlami St. Entrance
P.O. Box 7741
Lagos

Adeleke, A. K. A.
Assistant General Manager, Nigerian Industrial Development Bank
NIDB House
63/71 Broad Street
Lagos

Oyekunle, Tinuade O.
Barrister & Solicitor; Secretary, Association of Arbitrators of Nigeria;
ICCA member
P.O. Box 9433
Lagos

Norway

Mitsem, Paul
Supreme Court Attorney;
Advokatfirma Mitsem
Parkvn. 62, P.O. Box 2327
Solli
Oslo 2 0201

Poland

Gadomska, Jadwiga
Legal Adviser, Elektrim Ltd.
Inflancka 19, Apt. 291
Warsaw 00-189

Lisowski, Jan
Legal Adviser, Testilimpex Ltd., Lodz
102 Jaracza Street
Lodz 90–244

Maciuch, Zygmunt
Advocate; Arbitrator, Arbitration Court at the Polish Chamber of Foreign Trade;
Counsel, MINEX Foreign Trade Company
Kolowa Street 4/75
Warsaw 03-536

Mlynarczyk, Prof. Jerzy
Maritime Institute Gdansk
Doroszewskiego 21
Gdansk 80-319

Nanowski, Zbigniew L.
President, International Court of Arbitration for Marine and Inland Navigation in Gdynia
Natolinska 2/83
Warsaw 00-568

Pieckowski, Sylwester
General Counsel, Foreign Trade Enterprise PEZETEL, Ltd.
Aleja Stanow Zjednoczonych 61
Warsaw 00-991

Szurski, Tadeusz
President, Court of Arbitration at the Polish Chamber of Foreign Trade; ICCA member
Cieszkowskiego 1/3, Apt 102
Warsaw 01-636

Wilski, Krzysztof J.
Advocate, Centromor SA
Partyzantow 95/97/12
Gdansk 80–254

Zajaczkowski, Leszek
Legal Adviser, Metalexport Ltd.
Mokotowska 49
Warsaw 00-950

Romania

Costea Subert, Sorin Virgil
Advocate, Colegiul de Avocati
Prahova Str. Elena Doamna Nr. 69
Ploiesti Prahova 2000

Popescu, Prof. Dr. Tudor R.
ICCA member; President, Arbitration Commission Chamber of Commerce & Industry of the Social Republic of Romania
Boulevard N. Balcescu 22
Bucharest 70189

Saudi Arabia

Al Hejailan, Sheikh Salah I.
Legal Counsellor, The Law Firm of Salah Al-Hejailan
P.O. Box 1454
Riyadh 11431

Hoshan, Mohamed Hamad
Attorney-at-Law, Mohamed H. Hoshan Law Office
P.O. Box 2626
Riyadh 11461

Spain

Cremades, Prof. Dr. Bernardo M.
ICCA member;
Senior Partner, J. y B. Cremades, Abogados
Goya 18, 2nd Floor
Madrid 28001

Diez Clavero, José
General Secretary, Madrid Chamber of Commerce & Industry
c/Huertas 13
Madrid 28012

Gonzales-Soria, Julio
President, Arbitration Commission Madrid Chamber of Commerce & Industry
c/Sor Angela de la Cruz 6
Planta 10
Madrid 28020

Pombo, Fernando
Director;
Senior Partner, Gomez-Acebo & Pombo
Castellana 164
Madrid 28046

Sweden

Wetter, Dr. J. Gillis
Resident Partner, White & Case
Grev Turegatan 2
S-11435 Stockholm

Boholm, Per Chr.
Assistant Judge, Supreme Court of Sweden
Bragevägen 10-II
S-11424 Stockholm

Franke, Dr. Ulf
Secretary General, Arbitration Institute
Stockholm Chamber of Commerce
P.O. Box 16050
S-10322 Stockholm

Greene, David G.
White & Case
Grev Turegatan 2
S-11435 Stockholm

Hagberg, Lennart
Lawyer
Box 2235
S-40314 Gothenburg

Heuman, Prof. Lars
Professor of Law, University of Stockholm
S-10691 Stockholm

Hjerner, Prof. Lars A. E.
Professor, University of Stockholm
Villa Birka
S-17011 Drottningholm

Mangård, Judge Nils
ICCA member
29 Narvavägen
S-11460 Stockholm

Pedersen, Hans
Attorney-at-Law
Advokatfirman Hans Pedersen
Sveavägen 31, Box 3256
S-10365 Stockholm

Ramberg, Prof. Jan
Professor of Law
University of Stockholm
Vretvägen 13
S-18363 Taeby

Steen, Sverker
Attorney
Box 3083
S-10361 Stockholm

Strideberg, Seved
Attorney-at-Law
Advokatfirman Hans Pedersen
Box 3256
S-10365 Stockholm

Switzerland

Baladi, André
Chairman, ARICI
International Arbitration Association
Switzerland; Baladi & Company
8, Rue Töpffer
CH-1211 Geneva 12

Blessing, Dr. Marc
Partner, Bär & Karrer
Seefeldstrasse 19
CH-8024 Zurich

Briner, Dr. Robert R.
Member, Iran-United States Claims Tribunal
Partner, Lenz Schluep Briner & De Coulon
25 Grand' Rue
CH-1211 Geneva

Bucher, Prof. Eugene Ch.
Professor
University of Berne, Faculty of Law
Falkenplantz 18
CH-3012 Berne

Buresch, Dr. Michaela
Shearman & Sterling
17, Avenue des Cavaliers
CH-1224 Geneva

Cahier, Philippe
Professor, Graduate Institute of Inter. Studies
10 Pedro Maylan
Geneva

Carciente, Evelyne
Lawyer, Werner & Sieber
5, Place de la Fusterie
CH-1204 Geneva

Carrard, François
Attorney, Carrard Pashoud & Heim
6, Rue de la Grotte
CH-1003 Lausanne

Dohm, Dr. Jürgen A.
Attorney at Law,
Lalive & Budin
20, Rue Sénebier
CH-1205 Geneva

Grendelmeier, Dr. iur. Hans R.
Partner, Grendelmeier & Jenny
Dufourstrasse 116
CH-8008 Zurich

Hafter, Dr. iur. Peter
Lawyer, Stähelin Hafter Jagmetti
Lutz & Partners
In der Hinterzelg 12
CH-8700 Küssnacht/Zurich

Henchoz, Dominique
Lawyer, Lalive & Budin
26, Rue le Corbusier
CH-1208 Geneva

Kälin, Claudia
Partner, Froriep Renggli & Partners
General Wille-str. 10
CH-8002 Zurich

Karrer, Dr. iur. Pierre A.
Partner, Pestalozzi & Gmuer
Löwenstrasse 1
CH-8001 Zurich

Kaufmann, Gabrielle
Partner, Baker & McKenzie
6, Rue Bellot
CH-1206 Geneva

Lalive, Prof. Dr. Pierre A.
Professor, Univ. of Geneva;
Partner, Lalive & Budin; ICCA member
20, Rue Sénebier
CH-1205 Geneva

Levy, Laurent
Attorney, Brunschwig, Biaggi & Levy
23, Quai des Bergues
CH-1201 Geneva

Maire, Jean-Paul
Avocat, Reymond Bonnard Champoud
Maire & Barman
5, Rue du Grand-Chêne
CH-1003 Lausanne

Page, Dr. Gerald
Attorney, Poncet Turrettini
Amaudruz & Neyroud
22, Rue de la Corraterie
CH-1204 Geneva

Patocchi, Dr. Paolo M.
Maître-Assistant, Geneva University Law
School; Lalive & Budin
22, Avenue de Champel
CH-1206 Geneva

Pestalozzi, Dr. iur. Anton R.
Attorney at Law, Pestalozzi & Gmuer
Löwenstrasse 1
CH-8001 Zurich

Pestalozzi, Dr. iur. Regula E.
Attorney at Law, Pestalozzi & Gmuer
Löwenstrasse 1
CH-8001 Zurich

Peter, Wolfgang
Lawyer, Pirenne Python Schifferli
Peter & Associates
3, Rue Bellot
CH-1206 Geneva

Petitpierre, Dr. iur. Anne
Attorney at Law, Troller Vesely Petitpierre
15, Rue Toepffer
CH-1206 Geneva

Poncet, Dr. Charles
Partner, Lalive & Budin
20, Rue Sénebier
CH-1205 Geneva

Reymond, Prof. Claude J.
Avocat, Reymond Champoud Bonnard &
Maire
5, Rue du Grand-Chêne
CH-1003 Lausannc

Roncaglia, Renato
International Lawyer
40, Cret-de-Choully
CH-1242 Satigny (Geneva)

Schürmann, Hans-Jürg
Attorney at Law, Schürmann Rausch &
Rohrer
Limmatquai 3
CH-8001 Zurich

Stauffer, Dr. iur. Emmanuel
Partner, Stauffer and Partners
15, Rue Général Dufour
CH-1204 Geneva

Stoffel, Dr. iur. Walter A.
Vice Director, Swiss Institute of Comparative
Law
CH-1015 Lausanne

Wenger, Dr. iur. Werner
Partner, Wenger Mathys Mosimann & Cueni
Äschenvorstadt 55
CH-4010 Bâsle

Werner, Jacques
Lawyer, Werner & Sieber
5, Place de la Fusterie
CH-1204 Geneva

Wolfe, Suzanne R.
Senior Partner, Wolfe & Rogers
15, Rue du Cendrier
CH-1201 Geneva

Syria

El-Hakim, Prof. Jacques
Professor, Univ. of Damascus
P.O. Box 5788
Damascus

Sarkis, Dr. Sami
Attorney
Tajhiz Street 5
Damascus

Taiwan

Huang/Tsartsai, C. Y.
Attorney; Professor of Law
National Chung Hsing University
Taipei

Tunisia

Annabi, Samir
Attorney-at-Law, Annabi & Associates
83, Avenue Taieb Mehiri
Tunis Belvedere 1002

Malouche, Habib
General Delegate
Tunisian Bankers Association
Ave. Jugurtha-Rue 7001 No. 5
Tunis

United Kingdom

Alexander, Leslie W. M.
47 Menlove Avenue
Liverpool L18 2EH

Barclay, Cedric
ICCA member
London Maritime Arbitrator's Association
40 Stafford Court
Kensington High Street
London W8 7DL

Borley, Anthony P. G.
The Orchard, Cooper's Lane
Dedham Essex
Colchester CO7 6AX

Brown-Berset, Dominique
Lawyer, Froriep Renggli & Partners
58 Coleman Street
London EC2R 5BE

Cullen, Christopher W.
Beale & Co.
39 Green Lane
East Molesey, Surrey KT8 0PN

Geddes, Gerald
Gerald Geddes & Partners
6 Lloyds Avenue
London EC3N 3AX

Goode, Prof. Roy M.
Centre for Commercial Law Studies
Queen Mary College, Univ. of London
339 Mile End Road
London E1 4NS

Hacking, The Rt. Hon. Lord David
Richards Butler
5 Clifton Street
London EC2A 4DQ

Hunter, J. Martin H.
Solicitor, Freshfields
25 Newgate Street
London EC1A 7LH

Lew, Julian D. M.
S. J. Berwin
"Greystoke", Mayfield Drive
Pinner, Middlesex HA5 4EX

Littman, Mark
ICCA member
79 Chester Square
London SW1W 9DP

Lloyd, Humphrey J.
22 Old Buildings, Lincoln's Inn
London WC2A 3UJ

Marriott, Arthur L.
Marriott Harrison Bloom & Norris
34 Bedford Row
London WC1R 4JH

Micklethwaite, Neil P.
Litigation Assistant, Gouldens
118 Chancery Lane
London WC2 A1JJ

Minoprio, Lisa
Richards Butler
5 Clifton Street
London EC2A 4DQ

Redfern, Alan
Partner, Freshfields
25 Newgate Street
London EC1A 7LH

Redmond, Peter Dawson
Channel Islands Arbitration Centre
Lucas House – Sark
Channel Islands

Sabi, Hamid
Attorney, Sabi & Associates
169–173 Regent Street
London W1

Severn, Kenneth
11 Methley Street
London SE11 4AL

Shenton, David W.
Solicitor, Lovell White & King
21 Holborn Viaduct
London EC1A 2DY

Slade, Laurie G.
Deputy Registrar
Chartered Institute of Arbitrators
75 Cannon Street
London EC4N 5BH

St. John Sutton, David
Allen & Overy
9 Cheapside
London EC2

Tackaberry, John A.
22 Old Buildings
Lincoln's Inn
London NW5

Vigrass, Bert W.
Director and Registrar
London Court of International Arbitration
The Chartered Institute of Arbitrators
75 Cannon Street
London EC4N 5BH

Ward, Ian W. I. R.
Partner, Lovell White & King
21 Holborn Viaduct
London EC1A 2DY

Zaiwalla, Sarosh R.
Messrs. Zaiwalla & Company
95A Chancery Lane
London WC2A

USA

Acton, Peter
Managing Attorney, IBM Corporation
Old Orchard Road
Armonk, New York

Aibel, Howard J.
Senior Vice President & General Counsel
ITT Corporation
320 Park Avenue, 19th Floor
New York, NY 10022

Aksen, Gerald
Partner, Reid & Priest
40 West 57th Street
New York, NY 10019

Allison, Richard C.
Partner, Reid & Priest
40 West 57th Street
New York, NY 10019

Arkin, Harry L.
Principal, Harry L. Arkin, Counselor at Law
Suite 650, Ptarmigan Place
3773 Cherry Crk. North Drive
Denver, CO 80209-3816

Barisi, Jeffrey A.
Partner, White & Case
1155 Avenue of the Americas
New York, NY 10036

Barron, William M.
Partner, Walter Conston & Schurtman, P. C.
90 Park Avenue
New York, NY 10016

Beach, Charles A.
Counsel, Exxon Corporation
1251 Avenue of the Americas
New York, NY 10020–1198

Becker, Joseph D.
Partner, Fox Glynn & Melamed
One Broadway
New York, NY 10004

Belland, Stanton P.
Partner, Monteleone & McCrory
10 Universal City Plaza, Suite 2500
Universal City, CA 91608–7806

Berens, Sheldon L.
Senior Vice President & General Counsel
Continental Grain Company
277 Park Avenue
New York, NY 10172

Best, Geoffrey D. C.
Partner, LeBoeuf Lamb Leiby & MacRae
520 Madison Avenue
New York, NY 10022

Bianchi, Carlos J.
Attorney, Law Office of Thomas L. Hughes
2614 Pan Am Building
200 Park Avenue
New York, NY 10166

Botwinik, David A.
Partner, Pavia & Harcourt
600 Madison Avenue
New York, NY 10022

Boyd, Stephen M.
Lawyer, Bryan Care McPheeters & McRoberts
1015 Fifteenth Street NW
Washington, DC 20005

Branson, David J.
Attorney, Kaye Scholer Fierman
Hays & Handler
1575 I Street NW
Washington, DC 20005

Broches, Dr. Aron
ICCA member; Of Counsel, Holtzmann Wise
& Shepard
2600 Tilden Place, NW
Washington, DC 20008

Buchanan, Mark
Associate Professor, St. Cloud State University
126 Third Avenue NE
St. Cloud, MN 56301

Butler, E. Bruce
Senior Counsel
International Allied-Signal Corporation
P.O. Box 3000R
Morristown, NJ 07960

Carter, James H.
Partner, Sullivan & Cromwell
125 Broad Street
New York, NY 10004

Clark, Cameron
Partner, Paul Weiss Rifkind Wharton
& Garrison
345 Park Avenue
New York, NY 10154

Cohen, Michael Marks
Partner, Burlingham Underwood & Lord
One Battery Park Plaza
New York, NY 10005

Connelly, Albert R.
Partner, Cravath Swaine & Moore
One Chase Manhattan Plaza
New York, NY 10005

Coulson, Robert
ICCA member; President, American Arbitration
Association
140 West 51st Street
New York, NY 10020-1203

Cross, Wayne A.
Partner, Reboul, MacMurray, Hewitt, Maynard & Kristol
45 Rockefeller Plaza, 10th Floor
New York, NY 10111

Crowley, Christopher
Partner, Davis Polk & Wardwell
One Chase Manhattan Plaza
New York, NY 10005

Cuneo, Donald L.
Partner, Shearman & Sterling
50 Riverside Drive
New York, NY 10024

Curtin, Philip J.
Zock Petrie & Curtin
19 Rector Street
New York, NY 10006

De Goytisolo, Agustin
Attorney, Trenam Simmons Kemker Scharf Barkin Frye & O'Neill
169 East Flagler Street, Suite 1000
Miami, FL 33131

De Pombo, Joaquin
Deputy General Counsel, Inter-American Development Bank
808 17th Street, NW
Washington, DC 20577

De Vries, Oege H.
Counsel, General Electric Company
16 Sunnyside Road
Scotia, NY 12302

De Waard, Tom
Resident Partner, Stibbe Blaisse & De Jong
335 Madison Avenue, 17th Fl.
New York, NY 10017

Dodson, Charles P.
Lovell White & King
535 Madison Avenue
New York, NY 10022

Duckworth, Frank A.
Vice President & General Counsel, Pfizer, Inc.
235 East 42nd Street
New York, NY 10017

Ebb, Lawrence F.
Attorney
570 Lexington Avenue
New York, NY 10022

Ehrenbard, Robert
Partner, Kelley Drye & Warren
101 Park Avenue
New York, NY 10178

Everard Goodman, Rosabel E.
Director, World Arbitration Institute; Coordinator, 1986 ICCA International Arbitration Congress
American Arbitration Association
140 West 51st Street
New York, NY 10020–1203

Fenton, Heike
President, Transnational Publishers, Inc.
22 Myrtle Avenue
Dobbs Ferry, NY 10522

Fouchard, Isabelle
Avocat, Donovan Maloof Walsh & Kennedy
c/o Nancy Bell, 281 West 11th Street
New York, NY 10014

Freire, Antonio M.
Associate, Finley Kumble Wagner Heine Underberg Manley Myerson & Casey
707 Wilshire Boulevard
Los Angeles, CA 90017

Friedman, Andre H.
Attorney, Goetz Fitzpatrick & Flynn
1 Penn Plaza, 44th Floor
New York, NY 10119

Gans, Walter G.
Vice President & General Counsel
Siemens Capital Corporation
767 Fifth Avenue
New York, NY 10153

Gant, Ralph A.
General Attorney
International Minerals & Chemical Corporation
875 Third Avenue
New York, NY 10022

Gianni, Francesco
Res. Partner, Studio Legale Bisconti
660 Madison Avenue
New York, NY 10021

Gill, David G.
Counsel, Exxon Corporation
76 Greenleaf Avenue
Darien, CT 06820

Glass, Walter H.
General Electric Company
570 Lexington Avenue
New York, NY 10022

Golsong, Heribert
Attorney, Arent Fox Kintner Plotkin & Kahn
Washington Square
1050 Connecticut Avenue, NW
Washington, DC 20036-5339

Goodman, Dr. Ronald E. M.
Cleary Gottlieb Steen & Hamilton
One State Street Plaza
New York, NY 10005

Graving, Richard J.
Director, The Institute for Transnational Arbitration
1331 Lamar, Suite 1459
Houston, TX 77010

Haffer, Douglas P.
Attorney, ACA Joe, a California Corporation
915 Front Street
San Francisco, CA 94111

Hancock, Tila Maria de
Consultant
3307 N Street NW
Washington, DC 20007

Heineman, Paul L.
Partner, Howard Needles Tammen & Bergendoff
9200 Ward Parkway
Kansas City, MO 64114

Hill, Thomas W.
Consultant, Sidley & Austin
Palm Beach Polo & Country Club
2627 Muirfield Court
West Palm Beach, FL 33414

Hines, Jonathan H.
Associate, Debevoise & Plimpton
875 Third Avenue
New York, NY 10022

Hoellering, Michael F.
General Counsel
American Arbitration Association
140 West 51st Street
New York, NY 10020

Hsu, Roger Y. K.
Senior Vice President, Law
The Lubrizol Corporation
29400 Lakeland Boulevard
Wickliffe, OH 44092

Jackson, Owen E.
Vice President, Hill International, Inc.
1301 Pennsylvania Avenue, NW
Washington, DC 20011

Jones, J. Sorton
Managing Partner, Graham & James
One Maritime Plaza, Ste. 300
San Francisco, CA 94111

Karatz, William W.
Partner, Winthrop Stimson Putnam & Roberts
40 Wall Street, 24th Floor
New York, NY 10005

Karlson, Paul
Rutgers Camden Law School
5th and Penn Street
Camden, NJ 08102

Kaye, Stephen R.
Attorney, Proskauer Rose Goetz & Mendelsohn
300 Park Avenue
New York, NY 10022

Kostelanetz, Boris
Partner, Kostelanetz & Ritholz
80 Pine Street
New York, NY 10005

Krishnan, K. L.
Attorney-at-Law
One Allen Center 1000
Houston, TX 77002

Kuffler, Alfred J.
Partner, Palmer Biezup & Henderson
956 Public Ledger Building
Independence Square
Philadelphia, PA 19106

Lahne, Richard K.
Attorney, Wilmer, Cutler & Pickering
1666 K Street, NW
Washington, DC 20006

Lahne, Susan G.
Associate, Covington & Burling
10 Park Valley Road
Silver Spring, MD 20910

Lamm, Carolyn B.
Partner, White & Case
1747 Pennsylvania Avenue, NW
Washington, DC 20006

Lannon, Warren
Sales Representative, Butterworth
Legal Publishers
84 Montvale Avenue
Stoneham, MA 02180

Layton, Robert
Partner, Jones Day Reavis & Pogue
485 Madison Avenue
New York, NY 10022

Le Pera, Sergio
40 Sutton Place
New York, NY 10022

Lepp, Gerald P.
Counsel, Nourse & Bowles;
1 Exchange Plaza, at 55 Broadway
New York, NY 10005

Littman, Allan N.
Partner, Pillsbury Madison & Sutro
P.O. Box 7880 (225 Bush Street)
San Francisco, CA 94104

Lowenfeld, Andreas F.
Professor, New York University Law School
5776 Palisade Avenue
Riverdale, NY 10471

Matschullat, Dale L.
Vice President and General Counsel
Allis Chalmers Corp.
P.O. Box 512
Milwaukee, WI 53201

McClendon, J. Stewart
Vice Chairman, International Advisory
Committee
World Arbitration Institute
Counsel, Satterlee & Stephens
200 East 66th Street, Apt. B-405
New York, NY 10021

McCormack, Howard M.
Attorney, Healy & Baillie
29 Broadway
New York, NY 10006

McKenry, Prof. Carl. E. B.
Secretary General, International
Commercial Dispute Resolution Center
800 Douglas Entrance, Ste. 211
Coral Gables, FL 33134

McLaughlin, Joseph T.
Partner, Shearman & Sterling
Citicorp Center
153 East 53rd Street
New York, NY 10022

McLean, Robert D.
Partner, Sidley & Austin
One First National Plaza
Chicago, IL 60603

Mealy, Michael P.
President, Mealy Publications
P.O. Box 446
Wayne, PA 19087

Michida, Prof. Shinishiro
ICCA member;
Professor of Law, Kyoto Univ.
c/o Hastings College of Law
200 McAllister Street
San Francisco, CA 94102

Mifsud, Paul V.
General Counsel, USA KLM Royal Dutch
Airlines
437 Madison Avenue
New York, NY 10022

Molineaux, Charles B.
General Counsel, Perini Corp.
73 Mount Wayne Avenue
Framingham, MA 01701

Mosk, Richard M.
Attorney, Mitchell Silberberg & Knupp
11377 West Olympic Blvd. Suite 700
Los Angeles, CA 90064

Murphy, Gavin P.
Assistant General Counsel
J. P. Stevens & Company, Inc.
1185 Avenue of the Americas
New York, NY 10036

Myers, James J.
Gadsby & Hannah
One Post Office Square
Boston, MA 02109

Nattier, Frank E.
Attorney
1815 Richwood Drive
Austin, TX 78758

Newman, Edwin S.
Vice President, Oceana Publications
75 Main Street
Dobbs Ferry, NY 10522

Newman, Lawrence W.
Partner, Baker & McKenzie
805 Third Avenue
New York, NY 10022

Norberg, Charles R.
Director General,
Inter-American Commercial Arbitration
Commission
1819 H Street, NW, Suite 310
Washington, DC 20006

O'Connell, John F.
Partner, Burlingham Underwood & Lord
474 Union Avenue
Murray Hill, NJ 09794

O'Neill, Philip D.
Trial Attorney, Hale & Dorr
60 State Street
Boston, MA 02109

O'Sullivan, Thomas J.
Partner, White & Case
1155 Avenue of the Americas
New York, NY 10036

Oliensis, Sheldon P.
Partner, Kaye Scholer Fierman
Hays & Handler
425 Park Avenue
New York, NY 10022

Pallister, Timothy J. B.
Partner, Slaughter & May
c/o 126 East 56th Street
New York, NY 10020

Parlin, Charles C.
Partner, Shearman & Sterling
53 Wall Street
New York, NY 10005

Patterson, Robert P.
Partner, Patterson Belknap Webb & Tyler
30 Rockefeller Plaza
New York, NY 10112

Paulsen, The Hon. John R.
Partner, Healy & Baillie
29 Broadway
New York, NY 10006

Pechota, Prof. Vratislaw
Assistant Director
Parker School of Foreign and Comparative
Law
Columbia University
435 West 116th Street
New York, NY 10027

Peck, The Hon. David W.
Sullivan & Cromwell
250 Park Avenue
New York, NY 10177

Penegar, Kenneth
Dean, University of Tennessee
College of Law
1505 West Cumberland Avenue
Knoxville, TN 37996

Percival, Sir Ian
Partner, Sidley Austin, London
520 Madison Avenue
New York, NY 10022

Pietrowski, Jr., Robert F.
Partner, Bracewell & Patterson
1825 I Street NW
Washington, DC 20006

Politi, Mauro
Attorney, White & Case
1155 Avenue of the Americas
New York, NY 10036

Polvani, Giovanni
Attorney
1707, 240 Mercer Street
New York, NY 10012

Preston, John E.
Vice President and Group Counsel
Litton Industries
360 N. Crescent Drive
Beverly Hills, CA 90210

Quale, Jr., Andrew C.
Partner, Sidley & Austin
520 Madison Avenue
New York, NY 10022

Rachlin, Lauren D.
Partner, Kavinoky & Cook
120 Delaware Avenue
Buffalo, NY 14202

Ragan, Charles R.
Partner, Pillsbury Madison & Sutro
225 Bush Street
San Francisco, CA 94104

Raoul-Duval, Pierre
Partner, Gide Loyrette Nouel
900 Third Avenue, 27th floor
New York, NY 10022

Reboul, John W.
Partner, Reboul, MacMurray, Hewitt, Maynard & Kristol
45 Rockefeller Plaza, 10th Floor
New York, NY 10111

Rivkin, David W.
Associate, Debevoise & Plimpton
875 Third Avenue
New York, NY 10022

Robinson, Davis R.
Partner, Pillsbury Madison & Sutro
3729 Fordham Road, NW
Washington, DC 20016

Rooney, Thomas J.
Counsel, Allis-Chalmers Corporation
P.O. Box 512
Milwaukee, WI 53201

Rosenberg, Arthur
Associate, Gilbert, Segall and Young
430 Park Avenue
New York , NY 10022

Rovine, Arthur W.
Partner, Baker & McKenzie
150 East 61st Street
New York, NY 10021

Sandborg, David L.
Attorney, Bronson Bronson McKinnon
Bank of America Center (3400)
San Francisco, CA 94104

Saporta, Lionel
Attorney, Hill, Betts & Nash
1 World Trade Center
New York, NY 10048

Saravalle, Alberto
Attorney, Shearman & Sterling
53 Wall Street
New York, NY 10005

Shattuck, Jr. H. Francis
Outside Counsel, Mobil Oil Corporation
150 East 42nd Street
New York, NY 10017

Shifman, Bette E.
Associate Research Scholar
Parker School of Foreign & Comparative Law
Columbia University Law School
435 West 116 Street
New York, NY 10027

Silverman, Bennet H.
Attorney, Katz Wittenberg Levine & Silverman
New York, NY 10017

Skolnik, Steven D.
Partner, Bobrow Greenapple & Skolnik
630 Third Avenue
New York, NY 10017-6797

Smit, Prof. Hans
Fuld Professor of Law
Director, Parker School of Foreign & Comparative Law, Columbia University
435 West 116th Street
New York, NY 10027

Stats, Herbert E.
Member, AAA National Panel of Arbitrators
410 James Place
1077 30th Street NW
Washington, DC 20007

Stein, Steven J.
Partner, Proskauer Rose Goetz & Mendelsohn
300 Park Avenue
New York, NY 10022

Stevenson, Jr., Russell B.
Partner, Hale & Dorr
1201 Pennsylvania Ave
Washington, DC 20004

Stevenson, The Hon. John R.
Partner, Sullivan & Cromwell
125 Broad Street
New York, NY 10004

Stewart, David P.
2201 C Street NW
Washington, DC 20520

Straus, Michael S.
Attorney, Sullivan & Cromwell
125 Broad Street
New York, NY 10011

Straus, Donald B.
Past President, American Arbitration Association
1700 Broadway, Rm. 1702
New York, NY 10019

Taft, George
Attorney-Adviser, State Department, Office of the Legal Adviser
Washington, DC 20520

Thorsen, Madge S.
Attorney, Oppenheimer Law Firm
4824 IDS Center
Minneapolis, MN 55402

Townsend, John M.
Partner, Hughes Hubbard & Reed
One Wall Street
New York, NY 10005

Tupman, W. Michael
Associate, White & Case
1747 Pennsylvania Ave., NW Suite 500
Washington, DC 20006

Von Mehren, Prof. Arthur T.
Story Professor of Law, Harvard Law School
Langdell Hall
Cambridge, MA 02138

Von Mehren, Robert B.
Debevoise & Plimpton
875 Third Avenue
New York, NY 10022

Welch, Thomas A.
Partner, Brobeck Phleger & Harrison
38 Irving Lane
Orinda, CA 94563

Witz, Prof. Clade
Professor, University of Saarbrücken and Lyon
Visiting Scholar, Columbia University
71 East 77th Street, Apt 4C
New York, NY 10021

USSR

Festisov, Eveniy A.
Head Legal Department, V/O "Exportles"
Trubnikovsky per. 19
Moscow 121803 GSP

Filatov, Igor A.
Chief Expert, Legal & Treaties Department
Ministry of Foreign Trade
Smolenskaya-Sennaya Sq. 32/34
Moscow 121200

Komarov, Alexander S.
Deputy Head, Legal & Treaties Department
Ministry of Foreign Trade
Smolenskaya-Sennaya Sq 32/34
Moscow 121200

Lebedev, Prof. Sergei N.
President, Maritime Arbitration Commission at the USSR Chamber of Commerce & Industry, Moscow; ICCA Vice President
6 Kuibyshev Street
Moscow 103684

Pozdnyakov, Vladimir S.
ICCA member; President, Foreign Trade Arbitration Commission
USSR Chamber of Commerce and Industry
6 Kuibyshev Street
Moscow 103684

Razumov, Prof. Dr. Konstantin L.
Director, Arbitration Department of the USSR Chamber of Commerce & Industry, Moscow
6 Kuibyshev Street
Moscow 103684

Vassiliev, Igor D.
Chief Legal Department, V/O "Techmashexport"
Mosfilmovskaya 35
Moscow 117330

Yugoslavia

Djurović, Radomir M.
ICCA member; President, Foreign Trade Court of Arbitration at the Yugoslavian Economic Chamber
Knez Mihailo 10
Belgrade 11000

Ivanisević, Mirjana
Dipl. iur.,
Energoinvest Energokomerc Bratstva
Jedinstva 2
Sarajevo 71000

Lopicic, Pavle L.
Secretary General, Foreign Trade Court of Arbitration at the Yugoslavian Economic Chamber
Knez Mihailo 10
Belgrade 11000

Toplak, Prof. Dr. Ludwig
Professor of Law
Universities of Maribor and Ljubljana;
Vice President, Iskra Delta Parmova No. 37
Ljubljana

INTERNATIONAL COUNCIL FOR COMMERCIAL ARBITRATION (ICCA)

Correspondence address:
Dr. Werner Melis
Secretary-General ICCA
c/o Arbitration Centre,
Austrian Federal Economic Chamber
Wiedner Hauptstrasse 63
P.O. Box 190, A-1045 Vienna
Austria
Phone: (0222) 6505
Telex: 111871
Telefax 652501

LIST OF OFFICERS AND MEMBERS
1 December 1986

Honorary Presidents

MR. JEAN ROBERT
Paris (France)
President, Comité français de l'arbitrage

PROF. PIETER SANDERS
Schiedam (Netherlands)
Emeritus Professor, Erasmus University, Rotterdam

OFFICERS

President

PROF. GIORGIO BERNINI
Bologna (Italy)
Professor of Commercial Law, Bologna University; Member of the Executive Committee of the Associazione Italiana per l'Arbitrato; Lawyer

Vice-Presidents

MR. HOWARD HOLTZMANN
New York (United States)
Chairman, International Arbitration Committee and Past Chairman of the Board, American Arbitration Association; Member Iran-US Claims Tribunal

PROF. SERGEI LEBEDEV Moscow (USSR)	President, Maritime Arbitration Commission, USSR Chamber of Commerce & Industry; Head of the Chair of Private International and Civil Law, Moscow Institute of International Relations
MRS. TINUADE OYEKUNLE Lagos (Nigeria)	Barrister and Solicitor of the Supreme Court of Nigeria; Financial Secretary of the Nigeria Arbitration Association, Lagos, Nigeria
	Secretary-General
DR. WERNER MELIS Vienna (Austria)	Chairman of the Arbitration Centre, Austrian Federal Economic Chamber

MEMBERS

MR. CEDRIC BARCLAY London (United Kingdom)	Past President, London Maritime Arbitration Association and Institute of Arbitrators; President of the Society of Consulting Marine Engineers and Ship Surveyors
MR. ARON BROCHES Washington D.C. (United States)	Past Vice-President and General Counsel, International Bank for Reconstruction and Development; Past Secretary General, International Centre for Settlement of Investment Disputes; International Legal Consultant
MR. ROBERT COULSON New York (United States)	President, American Arbitration Association
PROF. BERNARDO M. CREMADES Madrid (Spain)	Professor, Law Faculty at the Madrid University; Lawyer
MR. YVES DERAINS Paris (France)	Past Secretary General, Court of Arbitration of the International Chamber of Commerce; Lawyer
PROF. RADOMIR DJUROVIĆ Belgrade (Yugoslavia)	President, Arbitration Court at the Federal Economic Chamber of Yugoslavia, Belgrade; Professor of Law, Belgrade University
PROF. AHMED S. EL KOSHERI Cairo (Egypt)	Professor of Law, Ain Chams University; Lawyer
PROF. DR. RAFAEL EYZAGUIRRE ECHEVERRIA Santiago (Chile)	President of the Inter-American Commercial Arbitration Commission (IACAC); Professor of Commercial Law, Chilean University
DR. MAURO FERRANTE Rome (Italy)	Secretary-General, Associazione Italiana per l'Arbitrato

M. MICHEL GAUDET Paris (France)	Conseiller d'Etat honoraire; Chairman, Court of Arbitration at the International Chamber of Commerce
DR. OTTOARNDT GLOSSNER Kronberg (F.R. Germany)	President, Arbitration Commission of the International Chamber of Commerce; President, Deutsches Institut für Schiedsgerichtswesen e.V.; Lawyer
DR. SVETOZAR HANÁK Prague (Czechoslovakia)	Director, Legal Department of the Chamber of Commerce of Czechoslovakia
PROF. PIERRE LALIVE Geneva (Switzerland)	President, Association Suisse de l'Arbitrage; Professor of Law, University of Geneva; Chairman, ICC Institute of International Business Law and Practice; Lawyer
MR. MARK LITTMAN, Q.C. London (United Kingdom)	Barrister; Vice-Chairman, London International Arbitration Trust
MR. NILS MANGÅRD Stockholm (Sweden)	Judge of Appeal (ret.); President of Chamber, Iran-US Claims Tribunal, The Hague (ret.); Advisor to the Stockholm Chamber of Commerce on Arbitration matters
PROF. SHINISHIRO MICHIDA Kyoto (Japan)	Professor, Faculty of Law of the Kyoto University
MR. FALI S. NARIMAN	Senior Advocate at the Supreme Court of India; Vice President Bar Association of India; Member, International Commission of Jurists; President, Law Asia
PROF. TUDOR R. POPESCU Bucharest (Romania)	President, Arbitration Commission at the Chamber of Commerce and Industry of the Socialist Republic of Romania; Professor of International Commercial Law, University of Bucharest
PROF. VLADIMIR POZDNYAKOV Moscow (USSR)	President, Foreign Trade Arbitration Commission, USSR Chamber of Commerce & Industry; Head of the Law Chair, the All-Union Academy of Foreign Trade
MR. EDILBERT P. RAZAFINDRALAMBO Antananarivo (Madagascar)	Honorary First President of the Supreme Court; Member of the International Law Commission
DR. JOSÉ LUIS SIQUEIROS Mexico City (Mexico)	President of Interamerican Bar Association; Past President of the Mexican Academy of International Commercial Arbitration

PROF. ZHIVKO STALEV Sofia (Bulgaria)	President, Court of Arbitration at the Bulgarian Chamber of Commerce and Industry
PROF. DR. ROLF STÖDTER Hamburg (F.R. Germany)	President, International Maritime Arbitration Organization (ICC/CMI), Paris; Past-President, International Chamber of Commerce, Paris; Past-President, International Law Association, London
PROF. DR. HEINZ STROHBACH Berlin (German Democratic Republic)	President, Court of Arbitration at the Chamber of Foreign Trade of the German Democratic Republic; Professor of Law, Academy of Political and Legal Science, Potsdam-Babelsberg
PROF. DR. IVÁN SZÁSZ Budapest (Hungary)	Professor of Law, Academy of Foreign Trade, Budapest; Honorary President of Legal Commission and member of the Presidential Council of the Arbitation Court at the Hungarian Chamber of Commerce
DR. HABIL. TADEUSZ SZURSKI Warsaw (Poland)	President of the Court of Arbitration at the Polish Chamber of Foreign Trade; Member of the Scientific Council of the Institute of International Law, Warsaw University; Member of the Polish Bar Association
MR. TANG HOUZHI Beijing (P.R. China)	Deputy Secretary-General, Foreign Economic and Trade Arbitration Commission; Advisor, Legal Affairs Department, China Council for the Promotion of International Trade

HONORARY MEMBERS

PROF. SERGUEI BRATUS Moscow (USSR)	Past President of the Foreign Trade Arbitration Commission, USSR Chamber of Commerce and Industry
PROF. ARTHUR BÜLOW Cologne (F.R. Germany)	Honorary Professor at the Faculty of Law of the University of Bonn; Past Secretary of State at the Federal Ministry of Justice, Bonn
DR. NARAYANASWAMI KRISHNAMURTHI New Delhi (India)	Past Executive Director, Indian Council of Arbitration; Past Vice President of ICCA
MR. DONALD B. STRAUS New York (United States)	President, Research Institute of the American Arbitration Association